Green Technology Book

Solutions for climate change mitigation

WIPO
WORLD
INTELLECTUAL PROPERTY
ORGANIZATION

Suggested citation: World Intellectual Property Organization (WIPO) (2023). *Green Technology Book: Solutions for Climate Change Mitigation.* Geneva: WIPO. DOI: 10.34667/tind.48717

First published 2023

World Intellectual Property Organization
34, chemin des Colombettes, P.O. Box 18
CH-1211 Geneva 20, Switzerland

wipo.int

ISBN: 978-92-805-3576-1 (print)
ISBN: 978-92-805-3577-8 (online)
ISSN: 3005-9402 (print)
ISSN: 3005-9410 (online)

Cover:
Getty Images and unsplash

WIPO Publication No. 1080EN-23

Contents

Foreword by WIPO

Daren Tang, Director General
World Intellectual Property Organization
(WIPO)

Because of the existential threat of climate change, there has been a tremendous amount of research, technology and innovation deployed to addressing this challenge over recent years. In fact, by some estimates, the world now has access to 80 percent of the technologies needed to halve global greenhouse emissions by 2030, with many more game-changing solutions in the pipeline.

The problem is therefore shifting from a scarcity of solutions to a scarcity of deployment. Breakthrough technologies and solutions are not yet getting to where they are most needed. Opportunities to finance and scale existing solutions are being missed. And adaptation must be stepped up so that local needs all over the world can be better met.

A big part of this problem is knowledge – there is a disconnect between those who have and want to offer the technology and those who need it.

It is this gap between what is available and what is needed that the *Green Technology Book* aims to bridge. Building on the theme of climate adaptation technologies in last year's inaugural edition, this 2023 report showcases more than 200 climate mitigation technologies in three areas – cities, agriculture and land use, and industry – where deployment is crucial.

In addition to being a practical guide for policymakers, industry, investors, researchers and many others, we hope that through providing information we inspire action. Action in the form of targeted interventions, as well as a deeper, more systemic change. Almost all the green technologies featured in this book are ready for use and available to all.

These and many other solutions can also be found on our tech-matching platform WIPO GREEN, which connects providers and seekers of green technologies from around the world. Its database now covers 130,000 technologies from over 140 countries, making it the biggest green-tech platform that the UN offers today.

We should take hope from the wealth of increasingly mature climate technologies at our fingertips

One of the key messages of this report is that, while we should take hope from the wealth of increasingly mature climate technologies at our fingertips, we must all work harder to get these solutions into the hands of those who can use them on the ground.

We hope that the *Green Technology Book* adds momentum to these efforts, and I would like to thank our partners at the Climate Technology Centre and Network (CTCN) and the Egyptian Academy of Scientific Research and Technology (ARST), not only for their cooperation, but also for their steadfast commitment to supporting accelerated climate action in each and every part of the world.

Foreword by partners

Climate Technology Centre and Network (CTCN)

COP28 is expected to conclude significant work on several long-awaited deliverables. They include decisions on a global adaptation goal, the specifics of a loss and damage finance facility, the closing of the substantial emissions gap, and expediting the transition to clean energy and a just transition. And technology plays a pivotal role in enabling climate action to address every one of these challenges.

Technology and innovation are imperative in addressing a wide range of factors associated with building sustainable cities, improving agricultural production and transforming food systems, and decarbonizing the steel and cement sectors etc.

Like no other organization, the CTCN Secretariat supports all aspects of technology innovation through providing technical assistance, fostering capacity building and facilitating knowledge sharing. At COP27, the CTCN launched its 3rd Programme of Work, highlighting the transformative potential of national system innovation and digitalization as key drivers of technology development and transfer.

The CTCN has maintained a longstanding partnership with the World Intellectual Property Organization (WIPO). It is not surprising that for this 2023 edition of the *Green Technology Book*, the CTCN has contributed to raising awareness about the diverse range of technologies available today, some of which are truly remarkable and accessible to all. Each year, the *Green Technology Book* sets out to demonstrate that solutions for climate-friendly technology do exist – the next step is a commitment to their implementation. This book is a practical guide for innovators, industry, researchers and agencies, and raises awareness of the technology solutions available for implementation by developing countries.

We at the CTCN express our gratitude and greatly appreciate our ongoing collaboration with WIPO, as together we continue to explore and showcase novel green technology climate solutions from around the world.

Rajiv Garg, CTCN Director ad interim

Academy of Scientific Research & Technology (ASRT), Egypt

The World Intellectual Property Organization's (WIPO) initiative to publish the *Green Technology Book* of those green technologies that could offer technological solutions to pressing challenges and accelerate efforts to mitigate climate change and foster sustainable development in the face of today's multiple global crises is critical. Egypt – one of the southern hemisphere countries most adversely affected by climate change and classified as one of the most vulnerable – is proud to support this initiative and has been firmly committed to its success since it was first announced jointly by WIPO, CTCN and the Academy of Scientific Research and Technology (ASRT) at COP 27 in Sharm El Sheik.

We invite all WIPO Member States to offer their locally available green technology and inventions for inclusion in the WIPO GREEN Database of needs and technologies for the mutual benefit of humanity. Knowledge sharing and exchange is one of the most powerful drivers in the fight against climate change.

This initiative will accelerate technology transfer, and encourage knowledge and experience to be relayed from developed to developing countries and vice versa. Such a transfer can assist developing countries in rapidly transitioning away from traditional, carbon-intensive development paths and toward cleaner, more sustainable technologies. In parallel, it will accelerate green patent technology diffusion and market expansion, allowing businesses to enter new markets and extend their client base. This should encourage private-sector investment in green technology research and development, and ultimately spur additional innovation.

Last but by no means least, making green technology and patent databases available and accessible to all is a human right and a main goal of the UNESCO Open Science initiative.

Thank you to WIPO and all of the Partners involved in this endeavor.

Professor Mahmoud M. Sakr, ASRT President

Acknowledgments

This second edition of the WIPO flagship *Green Technology Book* is a testament to the collective efforts of innovators paving the way for a more climate-friendly future. From the research labs to the households, from local communities to global partnerships, the pages that follow celebrate the scope of solutions that form the technological blueprint for reduced greenhouse gas emissions.

The book was prepared under the general auspices of WIPO Director General Daren Tang, and the Global Challenges and Partnerships Sector led by Assistant Director General Edward Kwakwa, as well as the Global Challenges Division led by Director Amy Dietterich.

Special thanks go to our partners at the Climate Technology Centre and Network (CTCN), represented by Director Rajiv Garg (ad interim) and the Egyptian Academy of Scientific Research and Technology (ASRT) represented by Prof. Mahmoud M. Sakr (President) for their vision, collaboration and continued dedication.

The *Green Technology Book* is an initiative under WIPO GREEN. It was conceived and led by Peter Oksen, Green Technology and Research Manager, who also acted as editor and co-writer. Shanar Tabrizi, Climate Technology Expert, is the main writer and co-editor of the book. Faisal Alenazi, Morven MacEwen, Clara Danbakli and Emma Francis supported the identification and management of technologies in the WIPO GREEN Database and Morven also contributed to the writing. Antonio Di Giamberardino (Solutions Design and Delivery Section) developed the GTB database collection. Other WIPO GREEN staff contributed important support, namely: Rishab Raturi, Sabrina de Souza Herzog, Dmitry Kalinin, Anja von der Ropp, Tatiana Hartop, Christy Nomura and Minna Guigon-Sell.

We extend our gratitude to Edwin Hassink (Graphic Designer) from WIPO Publications and Design Section for their meticulous work on the layout and design. Vanessa Harwood and Book Now Ltd. ensured the language was refined to a professional standard.

We also thank the team that made the digital iteration of this book come to life, namely: Dan Savu (Head) and Javier Aguilar López, both WIPO Solutions Design and Delivery Section, Virginie Roux and Spencer Cabildo, Web Communications Section and Daniel Pradilla, WIPO IP Portal team. Edward Harris, Senior Media Officer of the News and Media Division, helped us communicate our message effectively. The Language Division led by Mr. Lijun Fan provided translation expertise, extending our messages to a broader audience.

Our gratitude also extends to the invaluable contributions of the WIPO GREEN reference group, hailing from within WIPO and beyond, that helped us steer the *Green Technology Book* in the right direction. This cohort of experts and dedicated colleagues included: Amy Dietterich (Director, Global Challenges Division), Andrew Czajkowski (Director, Technology and Innovation Support Division), Carsten Fink (Chief Economist, Department for Economics and Data Analytics), Kevin Fitzgerald (Director, Information and Digital Outreach Division), Walid Abdelnasser (Director, Division for Arab Countries), Edward Harris (Senior Media Officer, News and Media Division), Charlotte Beauchamp (Head, Publications and Design Section), Victor Owade (Counsellor, WIPO Academy), Dan Savu (Head, Solutions Design and Delivery Section), Christopher Harrison (Patent Analytics Manager, Technology and Innovation Support Division),

Rajiv Garg (Director ad interim, CTCN), Cristina Comunian (Communications Specialist, CTCN), and Anastasiia Tiurmenko (Communications Specialist, CTCN). A distinguished assembly of experts graciously offered their time and expertise to review various segments of this publication, thereby making a profound impact on the publication's quality. We extend our heartfelt appreciation to the following individuals:

Rajiv Garg, Regional Manager and ad interim Director, UN Climate Technology Centre and Network (CTCN)

Tim Collins, Secretary-General, World Stainless Association

Andrew Purvis, Director Sustainable Manufacturing, World Steel Association

Åsa Ekdahl, Head, Environment and Climate Change, World Steel Association

Felipe Sanchez, Analyst, Leadership Group for Industrial Transition (LeadIT) Secretariat

Mahdi Shakouri, Industrial Energy Efficiency and Decarbonization Expert, Gen0

Dr. Rosie McDonald, Climate Change Officer, International Telecommunication Union (ITU)

Piotr Barczak, Circular Economy Program Manager at the African Circular Economy Network Foundation, Council Member at the European Environmental Bureau

Elisabeth Resch, Senior Advisor, United Nations Environment Program (UNEP) Copenhagen Climate Centre

Yoann Le Petit, Thought Leadership Manager, European Institute of Innovation and Technology (EIT) Urban Mobility

Dietram Oppelt, Advisor, NDE Germany

Dr. Romanas Savickas, Senior Advisor, UNEP Copenhagen Climate Centre

Santiago Hughes, Business Developer, Field Intelligence Energy

Gregory Kohler, PhD, Agriculture Expert, Climate and Clean Air Coalition (CCAC)

Francesco Carnevale Zampaolo, Programme Director, SRI-2030

Nikola Trendov, Digital Agriculture and Innovation Specialist, Food and Agriculture Organization of the United Nations (FAO)

Mikael Andersen, Product Specialist, Brøns Group AB

Acronyms

AC	air conditioner
AI	artificial intelligence
AM	additive manufacturing
ASRT	Egyptian Academy of Scientific Research and Technology
AWD	alternate wetting and drying
BF-BOF	blast furnace-basic oxygen furnace
BIM	building information modeling
BRT	bus rapid transit
CCS	carbon capture and storage
CCU	carbon capture and utilization
CCUS	carbon capture, utilization and storage
CDR	carbon dioxide removal
CGIAR	Consultative Group on International Agricultural Research
CHF	combined heat and power
CO_2	carbon dioxide
CO_2eq	CO_2 equivalent
CO_2eq/yr	CO_2 equivalent per year
CSA	climate-smart agriculture
CSS	carbon capture and storage
CTCN	Climate Technology Centre & Network
DRI	direct reduced iron
EAF	electric arc furnace
EO	Earth observation
ERC	Emission Reduction Credit
EU	European Union
GDP	gross domestic product
GHG	greenhouse gas
GIS	geographical information system
GPS	global positioning system
GtCO_2eq/yr	gigatonne CO_2 equivalent per year
GWP	global warming potential
HFC	hydrofluorocarbon
HTL	hydrothermal liquefaction
HVAC	heating, ventilation and air conditioning
ICT	information and communications technology
IGO	intergovernmental organization
IoT	internet of things
IP	intellectual property
IPCC	Intergovernmental Panel on Climate Change
IT	information technology
MBT	mechanical biological treatment
MOE	molten oxide electrolysis
NSI	national system of Innovation
PV	photovoltaics
R&D	research and development
RFID	radio frequency identification
SRI	System of Rice Intensification
TLR	Technology Readiness Level

Executive summary

Finding momentum

We are in a state of climate emergency. Limiting its catastrophic impact requires an unprecedented systems transformation. However, there is hope. The sources of greenhouse gas (GHG) emissions are many, but so are the technologies to address them.

There are sufficient options available across all sectors to at least halve emissions by 2030.[1] And technology and innovation are a key part of the solution. Eighty percent of the technologies we need to achieve the 2030 climate goals are already on the market[2] – with many more emerging. Technologies for lowering energy consumption, electrifying transport and enabling material efficiency are just some of the many options presented in this year's *Green Technology Book*. National innovation ecosystems are the source of all these new opportunities. A well-functioning innovation ecosystem is underpinned by an efficient and fair intellectual property rights system, which in itself stimulates innovation and disseminates technology to global markets.

This is the year of the Global Stocktake, where countries revise their national climate plans with the aim of raising ambitions for the coming years. And beyond nation-state level, a growing body of non-state actors, among them the private sector, academia and civil society, are working tirelessly to realize the vision set out in the Paris Agreement.

Photo: GettyImages / StockByM

80 percent of the technologies we need to achieve the 2030 climate goals are already on the market – with many more emerging

Knowledge that inspires action

The first edition of the *Green Technology Book* addressed climate change adaptation technologies. In this second edition, we make climate change mitigation solutions tangible by showing the wealth of mature and emerging innovation and technologies available. This publication analyses 10 sectors within three major categories:

- **Cities**
  - Efficient heating and cooling
  - Smart mobility
  - Material efficiency and sustainable waste management
- **Agriculture and land use**
  - Livestock
  - Soils, land use change and forestry
  - Rice cultivation
  - Data and precision farming

- **Industry**
  - Iron and steel
  - Cement
  - Industry 4.0

Over 600 climate mitigation and adaptation technologies - and growing - have been identified for the *Green Technology Book* collection in the WIPO GREEN Database of needs and technologies.[3] This publication showcases a selection of those related to climate mitigation. Solution providers can upload an overview of their technology to the Database, making it a continually expanding source of green innovation and technology. By bringing the technologies to the forefront, we aim to inspire action. Now is the time to rapidly develop and deploy solutions that overcome carbon lock-in and drive forward transformational change.

Solution providers can upload an overview of their technology to the Database, making it a continually expanding source of green innovation and technology

Designing circular and smart cities

Cities are where the climate battle will be largely won - or lost. They are where buildings are erected, energy and food consumed, waste generated and people and goods transported. On a vehicular level, the rapid scaling of electric cars has far exceeded expectations in many cities. Advances in battery technology, vehicle-grid integration and charging stations have been important enablers. However, while the electric vehicles market is growing, so is the trend toward highly fuel-consuming SUVs, which alone accounted for one-third of the total growth in oil demand between 2021 and 2022.[4] Furthermore, electric car prices are still out of reach for most people, particularly in emerging and developing countries. While many new electrified options for personal use and goods transport have emerged, including two-wheeled options, the effective reduction of transport sector emissions depends upon innovations that go beyond individual vehicles. For instance, better policies for compact cities and public transport can be practically supported by technologies such as intelligent traffic management systems, urban modelling tools and mobility-as-a-service platforms.

Energy-efficient heating and cooling technologies and alternative refrigerants are already on the market. Examples include new types of heat pumps, modern insulation materials and smart technologies able to adjust heating and cooling flow to match a building's demand. Yet, these are often not the foremost consumer choice, necessitating further innovation to make these solutions both more affordable and accessible. At the same time, the number of air conditioners installed worldwide is soaring, and heating is the biggest energy end-user. In a growing number of cities, district heating and cooling (district level centralized systems) helps reduce energy usage and enables renewable energy integration. However, emissions reduction in these sectors must go beyond improving operational efficiency. Technology can help address heating and cooling demand by enabling climate-smart design of buildings. Passive heating and cooling techniques have been around for centuries. Several countries are now modernizing these well-tried techniques and promoting their design principles through building codes and energy efficiency standards.

This publication further recognizes material efficiency and sustainable waste management in cities as a major lever for emissions reduction. From construction materials and wood to plastic and glass, the expected doubling of material use by 2050 urgently requires innovative solutions for enhanced circularity. Such solutions are no longer an option, but a necessity for climate action. Advances in sorting technologies, such as robotics and optical scanners, enable higher waste recovery rates. Innovative recycling technologies can now handle materials otherwise hard to recycle, such as tires and wind turbine blades.

Some waste management technologies are themselves a major source of emissions. Countries such as Denmark are moving away from materials incineration, because of its inefficiency and high emissions rate. Several emerging recycling technologies, such as chemical recycling, have been found to be energy-consuming, necessitating more focused life-cycle thinking directed at technology viability from a climate perspective. This also highlights the need for innovation and technologies that are more upstream. Deposit return and refill stations for anything from bottles and cans to water and detergents are growing in popularity in many cities. Meanwhile, digital tools support better building and product design to enable reusability, such as material passports. Furthermore, online platforms for co-ownership and the sharing of anything from cars and tools to office buildings reduce manufacturing demand for new things.

Regenerative agriculture and ag tech

Global food systems and the agricultural sector are under pressure. There is a pronounced need to produce more in order to feed a growing world population, often accompanied by a demand for more processed and high-emitting products. The environmental and climate change footprint of the agricultural sector is large, with methane emissions being particularly important. Agriculture, land use and land management account for around 22 percent of GHG emissions,[5] occupy 38 percent of the Earth's surface[6] and are responsible for 70 percent of global freshwater withdrawals.[7] It is therefore a sector where climate change mitigation is critical. Furthermore, the sector is highly vulnerable to climate change impacts and the type of climate change adaptation measures described in last year's *Green Technology Book* are urgently needed.

This edition focuses on the major emitting sectors within agriculture, and also considers the merits of the highly sophisticated technology frontier in data and precision farming. Livestock is a major source of emissions, primarily due to the methane produced by ruminant livestock. Emissions can be combatted through supply- and demand-side measures. On the supply side, there is strong correlation between productivity and emissions per amount of meat or milk produced, meaning meat and dairy product emissions can be reduced through increased productivity. Provided that such productivity increase does not create new environmental impacts or degrade animal welfare, it may contribute to limiting land and water usage.

Agriculture, land use and land management account for around 22 percent of GHG emissions, occupy 38 percent of the Earth's surface and are responsible for 70 percent of global freshwater withdrawals

But innovation is providing new options. One of the more promising is feed additives. Seaweed added to livestock feed can directly affect the enteric fermentation process to dramatically reduce methane production. Much innovation is also directed toward addressing meat demand through the quest for meat alternatives acceptable to the general consumer. Several such alternatives are currently being made available to consumers. However, while the benefits to avoided animal cruelty of this approach are obvious, the net environmental gains have yet to be determined. Replacing animal protein with plant and fungi-derived alternatives in the mass production of a broad range of processed food products may have a greater potential impact in this regard.

Chapter 3, Agriculture and land use, further touches upon range and land management. Soil stores vast amounts of carbon in a relatively stable form. Intensive agricultural practices and chemical fertilizers which cause soil degradation and erosion, as well as deforestation, lead to the release of this carbon stock. Careful management of land, regenerative agriculture and innovations that increase soil carbon all have a high mitigation potential. However, this is dependent on their becoming integral to the agricultural practice of a vast number of farmers.

Rice cultivation is a crop system of particular climate concern, because it involves flooding fields, which releases methane. In a rice producing region such as South East Asia, rice cultivation is responsible for between 25 and 33 percent of methane emissions.[8, 9, 10] It also uses a large amount of freshwater, making the practice highly vulnerable to climate change impacts. Productivity enhancements involving reduced water usage on less land can help reduce emissions. New cropping systems in which fields are flooded for a shorter period of time have shown promising results in those places where they can be implemented.

As in many other sectors, information technology and data can assist in a transition toward lower-emitting systems. In agriculture, advanced technologies are able to limit waste, reduce inputs such as fertilizer, pesticides and water, and optimize plant growth conditions. The drastic step of foregoing soil usage altogether and moving production indoors through hydroponics and vertical farming is already established and continually evolving, with important emissions reduction potential. Various semi- or fully autonomous farm machines are able to fulfill agricultural tasks more effectively, with a high degree of precision. Furthermore, systems and tools that support farmers in their decision-making and help them access funding for a shift to regenerative agricultural practices are becoming more widespread and simpler to use. Open access, high-resolution satellite images play an important role in this. Many of the advanced machines and new technologies are not yet a common sight in low-income rural areas. However, new modes of access, ownership and agricultural service-based business models may facilitate a broader deployment among smallholder farmers.

Decarbonizing steel and cement

Steel and cement are major GHG emitters. They are often considered to be two hard-to-decarbonize sectors. However, this narrative masks the fact that solutions do exist. One particularly high-impact way of reducing cement emissions is to reduce clinker usage. Clinker is a common ingredient in cement made by heating raw materials such as limestone in a process requiring high temperatures and emitting greenhouse gases. Partially replacing clinker with alternative materials has some of the greatest potential for reducing cement emissions. Yet, at the same time the clinker-to-cement ratio is increasing around the world.

Many steel furnaces are reaching their end of life. Replacing them with conventional high-emitting blast furnaces will cause a decades-long carbon lock-in until their investment value has depreciated. Decarbonization of steel and cement is challenging, but not impossible. We know which technologies are needed, but are not implementing them at the scale required. Several climate-friendly steel and cement production technologies are already mature and available, including direct reduced iron (DRI), electrification and the use of clinker substitutes.

However, simply reducing emissions from steel and cement production will not suffice. To effectively reduce total sector emissions amid booming demand, the management of these two materials, as well as their demand, warrants far greater attention. Construction projects often use excessive amounts of steel and cement. Millions of buildings and offices around the world either stand empty or are demolished before reaching their end of life. Extending a building's usefulness and lifetime, designing for efficient material usage and employing lightweight, low-carbon materials are all central to emissions reduction. Digital-sharing platforms and design tools, advanced recycling technologies and material innovation are key enablers of such a circular supply chain.

Technologies that enable more efficient steel and cement usage hold significant promise for achieving climate targets. Yet, more attention is currently directed toward emerging technologies, such as carbon capture and storage (CCS), carbon capture, utilization and storage (CCUS) and green hydrogen. It is likely that the focus on improving production processes and carbon capture rather than on efficient material usage reflects a lack of financial and market incentives for manufacturers. At the same time, the implementation of CCS, CCUS and green hydrogen technologies is still very slow and has made no significant impact, especially in the major steel- and cement-producing nations. These two sectors have also been slow in adopting frontier digital technologies to optimize energy usage and processes. Steel and cement are sectors in particular need of further technology research and development if they are to achieve net zero CO_2 emissions by 2050.

Climate technologies must address both supply and demand

Governments and cities must rapidly develop and scale climate mitigation technologies. However, now more than ever, the choice of technology matters. Simply optimizing current systems will not be enough to realize climate goals. In most countries, the central role of renewable energy in phasing out fossil fuels has been recognized. Less attention has been given to the role of technology and innovation in managing our growing material and resource demand, and in enhancing circularity. This is despite material usage being the main driver of a triple planetary crisis composed of climate change, biodiversity loss and health-related pollution impacts.

Many reports on climate technologies focus on their role in reducing supply-side emissions, for instance, through fuel switching and energy efficiency. The *Green Technology Book* is different in that it also recognizes the huge untapped potential of demand-side management. With resource demand growing exponentially, we need to rethink ways of providing basic human services, including food, shelter and mobility - and of doing more with less.

Technology is a key part of the puzzle. It can enable developed, emerging and developing economies to use resources more efficiently. It also allows us to substitute high-carbon materials and systematically integrate climate perspectives into the development of our cities, buildings, products and food systems. As stated recently by the Intergovernmental Panel on Climate Change (IPCC), *avoiding*, *shifting* and *improving* demand for services has the potential to reduce GHG emissions by between 40 and 70 percent globally by 2050.[11, 12]

This requires changes to our investments, policies and behavior. Technology and innovation have the power to enable systems change rather than ways of simply improving business as usual, with many technologies affording no-regret options for developed and developing economies alike. Digital technologies deserve special mention here, given their potential to better match supply and demand, avoid unnecessary production waste and enable the design and use of circular systems. This publication highlights a broad range of technologies addressing activities across cities, agriculture and land use, and industry.

Notes

1 IPCC (2022). *Climate change 2022: Mitigation of climate change – Technical summary, Working Group III contribution to IPCC sixth assessment report*. Cambridge, UK: Intergovernmental Panel on Climate Change (IPCC). Available at: https://www.ipcc.ch/report/sixth-assessment-report-working-group-3/.

2 IEA (2021). *Net Zero by 2050: A roadmap for the global energy sector.* Paris: International Energy Agency (IEA). Available at: https://www.iea.org/reports/net-zero-by-2050.

3 The Introduction provides more information on how we define, identify and select the proven, frontier and horizon technologies showcased in the *Green Technology Book*.

4 Cozzi, L., *et al.* (2023). As their sales continue to rise, SUVs' global CO_2 emissions are nearing 1 billion tonnes. International Energy Agency (IEA). Available at: https://www.iea.org/commentaries/as-their-sales-continue-to-rise-suvs-global-co2-emissions-are-nearing-1-billion-tonnes [accessed September 2023].

5 IPCC (2023). *Synthesis report (SYR) of the IPCC sixth assessment report (AR6): Summary for policymakers*. Geneva: Intergovernmental Panel on Climate Change (IPCC). Available at: https://www.ipcc.ch/report/ar6/syr/.

6 FAO (2023). Land use in agriculture by the numbers. Food and Agriculture Organization of the United Nations (FAO). Available at: http://www.fao.org/sustainability/news/detail/en/c/1274219/ [accessed May 2023].

7 World Bank (2023). Water in agriculture. World Bank. Available at: https://www.worldbank.org/en/topic/water-in-agriculture [accessed May 2023].

8 Umali-Deininger, D. (2022). *Greening the rice we eat*. Washington, DC: World Bank. Available at: https://blogs.worldbank.org/eastasiapacific/greening-rice-we-eat?cid=SHR_BlogSiteEmail_EN_EXT [accessed November 2023].

9 Kurnik, J. and K. Devine (2022). Innovation in reducing methane emissions from the food sector: Side of rice, hold the methane. World Wildlife Fund. Available at: https://www.worldwildlife.org/blogs/sustainability-works/posts/innovation-in-reducing-methane-emissions-from-the-food-sector-side-of-rice-hold-the-methane [accessed July 2023].

10 WRI (2023). Our world in data: Emissions by sector. World Resources Institute (WRI). Available at: https://ourworldindata.org/emissions-by-sector [accessed June 2023].

11 This estimate relates to potential emissions reduction in buildings, overland transport and food by 2050 (high confidence).

12 IPCC (2023). Synthesis report (SYR) of the IPCC sixth assessment report (AR6). Summary for policymakers. Geneva: Intergovernmental Panel on Climate Change (IPCC). Available at: https://www.ipcc.ch/report/ar6/syr/.

Key messages

Photo: Getty Images/Thirawatana Phaisalratana

The world is confronted by an ever-increasing and wide range of greenhouse gas emissions. But the good news is that there is an even wider range of technologies to mitigate them. By bringing to the forefront not only the technologies themselves but the systems in which they operate, this publication aims to inspire a broader conversation on technology and innovation's role in a low-carbon future. The mapping of more than 400 climate mitigation technologies allows us to make the following observations.

Demand-side measures deserve more attention: Climate technologies are often applied as single-level interventions. This misses the potential for deeper and longer-term systemic decarbonization. There needs to be a broader assessment of climate technology needs that considers both demand- and supply-side measures essential for total carbon emissions reduction. For instance, technology can support demand-side measures by enabling better buildings design and operation to reduce the need for energy-intensive heating and cooling technologies. Technology – especially digital technologies – further enables the smart planning of a city's infrastructure. This includes mapping waste collection routes and public transport networks in a manner that lowers dependency on privately-owned vehicles or the need to take long journeys. Technology and innovation also have a major role to play in developing novel types of material, advancing reuse and recycling methods and avoiding waste in the food supply chain. Meanwhile, plant and fungi-derived products can replace animal protein in food processing, thereby reducing demand for methane-emitting livestock. The climate mitigation potential of such technologies deserves to be fully recognized for a whole range of applications, from a country's climate roadmap to city planning and policymaking.

No time to wait for breakthrough technologies: We already have most of the technologies needed to reach our global 2030 climate targets. There is a growing recognition of the risks inherent in relying too heavily on the commercialization and widespread adoption of breakthrough technologies, such as green hydrogen and carbon capture and storage, for a solution. Mainly, this could result in a missed opportunity to finance and scale existing solutions within the time-critical framework demanded by the climate crisis. That said, innovation is still crucial. Existing climate technologies are often unaffordable and difficult to access in many parts of the world. Creative adaptation of existing solutions to meet the unique challenges of various regions and sectors is needed in order to facilitate their widespread uptake.

Key climate technologies are ineffective without fossil fuel phase-out: Fossil fuel dependence reduces the efficiency of many climate technologies. Electric arc furnaces, electric vehicles, hydrogen and heat pumps are all considered essential for the decarbonization of various sectors. However, the climate mitigation potential of these technologies is subject to renewable energy being available to power the electricity grids that feed them. For instance, hydrogen as an alternative steelmaking fuel is receiving attention as a climate technology. Yet, its decarbonization potential is highly dependent on how the hydrogen is produced in the first place. Hydrogen made from natural gas (a fossil fuel) rather than renewable electricity has limited emission reduction potential. Countries with electric grid systems that rely primarily on fossil fuels face major barriers to a sustainable and cost-effective implementation of hydrogen and other electricity-dependent decarbonization measures. As such, fossil fuel phase-out is not only an enabler but a precondition for the success and efficiency of many climate technologies.

Rapidly growing cities must be supported to avoid carbon lock-in: Globally, the climate technology landscape is dominated by a few countries with a strong national system of innovation, with developing countries having fewer opportunities to develop and access new technologies. All countries should be enabled, economically and technically, to harness climate technology opportunities. Collaborative innovation and technology transfer can make innovative solutions more accessible to developing nations. Rapidly growing cities are putting in place long-term infrastructure such as buildings, industrial assets and road networks. Slow adoption of climate technologies and their enabling opportunities increases the risk of stranded assets and carbon lock-in. At the same time, making careful technology choices is crucial if a dependence on suboptimal climate technologies is to be avoided. Examples of poor choices include cooling technologies with suboptimal refrigerants, downstream waste management technologies that impede recycling and extending a blast furnace's lifespan by relining instead of phasing it out for a better alternative.

Steel and cement are in particular need of R&D: In certain sectors, rapid technological advancements are vital to achieving long-term climate goals. Key technologies needed to reach net zero goals by 2050 are still emerging. Considered difficult-to-decarbonize, industrial sectors such as steel and cement are in particular need of further R&D of appropriate climate technologies. Innovation is most needed for technologies that enable electrification, fossil fuel phase-out and changes to production processes. However, at present, most patenting activity for low-emitting steel is focused on the processing and transport of iron ore rather than the more carbon-intensive stages of steelmaking and the current planned capacity for low-carbon steel and cement is not aligned with the emission reductions needed.

Agriculture and land use have a large mitigation potential: Innovation and technology can help enable the changes necessary. Together they offer a great variety of already available solutions able to make a real difference. However, it is likely that the greatest mitigation effects will come from a change in agricultural practices. A change in the way we cultivate the land and herd animals, in avoided deforestation and in consumer behavior. Such changes can prevent large-scale emissions from soil carbon. They can also reduce emission-intensive inputs and fuel usage, lower livestock methane emissions and increase productivity - something which in itself mitigates against climate change. Technologies are available to support such changes in practice. Satellite images can provide data for monitoring crops and forecasting yields. Feed additives can lower livestock methane emissions. Weeding robots and spraying drones can aid better soil management and advanced, data-driven ag tech can increase productivity and decrease chemical usage. Some of the more advanced technologies are yet to become mainstreamed. Most farmers are unlikely to make dramatic changes unless they come with limited risk and are economically sound. Innovative ways of making new advanced equipment accessible to farmers, such as leasing and through agricultural service companies, could accelerate the uptake of new solutions, which otherwise may seem out of reach to smaller farmers. But consumer demand, policy support, regulations and finance are all required for a new agricultural revolution in support of climate change mitigation to become a reality.

Introduction and methodology

Photo: Getty Images / ellenamani

The *Green Technology Book 2023* is for anyone who has ever wondered about climate mitigation technologies and wanted to know more. It is for those seeking tangible solutions for building homes, providing food and transforming industries, without contributing to the global climate disaster. It is for those curious to know precisely what mitigation technologies are available today and in the near future – and, importantly, how to access them. It is also for those seeking to invest, and for those who design our cities, transport and agricultural systems, and for those leading our communities and countries along a low-carbon path.

By showing examples of solutions, we aim to inspire action. The *Green Technology Book* is not a comprehensive collection of all mitigation technologies available. Nor does it cover all those many areas where mitigation technologies could be relevant. This year's *Green Technology Book* chooses instead to focus on three broad areas where we believe climate change mitigation is and will be particularly critical. They are cities, agriculture and land use, and industry. Energy as a sector in itself is not included, simply because it is too large a topic to fit into this edition.

We welcome greater visibility for local innovation, especially from those countries most affected by climate change. Often the best technology may not be the one on the market. It may instead be the one available locally but not widely known, maybe reviving ancient skills and insights. The *Green Technology Book* is more than a catalogue meant for inspiration – it is a living project to which everyone can contribute. This publication links to the free public WIPO GREEN Database of needs and green technologies, where users can create a profile and share their climate solutions and needs.

How we wrote the book

For the purposes of this publication, we considered a broad set of scientific articles, gray literature, together with technology databases developed by private, public and civil society entities and organizations. Search strings included broad terms related to climate mitigation paired with key terms for the three thematic areas, and key terms related to specific technologies ("heat pumps," "soil carbon," "direct reduced iron" and so on). Translation engines enabled us to search articles in several languages to ensure a broad geographical spread.

Owners of the technologies identified were contacted, and all have been uploaded to the WIPO GREEN Database of needs and green technologies, either by the technology owner or by us at WIPO.

How we found the technologies

Throughout the publication, we operate with three concepts: innovation, solution, and technology. While sometimes used almost interchangeably, they do have different meanings. We here use the term innovation to cover all intellectual creativity that could result in a solution. Solution is broadly taken to mean the deployment of an innovation output to solve a specific challenge. The third concept, technology, relates to any physical entity or technique, with or without additional equipment, that is deployed to resolve a specific challenge. We are primarily interested in a technology's potential for responding to climate change, ranging from the very simple to the highly complex. Often the scope of climate technologies is expanded to include enabling mechanisms such as ownership and the institutional arrangements that pertain to that technology (e.g., building codes or energy management systems). But, while recognizing the importance of such mechanisms, we focus primarily on tangible technologies or actual techniques.

It is important to emphasize that the technologies presented here have not been tested or in any way vetted by WIPO, and that we rely on publicly available material. Inclusion within the *Green Technology Book* is therefore not a recommendation of a particular technology. Technologies presented here should instead be seen simply as examples of a technology area, and that there may be many other similar offerings which to our knowledge are in no way inferior. Photos illustrating the technologies are reproduced with permission from the technology owners. When such permission could not be obtained, we have used relevant stock-photos, meaning photos of technologies may not always represent the actual technology example described.

The appropriateness of a technology is often highly context-specific and relates to factors other than geographical location. Therefore no recommendations on where, when or how the technologies are suitable have been provided. Such an assessment should always be made with the involvement of local experts and stakeholders. Technology owners can freely upload their technology to the WIPO GREEN Database and in doing so become part of the project.

The following criteria were used when selecting technologies for the *Green Technology Book*:

- relevance for climate change mitigation;
- relevance for the three thematic areas: 1) Cities, 2) Agriculture and land use, and 3) Industry;
- pertain to:
  - a product or service available for purchase or licensing;
  - a product or service available for free/open source;
  - a guidebook on application of a method or technique;
  - a research project or similar (for horizon technologies).

In addition, the following factors were taken into consideration:

- anticipated impact from implementation;
- availability of sufficient quality information or third-party endorsements;
- market availability (for proven and frontier technologies);
- cost in relation to impact;
- geographical balance;
- business balance (large- and small-scale businesses, start-ups, research teams, non-governmental organizations and so on);
- no harm principle.

We have divided technologies into three broad groups in order to indicate their maturity and availability. Proven technologies are those that have been on the market for some time and therefore rely on a tried and tested concept. Frontier technologies are those that are available, but still relatively new, and as such possibly less validated within a real-world setting. Horizon technologies are those new concepts currently at research or development stage expected to become available within a few years' time.

Technologies have been classified in order to give an easy guide to relevance for a reader. We have aimed for a broad representation of technologies at various levels of complexity and stages of readiness. Technologies are classified as having either a low, medium or high level of complexity. This is an indication only and does not adhere to a strict definition of complexity. Rather, it reflects the level of human, material and monetary resources required to implement the solution in question. Meanwhile, technology maturity is broadly assessed according to the quasi-standard Technology Readiness Level (TRL) definition. According to this measure, horizon technologies have the lowest readiness level, but are nonetheless close to full development (TRL 6–7), whereas proven and frontier technologies have been validated and are ready to be scaled-up, if this has not already been done (TLR 8–9).

We hope you will be inspired by the creativity, ingenuity and diversity of the technologies here presented. We welcome any feedback and suggestions, which can be sent to us through the WIPO GREEN website.

Disclaimer

This publication, WIPO, and WIPO GREEN are in no way affiliated with any of the featured companies. Nor does this publication imply that other non-featured companies or technology solutions do not exist. All content in this publication is provided in good faith and based on information provided directly from the providers and/or using publicly available materials. Photos of technologies may not necessarily depict the actual technology. Therefore WIPO and WIPO GREEN disclaim any warranties, express or implied, as to the accuracy, adequacy, validity, reliability, availability, or completeness of any information provided. WIPO and WIPO GREEN are not responsible for any negative outcomes as a result of actions taken based on information in this publication.

URL Links

This publication contains weblinks to external websites not provided nor maintained by WIPO or WIPO GREEN. Responsibility for the content of listed external sites lies with their respective publishers. Weblinks are provided solely for contact and informational purposes; WIPO and WIPO GREEN do not sponsor or endorse any of the content therein. While every effort has been made to establish the legitimacy of each linked website, WIPO and WIPO GREEN disclaim any warranties, express or implied, as to the accuracy of the information within the linked content, and also disclaim any responsibility regarding the potential for data breaches as a result of accessing the weblinks.

1 / Overview: technology and innovation for climate mitigation

Photo: GettyImages / Dhai Amponrdanai

Climate change mitigation technologies

Climate mitigation requires innovation

Every modelled pathway for limiting global warming to 1.5 or even 2 degrees Celsius relies on making rapid and deep GHG reductions *this decade*.[1] Although we may have the solutions needed to halve emissions by 2030, reaching net zero by 2050 continues to require significant and rapid technological innovation.

Almost half of the emission reductions in net-zero scenarios produced by the International Energy Agency (IEA) are projected to come from technologies currently at the demonstration or prototype stage.[2] Furthermore, only 26 pathways of the 1,200 scenarios assessed by the IPCC limit warming to 1.5 degrees Celsius using proven technologies.[3]

It takes time for innovation to mature into market-ready solutions. Technologies such as solar panels, wind turbines, light-emitting diode (LED) bulbs and lithium-ion batteries have played a significant role in reducing emissions. But their path to massive deployment took decades to achieve.[4] For new clean energy technologies there is a lag-time of up to 10 years between initial funding and their appearance within an academic article, and a further decade or more between the publication of such an article and the filing of a technology patent.[5] Furthermore, new technologies often face challenges related to first-of-kind costs, higher operation and investment costs and insufficient or uncertain carbon prices.[6]

Although we may have the solutions needed to halve emissions by 2030, reaching net zero by 2050 continues to require significant and rapid technological innovation

Proven technologies must first be scaled

The challenge is that time is short and we cannot wait around for technological breakthroughs to arrive. According to most projections, carbon-capture and storage (CCS) will not see a significant scale-up this decade.[7, 8] Only one of the 30 commercial CCS facilities in operation globally has been developed at an iron and steel plant, and none at a cement plant.[9] Large-scale green hydrogen production is still a long way off, especially in those countries dominating hard-to-abate sectors. In 2022, low-emission hydrogen production was under 1 percent of total global hydrogen production, the rest predominantly produced from natural gas, a fossil fuel.[10]

We must therefore invest significantly in the vast range of solutions already at hand. Simply relying on emerging and breakthrough technologies to enter the market risks missing the window of opportunity to act. Moreover, technologies such as CCS must not become an enabler of business as usual. The science is clear – there is no room for new fossil fuel developments, if we are to avoid dramatic climate change impacts. Beyond enabling cleaner energy sources, there are already proven technologies available that can transform how we build, eat, live and travel.

Climate technology adoption in most developing countries is slow, especially in the least developed.[11] Rapidly growing cities and economies have a massive potential for scaling existing solutions, which would bring with them economic development opportunities and green jobs creation. The International Finance Corporation estimates there is a climate investment opportunity in emerging market cities amounting to USD 29.4 trillion by 2030.[12] This relates to six main sectors, many of which are covered in the *Green Technology Book*, namely: waste, climate-smart water, renewable energy, electric vehicles, public transport and green buildings.

> Technologies such as CCS must not become an enabler of business as usual. The science is clear – there is no room for new fossil fuel developments

Several studies have chosen to focus on the barriers to scaling climate technologies. These include cost and risk, as well as institutional, regulatory and human resource constraints. The *Green Technology Book* chooses instead to highlight the opportunities by showcasing a variety of climate technologies and innovations that could well shape the future of cities, food systems and industry. The most appropriate technology may differ immensely depending upon region, income level and the availability of local resources. The *Green Technology Book* therefore reflects a broad and inclusive range of technology solutions.

Climate mitigation requires circular thinking and good design

Not all climate technologies are equal. In fact, certain options can create a lock-in effect in suboptimal solutions; for example, market penetration by a refrigerant that does not deplete the ozone layer but nonetheless contributes to climate change. Similarly, an incinerator might address plastic pollution, but emit harmful emissions, reduce the incentive to recycle and, in some cases, rely on imported waste from around the world. Yet another example is retrofitting conventional steel furnaces rather than exploring electrified alternatives.

The world has a clear mandate to scale ambition. Incremental efficiencies are unlikely to bring about the transformation required.

> This means rethinking the design of our cities, understanding the limits of recycling, valuing soil and acknowledging the important role of technology and innovation in managing humanity's collective demand for Earth's resources

Circular approaches have a massive climate mitigation potential. In the European Union, such approaches could reduce CO_2 emissions from material production by 56 percent by 2050.[13] Roughly 70 to 80 percent of the municipal solid waste generated in Africa is recyclable; yet, only 4 percent is currently recycled.[14] Placing material efficiency and circular economy at the center of decarbonization can reduce the risk of an over-reliance on breakthrough technologies that may or may not come to fruition in time. It also requires significantly lower up-front costs. Yet, this is an often-overlooked mitigation action.[15] Countries' national climate plans and strategies have largely ignored this perspective.[16] And even when material efficiency is discussed, it is mainly in the context of waste management, not GHG emissions.[17]

The *Green Technology Book* presents new perspectives on what can be termed climate mitigation technology. This means rethinking the design of our cities, understanding the limits of recycling, valuing soil and acknowledging the important role of technology and innovation in managing humanity's collective demand for Earth's resources.

International climate finance and cooperation

The cost of climate change is growing

Managing emissions is expensive. However, not managing them will cost us more - both in terms of assets and lives lost. The cost of averting the most severe consequences of climate change on a global scale is likely to be approximately USD 4 trillion a year by 2030.[18] We are currently far off-track. The global climate finance flow is estimated to have been between USD 850 and USD 940 billion in 2021, met equally by the public and private sectors.[19]

Investments into climate mitigation are dominated by renewable energy, followed by low-carbon transport and energy efficiency (figure 1.1). Private finance mobilization is crucial for achieving climate targets. But private finance is growing at a slower annual rate than public finance.[20] At the same time, there is a growing recognition of the financial gains that come from investing in climate technologies. Venture capital investments into climate technologies represented over a quarter of every venture dollar invested in 2022, with the vast majority spent on mobility followed by energy.[21]

Sometimes overlooked in conversations on climate finance, consumer spending plays an especially important role in the adoption of technologies such as solar panels, water heaters and electric cars. Global spending on electric cars in 2022 was up 50 percent on the previous year, exceeding USD 425 billion.[22]

Figure 1.1 Climate mitigation finance by solution, 2011–2020 (USD billion)

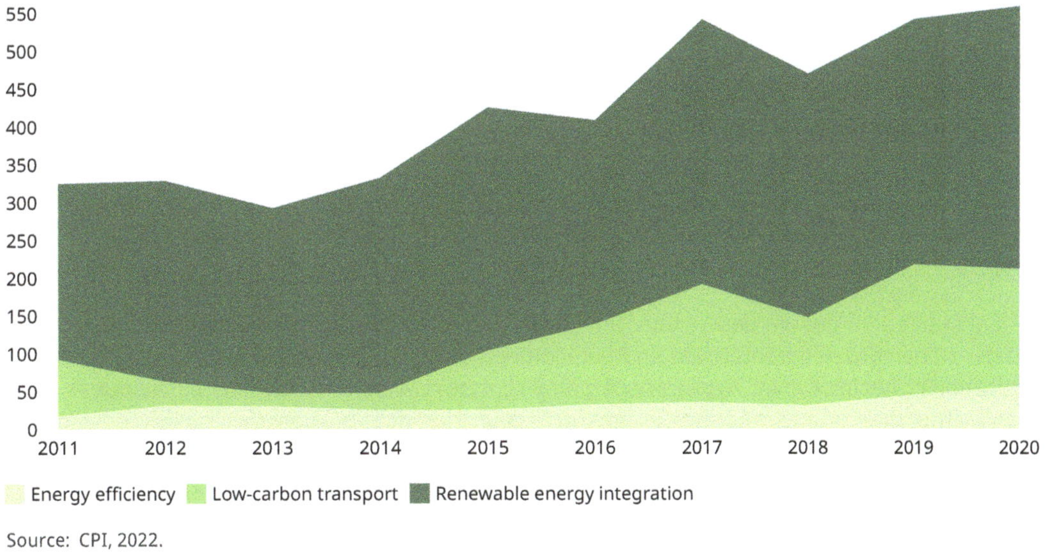

Source: CPI, 2022.

Given the gravity of climate change and its impacts, there is the question of whether certain climate technologies, such as early warning systems and climate datasets, ought to be considered a public good.[23, 24] Viewing climate technologies as a public good whose outcomes benefit everyone means setting aside market principles to some extent, or finding innovative measures to reward innovators, for instance, through an international mechanism.

International collaboration is essential, if developing countries are to have an equal opportunity to adopt climate technologies. Accepting responsibility for historical GHG emissions, developed countries have committed to providing USD 100 billion a year of climate finance to developing countries by 2025. The failure to provide this funding is clearly recognized. Meanwhile, the cost of climate change is rising. The external climate finance needs of developing countries and emerging markets (excluding China) have been estimated at USD 1 trillion a year from now until 2030.[25]

Countries are currently negotiating a New Collective Quantified Goal to replace the USD 100 billion commitment goal expiring in 2025. However, the conversation around international climate finance has expanded beyond discussions about how many billions of dollars are required. The questions now are who should be paying these billions and how new financial mechanisms and systems can be built that are fit for purpose.

Over 70 percent of global climate finance continues to be paid out as loans rather than grants, potentially adding to countries' debt burden

Climate finance, fossil fuels and public debt: balancing the scales

The flow of climate finance must be seen in relation to other relevant finance flows in order to get the bigger picture. Most notably this includes global fossil fuel funding and the annual debt repayments by developing countries (figure 1.2). Such a viewpoint is important in our understanding the full extent of the financial effort required to fund the climate transition, which goes beyond just positive climate finance flows. It also highlights what resources are available to dramatically scale and redirect funds toward global climate action. The COVID-19 pandemic recently demonstrated that a financial scaling of equivalent magnitude toward a global challenge is entirely possible. The investments in clean energy currently projected are a mere fraction of the amount committed to COVID-19 recovery.[26]

Figure 1.2 Global climate finance flows in relation to global debt and fossil fuel subsidies

* IMF estimate includes negative externalities such as health costs.
Source: UNCTAD 2023a; Black et al., 2023; IEA, 2023c; CPI, 2022.

Global public debt has increased more than fivefold since 2000, with developing countries owing almost 30 percent of the total debt. In Africa, more is spent in interest payments than on either education or health.[27] Over 70 percent of global climate finance continues to be paid out as loans rather than grants,[28] potentially adding to countries' debt burden. Civil society, developing countries, the United Nations and other actors have all called for a reform of international financial institutions, debt cancellations or new repayment policies, possibly as an alternative way of financing climate action.[29, 30]

In recent years, major institutions have shown some response to such calls. The World Bank recently announced an offer to developing countries hit by climate disaster to pause debt repayments on new loans. Furthermore, a new wave of debt-for-climate swaps is making it possible for countries to swap debt repayments for investment into climate projects. For example, the Seychelles is the first country to have shifted its loan repayments toward investment into marine protected areas.

Required financial return on a solar project can range from 7 percent in Germany to a staggering 52 percent in Argentina, regardless of identical solar arrays being deployed

Meanwhile, subsidies for global fossil fuel consumption continue to grow. Indeed, 2022 marked a record-breaking year for fossil fuel subsidies.[31] In 2023, 60 percent of global energy investment is expected to go into clean technologies, including into renewables, electric vehicles and heat pumps. The rest is expected to be invested into fossil fuel supply and power.[32] The World Trade Organization (WTO), led by New Zealand, is exploring fossil fuel subsidy reform. But global calls for fossil fuel subsidies and fossil fuel project loans to be cancelled have had very little impact to date.

De-risking climate technology innovation and deployment

Governments continue to lag behind on international collaboration for climate finance. Meanwhile, they have an equally important role to play in developing and deploying climate technologies. Technology-push and demand-pull drivers are both important when it comes to fostering technological innovation.

Regarding low-carbon technologies, markets are not always able to provide the right type of incentives. This justifies government intervention and spending. Governments stimulate technological innovation by sharing the risks and rewards between public and private actors.[33] They are also critical to the creation of new markets and for improving the innovation-cost balance. Carbon taxes, in particular, have been shown to positively impact innovation in mitigation technologies.[34]

Once developed, climate technologies face a further challenge - deployment. Lack of data and risk perception are important barriers to technology transfer, uptake efficiency and financial viability, especially in developing countries. The role of international institutions in providing project transparency and de-risking investments is widely recognized. The importance of de-risking becomes apparent in light of the tremendous variation in the credit required rate of return on investment, which is often linked to a project's location and the country's credit rating.

For instance, the required financial return on a solar project can range from 7 percent in Germany to a staggering 52 percent in Argentina, regardless of identical solar arrays being deployed (table 1.1).[35] Such assessments are linked to a country's credit rating issued by organizations such as S&P Global. There can therefore be a demand for developing mechanisms and support structures which can de-risk such climate technology deployment.

Table 1.1 **Required return on investment from solar projects in various countries**

Country	S&P rating	Required return on solar project (%)
Germany	AAA	7
United States	AA+	9
United Arab Emirates (UAE)	AA	10
Saudi Arabia	A-	12
Chile	A	12
Morocco	BBB-	15
India	BBB-	17
Algeria	B	18
Oman	BB-	18
Peru	BBB	20
Costa Rica	B	21
Namibia	BB-	21

Country	S&P rating	Required return on solar project (%)
Ghana	B–	22
Brazil	BB–	22
Nigeria	B+	22
Bolivia	B+	24
Tanzania	B	24
Egypt	B	28
Zambia	CCC–	38
Argentina	CCC+	52

Source: Adapted from Songwe, Stern and Bhattacharya, 2022.

The role of innovation and IP for the diffusion of low-emission technologies

Strengthening national systems of innovation

Innovation often builds on existing inventions. OECD countries usually have the most efficient national systems of innovation (NSIs). A great many factors and drivers determine a healthy NSI. They include education spending, small business and market support, institutional and infrastructural stability and well-managed intellectual property (IP) rights. These and more are described in the first edition of the *Green Technology Book*.

Pressing global challenges and climate change make it imperative that innovation and technology address real-world needs on the ground. A better understanding of how various actors and different parts of the innovation ecosystem interact make it possible for innovation systems to be strengthened across sectors and countries. This can in turn lead to insights into the appropriateness and social alignment of new technologies and practices. Partly, this requires going beyond traditional ways of measuring innovation, such as R&D investments and patents, to include the monitoring of systemic indicators, such as resource mobilization, entrepreneurial activity and market formation.[36, 37]

Strengthening innovation ecosystems requires a systemic approach enabled by supportive policies. The IPCC[38] highlights how important policies addressing innovation systems are in helping overcome the distributional, environmental and social barriers associated with low-emitting technologies. Increasingly, regulatory frameworks for addressing global challenges must consider the important role of scientific and technical knowledge, and the provision of secure IP rights and ownership.[39]

Technological adaptation and endogenous technologies

A majority of climate technology patents are filed at IP offices within developed countries (see next section). And there is a striking mismatch between the technology needed by developing countries and its availability. This has come to mean that a majority of climate technologies are a response to the needs and conditions of developed nations. More locally appropriate climate technologies can be promoted in a variety of ways. They include 1) adaptation of transferred technologies to local contexts, 2) innovation co-development and 3) the support and recognition of locally-invented, endogenous or indigenous peoples' technologies.

Successful technology uptake and adaptation requires effective participation by domestic labor and national skillsets building. The choice of technology is important. Consideration needs to be given to a technology's maturity, its complexity and its potential for scaling to a meaningful level. But perhaps even more importantly, successful uptake depends on understanding user needs. This warrants a broad-based, participatory approach, with the inclusion of a broad range of stakeholders, including farmers, youth, indigenous peoples, women and other groups, when deploying innovative climate technologies.

There is a growing debate around shifting the "technology transfer" paradigm to one of "co-development of technology" to highlight the importance of collaborative interventions in bringing climate innovations to market. Examples of such initiatives can already be seen, but are not widespread. Joint ventures, collaborative R&D, and technology collaboration programs have the potential to support localization in favor of imported technologies. Scaling this approach further could mean building on modalities such as IP rights co-ownership, pooled financial resources and shared responsibility for risk, liability and transparency.[40] However, while more support is undeniably needed for local technology development, climate targets are unlikely to be met without a transfer of technology and the sharing of know-how and skills at a global level.

In the process of identifying climate technologies for the *Green Technology Book*, the challenge of finding solutions from certain parts of the world has become clear. The reasons for this are manifold. Weaker national systems of innovation lead to fewer patents and a consequential absence from patent databases. Language barriers and a lack of documentation means negligible global online presence and a missed opportunity for attracting funding for locally appropriate technology dissemination and uptake. There is therefore a pressing need for greater recognition, visibility and support for technology solutions emerging from developing countries which may help increase the diversity of solutions available for a wider range of local conditions and contexts.

Climate technology patent trends

Patent trends can with due caution be used as a proxy for innovation activity and technology trends. Inventions in climate change mitigation technologies increased fivefold between 1995 and 2011.[41] But there was subsequently a notable slowdown in the total number of patent applications filed between 2014 and 2017 (figure 1.3).[42, 43]

Figure 1.3 Global patent applications for climate mitigation technologies in various sectors, 1990-2015

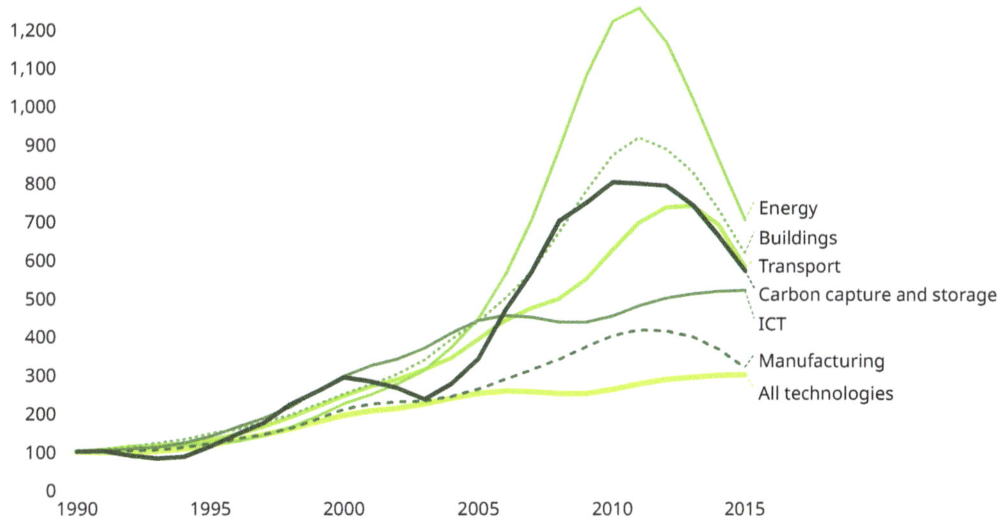

Note: ICT = Information and communication technologies
Source: IEA, 2019b.

One study shows that the climate mitigation technologies growth rate fell by 6 percent a year between 2013 and 2017, after having grown by 10 percent a year the decade before.[44] The drop in overall patent activity - mainly affecting the energy, building, manufacturing and CCS sectors - is likely to have been due to declining fossil fuel prices, low carbon prices and the "maturity" of certain climate mitigation technologies.

But, while growth is no longer at the level it was in the first decade of this century, the trend appears once again to be upward. Low-carbon energy technologies patenting grew in the three years following 2017, mainly driven by fuel switching and energy efficiency, as well as by cross-cutting technologies such as hydrogen and batteries for transport.[45]

The transport sector has maintained slow and steady growth over time, but activity has recently accelerated. There is a clear correlation between electric vehicle patent activity and the price of fossil fuels. Europe saw a drop in electric vehicle patent applications following the 2014 oil price plunge. Subsequently, 2017–2021 saw a significant increase in electric and hybrid vehicle technologies, while innovations related to conventional fossil-based engines declined markedly during the same period (figure 1.4).[46]

Figure 1.4 European Patent Office (EPO) applications for electric, hybrid and exhaust treatment technologies, 2012 and 2021

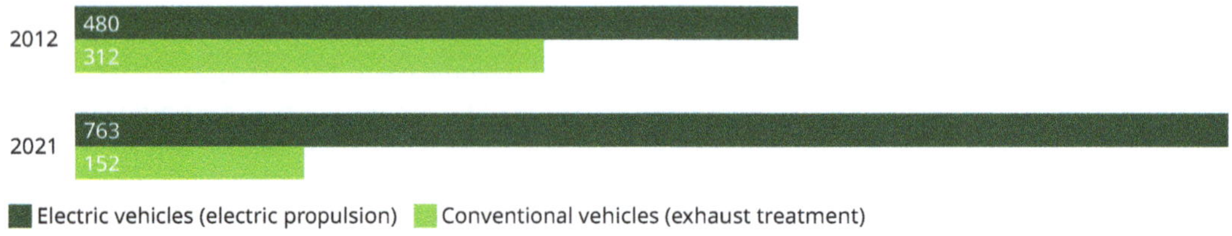

Source: EPO, 2022a.

Not all climate mitigation technologies are sensitive to oil price fluctuation. Digital technologies are increasingly considered important climate enablers and their rate of penetration in climate technologies is extremely high. In fact, 60 percent of climate-related trademarks are information and communication technology (ICT)-related.[47] Almost 40 percent of climate mitigation innovation within the energy and building sectors can be considered digital. Indeed, as patent activity within these two sectors slowed down, digital climate mitigation technologies related to energy and buildings grew markedly.[48]

What has not changed over the past decade is that inventions are concentrated in certain countries and among a few R&D investors.

Five countries alone represent nearly 76 percent of high-value climate mitigation innovation, namely China, Germany, Japan, the Republic of Korea and the United States, with China dominating a growing number of patent filings. The data refers to inventions developed between 2010 and 2015,[49] but the distribution is unlikely to have changed substantially since then. The top 10 countries in turn accounted for almost 90 percent of high-value climate innovation. These consist exclusively of high-income countries, with the sole exception of China. And the trend is toward increasing concentration of innovation. This underlines the need for greater technology transfer and innovation at the national level.[50] What is more, there is data to suggest that it is often inventors and young firms beyond the top few who develop the more radical innovations likely to spearhead much needed breakthrough discoveries.[51]

Notes

1 IPCC (2023). Synthesis report (SYR) of the IPCC sixth assessment report (AR6). Summary for policymakers. Geneva: Intergovernmental Panel on Climate Change (IPCC). Available at: https://www.ipcc.ch/report/ar6/syr/.

2 IEA (2021). Net Zero by 2050. A roadmap for the global energy sector. Paris: International Energy Agency (EIA). Available at: https://www.iea.org/reports/net-zero-by-2050.

3 IISD (2022). Lighting the path: What IPCC energy pathways tell us about Paris-aligned policies and investments. Canada: International Institute for Sustainable Development (IISD). Available at: https://www.iisd.org/system/files/2022-06/ipcc-pathways-paris-aligned-policies.pdf.

4 Sivaram, V. (2022). Climate change. *MIT Technology Review*, 125(4).

5 Noailly, J. (2022). Directing innovation towards a low-carbon future. *Economic Research Working Paper No. 72*. Geneva: World Intellectual Property Organization (WIPO). Available at: https://www.wipo.int/publications/en/details.jsp?id=4599&plang=EN.

6 Richstein, J.C. and K. Neuhoff (2022). Carbon contracts-for-difference: How to de-risk innovative investments for a low-carbon industry? *iScience*, 25(8), 104700.

7 IEA (2023). *CCUS project explorer*. Available at:: https://www.iea.org/data-and-statistics/data-tools/ccus-projects-explorer.

8 Martin-Roberts, E., *et al*. (2021). Carbon capture and storage at the end of a lost decade. *One Earth*, 4(11), 1569-84.

9 Global CCS Institute (2022). 2022 Status report: Appendices. Available at: https://status22.globalccsinstitute.com/2022-status-report/appendices [accessed May 2023].

10 IEA (2023). *Hydrogen: Tracking clean energy progress 2023*. International Energy Agency (IEA). Available at: https://www.iea.org/energy-system/low-emission-fuels/hydrogen#tracking [accessed August 2023].

11 IPCC (2023). Synthesis report (SYR) of the IPCC sixth assessment report (AR6). Summary for policymakers. Geneva: Intergovernmental Panel on Climate Change (IPCC). Available at: https://www.ipcc.ch/report/ar6/syr/.

12 CCFLA (2021). *The state of cities climate finance*. The Cities Climate Finance Leadership Alliance (CCFLA). Available at: https://www.climatepolicyinitiative.org/publication/the-state-of-cities-climate-finance/.

13 Material Economics (2018). *The circular economy – A powerful force for climate mitigation*. Stockholm, Sweden. Available at: https://circulareconomy.europa.eu/platform/en/knowledge/circular-economy-powerful-force-climate-mitigation.

14 UNEP (2023). *Harnessing technology in the circular economy for climate action in Africa*, CTCN knowledge brief series. Nairobi: United Nations Environment Programme. Available at: https://www.ctc-n.org/news/climate-action-africa-harnessing-technology-circular-economy.

15 IEA (2019). *Material efficiency in clean energy transitions*. Paris: International Energy Agency (IEA). Available at: https://www.iea.org/reports/material-efficiency-in-clean-energy-transitions.

16 Potochnik, J. and A. Wijkman (2022). From 'greening' the present system to real transformation – Transforming resource use for human wellbeing and planetary stability. Earth4all: Deep-dive paper 12. Earth4All. Available at: https://www.clubofrome.org/wp-content/uploads/2022/10/Earth4All_Deep_Dive_Wijkman-2.pdf.

17 International Resource Panel (2020). *Resource efficiency and climate change: Material efficiency strategies for a low-carbon future*. Nairobi, Kenya: United Nations Environment Programme International Resource Panel. Available at: https://www.resourcepanel.org/reports/resource-efficiency-and-climate-change.

18 CPI (2022). *Global landscape of climate finance: A decade of data*. Climate Policy Initiative (CPI). Available at: https://www.climatepolicyinitiative.org/publication/global-landscape-of-climate-finance-a-decade-of-data/.

19 CPI (2022). *Global landscape of climate finance: A decade of data*. Climate Policy Initiative (CPI). Available at: https://www.climatepolicyinitiative.org/publication/global-landscape-of-climate-finance-a-decade-of-data/.

20 CPI (2022). *Global landscape of climate finance: A decade of data*. Climate Policy Initiative (CPI). Available at: https://www.climatepolicyinitiative.org/publication/global-landscape-of-climate-finance-a-decade-of-data/.

21 PwC (2022). *State of climate tech 2022: Overcoming inertia in climate tech investing*. Available at: https://www.pwc.com/gx/en/services/sustainability/publications/overcoming-inertia-in-climate-tech-investing.html.

22 IEA (2023). *Global EV outlook 2023*. International Energy Agency (IEA). Available at: https://www.iea.org/reports/global-ev-outlook-2023.

23 ITU (2022). Tech transfer and digital public goods needed for climate action. The International Telecommunication Union (ITU). Available at: https://www.itu.int/hub/2022/03/tech-transfer-digital-public-goods-climate-action-africa/ [accessed August 2023].

24 United Nations (2020). *Roadmap for digital cooperation*. Available at: https://www.un.org/en/content/digital-cooperation-roadmap/assets/pdf/Roadmap_for_Digital_Cooperation_EN.pdf.

25 Songwe, V., N. Stern and A. Bhattacharya (2022). *Finance for climate action: Scaling up investment for climate and development*. London: Grantham Research Institute on Climate Change and the Environment, London School of Economics and Political Science. Available at: https://www.lse.ac.uk/granthaminstitute/wp-content/uploads/2022/11/IHLEG-Finance-for-Climate-Action.pdf.

26 Andrijevic, M., *et al*. (2020). COVID-19 recovery funds dwarf clean energy investment needs. Science, 370(6514), 298–300.

27 UNCTAD (2023a). *A world of debt: A growing burden to global prosperity*, United Nations Conference on Trade and Development (UNCTAD). Available at: https://unctad.org/publication/world-of-debt.

28 CPI (2022). Global landscape of climate finance: A decade of data. Climate Policy Initiative (CPI). Available at: https://www.climatepolicyinitiative.org/publication/global-landscape-of-climate-finance-a-decade-of-data/.

29 UNCTAD (2023b). *A world of debt: A growing burden to global prosperity*, United Nations Conference on Trade and Development (UNCTAD). Available at: https://unctad.org/publication/world-of-debt.

30 United Nations (2023). Finance & justice. Available at: https://www.un.org/en/climatechange/raising-ambition/climate-finance [accessed October 2023].

31 IEA (2023). Fossil fuel consumption subsidies 2022. Policy report, International Energy Agency (IEA). Available at: https://www.iea.org/reports/fossil-fuels-consumption-subsidies-2022.

32 IEA (2023). *World energy investment 2023*, Flagship report. Paris: International Energy Agency (IEA). Available at: https://www.iea.org/reports/world-energy-investment-2023.

33 UNEP-CCC (2022). *The climate technology progress report 2022*. Copenhagen, Denmark: Copenhagen Climate Centre (CCC), UNFCCC Technology Executive Committee (TEC) and United Nations Environment Programme (UNEP). Available at: https://unepccc.org/publications/the-climate-technology-progress-report-2022/.

34 van den Bergh, J. and I. Savin (2021). Impact of carbon pricing on low-carbon innovation and deep decarbonisation: Controversies and path forward. *Environmental and Resource Economics*, 80(4), 705-15.

35 Songwe, V., N. Stern, and A. Bhattacharya (2022). *Finance for climate action: scaling up investment for climate and*

development. London: Grantham Research Institute on Climate Change and the Environment, London School of Economics and Political Science. Available at: https://www.lse.ac.uk/granthaminstitute/wp-content/uploads/2022/11/IHLEG-Finance-for-Climate-Action.pdf.

36 IPCC (2022). *Climate change 2022: Mitigation of climate change - Summary for policymakers, Working Group III contribution to IPCC sixth assessment report*. Cambridge, UK: Intergovernmental Panel on Climate Change (IPCC). Available at: https://www.ipcc.ch/report/sixth-assessment-report-working-group-3/.

37 WIPO (2023). *Global Innovation Index (GII)*. World Intellectual Property Organization (WIPO). Available at: https://www.wipo.int/global_innovation_index/en/index.html.

38 IPCC (2022). *Climate change 2022: Mitigation of climate change - Summary for policymakers, Working Group III contribution to IPCC sixth assessment report*. Cambridge, UK: Intergovernmental Panel on Climate Change (IPCC). Available at: https://www.ipcc.ch/report/sixth-assessment-report-working-group-3/.

39 UNEP-CCC (2022). *The climate technology progress report 2022*. Copenhagen, Denmark: Copenhagen Climate Centre (CCC), UNFCCC Technology Executive Committee (TEC) and United Nations Environment Programme (UNEP). Available at: https://unepccc.org/publications/the-climate-technology-progress-report-2022/.

40 SEI and CEEW (2022). *Stockholm+50: Unlocking a better future*. Stockholm: Stockholm Environment Institute (SEI). Available at: https://www.stockholm50.report/unlocking-a-better-future.pdf.

41 EPO and UNEP (2015). *Climate change mitigation technologies in Europe - Evidence from patent and economic data*. Nairobi: United Nations Environment Programme (UNEP) and European Patent Office (EPO). Available at: https://www.epo.org/news-events/in-focus/sustainable-technologies/clean-energy/europe.html.

42 IEA (2019). *Global patent applications for climate change mitigation technologies - a key measure of innovation - are trending down*. Paris: International Energy Agency (IEA). Available at: https://www.iea.org/commentaries/global-patent-applications-for-climate-change-mitigation-technologies-a-key-measure-of-innovation-are-trending-down.

43 The IEA data draws upon information from the Patent Statistical Database (PATSTAT) and applies to those mitigation technologies related to buildings, CCS, manufacturing, transport and ICT.

44 Probst, B., *et al*. (2021). Global trends in the invention and diffusion of climate change mitigation technologies. *Nature Energy*, 6, 1077–86.

45 EPO and IEA (2021). *Patents and the energy transition*. European Patent Office (EPO) and International Energy Agency (IEA). Available at: https://iea.blob.core.windows.net/assets/b327e6b8-9e5e-451d-b6f4-cbba6b1d90d8/Patents_and_the_energy_transition.pdf.

46 EPO (2022). Insights into urban mobility. European Patent Office (EPO). Available at: https://www.epo.org/about-us/annual-reports-statistics/statistics/2021/insight-into-smart-urban-mobility.html [accessed August 2023].

47 Amoroso S., *et al*. (2021). *World corporate top R&D investors: Paving the way for climate neutrality - A joint JRC and OECD report*. Luxembourg: Publications Office of the European Union. Available at: https://www.oecd.org/sti/world-corporate-top-rd-investors-paving-the-way-for-climate-neutrality.pdf.

48 IEA (2019). Global patent applications for climate change mitigation technologies - a key measure of innovation - are trending down. Paris: International Energy Agency (IEA). Available at: https://www.iea.org/commentaries/global-patent-applications-for-climate-change-mitigation-technologies-a-key-measure-of-innovation-are-trending-down

49 Touboul, S. (2021). *Technological innovation and adaptation to climate change*. Paris: Université Paris sciences et lettres. Available at: https://pastel.hal.science/tel-03610832/document.

50 Probst, B., *et al*. (2021). Global trends in the invention and diffusion of climate change mitigation technologies. *Nature Energy*, 6, 1077–86.

51 Amoroso S., *et al*. (2021). *World corporate top R&D investors: Paving the way for climate neutrality - A joint JRC and OECD report*. Luxembourg: Publications Office of the European Union. Available at: https://www.oecd.org/sti/world-corporate-top-rd-investors-paving-the-way-for-climate-neutrality.pdf.

2 / Cities

Photos: Getty Images

Technological developments and trends

Cities cover just a small percentage of our planet's surface. Yet they generate 50 to 80 percent of the world's greenhouse gas (GHG) emissions and consume nearly 75 percent of global material resources.[1] Technology and innovation have vital roles to play in transforming cities from carbon emitters to carbon sinks.

This chapter explores proven, frontier and horizon technologies for decarbonizing cities. The topics addressed include low-carbon mobility, heating and cooling and material efficiency. Key trends are presented in the introductory section below, focusing on technology, finance and patents.

With the growth in transport demand offsetting efficiency gains, vehicle-level interventions alone may not be sufficient to decarbonize the mobility sector

Alternative fuels and material innovation

Many cities are witnessing a massive trend toward electrification of vehicle fleets, from cars and buses to rickshaws and scooters. Numerous startups are developing electric vehicle batteries that charge faster and run for longer with reduced reliance on critical minerals. Others are tackling barriers to electric vehicle use through battery-swapping stations and vehicle-grid integration enabled by charging apps, delayed charging technologies and real-time grid data.

Advances in waste valorization and non-food biomass could encourage biofuel use beyond its role as a transition fuel. The global micromobility market – such as electric bicycles and scooters – is bucking the trend toward larger and more energy-consuming cars and is currently estimated at around USD 180 billion.[2] Innovations in composite materials, carbon fiber technology and high-strength steels to reduce vehicle weight, and therefore fuel consumption, have an important mitigating effect if applied at scale.

Compact cities and smart mobility

However, with the growth in transport demand offsetting efficiency gains, vehicle-level interventions alone may not be sufficient to decarbonize the mobility sector. Compact cities offer better opportunities for walking, cycling, public transport and pooled mobility options. There is also growing momentum in favor of performing certain tasks without the need to travel altogether.

As the world has recently witnessed, a rapid and large-scale modal shift is possible. The COVID-19 pandemic prompted unprecedented growth in non-motorized transport and telecommunication technologies. The need to socially distance drove a massive increase in bicycle sales, while car use reduced drastically as people worked from home. Some cities seized this opportunity to redesign streets, reclaiming parking space for new pedestrian and cycle lanes.[3]

Digital technologies are increasingly allowing cities to plan and create sustainable urban environments for low-carbon mobility. For instance, mobility-as-a-service digital platforms enable bus/train intermodality and smart traffic management systems reduce traffic congestion. Shared mobility platforms were conceived to reduce car ownership but they can end up competing with public transport in cities where these services are dominant.

Addressing the cooling dilemma

Cooling is increasingly necessary for survival in a growing number of cities. But the energy use required for cooling contributes significantly to global warming. The most commonly available technologies are energy consuming, but significant advances to address this challenge are being made.

Although some regions are seeing a decrease in heating demand as a result of global warming,[4] it still makes up around half the world's energy consumption. Development and dissemination of highly efficient heat pumps that can both heat and cool features on many cities' decarbonization agendas. Innovations range from improvements in energy efficiency and solar integration to the use of refrigerants with lower climate impact. Research on refrigerant-free heat pumps is underway.

Heating and cooling demand is currently met by individual devices but district heating and cooling solutions that offer efficiency and climate mitigation benefits are expected to grow. Next-generation district technologies can enable simultaneous heating and cooling, and integration with smart energy systems.

Heating or cooling solutions depend on the local climate, economy and culture. Embracing vernacular techniques and materials within modern applications can enable passive heating and cooling. Nature-based solutions, such as green zones and waterways, reduce the urban heat island effect. In certain settings, energy-consuming heating and cooling technologies can be avoided altogether. Countries ranging from India to Switzerland are limiting the use and operating temperature of air conditioners. This energy-saving measure is enabled through legislation and minimum energy performance standards.

Smart technologies and return schemes enhance recycling

Material efficiency has a massive impact on GHG reduction by reducing energy consumption from production. An important aspect is how discarded products are handled and reintroduced into production and use cycles. At present, globally, waste is still generally dumped in open landfill sites that pollute soil and groundwater, spread disease and generate GHG emissions as organic materials decompose. Recycling is currently failing to keep pace with the waste generated by the ever-growing production of products such as packaging and construction material.

Technology and innovation play vital roles in sustainable waste management, with policy and local institutional capacities as key enablers. Smart cities in high-income countries are increasingly harnessing the power of data and automation. Sensors and digital technologies optimize waste collection and separation while optical scanners and robotics divert materials away from landfill. Deposit return schemes and technologies that recirculate bottles and cans are growing in popularity. Alternative recycling technologies, such as chemical recycling, have reemerged rapidly as a means of converting plastic waste into oils and fuel. However, their high costs and energy demands will likely limit their usefulness from a climate perspective.

Downstream waste management practices cannot adequately address the climate impact of our material consumption

Material efficiency beyond waste management

In lower-income countries advancing from open dumping and burning, the organic fraction of the waste is often high. Locally appropriate technological solutions include composting, anaerobic digesters and recycling processes that often rely on the important work of informal waste pickers. Transitioning from open dumping to semi-aerobic landfill solutions has the potential to reduce emissions by 40 percent.[5] While incineration technologies are gaining prominence in regions such as Southeast Asia, some countries in the European Union (EU) are phasing out such practices in favor of preserving materials for better uses.

Downstream waste management practices cannot adequately address the climate impact of our material consumption. Technologies and solutions that enable circular cities and upstream material efficiency are therefore taking precedence as climate mitigation measures. Innovations in lighter products and green manufacturing methods are ushering in a new era for material use in cities. Engineered wood and new applications for natural and sustainable construction materials offer both strength and sustainability. The substitution of timber for steel and concrete has significant potential to reduce embedded emissions in buildings if forests are managed sustainably and timber elements are reused or recycled at end of life.[6] Self-healing concrete, high-strength steel and deconstruction-ready design principles further extend the lifespan of materials and products, reducing the need for primary production.

Patents and finance

Electric vehicle patents dominating

The section on Mobility in this year's *Green Technology Book* focuses on road transport - the primary source of GHG emissions compared to rail, air and maritime transport. Road transport also dominates low-carbon innovation in the transport sector, with growth in electric vehicle technologies accelerating after 2005.[7] Electric vehicle uptake has been boosted by government subsidies, regulatory targets and technological advances. These have led to a price drop of nearly 90 percent since 2010 for lithium-ion batteries - the most commonly used battery for electric vehicles.[8]

Most low-carbon transport inventions relate to battery technology, with 9 of the top 10 filing companies based in Asia. Lithium-ion batteries still dominate research, with the greatest focus on extending battery life, increasing charging speed and facilitating recyclability. At the frontier, lithium-based solid-state batteries could offer longer lifespans and higher energy density. While these are not yet commercialized, they have seen an average 25 percent increase in patents since 2010. A number of companies have announced their intention to use this technology as an alternative to lithium-ion batteries in their vehicles in the next few years.[9]

Micromobility, fuel cells and smart mobility

Micromobility systems have expanded significantly in recent years, with e-bikes and step scooters seeing the most intense level of innovation among European patent applications.[10, 11] Research and development (R&D) activity in the field of hydrogen fuel cells has also accelerated with nearly 4,000 fuel cell patents filed in 2018 by applicants in China, which has overtaken Japan to become the leading patent country.[12]

Patent trend reports on climate change mitigation in the mobility sector mainly focus on vehicle-level interventions. But technologies that enable a more transformative shift in travel patterns have become increasingly important in the last decade, driven by the rise in artificial intelligence (AI) and the internet of things (IoT). Such technologies range from smart traffic management systems and smart parking and charging solutions to technologies for vehicle-grid integration and urban planning.

Heat pump innovation on the rise

The global patent landscape for efficient heating and cooling technologies has evolved in the last decade. Reflecting their growing importance, heat pump patents have increased substantially since 2015. While China is the country with most patents, Austria and Germany are more specialized in this field.[13] Meanwhile, conventional air-conditioner technology based on vapor-compression has witnessed slower growth.[14] Comprehensive patent trend assessments are not available for passive cooling technologies, such as insulation and radiative coatings.[15]

Advances in sustainable material alternatives

This chapter offers an overview of various technologies that reduce climate impact through material efficiency, ranging from lightweight and low-carbon materials to reuse and recycling. As this brief commentary on patent trends cannot address all these categories, examples of innovation activity are presented along the value chain of one specific material: plastic. After all, the United Nations Environment Programme (UNEP) estimates that the GHG emissions from plastic production, use and disposal could account for 19 percent of the global carbon budget by 2040.[16]

The production and conversion stage generates 90 percent of plastic-related emissions. Recycled, biodegradable or bio-based plastics are considered important mitigating measures, but their share of total plastic will remain limited under current policies.[17] The health-care sector is leading the way in bioplastic innovation with more than 19,000 international patent families in the period 2010–2019. The sector uses plastics for single-use or medical surgery tools and packaging.[18]

Recent studies have cautioned that with the current level of technology, increased consumption of bioplastics is likely to generate GHG emissions from cropland expansion, warranting further innovation in this space.[19] Plastic production also results in significant pre-consumer waste (i.e., waste generated during the manufacturing process that never reaches end-consumers). Material efficiency measures and innovation in this space are neither well understood nor discussed.

After all, the United Nations Environment Programme (UNEP) estimates that the GHG emissions from plastic production, use and disposal could account for 19 percent of the global carbon budget by 2040

Plastic recycling innovations

In terms of plastic recycling, there is a discrepancy between patenting activity and technology needs from a climate perspective. Most activity relates to chemical or biological recycling where microbes and bacteria break down the plastics. These methods saw twice the number of patents compared to mechanical recycling, which is currently the most common recycling method. However, successful commercialization of chemical or biological plastic recycling is yet to materialize. Moreover, these are energy-intensive processes that produce oil and other simpler compounds rather than direct generation of new plastic outputs.

More recently, innovations that focus on high-quality or easily recyclable plastics have grown exponentially. This includes research into so-called dynamic covalent bonding. The field addresses typical recycling challenges and plastic materials capable of self-repair. This could enhance recycling rates while minimizing the need for frequent replacements due to wear and tear.[20]

The urban climate finance gap

Climate finance for cities recently reached approximately USD 384 billion a year. Loans, rather than grants, represented a significant portion. Of the total climate finance flows assessed by the Cities Climate Finance Leadership Alliance, funding commitments through debt represented 42 percent. Regardless of the financing instrument, this sum is far from the estimated USD 4.5 to 5.4 trillion needed to transform cities' power and transport systems and buildings. Cities in developing countries face a particularly large climate finance gap. Furthermore, the global balance is uneven with more than 90 percent of finance going into mitigation rather than adaptation.[21]

Conversations on climate finance often relate to international grants and loans, or domestic public funding. For cities, however, household and individual spending on electric vehicles and energy efficiency improvements is a major growing contributor representing on average 32 percent of all private finance. This is particularly the case in developed country cities.

Meanwhile, public sector investments in urban climate finance represented 38 percent of the total funding sources mapped. There are significant data gaps due to data confidentiality issues and the lack of centralized databases. Thus, the remaining urban climate finance mapped originated from unknown sources (figure 2.1).[22]

Figure 2.1 Urban climate flows, annual average 2017–2018 (USD billion)

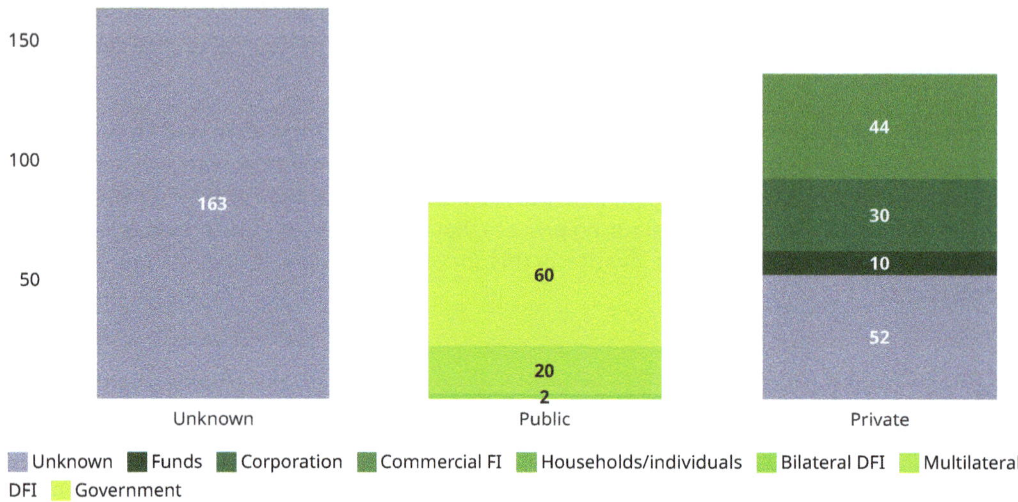

Source: CCFLA, 2021.

Investment trends in urban decarbonization

Nearly 54 percent of climate investments for decarbonization of cities were directed at transport. While electric vehicles and charging infrastructure received a fifth of the total investment, the vast majority went to public transport measures such as metro, tram and electric buses. It is also relevant to consider the nature of climate finance. International finance that targets climate technologies in the transport and storage sector offers few grants in comparison to the number of debt instruments.[23] This is surprising considering the dual challenge of climate change and urban air pollution addressed by investment in low-carbon urban transport.

The urban building sector attracts approximately 44 percent of total urban climate finance, representing an average USD 167 billion annually. Of this total, a little over USD 100 billion is directed toward energy efficiency and renewable heat investments.[24] This includes energy efficient heating and cooling systems, but also consideration of the embodied carbon in building materials. This figure excludes district heating and cooling networks.

Global finance for climate mitigation within the waste sector amounted to an average of USD 2 billion in 2019/2020. This was merely a fraction of the total global mitigation finance in that period.[25] When assessing climate finance figures, the waste sector typically does not include material efficiency measures such as demand management, waste prevention and material substitution. Generally, material efficiency has received less attention as a climate mitigation measure, meaning there is a lack of global aggregated data on related climate finance flows.

However, this does not mean that investments are not being made. For instance, the circular economy is a key pillar of the EU's USD 1.2 trillion European Green Deal Investment Plan. In 2020, assets managed through public equity funds with a circular economy focus increased more than sixfold to USD 2 billion, and startups developing plastic alternatives raised more than USD 850 million in funding in the three years leading up to 2020.[26]

Photo: Getty Images / 4FR

Efficient heating and cooling

Reducing the carbon footprint of heating and cooling is a key mitigation measure in cities. Beyond phasing out fossil fuels, this means electrifying heating and scaling energy-efficient heating and cooling technologies. It also means switching to refrigerants with low global warming potential (GWP). But, perhaps more importantly, it means limiting demand as far as possible. By harnessing the power of good design and nature-based solutions in cities, we can enhance energy efficiency in buildings that use heating and air conditioners (ACs) as a last resort.

Note: This chapter covers commercial and residential heating and cooling. See Chapter 3, Industry, for boilers and furnaces in the steel and cement sector.

Good design can go a long way

In ancient Persia, windcatchers - or *bâdgirs* - were a common architectural element. These towers would catch the breeze and channel it down through the house to cool the interior. Vernacular architecture around the world has provided thermal comfort through natural heating, cooling and ventilation solutions for centuries.

In many places, we are now constructing buildings in ways that make mechanical devices indispensable, adding to the growing climate impact of heating and cooling (see box 2.1).[27] Mechanical heat recovery systems have replaced natural ventilation in larger buildings and ACs have largely enabled us to disregard local climatic factors during building design. Meanwhile, the growing size of buildings has led to the replacement of local building materials in favor of concrete. Concrete can give rise to overheated indoor spaces in tropical regions during hot seasons, necessitating further use of ACs.[28]

Vernacular architecture elements can still play a major role in heating and cooling decarbonization today. This approach involves reestablishing a balance with the natural elements and reintroducing tried and tested techniques in modern ways, through passive design. To encourage this process, an increasing number of countries are now establishing mandatory or voluntary building energy codes and energy efficiency standards. Active and passive strategies, particularly for reducing heating demand, are popular in North America and Europe.

Passive heating and cooling

In cold or moderate climates, optimizing solar energy absorption through building and window orientation, insulation and improvements to the building shell are common strategies for reducing heating demand. Heat from the sun can also be absorbed by and transferred to building elements.[29] To stay cool in summer, the simple use of shades, window screens and appropriately sized openings can often be sufficient.

In hot climates, insulation and the careful selection of sustainable construction materials with the right thermal properties could reduce the energy required for cooling by 10 to 40 percent.[30] Depending on the region, passive cooling can also involve ventilation shafts, green roofs or reflective roof coatings and double-glazed windows as well as careful consideration of building layout.[31, 32]

Energy demand for heating and cooling can also be managed at consumer level. Technology can influence behavior and nudge us toward better use of heating and cooling devices. Examples include metering systems that increase awareness and offer financial incentives for reduced energy usage.

Box 2.1 GHG emissions from heating and cooling

Heating is the largest end-user of energy, accounting for 40 percent of energy-related CO_2 emissions. In buildings, heating accounts for 80 percent of the direct CO_2 emissions. Fossil fuels still dominate, with renewables making up just 11 percent in 2022.33 Meanwhile, global heat consumption is expected to increase by 6 percent between 2022 and 2027.34

While cooling is largely electrified, the heating sector is lagging behind in electrification. Whether for the homes, transport or industry, demand for cooling is also growing. Devices such as ACs are deeply embedded in society. In many countries, they are a symbol of rising income levels and comfort, with global warming contributing to their demand. By 2050, around two-thirds of households worldwide could have an AC (figure 2.2).[35] In 2020, GHG emissions associated with space cooling and refrigeration represented over 10 percent of global emissions.[36]

Energy usage accounts for 70 percent of AC emissions. The rest is due to refrigerant leakage.[37] While refrigerants such as hydrofluorocarbons (HFCs) are not major greenhouse gases, they are the fastest growing globally.[38] Refrigerants with low GWP are available on the market. However, this is a sector where policy intervention is crucial. Without policy intervention, emissions from AC and refrigeration are projected to rise 90 percent above 2017 levels by 2050.[39]

Figure 2.2 Global air conditioner stock, 1990–2050 (millions of units)

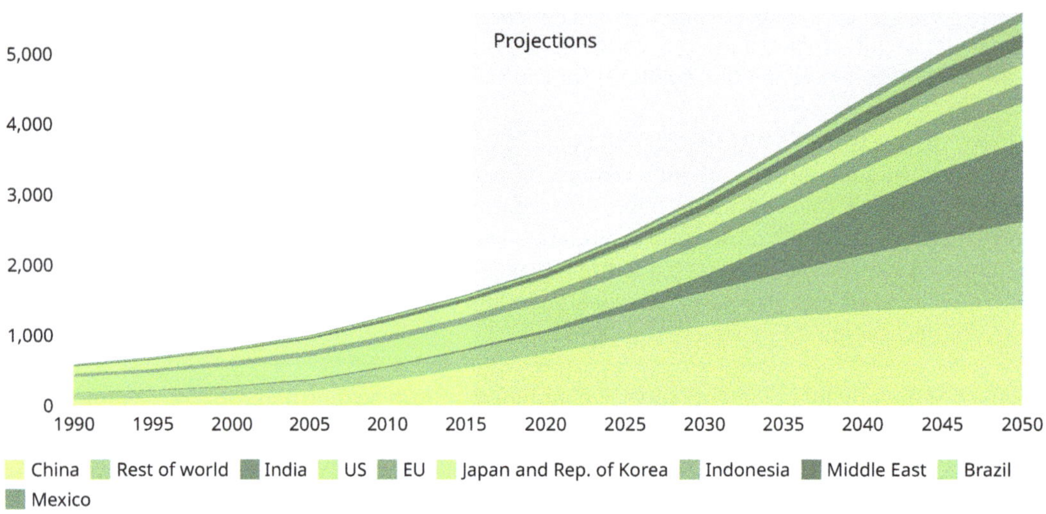

Source: IEA, 2018a.

Heating and cooling retrofits

Natural heating, cooling and ventilation is particularly important in emerging economies with rapidly growing cities as new construction offers opportunities to consider energy efficiency from the outset. Well-designed cities could save 25 percent of heating and cooling energy usage.[40] Meanwhile, cooling and heating retrofits are an important option in industrialized countries and cities with aging building stock. However, the rate of green retrofitting of existing buildings is low. For instance, although 75 percent of European buildings are energy inefficient, only between 0.4 and 1.2 percent of the whole stock is renovated annually.[41]

In addition to retrofitting and enhancing energy efficiency of buildings, heating and cooling systems themselves can benefit from retrofits. Replacing conventional heating systems with heat pumps can be challenging, generally necessitating renovation for their installation. Often, significant infrastructure is already in place - central heating, piped gas networks and boilers for apartment and office buildings. Combining hybrid heat pumps with existing gas-fired boilers can minimize efficiency drops. Another transitional alternative includes retrofitting existing heating systems by replacing fossil fuel boilers with natural gas or biomass boilers fueled by agricultural and forestry residues.

However, depending on the feedstock source, biomass boilers could exacerbate competition for agricultural land needed for food production. Electrification of heating, such as through heat pumps, is a far better option from a climate perspective. Furthermore, electrification allows for integration with renewable energy sources.

While passive design and retrofits may be more sustainable ways of managing demand, progress in these directions is not fast enough in some of the world's most rapidly expanding cities

Inefficient technologies are still dominant

Scaling the use of efficient heating and cooling technologies is a key measure for reducing the climate impact of these functions. While passive design and retrofits may be more sustainable ways of managing demand, progress in these directions is not fast enough in some of the world's most rapidly expanding cities.[42, 43, 44]

Minimum energy performance standards, energy efficiency labelling and incentive programs are important measures for stimulating uptake of energy-efficient technologies.[45] But generally, top-down regulation is sparse and, despite better alternatives being available on the market, the most commonly sold units are often several times less efficient.[46]

It is difficult to estimate the GHG mitigation potential of more energy-efficient technologies. But studies have shown that the world can avoid up to eight years of global emissions (at 2018 levels) over the next four decades through efficiency improvements and transitioning to refrigerants with a low GWP.[47] For instance, more efficient ACs could reduce cooling energy demand by 45 percent.[48]

The growing impact of heat pumps

Over the past five years, global sales of heat pumps have grown at an average rate of 10 percent per year.[49] Europe is seeing the fastest growth (figure 2.3) and nearly half of the installed capacity today is in North America with the other half in China. In colder regions, like Scandinavia, heat pumps already meet between 40 and 60 percent of heating needs.[50]

Figure 2.3 Increase in heat pump sales between 2020 and 2021

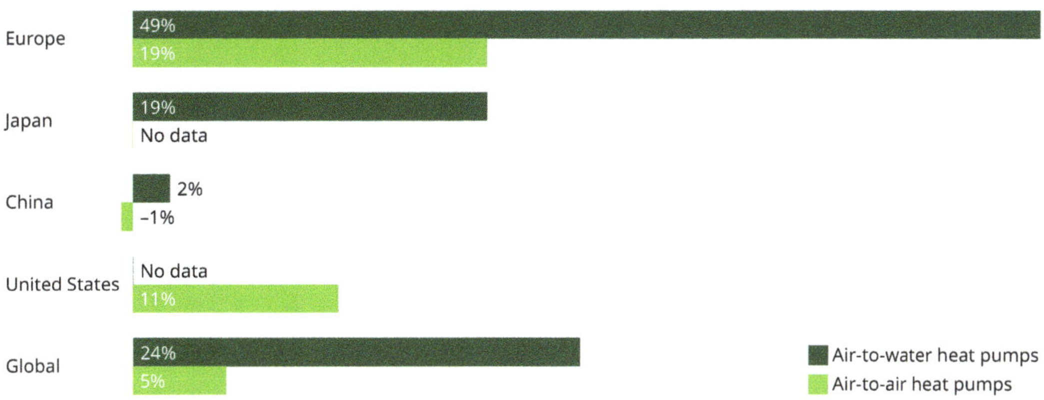

Source: IEA, 2023e.

ACs and heat pumps are technically similar. However, heat pumps can offer both heating and cooling. They can therefore replace both fossil fuel boilers and inefficient ACs. The climate mitigation potential of heat pumps relies largely on the technology that it is replacing, the share of renewable energy in the electricity grid and the type of refrigerant used. However, the International Energy Agency (IEA) estimates that replacing fossil fuel boilers with heat pumps could reduce GHG emissions by 500 million metric tonnes by 2030.[51]

Heat pumps and ACs transfer heat from one location to another through compression and decompression of a heat-absorbing refrigerant. Such systems can require ductwork, with pipes and tunnels running through the building. They can also be ductless, in which case they are suited for retrofitting buildings or adding heating, ventilation and air conditioning (HVAC) such as geothermal HVAC to specific rooms. Heat pumps draw heat from air, water or geothermal sources, often via separate indoor and outdoor components.[52] While they are more efficient than ACs, they do have drawbacks such as noise, outdoor space use and exhaust heat emission which exacerbates the urban heat island effect.[53]

The need to reduce heating and cooling energy consumption has fostered innovative new technologies. Electrocaloric heat pumps could offer refrigerant-free cooling in the future, but are still at R&D level. Other solutions, such as solar-driven heating and cooling units, could become a more common alternative sooner, especially considering that cooling units are needed most in solar-intense regions and seasons. Examples include solar concentrator collectors that are integrated with absorption chillers to provide the chilled water used in ACs, or ACs that are sold packaged with accompanying solar panels and converters. However, solar-driven systems are space consuming and typically not the most efficient or cost-effective solutions. Scaling renewable energy grid integration should be a priority.

Alternative refrigerants

A major problem of ACs and heat pumps is the negative climate impact from refrigerants. Although regular maintenance can prevent many leaks, gases may escape when the units are repaired or decommissioned. Naturally, leakage is less of a problem when using refrigerants with a lower GWP.

The production of harmful chlorofluorocarbons (CFCs) as refrigerants in ACs and heat pumps has been phased out under the globally agreed Montreal Protocol on Substances that Deplete the Ozone Layer. While their most common replacement - HFCs - have no impact on the ozone layer, they are still potent greenhouse gases. Therefore, the Kigali Amendment to the Montreal Protocol aims to also phase out HFCs.[54]

Replacing refrigerants with a high GWP with better alternatives could avoid 0.1 degrees Celsius of global warming by 2050.[55] Several promising alternatives have emerged, including natural refrigerants such as ammonia, propane (R290) and CO_2. However, some refrigerants face challenges related to flammability and cost, and require technological improvements.

Refrigerant leakage represents less than a third of the GHG emissions from cooling technologies. The rest is due to energy usage. Therefore, the use of low-GWP refrigerants alone will not be sufficient to tackle the overall climate impact from the sector.[56] However, switching to better alternatives is a no-regret solution with low marginal abatement costs, and alternatives are available.

As cities grow large and dense, centralized energy distribution systems such as district heating and cooling supply becomes an increasingly relevant alternative

From individual to district heating and cooling

As cities grow large and dense, centralized energy distribution systems such as district heating and cooling supply becomes an increasingly relevant alternative. Compared to individually installed heat pumps, boilers and ACs, district systems can reduce energy usage and cost while enabling renewable energy integration.[57] Cities like Copenhagen, Denmark and Geneva, Switzerland have combined their district systems with heating from external heat pumps and natural cooling from surrounding seawater and lakes. Next-generation district heating and cooling systems can provide both heating and cooling simultaneously by recycling waste heat from chillers.

District cooling consumes between 20 and 30 percent less power than conventional alternatives. Efficiency is, however, highly dependent on the availability of natural heat sinks and vapor absorption systems as well as larger chiller systems.[58, 59] District heating systems are more common than district cooling. In 2021, more than 10 percent of buildings' heat demand was met by district heating networks globally.[60] However the implementation of both district heating and cooling is still relatively limited and installation is uneven across the world.[61]

Equal access to cooling is a growing concern

Between 1.8 and 4.1 billion people in the Global South are believed to lack access to residential cooling.[62] In addition to structural measures to reduce people's vulnerability to extreme heat, achieving equity in terms of cooling necessitates the provision of public spaces to cool down. Air-conditioned cooling centers, such as libraries and malls, or even dedicated chilled facilities during extreme heatwaves, are becoming important means for adapting to climate change in cities.

But local and public cooling can also be provided through urban greening.[63] Trees and water bodies that offer temperature relief and shade are great nature-based alternatives with a multitude of co-benefits. As the urban heat island effect takes its toll on increasingly warmer cities, equal access opportunities to cool down are imperative for maintaining decent living standards and saving lives.

Leapfrogging done right

Emerging technologies present an opportunity for countries to make significant progress toward low-carbon heating and cooling. Countries experiencing a surge in sales of ACs can benefit greatly from adopting low-GWP refrigerants and high-efficiency heaters and coolers. However, the technology choices are numerous and require ambitious investment. The right solutions must urgently be made affordable and accessible to avoid a wrong leapfrog approach and cause a lock-in effect for suboptimal refrigerants and technologies.[64]

Similarly, the energy to fuel these solutions must be carefully chosen. For instance, many residential and district heating systems are increasing the share of biomass, often using wood pellets and wood chips. The risk of exacerbating competition for land needed to produce biomass feedstock must be considered. As appliances and systems for heating and cooling last longer than a decade, converting fossil fuel boilers to systems that burn biomass could result in a potentially damaging fuel lock-in for European countries.[65]

Wood is still the largest biomass energy source today. However, some scientists and environmental groups have raised concerns that simply cutting down trees and burning them can release more CO_2 emissions and be even more harmful than burning fossil fuels.[66] Growing biomass on already cleared land with measures in place to restore soil carbon can mitigate this challenge to some extent.

Innovation examples

Photo: Getty Images / C. mathess

Shavadoon natural ventilation systems in Iran
Shavadoon is an Iranian indigenous technique for natural ventilation developed in the city of Dezful. It consists of an underground cavity that utilizes the Earth's average temperature to provide thermal comfort in the hot and semi-humid climate. Shavadoons have traditionally been used as resting places, or for storing and refrigerating food. They are constructed between 5 and 12 meters underground where temperatures are around 20°C cooler than the outside temperature during the hottest days of summer. They consist of various components, including a wide entrance located in the courtyard and a stairway leading to the main hall, which serves as the central activity area. Shavadoons also feature small rooms separated from the main hall by a maximum one-level difference. Some Shavadoons have interconnected rooms with vertical canals for light and ventilation purposes. Integrating this traditional technique into modern apartments can help reduce energy consumption and modern studies have investigated the optimal Shavadoon shapes to offer maximum ventilation rates.[67, 68]

Photo: Getty Images / © apomares

Giant "wind garden" to cool Madrid

A giant "wind garden" inspired by ancient Middle Eastern wind towers is being built in a park in Madrid, Spain. The architectural structure applies nature-based solutions and has a spiral form made of mosses and ferns. This draws down cool breezes from above the treetops into the garden and nearby streets, acting as a giant air conditioner. The park structure is designed to lower local temperatures by 4°C and reduce cooling needs in nearby buildings. The 14.5 hectare park, to be developed by landscape architecture firms West 8 and Porras Guadiana, will open in 2025.

Photo: Getty Images / © Scharvik

District cooling lowers Copenhagen's cooling emissions by 70 percent

In Copenhagen, Denmark, district cooling has proven to be a highly effective solution for reducing CO_2 emissions and cutting costs in comparison to conventional cooling methods. The city has experienced increasing demand for cooling due to rising temperatures, leading the Greater Copenhagen Utility Company (HOFOR) to implement the district cooling system. This comprises an underground network of pipes and multiple cooling plants that primarily use seawater to chill the water supplied to customers. During the winter months, the system utilizes seawater pumped to the cooling plant to produce chilled water for customers, which is considered zero-carbon cooling. Seawater with a temperature of 6°C or lower is directly used to cool the water. However, in the summer months when seawater is not sufficiently cold, energy is required to cool the water. The system serves commercial buildings, such as banks, hotels, department stores and offices, as well as providing year-round cooling for servers and other processes. The district cooling system is continually expanding to accommodate future customers and meet growing demand. HOFOR opened the first cooling plant in 2010 and a second in 2013. In 2019, a new cooling plant was built in the Ørestad area to provide climate-friendly cooling to numerous office buildings.

Technology solutions

Proven technologies

Plug-and-play solar water heaters

Nexol Photovolthermic AG

Photo: Getty Images / © KangeStudio

Nexol's photovoltaic (PV) water heaters are a plug-and-play solution that can operate using either heating rods or a heat pump. They can also be fitted with a smart controller powered by either alternating or direct current (AC or DC) that autonomously determines whether grid electricity or PV energy should be used – with a preference for the latter. At the technology's core is a semiconductor element, which absorbs thermal energy from the ambient air and feeds it into a water tank. The company supplies various products. The NEX P40, for example, is a PV water heater that could reduce the electricity needed to heat water by half.

- Contracting type: For sale
- Technology level: High
- Country of origin: Germany
- Availability: Worldwide
- Contact: WIPO GREEN Database

Waste heat recovery for cooling and heating in buildings
iHandal Energy Solutions

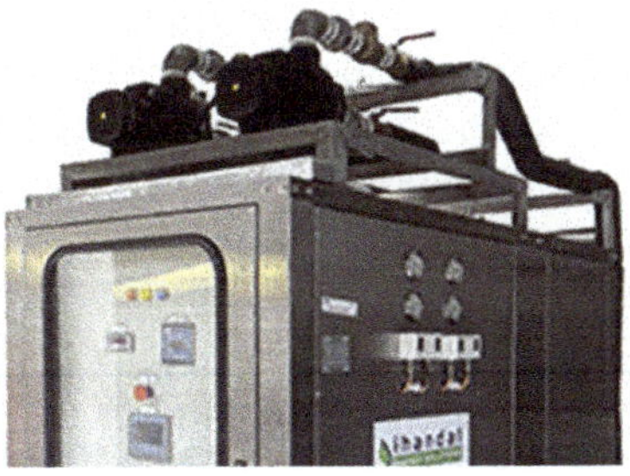

Photo: © iHandal

Recovered waste heat from buildings' gas boilers is compressed using iHandal's Heatfuse™ technology. The energy is then channeled into reheating and/or cooling the building through an energy-efficient heat pump. The Heatfuse™ technology aims to replace inefficient boilers and chillers and use recovered waste heat from AC condenser units or other equipment. As the technology can operate at very high temperatures and deliver water up to 140°C, their biggest market growth is currently in industrial sectors such as food and beverage, health care and pharmaceuticals.

- Contracting type: For sale
- Technology level: High
- Country of origin: Malaysia
- Availability: Asia
- Contact: WIPO GREEN Database

Micro combined heat and power (CHP) technology
Micro Turbine Technology BV

Photo: © Micro Turbine Solutions

The EnerTwin is a small-sized power cogeneration system that uses a boiler and micro turbine to generate electricity for domestic use. While the EnerTwin needs energy from a grid to start up, it can operate on fuels such as liquefied petroleum gas (LPG), biogas or biomethane provided decent quality fuels are fed into the system. It is also certified for 23 percent hydrogen mix and models suitable for higher proportions of hydrogen will be released in the future. The EnerTwin currently works with the standard European grid system but a version is planned for the North American market. For cooling needs rather than heating, the EnerTwin would need to be combined with a cooling device such as an absorption chiller to convert the heat output into cooling output. For both power and heating needs, the EnerTwin's microturbine solution uses off-the-shelf components combined with in-house fuel-saving components.

- Contracting type: For sale
- Technology level: High
- Country of origin: Netherlands (Kingdom of the)
- Availability: Europe
- Contact: WIPO GREEN Database

Absorptive cooling from industrial waste heat

AGO GmbH

Photo: Getty Images /© BrianBrownImages

AGO GmbH provides absorption chillers for industrial use that reuse industry process heat waste for cooling purposes. Using natural refrigerants such as ammonia and water, the absorption chillers can meet the cooling needs of food, beverage, chemical, pharmaceutical and other industries (between +5°C and -40°C). The basic technology behind absorption chillers was patented in 1859. The heat source, such as hot water or steam, causes the absorbent to release the refrigerant gas, which then goes through a condensing process to convert it into a liquid. The liquid refrigerant absorbs heat from the surrounding areas, creating a cooling effect, and then returns to the absorbent to restart the cycle.

- Contracting type: For sale
- Technology level: High
- Country of origin: Germany
- Availability: Worldwide
- Contact: WIPO GREEN Database

Intelligent whole-house HVAC system with heat recovery

Ventive

Photo: © Ventive

This product is a fully integrated household solution combining exhaust-air and air-sourced heat pump technologies for ventilation, heating and hot water systems. It replaces traditional boilers, hot water cylinders and ventilation units and is suitable for energy retrofits. An internal heat recovery system enables further efficiencies and real-time performance monitoring helps optimize its energy use and performance. A 10 kWh thermal store enables the heat pump to generate heat at night using off-peak electricity and in the summer the heat pump tempers the incoming air to cool down the house without using extra electricity.

- Contracting type: For sale
- Technology level: High
- Country of origin: United Kingdom
- Availability: United Kingdom
- Contact: WIPO GREEN Database

Transpired solar air collector
Conserval Systems Inc.

Photo: Getty Images / © Helmut Feil

Transpired solar air collectors are a type of solar heating technology of relatively simple design using dark-colored perforated metal cladding mounted on a south-facing wall of a building. The cladding is mounted with a gap between it and the building's structural wall. As sunlight heats up the metal, a fan pulls outside air through the perforations and into the space behind the cladding. The air that passes through – which can be heated up to 22°C above the ambient air temperature – is drawn into the building and distributed through the ventilation system. Researchers at the National Renewable Energy Laboratory (NREL) and engineers at Conserval Systems Inc. have developed the technology, currently marketed as the SolarWall system. The system has a short payback period and can convert up to 80 percent of the solar energy into usable heat.

- Contracting type: For sale
- Technology level: Low
- Country of origin: United States
- Availability: Worldwide
- Contact: WIPO GREEN Database

Nubian vaults
La Voûte Nubienne

Photo: Getty Images / © Dina Muanes

The association La Voûte Nubienne is addressing the issue of affordable housing in sub-Saharan Africa with a traditional, low-carbon building technique that uses only earth bricks and earth mortar, thereby reducing deforestation pressures. The Nubian Vault structure has thick raw earth walls, which significantly alleviate high temperatures inside the building. Studies on Nubian Vault design in Burkina Faso and Senegal have validated the significant thermal comfort increase compared to houses with corrugated metal roofs. The association trains local builders to create a market for the building technique while adapting it to the climatic conditions and traditional know-how of the Sahel region. Properly maintained, the homes can last for 50 years or more.

- Contracting type: Service
- Technology level: Low
- Country of origin: Egypt
- Availability: Sahel region
- Contact: WIPO GREEN Database

Evacuated tube solar collectors

Hydro Solar Innovative Energy

Photo: Getty Images/© Lex20

The product is a solar collector for space and domestic hot water heating using evacuated tubes filled with fluid. Evacuated tube collectors can produce higher temperatures than flat-plate solar collectors as they increase the surface area available to the sun and absorb heat from different angles. They are thin tubes, often made of copper, filled with a fluid such as water. The tubes are situated inside a larger sheet of glass or in plastic tubes. As the system is partially in a vacuum, heat loss to the outside environment is reduced. Hydro Solar's evacuated tube collectors are particularly suitable for cold Northern climates.

- Contracting type: For sale
- Technology level: Medium
- Country of origin: Canada
- Availability: Worldwide
- Contact: WIPO GREEN Database

Modular ice storage cell for cold energy storage in commercial buildings

Nostromo

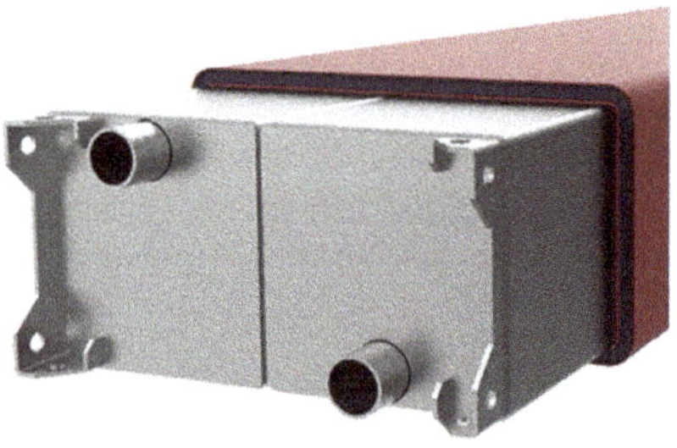

Photo: © Nostromo

This technology offers a modular energy storage solution for HVAC systems. It involves transforming commercial building cooling systems into efficient energy storage assets. Using water as the primary medium for energy storage, Nostromo's IceBrick system consists of a modular unit that integrates with commercial building cooling systems. During periods of low electricity demand, excess energy is used to freeze water within the IceBrick, creating ice as a form of energy storage. When energy demand is high, the IceBrick utilizes the stored ice to provide cooling without the need for additional energy consumption.

- Contracting type: For sale
- Technology level: Medium
- Country of origin: Israel
- Availability: Israel, United States
- Contact: WIPO GREEN Database

Ventilated facade

Eliane TEC

Photo: Getty Images/© Lari Bat

Eliane TEC provides ventilated facades that regulate temperature, air and light. The ventilated facades are integrated into a building's envelope to create a gap between the exterior and inner walls. As air circulates between the walls during warm weather, it is heated through a "chimney effect," whereby air is pushed upward and building temperature reduced. Conversely, during cold weather, the air gap balances the temperature of the building and reduces moisture risk.

- Contracting type: For sale
- Technology level: Medium
- Country of origin: Brazil
- Availability: Worldwide
- Contact: WIPO GREEN Database

Cooling system heat recovery units

Ecolactis Boostherm

Photo: Getty Images/© Ronstik

Boostherm's heat recovery technology enables waste heat from cooling operations to be recycled for hot water use in residential and commercial buildings, or for low temperature space heating. The company claims that 100 percent of the heat normally rejected by cooling system condensers can be recovered to preheat sanitary hot water at 55°C and above. This reduces both energy usage and costs associated with heating and cooling needs. Advanced simulation tools assess total energy needs before installation.

- Contracting type: For sale/service
- Technology level: High
- Country of origin: France
- Availability: Worldwide
- Contact: WIPO GREEN Database

Frontier technologies

Natural passive cooling for outdoor use and building facades

Ant Studio Pvt. Ltd.

Photo: © CoolAnt

This modular passive cooling system harnesses natural elements to create thermal comfort without relying on electricity. Combining evaporative cooling and natural ventilation, the modular design allows for easy installation. The design resembles a beehive structure with cylindrical pots. Water runs over the surface of the cylinders in a circulating system to cool the hot air passing through the terracotta cones. The studio offers customized building facades as well as passive cooling structures for outdoor use, including as art installations in public spaces. To enhance the cooling effect, the outdoor systems incorporate water features such as misters, fountains or water walls, which utilize the evaporative cooling process to lower temperatures further.

- Contracting type: For sale/service
- Technology level: Low
- Country of origin: India
- Availability: India
- Contact: WIPO GREEN Database

Low-cost solar heating and cooling

Solar Polar Ltd

Photo: Getty Images / © Dovapi

Solar Polar is a startup that designs and makes low-cost, modular solar thermal technologies for heating and cooling. As an off-grid system, their technology can replace gas and electrical heating and cooling and is specifically adapted to rural areas. Their cooling technology uses an absorption refrigeration system that operates with lower-GWP refrigerants. The company is currently developing a solar heater which stores energy in thermal slats that sit under a concentrator lens on a double-glazed glass panel. When needed, the slats are turned over, and the stored energy is projected downward onto the heater which gives off heat at very long-wave infrared radiation.

- Contracting type: For sale/service
- Technology level: High
- Country of origin: United Kingdom
- Availability: United Kingdom
- Contact: WIPO GREEN Database

Compact solar desiccant cooling air conditioner

Solarinvent

Photo: Getty Images/©RonFullHD

Freescoo is a compact plug-and-play solar air conditioning system for ventilation, heating and cooling of buildings. Its key feature is its compactness, with every component available in a single casing. The sun's heat is used to drive the cooling process based on the phenomenon of adsorption, which enables the extraction of moisture from the air through microporous materials. Water is used as a refrigerant and heat is stored in the form of dry silica gel (a desiccant material). The device can be integrated with a solar PV panel for off-grid applications.

- Contracting type: For sale/collaboration
- Technology level: Medium
- Country of origin: Italy
- Availability: Italy
- Contact: WIPO GREEN Database

Linear electric motor for energy-efficient heating and cooling

Magtor Compressor Limited

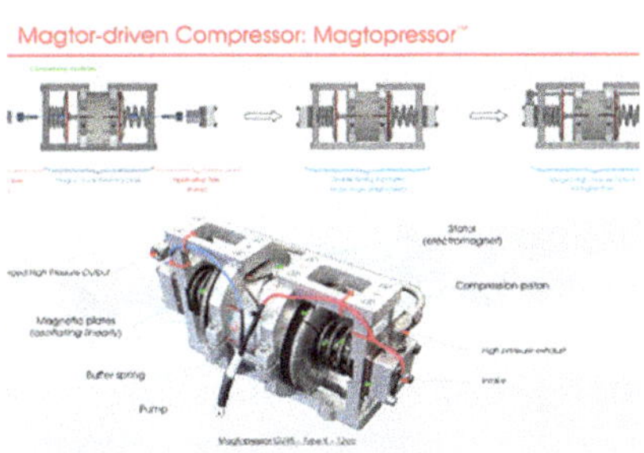

Photo: © Magtor

Cooling and heating devices are often limited in their efficiency. Traditional rotary motor technology, which is central to compression requirements in many cooling and heating devices, has been around for many years and achieved few efficiency improvements in the past decade. Magtor aims to replace the traditional rotary-based electric motors that currently dominate the market with their direct linear electric motor that can achieve higher levels of energy efficiency. The technology uses long-distance magnetic attraction and repulsion to deliver linear power on both the outstroke and the backstroke of the motor. Magnetic plates on both sides of a fixed electromagnet are connected via a shaft and move from side to side based on single-phase voltage. As this proprietary technology removes the need for a crankshaft, the company claims that energy efficiency can be improved by more than 30 percent. The technology is currently in the deployment phase.

- Contracting type: For sale/licensing
- Technology level: High
- Country of origin: Monaco
- Availability: Austria
- Contact: WIPO GREEN Database

Horizon technologies

Cooling device combining vapor compression, evaporative cooling and renewable energy

Gree + Tsinghua University

Photo: Getty Images/© brebca

Gree, the world's largest manufacturer of residential ACs, and Tsinghua University have developed a cooling technology with a climate impact five times lower than currently available ACs. The technology combines vapor compression refrigeration, evaporative cooling and ventilation with renewable energy sources and free cooling whenever possible. The technology's various cooling and ventilation modes operate automatically, either individually or in parallel, depending on external weather conditions. Key elements that enable a lower carbon footprint are the integration of photovoltaics that reduce dependency on the grid, as well as an efficient compressor and low-GWP refrigerant.

- Contracting type: For collaboration
- Technology level: High
- Country of origin: China
- Availability: Under development
- Contact: WIPO GREEN Database

Cooling surface coating harnessing the power of the sun

SolCold

Photo: © SolCold

SolCold's cooling coating film uses sunlight radiation to cool down objects. The stronger the sun, the stronger the cooling effect. This active cooling coating can be applied to any surface exposed to sunlight, such as cars, reducing the need for air conditioning. This technology can save over 50 percent in cooling consumption and costs while reducing carbon emissions. During tests, the air inside a car whose rooftop and dashboard were coated with the film was found to be 13°C cooler than in one without. The patented technology is based on "anti-stokes fluorescence" technology that combines nanotechnology, physics and chemistry. Four main layers of films and filters are applied to the targeted surface: (i) a smart filter layer that blocks sunlight's heating wavelengths and amplifies "useful" wavelengths; (ii) an active cooling layer that uses solar radiation; (iii) a cooling matrix layer; and (iv) a reflective and radiative cooling layer. The technology is currently in the development stage.

- Contracting type: For collaboration
- Technology level: Medium
- Country of origin: Israel
- Availability: Israel, Singapore
- Contact: WIPO GREEN Database

No-refrigerant heat pump component

Blue Heart Energy

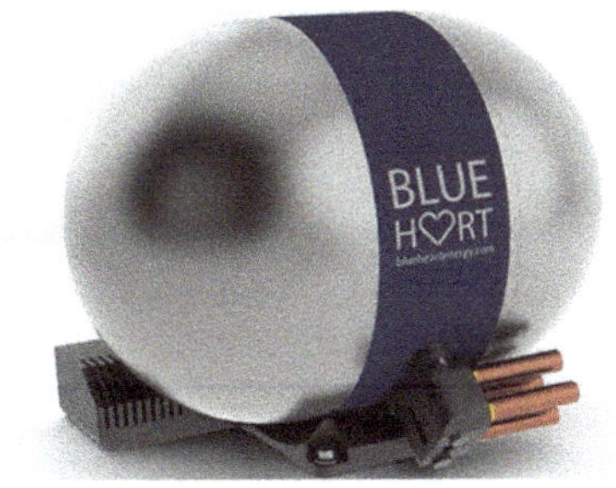

Photo: © Blue Heart Energy

Blue Heart has developed an engine for use in heat pumps that replaces the cold circuit part that otherwise contains refrigerants. Blue Heart's solution consists of a sealed tubular circuit filled with helium, which has zero GWP. Using thermoacoustics, the technique creates sound waves in a closed circuit to generate heat and cold. The compact size of the product compared to the conventional cold circuits in heat pumps means that the final devices are smaller and more affordable. The technology works with various heat sources, including ground, brine, water, air, photovoltaics and district heating.

- Contracting type: For collaboration
- Technology level: High
- Country of origin: Netherlands (Kingdom of the)
- Availability: Under development
- Contact: WIPO GREEN Database

Electrocaloric heat pump

Fraunhofer IPM

Photo: Getty Images / © NAPA74

Heat pumps often use compressor technology that relies on refrigerants which contribute to global warming. Solid-state heat pumps, by contrast, include electrocaloric systems that can operate using fluids such as water instead of refrigerants and which are significantly more energy efficient. When an electric field is applied to electrocaloric materials, the material heats up and the heat is dissipated via a heat sink, cooling the material down again. When the electric field is removed, the material instead cools down and can absorb thermal energy from a heat source. The effect is reversible, so that the heat pump can be used for both heating and cooling. Researchers at the Fraunhofer Institute for Physical Measurement Techniques (IPM) are working on the development of electrocaloric heat pumps, which they believe to be a disruptive technology for the industry that will completely replace compressor-based heat pumps and mitigate global warming impact from heating and cooling.

- Contracting type: For collaboration
- Technology level: High
- Country of origin: Germany
- Availability: Under development
- Contact: WIPO GREEN Database

Photo: Getty Images / peeterv

Smart mobility

Transport emits 23 percent of the world's energy-related CO_2 emissions.[69] Low-carbon technologies and demand-side measures are crucial for mitigating the sector's climate impact, while providing important co-benefits for air quality and human health.[70,71] From digital planning tools to electric vehicles, this section explores a range of technological solutions essential for the green mobility transition.

Urban planning and compact cities

Good urban planning is critical for reducing greenhouse gas (GHG) emissions in the mobility sector. The design of our cities influences the length of trips and the choice of transport. For instance, urban sprawl increases commuting distance, car ownership and emissions.[72] Compact, mixed-use developments, by contrast, facilitate walking or cycling, reducing the need for car travel.[73]

The climate implications can be massive. Cycling reduces transport emissions by 84 percent.[74] Public transport is among the most direct and equitable ways to reduce traffic congestion and fuel consumption.[75,76] Estimates of public transport promotion's mitigation potential range from 25 percent to 47 percent compared to business-as-usual scenarios.[77]

From subways and trams to sky trains and driverless buses, the urban landscape continues to evolve. Technology can contribute to scaling public transport solutions. Digitalization of fare payment systems, e.g. through mobile phones, is growing rapidly worldwide and contributing to the efficiency of public transportation.[78] Electrification of public transport systems is another priority measure.

Good urban planning is critical for reducing greenhouse gas (GHG) emissions in the mobility sector

Global variations in urban modality choices

The choice of modality differs greatly between countries. For instance, bus rapid transit (BRT) systems with designated lanes and specifically adapted stations are relatively low-cost and flexible alternatives for relieving traffic problems in urban areas. They are especially common in countries in Latin America and Asia, with growing popularity in Africa.[79] Currently, more than 180 cities across the globe have implemented BRT systems, carrying over 34 million passengers each day.[80]

As cities grow and more people can afford private vehicles, increased demand has offset significant GHG reduction in the mobility sector.[81,82] Transport activity is expected to double by 2050.[83] There is also a trend toward increased size of vehicles and distance travelled per person.[84] Yet, climate efforts often focus on technologies and innovations at vehicle level rather than promoting public transport through urban planning.[85]

Digital technologies for smart traffic management systems

Municipalities and urban planners are increasingly relying on georeferenced data systems, scenario building tools and algorithms to predict and optimize greener transport routes. By developing a complete, dynamic picture of the urban landscape, cities can make better use of land and integrate public transport, pedestrian zones and bicycle lanes. Interactive and predictive digital twins for mobility planning, such as for bus systems and routes, can also help to involve citizens in the planning process.

Digital technologies can alleviate real-time traffic congestion. Advances in smart traffic management systems apply internet of things, artificial intelligence (AI) and machine learning technologies in response to data from video cameras, sensors and radars. Real-time traffic data allows cities to forecast traffic flows, tailor traffic lights to meet demand, suggest alternative routes and restrict access to low-carbon emission zones through smart pricing systems.[86]

Technologies that reduce the time cars spend on the road are highly relevant from a climate perspective. In Mumbai, India, 53 percent of GHG emissions from the transport sector were attributed to traffic congestion.[87] Studies have shown that staggered office hours and remote working, enabled by digital teleconferencing solutions, can have a significant impact on traffic congestion and climate change. By early April 2020, in the midst of the COVID-19 pandemic, global emissions from surface transport fell by 36 percent compared with the 2019 mean levels.[88]

As cities grow and more people can afford private vehicles, increased demand has offset significant GHG reduction in the mobility sector

Shared micromobility systems: not necessarily a game-changer

E-scooters and e-bikes have transformed the urban landscape in many cities in Europe and North America, while non-electric two-wheelers have long been a common sight in many developing countries. In countries such as India, Indonesia and Thailand, sales of electric two- or three-wheelers now outnumber electric cars.[89] This is a positive development as smaller electric vehicles could reduce battery size and hence demand for critical metals by almost a quarter.[90]

Digital technologies are enabling cities to integrate micromobility vehicles through a single interface, such as mobile apps and ride-sharing platforms. In the United States, 136 million shared micromobility rides were recorded in 2019[91] with substantial expansion likely since. Such ride-sharing platforms are often viewed as a climate-friendly transport solution with the potential to reduce global urban transport emissions by 6 percent, on average.[92]

However, the climate mitigation potential of micromobility systems and ride-sharing depends on the urban environment. Ride-sharing may be more suitable in car-dependent urban areas. In cities where public transport infrastructure is dominant, ride-sharing may instead draw users away from public transport.[93] For instance, one study in Switzerland found that only 12 percent of e-scooter trips replace car trips, while 50 percent simply replaced walks.[94] In major US cities, ride-sharing was found to double vehicle mileage as travelers often shifted away from public transportation.[95]

These findings stress the need for cities to understand travel behavior and mode choices from a systems perspective to achieve low-carbon mobility. However, they also emphasize the role of the urban landscape, as well as the need to transform micromobility systems and ride-sharing fleets to low- and zero-emission vehicle types.

Electric vehicles hold largest potential

In 2022, 14 percent of all cars sold were electric cars, up from less than five percent just two years earlier. Sales are concentrated in China, Europe and the United States.[96] Electric vehicles can reduce reliance on fossil fuels, especially if the electricity in the grid is based on renewable sources. If powered by low-emission electricity, electric vehicles offer the largest decarbonization potential for land-based transport, when considered from a life-cycle perspective.[97]

Regardless of the energy mix of a country's electricity grid, the life-cycle emissions of an electric car are still approximately 40 percent lower than a conventional car.[98, 99] While they do not solve the problem of traffic congestion, they make a positive contribution to air quality in cities.

Growing concerns about critical minerals used for electric batteries can be addressed by diversification strategies, efficiency improvements and battery recycling. Advances in battery technologies are facilitating the electrification of heavy-duty trucks and complement conventional electric rail systems.[100] Electrification of all these transport systems requires significant additional renewable electricity capacity, upgrades to grid infrastructure and rollout of electric vehicle charging networks.[101]

Regardless of the energy mix of a country's electricity grid, the life-cycle emissions of an electric car are still approximately 40 percent lower than a conventional car

Vehicle–grid integration a key enabler

The growing number of electric vehicles can put pressure on cities' electric grid systems. Innovations in smart grids and charging apps aim to improve vehicle–grid integration in the future and address electricity fluctuations and demand. Real-time grid data enables flexible electric vehicle tariffs so car users can be rewarded for charging their vehicles overnight when demand is low. Alternatively, users can discharge their vehicles' batteries and sell the electricity back to the grid through so-called bidirectional charging. Such trials are currently underway in countries such as the United Kingdom, and in California a recent bill approved by the US State Senate would require all new electric cars sold to be equipped with bidirectional charging technology by 2030.[102]

Systems that initiate delayed charging at off-peak times increase the reliability of power systems and make better use of renewable energy sources. Delayed charging technologies combined with strategic placement of charging stations at workplaces could eliminate the need for new power plants altogether. Simple technologies and planning of this kind could also avoid the need for more advanced systems of connected devices and real-time communications.[103] While connected devices and delayed charging technologies have been piloted, they must be better understood and accepted by consumers.[104, 105]

Fast technological advances in battery design

Most electric vehicles today run on lithium-ion batteries – a technology used for decades that offers limited energy density. Advances in the energy performance of electric batteries aim to respond to growing demand for more and larger electric batteries worldwide, while diversifying material sources in light of mineral shortages. This approach also aims to ensure autonomy and access to critical raw materials as production is becoming increasingly concentrated in a few countries, such as China.

Innovations include the use of lithium iron phosphate and the replacement of graphite with silicon to make vehicle batteries lighter and more energy dense. Such advances offer longer life and faster charging times. Solid-state batteries, such as lithium metal, hold even more potential to overcome the limitations of current lithium-ion batteries. These are not yet commercially available, but progress is being made on advanced electrolytes, cathodes and production of the lithium metal anodes needed to achieve industrial scalability.[106, 107]

In recent years, sodium-ion (Na-ion) batteries have seen rapid technological progress. They have the advantage of being cheaper and avoid the need for critical minerals, such as lithium. With their lower energy density, the batteries could be ideal for urban vehicles with a shorter range. Currently, there are nearly 30 sodium-ion battery manufacturing plants operating, planned or in construction, mainly in China, with mass production rollout expected this year.[108]

Biofuels: a complementary strategy in the short-to-medium term

Electrification alone is unlikely to meet the growing low-carbon energy demand for transport. New propulsion technologies for vehicles and alternative low-carbon fuels can make a significant difference in reducing transport emissions and diversifying fuel types.

Biofuels represented over 3.5 percent of global transport energy demand in 2022. These were mainly ethanol and conventional biodiesel based on sugarcane, corn and soybeans.[109] For instance, in France and Sweden, the E85 fuel type, containing up to 85 percent ethanol, is widely available for privately owned cars. While E85 contains less energy than gasoline, it can sell at almost half the price.

While biofuel usage is growing, its potential to reduce emissions in comparison to conventional fuels depends on its biomass source. Using crop-based biofuels significantly increases the agricultural land area needed. The resulting land-use change and forest clearing could potentially release more GHG emissions than simply using fossil fuels, necessitating stronger global protections of natural land.[110, 111]

Future of biofuel technologies

The development of second-generation biofuel technologies from non-food biomass may help to avoid both competition for arable land and land-use change emissions. Countries with abundant available biomass are exploring the production of methanol from forestry products. Innovations are also focusing on using a wider range of vegetal material, such as grass, or converting waste cooking oil or food waste such as corncobs into biodiesel using enzymes.

Frontier solutions include direct thermochemical liquefaction (DTL) technologies such as hydrothermal liquefaction (HTL) and fast pyrolysis. These are means for converting biomass into liquid products. First investigated in the 1970s, as of June 2023 there were 11 commercial and 15 demonstration-scale plants either operational or in development across 14 countries. While most of the liquid products are developed for heating applications, more and more processes include upgrading of the liquid product into transportation fuels due to the growing need for low-carbon mobility.[112]

Scaling more sustainable biofuel alternatives and bringing them to market is challenging. Success is highly dependent on the price of conventional fuels. Novel fuel sources such as algae have been tried, tested and abandoned over the years.[113] Nevertheless, while they are constrained by feedstock availability and sustainability concerns, biofuels can offer a complementary mitigation strategy for land-based transport in the short-to-medium term.[114]

Several car manufacturers are now developing autonomous vehicles. From a climate perspective, the best-case scenario will see them run on renewable electricity and be available on demand as part of shared car fleets. In the worst-case scenario, they would have conventional engines and be attractive to private car owners

Alternative fuels risk creating lock-in effect

Some alternative fuels marketed as low-carbon may risk creating a distracting lock-in effect for both climate and health. For instance, compressed natural gas is already widely used, but unless the technology is based on biogas, it relies on fossil fuels and emits high levels of toxic pollutants. However, it could be relevant as a complementary fuel for long-distance journeys.[115, 116]

Similarly, renewable fuels of non-biological origin (RFONBOs) or recycled carbon fuels (RCFs) are fuels derived from plastic waste or bacterial fermentation of industrial off-gases. As these too rely on fossil-based products or processes, they could delay the transition to low-carbon mobility.[117]

Finally, while so-called synthetic e-fuels are receiving growing attention, their climate effectiveness is unclear. Synthetic fuels such as ammonia, methanol and methane can be used as additives in conventional cars but are currently neither financially competitive nor produced at scale. Furthermore, powering cars with e-fuels may require about five times more renewable electricity than running an electric car.[118]

Moderate interest in hydrogen and automated transport

Interest in hydrogen as a transport fuel source is still subdued. Hydrogen is highly reliant on the development of cost-competitive fuel cells and infrastructure for production, distribution and storage. While the number of hydrogen fuel cell electric vehicles increased by 40 percent in 2022 compared to the previous year, the total of 72,000 vehicles was still marginal in comparison to the total number of cars sold that year.[119] Nevertheless, several countries including China, Japan, as well as the EU have launched ambitious hydrogen plans and strategies which also include the transport sector.[120]

Several car manufacturers are now developing autonomous vehicles. From a climate perspective, the best-case scenario will see them run on renewable electricity and be available on demand as part of shared car fleets. In the worst-case scenario, they would have conventional engines and be attractive to private car owners. Major urban areas such as Beijing, London and San Francisco could become early markets for autonomous vehicles. Currently, no commercial-scale applications are available and their environmental impact is largely uncertain.[121] However, consultancies such as McKinsey believe autonomous driving could generate USD 300 to 400 billion in revenue by 2035.[122]

In terms of autonomous vehicles, drone delivery services may have more potential for climate mitigation. Increased demand for delivery services prompted a study looking at last-mile transport modes which found that GHG emissions per package were 84 percent lower for drones compared to diesel trucks. This could become relevant for deliveries of smaller items such as medicines or food[123] and in certain countries such as Rwanda drone delivery of medical supplies has already seen significant success (see the Innovation example below). Experts anticipate acceptance of drones and that their applicability will be greater for medical transport and packages in industrial spaces than for e-commerce and food deliveries.[124]

Efficiency improvements and greener transport

Improving the efficiency of vehicles can contribute to fuel savings and emission reduction. Improvements in the internal combustion engine and aerodynamics of vehicles are resulting in continual efficiency gains.[125] Progress is being made on energy-efficient engines that run on two cylinders. Research is also addressing the possibility of electronically deactivating some cylinders in a multi-cylinder engine. Electronics will play a growing role in operating engines at even lower fuel consumption levels, such as through better control of fuel injection and ignition. Sensors and controllers can also be used to monitor and optimize fuel consumption.

Making vehicles lighter, known as *lightweighting*, also reduces fuel consumption. This includes replacing some of the steel with aluminum, composite materials and carbon fiber technology. New high-strength steels can achieve weight savings of 30 percent. Therefore, fundamental research into materials is important for improving efficiency in transportation.[126]

Innovation examples

Photo: Getty Images/© metamorworks

Using ICT to manage traffic flow in Moscow

Moscow City Government has improved management of its urban traffic flows, with significant benefits for the environment and climate, by applying information and communications technology (ICT) infrastructure. To reduce traffic congestion and lower carbon emissions, the city implemented various ICT-driven initiatives such as smart traffic management systems consisting of 2,000 traffic lights, 3,500 traffic detectors and 2,000 closed circuit television (CCTV) cameras, all feeding real-time data to the Traffic Management Centre. This data enables informed decisions on traffic management, reducing idling time for drivers and consequently cutting carbon emissions. Additionally, Moscow introduced measures to promote public transport use, such as parking fees and fewer free parking spots. Online maps and payment systems have enhanced efficiency while the city's Troika transport card facilitates seamless transfers between different transport modes. The city also monitors over half of its signal-controlled intersections with adaptive traffic-control measures, using embedded road sensors to optimize traffic flow.

Photo: Getty Images/© helivideo

Drone-delivery of packages in Rwanda

Delivery of packages to last-mile users using drones instead of diesel trucks can significantly reduce GHG emissions. In Rwanda, the company Zipline has successfully delivered medical products using drone technology for the past six years. Operations have also expanded to Ghana, Nigeria and the United States. The packages are delivered in plastic boxes lowered by parachute. The unmanned and self-piloted drones have made a total of 450,000 deliveries to date. Partnership with the Government of Rwanda is now expanding with a contract for a further 2 million deliveries by 2029, covering postal service items, food and agricultural products.

Technology solutions

Proven technologies

Urban planning: data for cyclist and pedestrian planning

Strava

Photo: Getty Images/© seamartini

Strava provides the world's largest data set of transport information. The data is gathered through more than 100 million people's phones or global positioning system (GPS) devices. The company aggregates and analyzes the data to support urban planners, trail network designers and city authorities in understanding the needs and mobility patterns of cyclists and pedestrians. The result is a valuable tool for planning investments and urban infrastructure. Their Strava Metro web platform is easily accessible and requires no technical expertise such as geographical information system (GIS) experience. As of 2020, organizations who aim to enhance cyclist and pedestrian conditions in cities can apply to access the web platform and data free of charge.

- Contracting type: Service/free
- Technology level: Medium
- Country of origin: United States
- Availability: Worldwide
- Contact: WIPO GREEN Database

Urban planning: digital tool for traffic congestion planning

Intelligent Traffic Control

Photo: Getty Images / © choi dongsu

Intelligent Traffic Control helps cities reduce traffic congestion using traffic data and planning software. Their software uses machine learning and AI algorithms based on live traffic data gathered from off-the-shelf cameras. These detect the behavior of private cars, public transport vehicles and pedestrians with a high degree of accuracy both day and night. The data is then analyzed to help cities predict congestion and mitigate it through smart traffic light manipulation. The company has completed projects in Australia, Brazil, Israel and the United States.

- Contracting type: Service
- Technology level: Medium
- Country of origin: Israel
- Availability: Worldwide
- Contact: WIPO GREEN Database

Modal shift + electric vehicles: electric two-wheeler micromobility system

Yulu

Photo: Getty Images / ©Arkadij Schell

Micromobility solutions such as scooters and motorbikes are commonplace and help reduce both traffic congestion and car dependency in cities. Yulu operates India's first electric micromobility service with keyless access. It is a technology-driven mobility platform based on technologies such as machine learning, AI and a global positioning system (GPS) tracking system for management of supply, demand and operations. The company rents electric bikes and scooters to other companies, such as delivery partners with last-minute connectivity needs. The service is based on a kilometer-based pricing model and hundreds of battery-swapping stations have been installed a cross the participating cities. Fully charged batteries can be reserved in advance through the app on a needs basis.

- Contracting type: Service
- Technology level: Medium
- Country of origin: India
- Availability: India
- Contact: WIPO GREEN Database

Modal shift + electric vehicles: mass transit electric vehicles with pay-as-you-drive subscription

BasiGo

Photo: © Basigo

BasiGo is an e-mobility startup based in Kenya that provides electric public transport buses. Having identified the upfront cost of purchasing electric buses as a major barrier, the company offers pay-as-you-drive subscriptions to public service vehicle operators, currently mainly in the Nairobi area. Operators then pay a fee for every kilometer traveled that covers the cost of leasing the e-bus battery, charging services and general vehicle maintenance. The company has also installed Kenya's first publicly accessible fast-charging stations for electric buses and rolled out an app that allows travelers to plan their routes and book and pay for their trip in advance. BasiGo plans to supply over 1,000 mass transit electric buses to transport operators in Kenya over the next five years.

- Contracting type: Service
- Technology level: Medium
- Country of origin: Kenya
- Availability: Kenya
- Contact: WIPO GREEN Database

Ride-sharing: car-sharing platform with hourly or daily rental options

Awto

Photo: Getty Images / © Tero Vesalainen

Awto is Chile's first car-sharing service. It was founded with the intention of addressing traffic congestion in Santiago and reducing the number of privately owned cars by introducing an hourly or daily car rental service. Their fleet of cars now ranges from two-wheelers to large cargo vehicles. Vehicles are shared using a mobile app that identifies, books and pays for vehicle use on a needs basis.

- Contracting type: Service
- Technology level: Low
- Country of origin: Chile
- Availability: Chile
- Contact: WIPO GREEN Database

Electric vehicles: smart charging stations
XCharge

Photo: Getty Images / © piranka

XCharge is an electric vehicle charging solution provider with a wide range of products, including energy storage and load management. Their charging stations meet diverse electric vehicle charging needs, including for private cars and public buses. Since 2015, more than 40,000 chargers have been installed in more than 25 countries worldwide. The chargers are equipped with liquid cooled lithium-ion battery packs for energy storage and can support simultaneous charging for two vehicles.

- Contracting type: For sale
- Technology level: Medium
- Country of origin: China
- Availability: Worldwide
- Contact: WIPO GREEN Database

Electric vehicles: battery-as-a-service for electric motorbikes
Ampersand

Photo: © Ampersand

Ampersand offers electric motorcycles and a battery-swapping network for motorcycle taxi drivers in Rwanda. A driver can purchase or lease a motorcycle from Ampersand at a competitive price. Batteries are owned by the company and provided to drivers as a service. This means that drivers pay for the electricity as they would petrol – paying only for what they use. When the driver's battery runs out, they can swap it for a fully charged battery at one of the company's swap stations located around the city. This avoids having to wait while the battery charges. The company currently hosts around 35 motorbikes in Kigali with 7,200 drivers on the waiting list.

- Contracting type: Service
- Technology level: Medium
- Country of origin: Rwanda
- Availability: Rwanda
- Contact: WIPO GREEN Database

Electric vehicles: electric vehicles and charging stations in the Arab States

NEV Enterprise Trading L.C.C.

Photo: Getty Images / © Marcus Lindstrom

NEV Enterprise provides tailored solutions to facilitate the scale-up of electric vehicle use in the Arab States. Services include the supply of electric vehicle charging stations for supermarkets, stores, hotels and other establishments. For larger fleets, charging infrastructure can be optimized through a user-friendly back-end management system that tracks and controls usage and costs.

- Contracting type: For sale/service
- Technology level: Medium
- Country of origin: United Arab Emirates
- Availability: Middle East
- Contact: WIPO GREEN Database

Electric vehicles: retrofitted electric cars for emerging economies

Advanced Dynamics

Photo: Getty Images / © anon-tae

Advanced Dynamics transforms conventional used cars into electric vehicles using a complete electrification package consisting of an electric vehicle motor, battery, control system, solar body parts and other supporting components. Their mission is to help fast-growing economies to shift toward electric vehicle use in an affordable manner. Their technology can be adapted to various vehicles, from midsize cars to large commercial trucks.

- Contracting type: Service
- Technology level: Medium
- Country of origin: Singapore/Bangladesh
- Availability: Asia
- Contact: WIPO GREEN Database

Modal shift: app that incentivizes walking

Walk15, UAB

Photo: Getty Images / © Hanna Siamashka

#walk15 is an activity app developed in Lithuania and available worldwide free of charge. Hundreds of thousands of users, as well as over 1,000 companies, have used the app as a tool to encourage their employees to walk more. The app counts steps, creates challenges, enables competitions, shares educational messages relating to the location along the selected route and offers discounts for walking.

- Contracting type: Free
- Technology level: Medium
- Country of origin: Lithuania
- Availability: Worldwide
- Contact: WIPO GREEN Database

Urban planning: local air quality data for mobility planning

Lobelia Earth

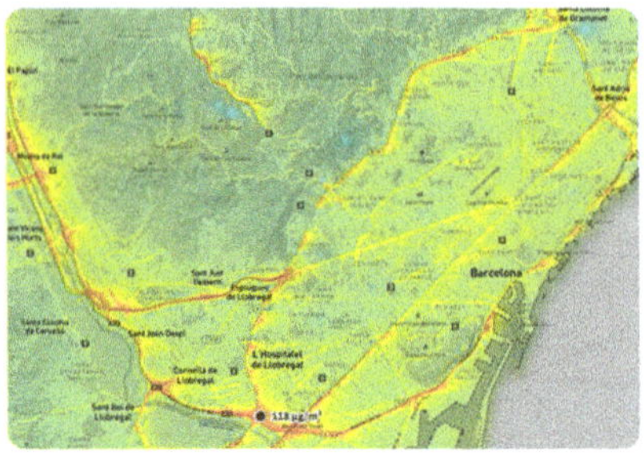

Photo: © Lobelia Earth

Lobelia Earth offers highly localized air quality information at street-level resolution using a combination of local data sources and satellite observations. The platform addresses the need for accurate local air quality measurement and tackles the limitations imposed by in-situ monitoring infrastructure, such as sparse coverage and high cost. The service is currently accessible and utilized in major European cities, assisting city authorities in promoting low-emission zones and mobility planning. The approach relies on meteorological and emission proxy data to generate regular updates on particulate matter (PM) and nitrogen dioxide (NO_2) levels on an hourly basis. The data is based on satellite technologies utilizing radar and optical remote sensing, complemented by on-the-ground monitoring and modeling supported by machine learning algorithms.

- Contracting type: Service
- Technology level: Medium
- Country of origin: Spain
- Availability: Europe
- Contact: WIPO GREEN Database

Biofuel: E85 conversion kit

BioMotors

Photo: © Peter Olsen

In order to fuel a vehicle with E85 (85 percent ethanol 15 percent gasoline) the best option is to buy a flex-fuel vehicle or a vehicle specifically designed to run on E85. However, some cars can be retrofitted to use E85 through conversion kits that typically include components such as modified fuel injectors, fuel lines and pumps and systems to handle the higher ethanol content. As E85 is widely available in France, the French company BioMotors provides E85 conversion kits that allow a car to run on multiple types of fuel. The kit enables real-time detection of the fuel in the vehicle, allowing automatic adjustment of the settings.

- Contracting type: For sale
- Technology level: Medium
- Country of origin: France
- Availability: France
- Contact: WIPO GREEN Database

Hydrogen: on-site hydrogen production and vehicle charging

Atawey Hydrogen

Photo: Getty Images / © Schafsinn86

Atawey Hydrogen designs and develops autonomous, green hydrogen refueling stations. The technology is based on electrolysis (i.e., extracting hydrogen from water using electricity). The water molecule is split into oxygen and hydrogen, with the hydrogen recovered, compressed and stored in vessels. The hydrogen can then be used to refuel vehicles such as cars and bikes. The refueling stations also include charging points for electric vehicle batteries, offering multiple charging options at the same station. Currently, 24 Atawey hydrogen stations have been installed in France and one in New Caledonia.

- Contracting type: For collaboration
- Technology level: High
- Country of origin: France/United States
- Availability: France, New Caledonia
- Contact: WIPO GREEN Database

Hydrogen: converting conventional engines to hydrogen combustion engines

KEYOU

Photo: © Keyou

German startup KEYOU specializes in the transformation of conventional engines into hydrogen combustion engines. The technology has been successfully implemented in an 18-tonne truck and the company aims to rent these converted vehicles on a hydrogen mobility-as-a-service model, where end customers pay a monthly kilometer-based price depending on their actual mileage. The complete package includes the hydrogen vehicle, fuel, service, maintenance and insurance. The basis for the converted engine is a diesel engine platform sourced from an established manufacturer with a power output of 210 kW. It complies with EU emission standards and consumes about 7.5 kg of hydrogen per 100 km with a storage capacity of about 27 kg hydrogen enabling a range of 350 km. Refueling with hydrogen takes approximately 15 minutes. The company premiered their trucks in 2022 and customer operations are set to begin soon.

- Contracting type: For sale/service
- Technology level: High
- Country of origin: Germany
- Availability: Germany
- Contact: WIPO GREEN Database

Ride-sharing + autonomous vehicles: autonomous robotaxis

Zoox Inc.

Photo: Getty Images/© Kinwun

Zoox robotaxis are on-demand autonomous vehicles designed for moving people via a ride-hailing service platform. They have been piloted and are currently in operation as an employee shuttle service in Las Vegas, Nevada. The vehicle is fully electric and driverless. It uses sensors, cameras, lidars and radars to navigate through its surroundings.

- Contracting type: Service/collaboration
- Technology level: High
- Country of origin: United States
- Availability: United States
- Contact: WIPO GREEN Database

Electric vehicles: solid-state lithium batteries

Chongqing Talent New Energy Co., Ltd.

Photo: © Chongqing Talent New Energy

Talent New Energy develops next-generation batteries with a focus on solid-state lithium batteries. Their semi-solid lithium batteries use a solid electrolyte similar to ceramics, which increases mechanical and chemical strength and stability and improves the safety of the battery. The batteries display extended lifetimes and their higher energy density in comparison to traditional liquid lithium batteries results in faster charging times.

- Contracting type: For sale
- Technology level: High
- Country of origin: China
- Availability: China
- Contact: WIPO GREEN Database

Electric vehicles: automatically rechargeable e-bike

byAr Volta

Photo: Getty Images/© ABBPhoto

The byAr Volta electric bicycle features a shaft-driven design that uses energy produced by backpedaling to recharge its battery. The longer you backpedal, the more energy is produced to recharge the battery, saving on charging time. The company claims the battery can be nearly fully charged during use.

- Contracting type: For sale
- Technology level: Medium
- Country of origin: Netherlands (Kingdom of the)
- Availability: Netherlands (Kingdom of the)
- Contact: WIPO GREEN Database

Modal shift + electric vehicles: electrified buses in sub-Saharan Africa

Kiira Motors

Photo: Getty Images / © FullFrameFactory

Kiira Motors has designed a fully electric low-floor bus for urban mass transportation in sub-Saharan Africa. Fully charged, the Kayoola EVS™ bus has a range of up to 300 km, with capacity to seat up to 90 passengers. The bus is also equipped to transport passengers with special needs, with special seats and a ramp for easy onboarding of people in wheelchairs. The company is currently taking orders to produce the buses.

- Contracting type: For sale/collaboration
- Technology level: Medium
- Country of origin: Uganda
- Availability: Uganda
- Contact: WIPO GREEN Database

Horizon technologies

Electric vehicles: graphene electric vehicle battery

Graphenano

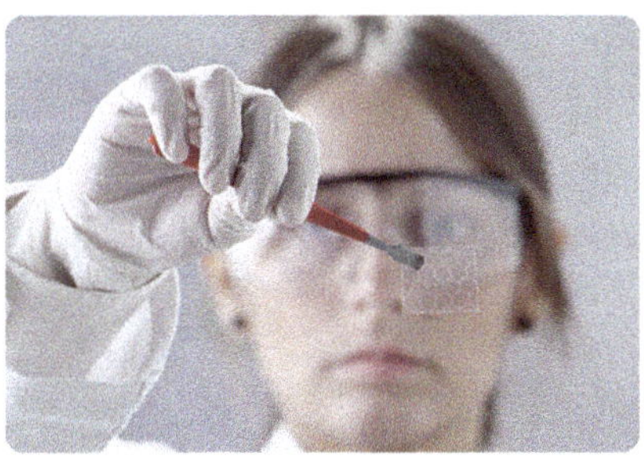

Photo: Getty Images / © BONNINSTUDIO

Graphene batteries have the potential to be the electric vehicle battery of the future, as they charge much faster than conventional electric vehicle batteries and store more energy. The Spanish company Graphenano is developing a graphene polymer-based battery for use in electric vehicles with a 500 km range. Their aim is to produce a battery that is rechargeable in less than five minutes.

- Contracting type: Service/collaboration
- Technology level: High
- Country of origin: Spain
- Availability: Under development
- Contact: WIPO GREEN Database

Electric vehicles: sodium-ion battery

Contemporary Amperex Technology Co. (CATL)

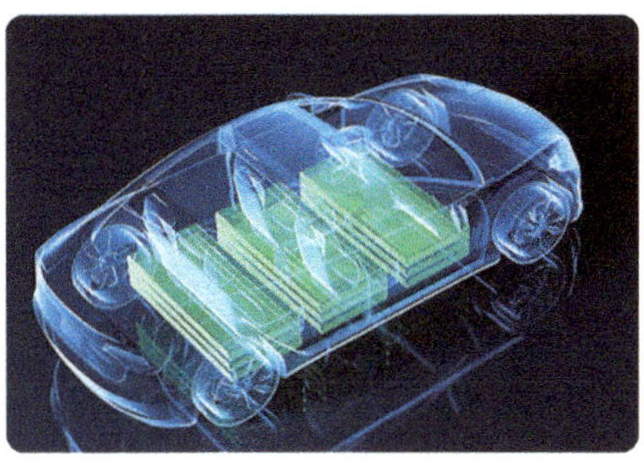

Photo: Getty Images / © Just_Super

Sodium-ion batteries could become an important alternative to conventional lithium-ion batteries in the future. While they have the advantages of being cheaper and not relying on lithium, their energy density is lower which may make them more suitable for vehicles with a shorter range. However, research into strengthening their performance is ongoing and the leading electric vehicle battery manufacturer, Contemporary Amperex Technology Co. (CATL), plans mass production of sodium-ion batteries this year.

- Contracting type: For collaboration
- Technology level: High
- Country of origin: China
- Availability: Under development
- Contact: WIPO GREEN Database

Biofuel: hydrothermal liquefaction (HTL) of biomass for transport fuel
Licella

Photo: Getty Getty Images/© Toa55

Hydrothermal liquefaction (HTL) is a thermochemical conversion process that converts wet biomass, such as sewage sludge, agricultural residues and other organic materials, into a liquid biofuel. This process takes place in conditions of high temperature and pressure to break down the organic material and form a mixture of volatile organic compounds. Mixed with water, this compound forms a liquid known as bio-oil or bio-crude, which can be refined for use as transport fuel. Unlike pyrolysis or gasification processes, this technology can process feedstock with high moisture content, avoiding the need for energy-intensive drying. No commercial-scale plants are currently operational. However, several plants from demonstration to commercial scale are in development, including one plant in Canada that aims to apply the Licella technology for development of bio-crude which can be further refined into transport fuel.

- Contracting type: For collaboration
- Technology level: High
- Country of origin: Canada
- Availability: Under development
- Contact: WIPO GREEN Database

Biofuel: fast pyrolysis of biomass for transport fuel
Pyrocell AB

Photo: Getty Images/© Bill Oxford

Fast pyrolysis of biomass to produce liquid bio-oil is a well-established technology but high oxygen content limits its potential as a transport fuel.[127] Current research is focusing on improving the upgrading process of such bio-fuels for use in transport. Pyrocell is a pyrolysis plant commissioned in 2021 for the conversion of sawdust into pyrolysis oil with a capacity of 25,000 tonnes of bio-oil per year. Here, the fast pyrolysis technology developed by Dutch companies TechnipFMC and BTG BioLiquids has been utilized to produce bio-oil destined for upgrading to transport fuel at a refinery in Sweden.

- Contracting type: For collaboration
- Technology level: High
- Country of origin: Sweden
- Availability: Under development
- Contact: WIPO GREEN Database

Electric vehicles: "massless" energy storage in electric vehicles
Chalmers University of Technology

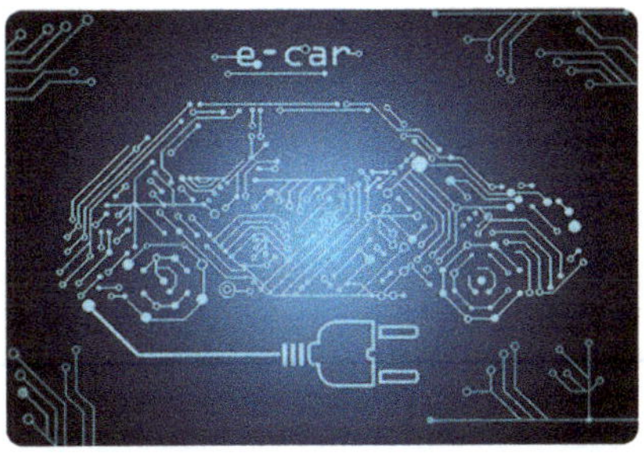

Photo: Getty Images / © kaptnali

Electric vehicles' batteries today constitute a large part of the vehicle's weight, thereby adding to the energy needed to drive the car. However, a so-called structural battery (or "massless" energy storage) is one that is integrated into the load-bearing structure of a vehicle. While attempts to develop such batteries first started in 2007, a recent breakthrough at Chalmers University of Technology, Gothenburg, has led to structural batteries with improved energy storage. While lighter consumer products such as computers and bicycles are currently more within reach for this technology, continued research aims to make structural batteries a reality for electric vehicles.

- Contracting type: For collaboration
- Technology level: High
- Country of origin: Sweden
- Availability: Under development
- Contact: WIPO GREEN Database

Material efficiency and sustainable waste management

The past 50 years have seen the world's resource use more than triple while the global population doubled.[128, 129] This is the main driver of the current triple planetary crisis. In fact, resource use represents half of total greenhouse gas (GHG) emissions, more than 90 percent of land-related biodiversity loss and water stress, and a third of health-related pollution impacts.[130] This section explores how technology and innovation, from simple water fountains to digital solutions, can support a transformational shift in how we produce, consume and dispose of materials.

Photo: Getty Images / Kyryl Gorlov

The growth in material demand is not only depleting natural resources such as minerals and water, but it nearly doubled the GHG emissions caused by material production from 1995 to 2015

Emissions from materials are growing rapidly

Construction materials, metals, plastics and wood are essential in building a city. More than half of the world's urban population lives in cities[131] and urbanization is increasing exponentially along with material consumption rates. The rapid scaling of electric vehicles, solar panels and wind turbines is also driving up demand for critical raw materials. Material use is expected to double between 2020 and 2050.[132] Exponential growth in production and consumption is seen in all resource types, with some growing faster than others. Plastics, which account for nearly 5 percent of global GHG emissions,[133] are expected to nearly triple by 2060 at the current rate (figure 2.4).[134, 135]

Figure 2.4 The current and projected growth in global plastics usage (in million tonnes), 1980–2060

Source: OECD, 2022b.

The growth in material demand is not only depleting natural resources such as minerals and water, but it nearly doubled the GHG emissions caused by material production from 1995 to 2015 (figure 2.5). The rapid growth in demand is thus offsetting policy and technology measures to reduce emissions from production and manufacturing processes. Therefore, material demand management is essential for meaningful climate action (box 3.2). Many technologies are responding to this challenge, and as is often the case, they start by supporting climate-smart design.

Figure 2.5 Emissions (in gigatons) caused by material production as a share of global emissions, 1995 versus 2015[136]

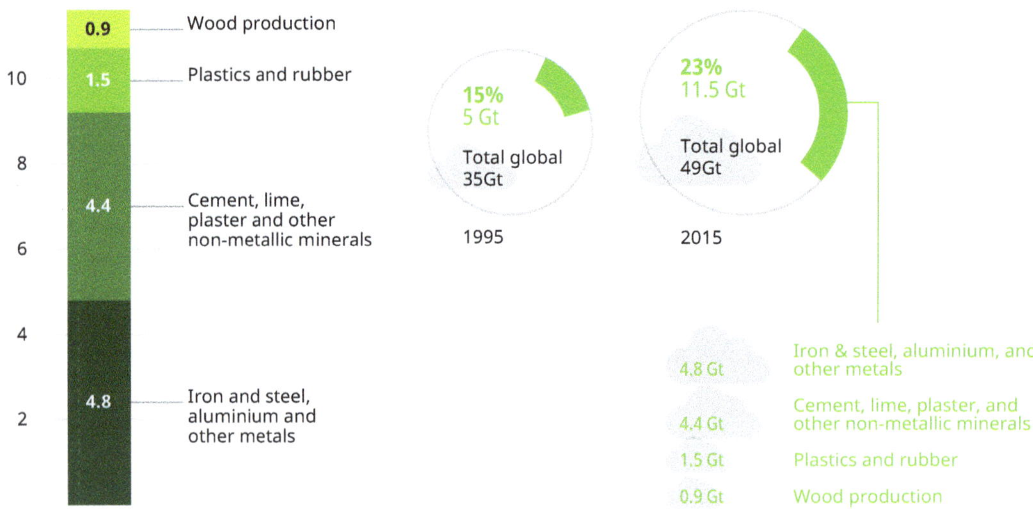

Source: International Resource Panel, 2020.

Climate-smart design for circular cities

Designing lighter products reduces the embodied carbon in assets such as homes and cars. Using less steel in the loadbearing structure of buildings is one example. Another is replacing some of the steel in vehicles with aluminum. Aluminum has a higher carbon footprint than steel but overall emissions are reduced through fuel-savings gained by having a lighter car.[137] These so-called lightweighting solutions must not come at the expense of durability or recyclability of a product.

There is growing interest in applying proven tools such as computer-aided design (CAD) and building information modeling (BIM) for climate-smart design.[138] For instance, BIM is used in design processes to locate areas of medium and low structural load that allow for lightweighting without losing functionality. The technology can also produce a virtual representation of a building to see how prefabricated components and modules can best fit together. This supports material use optimization and waste reduction.[139]

Climate-smart design also means considering materials' end-of-life stage and the design of products for easy and affordable reuse and recycling. For instance, transparent and unmixed plastic is easier to recycle than black plastic products that combine multiple material types. Bolting construction materials together instead of welding allows for easier and less destructive material recovery at the end-of-life stage.

Reviving natural building materials

Wood, rammed earth and adobe bricks made from materials such as mud are re-emerging as natural alternatives to carbon-intensive steel and cement in various parts of the world, depending on the climatic zone. While these are traditional solutions, they are easily overlooked in the face of rapid urbanization and restrictive building codes. A common barrier to uptake of low-carbon and local materials is the inability to produce them at scale. Limited availability of demonstration projects and a lack of supportive regulation further inhibits their adoption.[140, 141] However, technological developments and growing interest in state-of-the-art advanced manufacturing methods can enable a modern approach to the use of such materials in cities.[142, 143]

Wooden high-rise constructions are increasing in number thanks to advances in engineered wood, such as cross-laminated timber and glued laminated timber.[144] Reinforced timber beams and modern adhesive technologies have helped overcome barriers to tensile strength. Additionally, moisture monitoring and non-flammable surface materials have increased resistance to moisture damage and fire. However, it is important to note that the climate benefits of using wood as a construction material have recently been disputed, and the right conditions must be ensured to limit associated emissions.[145]

Innovations in material sustainability

Material science innovation is also leading to eco-friendly materials, sustainable building materials and the valorization of waste for new uses. This applies to a range of sectors, including for construction material, proteins, fertilizers and plastics. In the case of plastics, biodegradable and bio-based plastics have been championed for some time. Their production still represents less than 1 percent of all plastic but they are expected to witness an annual growth rate of 14 percent between 2022 and 2027.[146]

Notably, many institutions including the United Nations Environment Programme (UNEP) now highlight the fact that biodegradable plastic items often do not degrade in the environment but require special composting facilities. And while bio-based plastics can be a good alternative if there is appropriate collection and recycling infrastructure in place, they may not always lead to better outcomes.[147] In any case, material substitution considerations must be guided by life-cycle thinking to understand the trade-offs and overall impact.

For municipal waste, optical scanners and robotics are now merging with artificial intelligence (AI) technology to offer efficient screening, identification and separation of waste streams. Hundreds of sorting facilities around the world have already implemented such technologies

Policies for sustainable waste management

Less than 14 percent of global waste is recycled, mainly due to a lack of waste management infrastructure.[148] While this chapter explores the role of technology and innovation, such applications have limited impact on improved collection and sorting if the enabling environment is weak. Primarily, ambitious policies and economic measures such as extended producer responsibility (EPR) schemes are essential to incentivize better waste separation at source by citizens.

In more than 40 countries, mainly in Europe, deposit return schemes have helped increase the recycling rate for glass and plastic, and the number participating is growing.[149] In many countries, the scheme also extends to metal cans. A small fee is added to the price of products such as drinking containers, which is refunded to the consumer when they bring them back to a collection point.

The digital revolution in waste management

Cities in many developing countries rely on the support of formal or informal waste pickers to sort and collect waste for recycling. In some cities, waste pickers have started to use mobile apps that connect them directly with customers and enable door-to-door collection or organize pick-up points under more sanitary conditions than landfill sites.[150] For municipal waste, optical scanners and robotics are now merging with artificial intelligence (AI) technology to offer efficient screening, identification and separation of waste streams. Hundreds of sorting facilities around the world have already implemented such technologies[151] and Danish researchers recently revealed a near-infrared technology that could distinguish between 12 types of polymers.[152] Geographical information systems (GIS) enable optimization of collection routes in cities. Other innovations such as chemical tracers and digital watermarks are just emerging.

Beyond municipal waste, advances in automation technologies could also enable easier deconstruction and dismantling of buildings and products in the future.[153, 154] While mixed construction and demolition waste is difficult to recover and is often downcycled as aggregate, advances in robotics have shown a positive impact on separation and recycling rates. In the vehicles sector, machine-based vehicle recycling systems can dismantle cars with precision to extract valuable materials. With appropriate investment, many more parts could already be salvaged today, from tires and batteries to plastic bumpers and air conditioning compressors.

Waste management technologies have varying climate impact

For municipal waste that is not presorted, mechanical and biological treatment (MBT) plants are increasingly recognized for their ability to recover more materials and reduce methane emissions from landfill. At these plants, a mix of technologies and biological processes is used to sort out metal, glass and plastics and turn the remaining waste into refuse-derived fuel. For instance, studies have shown that MBT prior to landfilling is one of the most favorable options from a climate impact standpoint, and can be more cost-effective than incineration.[155, 156]

Several advances in recycling technologies themselves are also emerging, focusing on hard-to-recycle products such as car tires and wind turbine blades. However, as many of these recycling technologies rely on energy-intensive processes like pyrolysis, the full life-cycle implications need to be considered before they can be viewed as viable from a climate perspective.[157]

Recycling does not sufficiently address climate change

While several innovative recycling technologies are emerging, numerous studies have shown that recycling can never respond to the growing production of materials fast enough to make a meaningful contribution to climate mitigation. The numbers simply do not add up. For instance, at 9 percent the current rate of plastics recycling will never catch up with the exponential growth in plastic production. This is particularly problematic from a climate perspective, as more than 60 percent of plastic's emissions occur during plastic pellet production stage.[158, 159, 160] Therefore, any meaningful mitigation strategy requires a major shift in terms of investments toward a circular economy, with a particular focus on phasing out single-use and unnecessary plastic production. A circular economy approach would also go beyond recycling to support climate-smart design and material choices, and facilitate collective ownership, repair and reuse.

Reducing GHG emissions from incineration

Of all the waste generated in the world, around 11 percent is incinerated.[161] This occurs mainly in upper middle-income and high-income countries where waste-to-energy incineration is a common practice. While waste-to-energy technologies can contribute to global energy supply and address the need for waste management[162], municipal solid waste incinerators themselves are highly polluting.

In fact, incinerators can emit more GHG emissions per unit of electricity produced than any other power source, as they often operate under conditions of low efficiency.[163] Targeting the pressure and temperature of the steam cycle can improve efficiency of incinerators, while better plant capacity design can help reduce the need for imported waste. Yet, typical efficiencies of EU incinerators are as low as 25 percent, compared to 55 percent for combined cycle gas turbine plants.[164]

In developing countries, where municipal waste often contains more organic matter, efficiencies are even lower and air pollutants are a common problem. Here, technologies such as anaerobic digestion – in which microorganisms break down organic matter in the absence of oxygen – are more appropriate options.[165] However, it is expected that modern waste incinerators could be built in some middle-income countries in the near future and China is seeing rapid implementation of the technology.[166]

Carbon capture and storage technologies are now being considered to mitigate the climate impact of incinerators. Meanwhile, countries such as Denmark, where incineration has completely replaced landfills, have embarked on a journey to limit their incineration capacity in order to reach stated climate goals.[167]

Reducing methane emissions from landfills and open dumps

Globally, around 5 percent of global GHG emissions derive from solid waste treatment and disposal – mainly as methane – from open dumps and landfills without gas capture systems. In fact, landfill waste accounts for around 11 percent of global methane emissions.[168]

Satellite-based technologies can now measure site-specific emissions, which can vary greatly between different landfills.[169] Gas drainage and leachate control systems help reduce emissions from landfills caused by the degradation of organic matter into methane and other gases. Bioreactor landfills are a relatively new approach involving recirculation of leachate to support the degradation process of organic waste and increase gas generation and capture in controlled forms. Captured gases can even be used to generate electricity on site.

However, controlled landfills are almost exclusively found in high- or upper middle-income countries, while 93 percent of waste in low-income countries ends up in open dumps.[170] There have been rehabilitation efforts all over the world. Yet, the handling of open landfills and the environmental and health hazards they pose is a major unsolved challenge that cannot be addressed by the application of technology alone.

Any innovation in the management of open dumps would also need to consider the working conditions and rights of informal waste pickers who earn a daily living by collecting waste. This is particularly relevant considering their major contribution to recycling rates; nearly 60 percent of the world's recycled plastic is collected by waste pickers.[171]

Satellite-based technologies can now measure site-specific emissions, which can vary greatly between different landfills

The climate justice rationale for material sustainability and efficiency

Emerging economies show the steepest rise in consumption, driven by increased population density and industrialization. However, the per capita material footprint of high-income countries is still around 60 percent higher than upper middle-income countries, and more than 13 times the level of low-income countries.[172, 173]

Furthermore, material-intensive production is increasingly being outsourced from developed to developing countries.[174] In a global market, more cities are now estimating their GHG emissions based on consumption parameters, with the results pointing to large differences between those considered "producer" cities and "consumer" cities.[175]

Consumption-based emissions are much higher in European and North American cities, while several cities in Asia and Africa have higher sector-based GHG emissions due to the location of manufacturing industries.[176] Therefore, managing material demand and efficiency not only leads to greater overall GHG emission reductions, but also helps balance the responsibility for mitigation efforts more evenly between producers and consumers.

While economic development has historically relied on increasing material demand, the science around dematerializing economic growth is clear and the Intergovernmental Panel on Climate Change (IPCC) clearly refers to demand reduction as a key necessity for staying within the boundaries of what the planet can sustain (box 2.2). Meanwhile, research shows that the circular economy offers a USD 4.5 trillion economic opportunity and has massive potential for growth generation and job creation – while remaining within the planetary boundaries.[177]

Box 2.2 Managing material demand through technology and innovation

The need for sustainable resource management has been recognized as a prioritized principle in the landmark IPCC report on climate change mitigation. The report refers to the need to "avoid demand for energy, materials, land and water while delivering human well-being-for-all within planetary boundaries".[178]

Managing demand and ensuring sufficient access to resources relates to many spheres of life, including access to shelter, nutrition, basic amenities, health care, transportation, information, education and public space. Here, the principle of fair consumption of space and resources is central. This further recognizes the need for affluent countries to embrace resource conservation through measures such as better design and circulation of materials, while simultaneously enabling the sustainable growth of developing and emerging economies. The IPCC defines the upper limit of sufficiency as the remaining carbon budget, while a decent living standard defines the minimum level of sufficiency for basic human well-being.

Indeed, technology and innovation play a crucial role in achieving efficiency and shifting to low-carbon fuels and feedstock. However, more recognition is needed of the role of technology and innovation for managing the demand for materials throughout their life cycle.

There is an important distinction to be made here. While technologies that enable efficiency are the result of continuous technological improvements that allow more to be done with less, they do not necessarily consider the planetary boundaries. While efficiency gains are needed, taking demand and sufficiency of materials into consideration goes beyond efforts to support incremental change. It acknowledges strategies that use less material by design, extend product lifetimes, provide more efficient services, and reuse and recycle materials. Here, technology can play a major role.

Innovation examples

Photo: Getty Images / © JohnnyH5

Gaia – largest wooden building in Asia

Using wood instead of steel and cement in construction could save significant amounts of GHG emissions. Gaia, the largest wooden building in Asia, is located at Nanyang Technological University in Singapore. The six-storey development was constructed using mass-engineered timber – a material created by layering and bonding wood to achieve enhanced strength. The technology involves gluing, nailing or doweling wooden products together in layers, resulting in large structural panels. As a certified zero-energy building, the building generates the same amount of energy as it consumes through the use of solar panels, passive ventilation systems and other technologies.

Note: The climate benefits of using wood as a construction material have recently been disputed, and the claim lacks consensus.[179]

Photo: Getty Images / © Bim

Austin's online Materials Marketplace

The City of Austin, Texas has implemented the Austin Materials Marketplace, an online platform serving as an electronic clearinghouse that connects businesses seeking to dispose of materials with those in need of such materials. Additionally, the platform incorporates reporting functionality to track trades, measure the value of exchanges and monitor the diversion of materials from landfill. It is developed and managed by the United States Business Council for Sustainable Development and covers a wide range of materials, including construction and demolition materials, plastics, organics and packaging, attracting users from various sectors. Over 500 businesses, institutions and non-profit organizations have already signed up as participants. Notable outcomes include diverting over 400 tonnes of material from landfills and saving over 950 million tonnes of CO_2 equivalent emissions.

Photo: © Peter Oksen

Sudokwon landfill site in the Republic of Korea

The Sudokwon landfill site is a state-of-the art waste treatment facility based in South Korea (Republic of Korea). The site incorporates a 50 MW power plant fueled by gas collected from the landfill – one of the largest of its kind in the world. The captured methane would otherwise be emitted to the atmosphere as a greenhouse gas. Repurposing the gas for energy supply therefore makes an important contribution to climate mitigation. The facility also produces biogas for fueling buses and hosts a sludge recycling facility. The site covers 14 km2 of land with a daily capacity of around 12,000 tons of waste. The site's landfill capacity will eventually be used up and a replacement site required for handling more waste. This highlights the important limitations of landfills and the need to move toward a circular approach to waste management. Nevertheless, Sudokwon's efficient capturing of landfill gases marks an innovative and useful example for landfill climate mitigation.

Technology solutions

Proven technologies

Demand management: digital tool for climate-smart design

Dassault Systemes

Design for Manufacture and Assembly (DfMA) is a set of design principles traditionally used in the automotive industry and for consumer products. It is now increasingly being adopted by construction contractors. The approach focuses on designing for ease of assembling and disassembling components, with the co-benefit of reduced waste generation. Dassault Systemes offers architects, engineers and contractors a suite of digital tools to support them in designing for material efficiency via its 3DEXPERIENCE platform. For instance, the platform enables the creation of virtual twins to test ideas and real-life scenarios allowing design iteration before construction takes place. The software was used to design Brock Commons Tallwood House, the world's tallest mass-timber building in 2016.

- Contracting type: For sale/service
- Technology level: High
- Country of origin: France
- Availability: Worldwide
- Contact: WIPO GREEN Database

Demand management: public drinking water fountains

Elkay

The idea of public drinking fountains dates back thousands of years. Cities that provide free drinking water through drinking water fountains notice a significant reduction in plastic waste. Over time, technology has improved the accessibility and sanitary conditions of public water fountains. Elkay's bottle-refilling stations include features such as antimicrobial plastic components and hands-free operation.

- Contracting type: For sale
- Technology level: Medium
- Country of origin: United States
- Availability: Worldwide
- Contact: WIPO GREEN Database

Demand management: purified water refill stations
I-Drop

Photo: Getty Images /© Jatuporn Tansirimas

The Waterpod is a self-service purified drinking water refill dispenser for use in supermarkets and grocery stores. While the dispensers are connected to the main water supply, the in-built filtering consists of several layers including nanomesh technology, ultraviolet sterilization, activated carbon and alkaline cartridge mineralization. The design allows users to buy or dispense purified water using both reusable bottles and larger water containers for household consumption. An internet of things device enables timely changing of the filters.

- Contracting type: For sale/service
- Technology level: Medium
- Country of origin: South Africa
- Availability: Africa
- Contact: WIPO GREEN Database

Demand management: vending machines for consumer products in reusable containers
Algramo

Photo: Getty Images /© Space_Cat

Algramo is a Chilean enterprise that offers small quantities of bulk products in reusable containers. Since starting up in 2019, more than 2,000 stores have installed their vending machines, reaching over 350,000 customers. The vending machines enable customers to purchase household essentials in desired quantities dispensed into reusable containers. Customers save up to 40 percent by buying products in small quantities at bulk prices, which is an important incentive for minimizing the purchase of products in sachets and other single-use plastics.

- Contracting type: For sale/service
- Technology level: Medium
- Country of origin: Chile
- Availability: Chile
- Contact: WIPO GREEN Database

Demand management: interlocking bricks reduce demand for cement and mortar

Hydraform

Photo: © Hydraform

Hydraform is a South African manufacturer of brick- and block-making machines for construction, using stabilized soil cement blocks or compressed earth blocks. The blocks can be constructed on site, using locally available materials. The machines enable bricks and blocks to be hydraulically compressed to form interlocking blocks, which reduces the need for mortar joints, saving costs and emissions.

- Contracting type: For sale
- Technology level: Low/medium
- Country of origin: South Africa
- Availability: Worldwide
- Contact: WIPO GREEN Database

Material substitution: digital tool for calculating the climate impact of building with wood

Ruhr-Universität Bochum

Photo: © RUB, Roberto Schirdewahn

Substituting wood for conventional building materials can significantly reduce emissions – if done right. In order to scale these practices, researchers at the Ruhr-Universität Bochum, Germany have recently developed a web-based GIS tool, called the Holzbau-GIS system, to help municipalities and local authorities estimate the GHG reduction and carbon storage potential of building and renovating with wood.[180]

- Contracting type: For collaboration
- Technology level: Medium
- Country of origin: Germany
- Availability: Worldwide
- Contact: WIPO GREEN Database

Material substitution: locally manufactured construction materials in Cameroon

MIPROMALO

Photo: Getty Images /© ivanastar

The Local Material Promotion Authority (MIPROMALO) promotes the use of locally manufactured materials and the development of innovative materials for construction in Cameroon. Among the products they provide are compressed earth blocks, fired clay bricks and roof tiles. By favoring these materials over resource-intensive alternatives, the carbon footprint associated with transportation and manufacturing processes is reduced.

- Contracting type: For sale
- Technology level: Low
- Country of origin: Cameroon
- Availability: Cameroon
- Contact: WIPO GREEN Database

Material substitution: PHA-based bioplastics combining the use of plant oil and CO_2

Bluepha Co. Ltd.

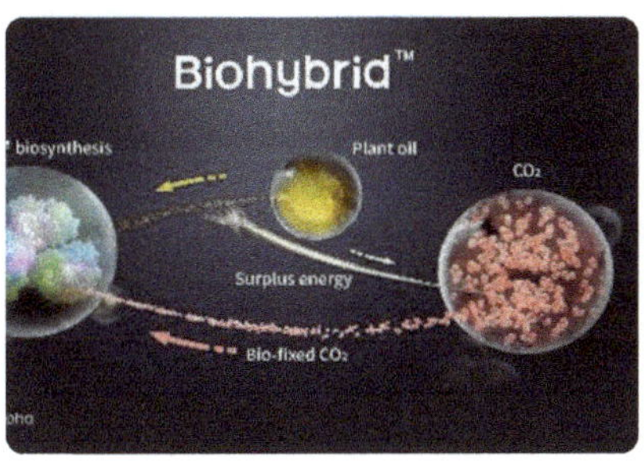

Photo: © Bluepha

Bluepha develops biodegradable alternatives to petroleum-derived plastic products ranging from packaging to agricultural materials. The technology utilizes organic feedstock such as starch, plant oil and sugarcane in a microbial fermentation process to produce a biodegradable polymer known as PHA (polyhydroxyalkanoate). Bluepha's specific type of PHA, made through their patented Biohybrid™ technology, is also capable of carbon fixation in the production process.

- Contracting type: For sale/service
- Technology level: High
- Country of origin: China
- Availability: Worldwide
- Contact: WIPO GREEN Database

Waste management: mechanical recycling of textile stock

Weturn

Weturn purchases unsold textile stock and recycles the textiles into new fabric, preventing the incineration of the material and displacing virgin material production. Raw materials such as cotton, wool, cashmere and mixed materials can be recycled through mechanical recycling if the synthetic fiber content is less than 20 percent. The fabric is collected and shredded then spun, weaved or knitted into new products.

- Contracting type: Service
- Technology level: Medium
- Country of origin: France
- Availability: France
- Contact: WIPO GREEN Database

Waste management: reverse vending machines

TOMRA Systems ASA

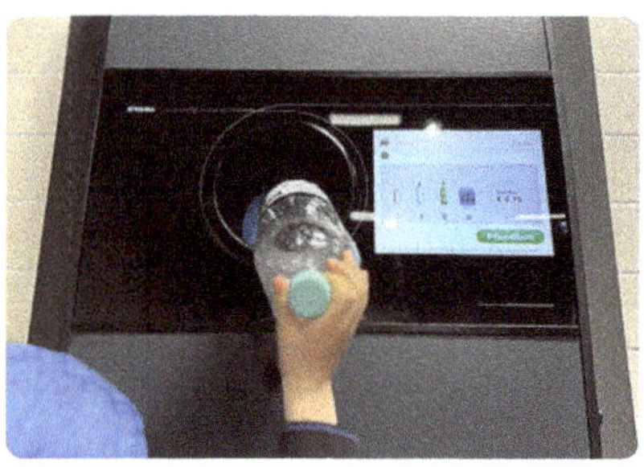

TOMRA provides various reverse vending machines for outlets ranging from small stores to large supermarkets. The machines provide an automated method for collecting, sorting and handling the return of cans, plastic and glass bottles and crates through more than 80,000 installations across more than 60 markets. The instant deposit received for each container recycled provides financial motivation for consumers to continue bringing back the containers. In many countries, such deposit return schemes have become a routine part of community life and systematically contribute to climate mitigation by increasing the number of refillable products on the market and promoting high-quality closed-loop recycling, thus reducing reliance on virgin materials. In Scotland, for example, a deposit return scheme for cans and bottles is estimated to reduce GHG emissions by 160,000 tonnes of CO_2 per year (equivalent to taking 85,000 cars off the road).[181]

- Contracting type: For sale/service
- Technology level: Medium
- Country of origin: Norway
- Availability: Worldwide
- Contact: WIPO GREEN Database

Demand management: digital material passports for increased circularity

Loopfront

Photo: © HildaWeges

Loopfront's digital platform and surveying tool enables new life and value from used building materials and interiors. The tool allows users to quickly map out what they already have and what can be reused. The platform offers a material overview and "material passport" for every product, including specifications and documentation. There is also the possibility to automatically generate reports of financial savings and CO_2 reductions.

- Contracting type: For collaboration
- Technology level: Medium
- Country of origin: Norway
- Availability: Norway
- Contact: WIPO GREEN Database

Demand management: blockchain-enabled construction project management tool

DigiBuild

Photo: Getty Images/© NatalyaBurova

Reuse and recycling of construction and demolition waste relies on a coordinated supply chain and strong stakeholder collaboration. The DigiBuild project management tool enables an overview of the construction project and automates the process of finding, ordering, tracking and managing materials. A key element of the blockchain-enabled software is a construction management and central data storage platform. It has built-in workflow approvals and audit trails providing a material visibility overview.

- Contracting type: For sale/service
- Technology level: High
- Country of origin: United States
- Availability: Worldwide
- Contact: WIPO GREEN Database

Demand management: upcycling industrial by-products into high-value ceramic tiles
Seramic Materials

Photo: Getty Images/© cnikola

Seramic recycles industrial solid waste such as sludge, ceramic waste and ashes into new products. Currently considered low-value by-products, these materials are otherwise consigned to landfills or sold as aggregates for roads and cement. Upcycling the waste into more high-value ceramic products, such as floor and wall tiles or for use in thermal storage systems, saves energy and helps displace waste from landfills. The patented recycling process is under continuous development and new applications for its products are currently being explored.

- Contracting type: For sale
- Technology level: Medium
- Country of origin: United Arab Emirates
- Availability: Worldwide
- Contact: WIPO GREEN Database

Waste management: app-based plastic waste collection and recycling system
Coliba Ghana Ltd

Photo: Getty Images/© Will Cormack

Coliba Ghana is a startup offering plastic recovery, collection and recycling services through tailored digital solutions integrated with a network of local waste pickers. A digital app combined with a simple SMS service enables clients to request collection of waste. The company's facilities and recycling centers then wash and crush the plastic material before packaging it into bales ready for mechanical recycling. Here, the plastic is shredded into flakes and processed into pellets to be used in new plastic products, displacing the demand for virgin materials.

- Contracting type: Service
- Technology level: Medium
- Country of origin: Ghana
- Availability: West Africa
- Contact: WIPO GREEN Database

Waste management: digital waste detection tool

iNex Circular

Photo: Getty Images /© bymuratdeniz

The iNex Sourcing solution is a predictive waste detection tool that enhances the supply chain overview in sectors such as biogas, construction, solar and recycling. For the recycling sector, the tool enables users to map, source and trace materials. It also helps identify suppliers and partners to connect, for instance, local waste producers and recyclers. The tool permits calculation and visualization of environmental impact in real time.

- Contracting type: Service
- Technology level: Medium
- Country of origin: France
- Availability: Europe
- Contact: WIPO GREEN Database

Waste management: thermoplastic from unsorted landfill waste

UBQ Material

Photo: Getty © UBQ Materials

UBQ™ is an eco-friendly thermoplastic produced entirely from unsorted household waste, comprising both organic and non-recyclable materials. It can integrate seamlessly into current manufacturing methods and has already been adopted in various sectors as a substitute for oil-based resins. Manufacturers utilizing the technology are effectively redirecting waste away from landfills and incineration, thus diminishing the overall carbon impact of their final products and actively promoting a circular economy. By reassembling the basic components of the waste, such as lignin, cellulose, fibers and sugars, while incorporating residual plastics, UBQ offers a sustainable alternative to conventional methods. This process operates at lower temperatures and requires less energy, and in 2021 UBQ achieved 100 percent energy self-sufficiency through the company's solar array.

- Contracting type: For sale/service
- Technology level: High
- Country of origin: Israel
- Availability: Worldwide
- Contact: WIPO GREEN Database

Waste management: advanced water-based recycling system for mixed waste

Fiberight Ltd

Photo: © Fiberight

Fiberight's HYDRACYCLE™ technology segregates and recovers material such as paper, card, plastics, metals and food waste from mixed residual-waste streams, using water as a separation medium within a closed-loop water-recycling process. The recovered materials are upgraded into high-value market-ready products following a valorization process. For instance, plastics are purified and sorted into polymer fractions for onward manufacturing. Paper/card is valorized into bio-based sugars for bio-manufacturing, or utilized in cellulose-based products. The process works with mixed household wastes that are typically burnt or buried. Fiberight's first UK commercial facility came online in April 2023 in Swansea, Wales, and is processing rejected material from material recovery facilities.

- Contracting type: For sale/service
- Technology level: High
- Country of origin: United Kingdom
- Availability: United Kingdom, United States
- Contact: WIPO GREEN Database

Horizon technologies

Demand management: 3D-printing mineral foam for complex formwork

ETH Zurich/FoamWork

Photo: © ETH Zurich

Researchers from ETH Zurich university, Switzerland have developed a system that uses 3D-printed elements to create a pre-cast concrete slab, which they claim uses 70 percent less material than a conventional slab. The 3D-printed material is made from recyclable mineral foam. The foam is filled into a rectangular mold to create a hollow cell structure before concrete is cast around the foam and left to cure. The hollow cells throughout the slab are reinforced along critical pressure points to create the necessary strength and reduce the amount of concrete needed. Once the hollow slabs are created, the foam can either be left in place as insulation material or recycled to create new formwork. As custom formwork geometries are otherwise wasteful to produce, the 3D-construction of the formwork may make the process more feasible.

- Contracting type: For collaboration
- Technology level: Medium
- Country of origin: Switzerland
- Availability: Under development
- Contact: WIPO GREEN Database

Material substitution: bio-based and compostable food packaging from cassava starch and banana fibers

Hya Bioplastics

Photo: Getty Images / © FreshSplash

Hya Bioplastics, a startup in Uganda, has developed a bio-based and fully home-compostable food packaging alternative to paper or petroleum-based plastics. The company uses cassava starch – a cheaper alternative to maize – and pulped fibers as their key raw material. The fibers are from the lower part of banana leaves, otherwise treated as waste. Products include a range of food packaging including fruit and vegetable trays, takeaway food boxes and disposable plates. The technology is currently in pilot phase.

- Contracting type: For sale/collaboration
- Technology level: Medium
- Country of origin: Uganda
- Availability: Uganda
- Contact: WIPO GREEN Database

Material substitution: water hyacinth fibers for use as insulation, packaging and wood-plastic composites

In-Between International

Photo: Getty Images / © Bkamprath

CYNTHIA® is a patented bio-based fiber made from water hyacinth – a common invasive species in many rivers where it blocks sunlight and threatens aquatic ecosystems. The fiber can be produced in various shapes and sizes making it suitable for several use cases. These include insulation for construction and building applications, packaging and wood-plastic composites. The products are currently available as laboratory prototypes and samples, but the company aims to bring the products to market.

- Contracting type: For collaboration
- Technology level: Medium
- Country of origin: Belgium
- Availability: Under development
- Contact: WIPO GREEN Database

Waste management: Advanced Dry Recovery (ADR) for on-site concrete recycling

C2CA Technology

Photo: Getty Images / © ghornephoto

Researchers from Delft University, the Netherlands are developing a low-cost technology for in-situ recycling of construction and demolition waste. The aim is to recycle aggregates from concrete for use in new mortar and concrete. Advanced Dry Recovery (ADR) relies on mechanical recycling of concrete while in the moist state. This means energy can be saved by avoiding the need for drying or wet screening the waste. Light contaminants are removed by using kinetic energy to break the bonds between fine particles formed by moisture. Materials are subjected to an acceleration of up to 1,000 G, which separates light materials from heavy ones. A sensor has also been developed to document and monitor the properties of the secondary material and classify the different waste components. The team has now formed a company, C2CA Technology, to build a mobile pilot plant and test the technology.

- Contracting type: For collaboration
- Technology level: Medium
- Country of origin: Netherlands (Kingdom of the)
- Availability: Under development
- Contact: WIPO GREEN Database

Waste management: high-value mechanical tire recycling

Tyre Recycling Solutions

Photo: Getty Images / © DedMityay

Tyre Recycling Solutions create a high-quality rubber powder, TyreXol™, through mechanical recycling of tires. Discarded tires are cut up then pulverized into fine powder using a proprietary water-jet system. The powder is then chemically treated before incorporation into complex polymer mixtures relevant for industries such as construction, automotive and 3D-printing. The material has the ability to alter or improve materials including rubber, polyurethane, plastics, bitumen and concrete. The technology can be part of a greenfield project or added to existing tire recycling facilities.

- Contracting type: Service
- Technology level: Medium
- Country of origin: Switzerland
- Availability: Under development
- Contact: WIPO GREEN Database

Notes

1 Lucertini, G. and F. Musco (2020). Circular urban metabolism framework. *One Earth*, 2(2), 138–22.

2 McKinsey (2023). *The future of mobility*, McKinsey Quarterly – McKinsey Center for Future Mobility. Available at: https://www.mckinsey.com/industries/automotive-and-assembly/our-insights/the-future-of-mobility-mobility-evolves.

3 Bernhard, A. (2021). The great bicycle boom of 2020. BBC. Available at: https://www.bbc.com/future/bespoke/made-on-earth/the-great-bicycle-boom-of-2020.html [accessed July 2023].

4 Mutschler, R., *et al.* (2021). Benchmarking cooling and heating energy demands considering climate change, population growth and cooling device uptake. *Applied Energy*, 288, 116636.

5 dos Muchangos, L.S. and A. Tokai (2020). Greenhouse gas emission analysis of upgrading from an open dump to a semi-aerobic landfill in Mozambique – The case of Hulene dumpsite. *Scientific African*, 10, e00638.

6 Churkina, G. and A. Organschi (2022). Will a transition to timber construction cool the climate? *Sustainability*, 14(7), 4271.

7 Noailly, J. (2022). *Directing innovation towards a low-carbon future*. Economic Research Working Paper No. 72. Geneva: World Intellectual Property Organization (WIPO). Available at: https://www.wipo.int/publications/en/details.jsp?id=4599&plang=EN.

8 EPO and IEA (2020). *Innovation in batteries and electricity storage*. International Energy Agency (IEA) and European Patent Office (EPO). Available at: https://www.iea.org/reports/innovation-in-batteries-and-electricity-storage.

9 EPO and IEA (2020). *Innovation in batteries and electricity storage*. International Energy Agency (IEA), European Patent Office (EPO). Available at: https://www.iea.org/reports/innovation-in-batteries-and-electricity-storage.

10 Olabi, A.G., *et al.* (2023). Micromobility: Progress, benefits, challenges, policy and regulations, energy sources and storage, and its role in achieving Sustainable Development Goals. *International Journal of Thermofluids*, 17, 100292.

11 EPO (2022). Insights into urban mobility. European Patent Office (EPO). Available at: https://www.epo.org/about-us/annual-reports-statistics/statistics/2021/insight-into-smart-urban-mobility.html [accessed August 2023].

12 Xie, H., *et al.* (2022). *Progress in hydrogen fuel cell technology development and deployment in China*. Geneva: WIPO, Global Challenges Division. Available at: https://dx.doi.org/10.34667/tind.44764.

13 UK IPO (2021). *Greener buildings and heat pumps*. Newport: United Kingdom Intellectual Property Office (UK IPO). Available at: https://www.gov.uk/government/publications/a-worldwide-overview-of-greener-buildings-and-heat-pump-patents.

14 Renaldi, R., *et al.* (2021). Patent landscape of not-in-kind active cooling technologies between 1998 and 2017. *Journal of Cleaner Production*, 296, 126507.

15 Wijewardane, S. (2022). Inventions, innovations, and new technologies: Paints and coatings for passive cooling. *Solar Compass*, 3–4, 100032.

16 UNEP (2021). *From pollution to solution: A global assessment of marine litter and plastic pollution*. Nairobi, Kenya: United Nations Environment Programme (UNEP). Available at: https://www.unep.org/resources/pollution-solution-global-assessment-marine-litter-and-plastic-pollution.

17 OECD (2023). *Climate change and plastic pollution*, Policy highlights. Organisation for Economic Co-operation and Development (OECD). Available at: https://www.oecd.org/environment/plastics/Policy-Highlights-Climate-change-and-plastics-pollution-Synergies-between-two-crucial-environmental-challenges.pdf.

18 EPO (2021). *Patents for tomorrow's plastics: Global innovation trends in recycling, circular design and alternative sources*. Munich, Germany European Patent Office (EPO). Available at: https://www.ovtt.org/wp-content/uploads/2021/10/patents_for_tomorrows_plastics_study_en.pdf.

19 Escobar, N., *et al.* (2018). Land use mediated GHG emissions and spillovers from increased consumption of bioplastics. *Environmental Research Letters*, 13, 125005.

20 EPO (2021). *Patents for tomorrow's plastics: Global innovation trends in recycling, circular design and alternative sources*. Munich, Germany European Patent Office (EPO). Available at: https://www.ovtt.org/wp-content/uploads/2021/10/patents_for_tomorrows_plastics_study_en.pdf.

21 CCFLA (2021). *The state of cities climate finance*. The Cities Climate Finance Leadership Alliance (CCFLA). Available at: https://www.climatepolicyinitiative.org/publication/the-state-of-cities-climate-finance/.

22 CCFLA (2021). *The state of cities climate finance*. The Cities Climate Finance Leadership Alliance (CCFLA). Available at: https://www.climatepolicyinitiative.org/publication/the-state-of-cities-climate-finance/.

23 UNEP-CCC (2022). *The climate technology progress report 2022*. Copenhagen, Denmark: Copenhagen Climate Centre (CCC), UNFCCC Technology Executive Committee (TEC) and United Nations Environment Programme (UNEP). Available at: https://unepccc.org/publications/the-climate-technology-progress-report-2022/.

24 CCFLA (2021). *The state of cities climate finance*. The Cities Climate Finance Leadership Alliance (CCFLA). Available at: https://www.climatepolicyinitiative.org/publication/the-state-of-cities-climate-finance/.

25 CPI (2021). *Global landscape of climate finance 2021*. Climate Policy Initiative. Available at: https://www.climatepolicyinitiative.org/publication/global-landscape-of-climate-finance-2021/.

26 EMF (2020). *Financing the circular economy: Capturing the opportunity*. Ellen MacArthur Foundation (EMF). Available at: https://ellenmacarthurfoundation.org/financing-the-circular-economy-capturing-the-opportunity.

27 Aflaki, A., *et al.* (2015). A review on natural ventilation applications through building façade components and ventilation openings in tropical climates. *Energy and Buildings*, 101, 153–62.

28 Anand, V., V.L. Kadiri and C. Putcha (2023). Passive buildings: A state-of-the-art review. *Journal of Infrastructure Preservation and Resilience*, 4(1), 3.

29 Cojocaru, A. and D. Isopescu (2021). Passive strategies of vernacular architecture for energy efficiency. *Bulletin of the Polytechnic Institute of Iași. Construction. Architecture Section*, 67, 33–44.

30 UNEP (2020). *Cooling emissions and policy synthesis report*. Nairobi and Paris: United Nations Environment Programme (UNEP) and International Energy Agency (IEA). Available at: https://www.unep.org/resources/report/cooling-emissions-and-policy-synthesis-report.

31 Aflaki, A., *et al.* (2015). A review on natural ventilation applications through building façade components and ventilation openings in tropical climates. *Energy and Buildings*, 101, 153–62.

32 Taleb, H.M. (2014). Using passive cooling strategies to improve thermal performance and reduce energy consumption of residential buildings in U.A.E. buildings. *Frontiers of Architectural Research*, 3(2), 154–65.

33 IEA (2022). *Heating*. International Energy Agency (IEA). Available at: https://www.iea.org/reports/heating.

34 IEA (2022). Renewable heat. International Energy Agency (IEA). Available at: https://www.iea.org/reports/renewables-2022/renewable-heat [accessed November 2023].

35 IEA (2018). *The future of cooling: Opportunities for energy-efficient air conditioning.* International Energy Agency. Available at: https://iea.blob.core.windows.net/assets/0bb45525-277f-4c9c-8d0c-9c0cb5e7d525/The_Future_of_Cooling.pdf.

36 Dong, Y., M. Coleman and S. Miller (2021). Greenhouse gas emissions from air conditioning and refrigeration service expansion in developing countries. *Annual review of environment and resources*, 46.

37 Dong, Y., M. Coleman, and S. Miller (2021). Greenhouse gas emissions from air conditioning and refrigeration service expansion in developing countries. *Annual review of environment and resources*, 46.

38 CCAC (2023). Promoting HFC alternative technology and standards. Climate & clean air coalition (CCAC). Available at: https://www.ccacoalition.org/fr/node/73 [accessed June 2023].

39 UNEP (2020). *Cooling emissions and policy synthesis report.* Nairobi, Paris: United Nations Environment Programme (UNEP) - International Energy Agency (IEA). Available at: https://www.unep.org/resources/report/cooling-emissions-and-policy-synthesis-report.

40 UNEP (2020). *Cooling emissions and policy synthesis report.* Nairobi, Paris: United Nations Environment Programme (UNEP) - International Energy Agency (IEA). Available at: https://www.unep.org/resources/report/cooling-emissions-and-policy-synthesis-report.

41 Pombo, O., B. Rivela and J. Neila (2019). Life cycle thinking toward sustainable development policy-making: The case of energy retrofits. *Journal of Cleaner Production*, 206, 267–81.

42 Anand, V., V.L. Kadiri, and C. Putcha (2023). Passive buildings: a state-of-the-art review. *Journal of Infrastructure Preservation and Resilience*, 4(1), 3.

43 Pombo, O., B. Rivela, and J. Neila (2019). Life cycle thinking toward sustainable development policy-making: The case of energy retrofits. *Journal of Cleaner Production*, 206, 267–81.

44 Menon, J.S. and R. Sharma (2021). Nature-based solutions for co-mitigation of air pollution and urban heat in Indian cities. *Frontiers in Sustainable Cities*, 3.

45 Dong, Y., M. Coleman, and S. Miller (2021). Greenhouse gas emissions from air conditioning and refrigeration service expansion in developing countries. *Annual review of environment and resources*, 46.

46 IEA (2018). *The future of cooling: opportunities for energy-efficient air conditioning.* International Energy Agency. Available at: https://iea.blob.core.windows.net/assets/0bb45525-277f-4c9c-8d0c-9c0cb5e7d525/The_Future_of_Cooling.pdf.

47 UNEP (2020). *Cooling emissions and policy synthesis report.* Nairobi, Paris: United Nations Environment Programme (UNEP) - International Energy Agency (IEA). Available at: https://www.unep.org/resources/report/cooling-emissions-and-policy-synthesis-report.

48 IEA (2018). *The future of cooling: opportunities for energy-efficient air conditioning.* International Energy Agency. Available at: https://iea.blob.core.windows.net/assets/0bb45525-277f-4c9c-8d0c-9c0cb5e7d525/The_Future_of_Cooling.pdf.

49 IEA (2022). *Heating.* International Energy Agency (IEA). Available at: https://www.iea.org/reports/heating.

50 IEA (2023). Heat pumps. International Energy Agency (IEA). Available at: https://www.iea.org/fuels-and-technologies/heat-pumps [accessed June 2023].

51 IEA (2023). Heat pumps. International Energy Agency (IEA). Available at: https://www.iea.org/fuels-and-technologies/heat-pumps [accessed June 2023].

52 Almogbel, A., *et al.* (2020). Comparison of energy consumption between non-inverter and inverter-type air conditioner in Saudi Arabia. *Energy Transitions*, 4(2), 191–97.

53 De Munck, C., *et al.* (2013). How much air conditioning can increase air temperatures for a city like Paris (France)? *International Journal of Climatology*, 33, 210–27.

54 Dong, Y., M. Coleman, and S. Miller (2021). Greenhouse gas emissions from air conditioning and refrigeration service expansion in developing countries. *Annual review of environment and resources*, 46.

55 Xu, Y., *et al.* (2013). The role of HFCs in mitigating 21st century climate change. *Atmospheric Chemistry & Physics*, 13, 6083–89.

56 Dong, Y., M. Coleman, and S. Miller (2021). Greenhouse gas emissions from air conditioning and refrigeration service expansion in developing countries. *Annual review of environment and resources*, 46.

57 Dong, Y., M. Coleman, and S. Miller (2021). Greenhouse gas emissions from air conditioning and refrigeration service expansion in developing countries. *Annual review of environment and resources*, 46.

58 UNEP (2020). *Cooling emissions and policy synthesis report.* Nairobi, Paris: United Nations Environment Programme (UNEP) - International Energy Agency (IEA). Available at: https://www.unep.org/resources/report/cooling-emissions-and-policy-synthesis-report.

59 Dong, Y., M. Coleman, and S. Miller (2021). Greenhouse gas emissions from air conditioning and refrigeration service expansion in developing countries. *Annual review of environment and resources*, 46.

60 IEA (2022). *Heating.* International Energy Agency (IEA). Available at: https://www.iea.org/reports/heating.

61 Werner, S. (2017). International review of district heating and cooling. *Energy*, 137.

62 Mastrucci, A., *et al.* (2019). Improving the SDG energy poverty targets: Residential cooling needs in the Global South. *Energy and Buildings*, 186, 405–15.

63 IPCC (2023). *Synthesis report (SYR) of the IPCC sixth assessment report (AR6): Summary for policymakers.* Geneva: Intergovernmental Panel on Climate Change (IPCC). Available at: https://www.ipcc.ch/report/ar6/syr/.

64 Dong, Y., M. Coleman, and S. Miller (2021). Greenhouse gas emissions from air conditioning and refrigeration service expansion in developing countries. *Annual review of environment and resources*, 46.

65 EEA (2023). *Decarbonising heating and cooling - A climate imperative.* Copenhagen, Denmark: European Environment Agency (EEA). Available at: https://www.eea.europa.eu/publications/decarbonisation-heating-and-cooling.

66 PFPI (2018). Letter from scientists to the EU Parliament regarding forest biomass. Partnership for Policy Integrity (PFPI). Available at: https://www.pfpi.net/wp-content/uploads/2018/04/UPDATE-800-signatures_Scientist-Letter-on-EU-Forest-Biomass.pdf [accessed July 2023].

67 Rahaee, O. (2013). Cultural identity and its effects on indigenous methods of natural ventilation passage of metal smiths in Dezful's Old Bazzar. *The Monthly Scientific Journal of Bagh-e Nazar*, 10(24), 39–46.

68 Mohammadshahi, S., *et al.* (2019). Investigation of naturally ventilated shavadoons component: Architectural underground pattern on ventilation. *Tunnelling and Underground Space Technology*, 91, 102990.

69 ITF (2023). *ITF transport outlook 2023.* International Transport Forum (ITF). Available at: https://www.oecd-ilibrary.org/transport/itf-transport-outlook-2023_b6cc9ad5-en.

70 IPCC (2023). *Synthesis report (SYR) of the IPCC sixth assessment report (AR6): Summary for policymakers.* Geneva: Intergovernmental Panel on Climate Change (IPCC). Available at: https://www.ipcc.ch/report/ar6/syr/.

71 WHO (2012). *Health in the green economy: Health co-benefits of climate change mitigation – Transport sector.* World

Health Organization (WHO). Available at: https://apps.who.int/iris/handle/10665/70913.

72 Kinigadner, J., *et al.* (2020). Planning for low carbon mobility: Impacts of transport interventions and location on carbon-based accessibility. *Journal of Transport Geography*, 87, 102797.

73 IPCC (2023). *Synthesis report (SYR) of the IPCC sixth assessment report (AR6): Summary for policymakers*. Geneva: Intergovernmental Panel on Climate Change (IPCC). Available at: https://www.ipcc.ch/report/ar6/syr/.

74 Brand, C., *et al.* (2021). The climate change mitigation effects of daily active travel in cities. *Transportation Research Part D: Transport and Environment*, 93, 102764.

75 AlKheder, S. (2021). Promoting public transport as a strategy to reduce GHG emissions from private vehicles in Kuwait. *Environmental Challenges*, 3, 100075.

76 Buchanan, M. (2019). The benefits of public transport. *Nature Physics*, 15(9), 876–76.

77 UDP (2021). *Climate technologies in an urban context*. Copenhagen, Denmark: UNEP DTU Partnership (UDP). Available at: https://tech-action.unepccc.org/publications/climate-technologies-in-an-urban-context/.

78 Frączek, B. and A. Urbanek (2021). Financial inclusion as an important factor influencing digital payments in passenger transport: A case study of EU countries. *Research in Transportation Business & Management*, 41, 100691.

79 Nikitas, D.A. and P.M. Karlsson (2015). A worldwide state-of-the-art analysis for bus rapid transit: Looking for the success formula. *Journal of Public Transportation*, 18(1), 1–33.

80 WRI Brazil (2023). *Global BRT data*. World Resources Institute (WRI) Brasil Ross Center for Sustainable Cities. Available at: https://brtdata.org/.

81 EEA (2023). *Transport and environment report 2022*. European Environment Agency (EEA). Available at: https://www.eea.europa.eu//publications/transport-and-environment-report-2022.

82 Furfari, S. (2016). Energy efficiency of engines and appliances for transport on land, water, and in air. *Ambio*, 45(1), 63–68.

83 ITF (2023). *ITF transport outlook 2023*. International Transport Forum (ITF). Available at: https://www.oecd-ilibrary.org/transport/itf-transport-outlook-2023_b6cc9ad5-en.

84 Ivanova, D., *et al.* (2020). Quantifying the potential for climate change mitigation of consumption options. *Environmental Research Letters*, 15(9).

85 Schwanen, T., D. Banister and J. Anable (2011). Scientific research about climate change mitigation in transport: A critical review. *Transportation Research Part A: Policy and Practice*, 45(10), 993–1006.

86 Musa, A.A., *et al.* (2023). Sustainable traffic management for smart cities using Internet-of-Things-oriented intelligent transportation systems (ITS): Challenges and recommendations. *Sustainability*, 15(13), 9859.

87 Bharadwaj, S., *et al.* (2017). Impact of congestion on greenhouse gas emissions for road transport in Mumbai metropolitan region. *Transportation Research Procedia*, 25, 3538–51.

88 Le Quéré, C., *et al.* (2020). Temporary reduction in daily global CO_2 emissions during the COVID-19 forced confinement. *Nature Climate Change*, 10(7), 1–7.

89 IEA (2023). *Global EV outlook 2023*. International Energy Agency (IEA). Available at: https://www.iea.org/reports/global-ev-outlook-2023.

90 Transport & Environment (2023). *Clean and lean: Battery metals demand from electrifying passenger transport*. Brussels, Belgium: Transport & Environment. Available at: https://www.transportenvironment.org/discover/clean-and-lean-battery-metals-demand-from-electrifying-cars-vans-and-buses/.

91 Reck, D.J., H. Martin and K.W. Axhausen (2022). Mode choice, substitution patterns and environmental impacts of shared and personal micro-mobility. *Transportation Research Part D: Transport and Environment*, 102, 103134.

92 Tikoudis, I., *et al.* (2021). Ridesharing services and urban transport CO_2 emissions: Simulation-based evidence from 247 cities. *Transportation Research Part D: Transport and Environment*, 97, 102923.

93 Tikoudis, I., *et al.* (2021). Ridesharing services and urban transport CO_2 emissions: Simulation-based evidence from 247 cities. *Transportation Research Part D: Transport and Environment*, 97, 102923.

94 Reck, D.J., H. Martin, and K.W. Axhausen (2022). Mode choice, substitution patterns and environmental impacts of shared and personal micro-mobility. *Transportation Research Part D: Transport and Environment*, 102, 103134.

95 Schaller, B. (2021). Can sharing a ride make for less traffic? Evidence from Uber and Lyft and implications for cities. *Transport Policy*, 102, 1–10.

96 IEA (2023). *Global EV outlook 2023*. International Energy Agency (IEA). Available at: https://www.iea.org/reports/global-ev-outlook-2023.

97 IPCC (2023). *Synthesis report (SYR) of the IPCC sixth assessment report (AR6). Summary for policymakers*. Geneva: Intergovernmental Panel on Climate Change (IPCC). Available at: https://www.ipcc.ch/report/ar6/syr/.

98 ITF (2023). *ITF transport outlook 2023*. International Transport Forum (ITF). Available at: https://www.oecd-ilibrary.org/transport/itf-transport-outlook-2023_b6cc9ad5-en.

99 EEA (2018). *Electric vehicles from life cycle and circular economy perspectives*. European Environment Agency (EEA). Available at: https://www.eea.europa.eu/publications/electric-vehicles-from-life-cycle.

100 IPCC (2023). *Synthesis report (SYR) of the IPCC sixth assessment report (AR6). Summary for policymakers*. Geneva: Intergovernmental Panel on Climate Change (IPCC). Available at: https://www.ipcc.ch/report/ar6/syr/.

101 ITF (2023). *ITF transport outlook 2023*. International Transport Forum (ITF). Available at: https://www.oecd-ilibrary.org/transport/itf-transport-outlook-2023_b6cc9ad5-en.

102 Traugott, J. (2023). California wants to make bidirectional charging mandatory for new electric vehicles. Carbuzz. Available at: https://carbuzz.com/news/california-wants-to-make-bidirectional-charging-mandatory-for-new-electric-vehicles [accessed July 2023].

103 MIT (2023). Minimizing electric vehicles' impact on the grid. Massachusetts Institute of Technology (MIT). Available at: https://www.sciencedaily.com/releases/2023/03/230315132448.htm [accessed July 2023].

104 EEA (2023). *Transport and environment report 2022*. European Environment Agency (EEA). Available at: https://www.eea.europa.eu//publications/transport-and-environment-report-2022.

105 Daziano, R.A. (2022). Willingness to delay charging of electric vehicles. *Research in Transportation Economics*, 94, 101177.

106 IEA (2023). *Global EV outlook 2023*. International Energy Agency (IEA). Available at: https://www.iea.org/reports/global-ev-outlook-2023.

107 Acebedo, B., *et al.* (2023). Current status and future perspective on lithium metal anode production methods. *Advanced Energy Materials*, 13(13), 2203744.

108 IEA (2023). *Global EV outlook 2023*. International Energy Agency (IEA). Available at: https://www.iea.org/reports/global-ev-outlook-2023.

109 IEA (2023). Biofuels. International Energy Agency (IEA). Available at: https://www.iea.org/energy-system/low-emission-fuels/biofuels [accessed July 2023].

110 WRI (2023). *The global land squeeze: Managing the growing competition for land*. World Resources Institute (WRI). Available at: https://www.wri.org/research/global-land-squeeze-managing-growing-competition-land.

111 Merfort, L., *et al.* (2023). State of global land regulation inadequate to control biofuel land-use-change emissions. *Nature Climate Change*, 13(7), 610–12.

112 IEA Bioenergy (2023). *Commercial status of direct thermochemical liquefaction technologies*. International Energy Agency (IEA). Available at: https://www.ieabioenergy.com/blog/publications/commercial-status-of-direct-thermochemical-liquefaction-technologies/.

113 Westervelt, A. (2023). Big oil firms touted algae as climate solution: Now all have pulled funding. *The Guardian*. Available at: https://www.theguardian.com/environment/2023/mar/17/big-oil-algae-biofuel-funding-cut-exxonmobil.

114 IPCC (2022). *Climate change 2022: Mitigation of climate change – Technical summary, Working Group III contribution to IPCC sixth assessment report*. Cambridge, UK: Intergovernmental Panel on Climate Change (IPCC). Available at: https://www.ipcc.ch/report/sixth-assessment-report-working-group-3/.

115 EEA (2023). *Transport and environment report 2022*. European Environment Agency (EEA). Available at: https://www.eea.europa.eu//publications/transport-and-environment-report-2022.

116 IEA (2023). Transport. International Energy Agency (IEA). Available at: https://www.iea.org/energy-system/transport.

117 ICCT (2020). *Beyond biomass? Alternative fuels from renewable electricity and carbon recycling*. The International Council on Clean Transportation (ICCT). Available at: https://theicct.org/publication/beyond-biomass-alternative-fuels-from-renewable-electricity-and-carbon-recycling/.

118 Ueckerdt, F., *et al.* (2021). Potential and risks of hydrogen-based e-fuels in climate change mitigation. *Nature Climate Change*, 11(5), 384–93.

119 IEA (2023). *Global EV outlook 2023*. International Energy Agency (IEA). Available at: https://www.iea.org/reports/global-ev-outlook-2023.

120 Xie, H., *et al.* (2022). *Progress in hydrogen fuel cell technology development and deployment in China*. Available at: https://dx.doi.org/10.34667/tind.44764.

121 EEA (2023). *Transport and environment report 2022*. European Environment Agency (EEA). Available at: https://www.eea.europa.eu//publications/transport-and-environment-report-2022.

122 McKinsey (2023). Autonomous driving's future: Convenient and connected. McKinsey & Company. Available at: https://www.mckinsey.com/industries/automotive-and-assembly/our-insights/autonomous-drivings-future-convenient-and-connected [accessed September 2023].

123 Kreier, F. (2022). Drones bearing parcels deliver big carbon savings. *Nature*.

124 EIT Urban Mobility (2022). *Urban mobility next 8: Expectations and success factors for urban air mobility in Europe*. Barcelona, Spain: EIT Urban Mobility. Available at: https://www.eiturbanmobility.eu/wp-content/uploads/2022/11/EIT-UrbanAirMobility.pdf.

125 Furfari, S. (2016). Energy efficiency of engines and appliances for transport on land, water, and in air. *Ambio*, 45(1), 63–68.

126 Furfari, S. (2016). Energy efficiency of engines and appliances for transport on land, water, and in air. *Ambio*, 45(1), 63–68.

127 Dabros, T.M.H., *et al.* (2018). Transportation fuels from biomass via fast pyrolysis, catalytic hydrodeoxygenation, and catalytic fast hydropyrolysis. *Progress in Energy and Combustion Science*, 68, 268–309.

128 International Resource Panel (2019). *Global Resources Outlook 2019: Natural resources for the future we want*. Nairobi, Kenya: United Nations Environment Programme International Resource Panel. Available at: https://wedocs.unep.org/handle/20.500.11822/27518.

129 World Bank (2022). Population, total: *World population prospects, 2022 Revision*, Available at: https://data.worldbank.org/indicator/SP.POP.TOTL?end=2022&start=1973 [accessed November 2023].

130 International Resource Panel (2019). *Global Resources Outlook 2019: Natural resources for the future we want*. Nairobi, Kenya: United Nations Environment Programme International Resource Panel. Available at: https://wedocs.unep.org/handle/20.500.11822/27518.

131 UN Habitat (2022). *World cities report 2022: Envisaging the future of cities*. Nairobi, Kenya: UN Habitat. Available at: https://unhabitat.org/wcr/.

132 International Resource Panel (2020). *Resource efficiency and climate change: Material efficiency strategies for a low-carbon future*. Nairobi, Kenya: United Nations Environment Programme International Resource Panel. Available at: https://www.resourcepanel.org/reports/resource-efficiency-and-climate-change.

133 Cabernard, L., *et al.* (2022). Growing environmental footprint of plastics driven by coal combustion. *Nature Sustainability*, 5.

134 OECD (2022). Plastic pollution is growing relentlessly as waste management and recycling fall short, says OECD. Organisation for Economic Cooperation and Development (OECD). Available at: https://www.oecd.org/environment/plastic-pollution-is-growing-relentlessly-as-waste-management-and-recycling-fall-short.htm [accessed July 2023].

135 OECD (2022). *Global plastics outlook: Policy scenarios to 2060*. Paris: Organisation for Economic Cooperation and Development (OECD). Available at: https://www.oecd-ilibrary.org/environment/global-plastics-outlook_aa1edf33-en.

136 International Resource Panel (2020). *Resource efficiency and climate change: Material efficiency strategies for a low-carbon future*. Nairobi, Kenya: United Nations Environment Programme International Resource Panel Available at: https://www.resourcepanel.org/reports/resource-efficiency-and-climate-change.

137 International Resource Panel (2020). *Resource efficiency and climate change: Material efficiency strategies for a low-carbon future*. Nairobi, Kenya: United Nations Environment Programme International Resource Panel Available at: https://www.resourcepanel.org/reports/resource-efficiency-and-climate-change.

138 Aziminezhad, M. and R. Taherkhani (2023). BIM for deconstruction: A review and bibliometric analysis. *Journal of Building Engineering*, 73, 106683.

139 Global Infrastructure Hub (2020). Pre-fabrication technology for modular construction. Global Infrastructure Hub. Available at: https://www.gihub.org/infrastructure-technology-use-cases/case-studies/pre-fabrication-technology-for-modular-construction/ [accessed July 2023].

140 Dosumu, O. and C. Aigbavboa (2019). An investigation of the barriers to the uptake of local materials in Africa: A literature review approach. *African Journal of Science, Technology, Innovation and Development*.

141 Chan, M., M.A.N. Masrom and S.S. Yasin (2022). Selection of low-carbon building materials in construction projects: Construction professionals perspectives. *Buildings*, 12(4), 486.

142 Gomaa, M., *et al.* (2022). Digital manufacturing for earth construction: A critical review. *Journal of Cleaner Production*, 338, 130630.

143 Gomaa, M., *et al.* (2023). Automation in rammed earth construction for industry 4.0: Precedent work, current progress and future prospect. *Journal of Cleaner Production*, 398, 136569.

144 Svatoš-Ražnjević, H., L. Orozco and A. Menges (2022). Advanced timber construction industry: A review of 350 multi-storey timber projects from 2000 and 2021. *Buildings*, 12(4), 404.

145 WRI (2023). *The global land squeeze: Managing the growing competition for land.* World Resources Institute (WRI). Available at: https://www.wri.org/research/global-land-squeeze-managing-growing-competition-land.

146 Skoczinski, P., *et al.* (2023). *Bio-based building blocks and polymers: Global capacities, production and trends 2022–2027.* Nova-Institute. Available at: https://renewable-carbon.eu/publications/product/bio-based-building-blocks-and-polymers-global-capacities-production-and-trends-2022-2027/.

147 UNEP (2023). *Turning off the tap: How the world can end plastic pollution and create a circular economy.* Nairobi, Kenya: United Nations Environment Programme (UNEP). Available at: https://www.unep.org/resources/turning-off-tap-end-plastic-pollution-create-circular-economy.

148 Kaza, S., *et al.* (2018). *What a waste 2.0: A global snapshot of solid waste management to 2050.* Washington, DC: World Bank. Available at: https://openknowledge.worldbank.org/entities/publication/d3f9d45e-115f-559b-b14f-28552410e90a.

149 Zero Waste Europe (2020). *Reusable VS single-use packaging: A review of environmental impact.* Brussels: Zero Waste Europe. Available at: https://zerowasteeurope.eu/library/reusable-vs-single-use-packaging-a-review-of-environmental-impact/.

150 ITU (2021). Indian firm's digital solution for urban waste pickers. International Telecommunication Union (ITU). Available at: https://www.itu.int/hub/2021/07/indian-firms-digital-solution-for-urban-waste-pickers/ [accessed July 2023].

151 Calaiaro, J. (2022). AI-guided robots are ready to sort your recyclables. Institute of Electrical and Electronics Engineers (IEEE). Available at: https://spectrum.ieee.org/ai-guided-robots-are-ready-to-sort-your-recyclables [accessed July 2023].

152 Bruun, J. (2022). Breakthrough in separating plastic waste: Machines can distinguish 12 different types of plastic. Aarhus University. Available at: https://ingenioer.au.dk/en/current/news/view/artikel/gennembrud-i-plastsortering-maskiner-kan-nu-se-forskel-paa-12-forskellige-typer-plastik [accessed July 2023].

153 Li, J., M. Barwood and S. Rahimifard (2018). Robotic disassembly for increased recovery of strategically important materials from electrical vehicles. *Robotics and Computer-Integrated Manufacturing*, 50, 203–12.

154 Poschmann, H., H. Brüggemann and D. Goldmann (2020). Disassembly 4.0: A review on using robotics in disassembly tasks as a way of automation. *Chemie Ingenieur Technik*, 92.

155 Zero Waste Europe (2023). *Nothing left behind: Modelling material recovery and biological treatment's contribution to resource recovery and fighting climate change.* Brussels, Belgium: Zero Waste Europe. Available at: https://zerowasteeurope.eu/library/nothing-left-behind-mrbt-costs-study/.

156 Hogg, D. (2006). *A changing climate for energy from waste? Final report for Friends of the Earth.* Eunomia Research & Consulting. Available at: https://www.friendsoftheearth.ie/assets/files/pdf/report_on_incineration_and_climate.pdf.

157 Tabrizi, S., *et al.* (2020). *Understanding the environmental impacts of chemical recycling – Ten concerns with existing life cycle assessments.* Brussels, Belgium: Zero Waste Europe. Available at: https://zerowasteeurope.eu/library/understanding-the-environmental-impacts-of-chemical-recycling-ten-concerns-with-existing-life-cycle-assessments/.

158 OECD (2022). Plastic pollution is growing relentlessly as waste management and recycling fall short, says OECD. Available at: https://www.oecd.org/environment/plastic-pollution-is-growing-relentlessly-as-waste-management-and-recycling-fall-short.htm [accessed July 2023].

159 OECD (2022). *Global plastics outlook: Policy scenarios to 2060* Paris. Available at: https://www.oecd-ilibrary.org/environment/global-plastics-outlook_aa1edf33-en.

160 Zheng, J. and S. Suh (2019). Strategies to reduce the global carbon footprint of plastics. *Nature Climate Change*, 9, 374–378

161 Kaza, S., *et al.* (2018). *What a waste 2.0: A global snapshot of solid waste management to 2050.* Washington, DC: World Bank. Available at: https://openknowledge.worldbank.org/entities/publication/d3f9d45e-115f-559b-b14f-28552410e90a.

162 Castaldi, M.J. and N.J. Themelis (2010). The case for increasing the global capacity for waste to energy (WTE). *Waste and Biomass Valorization*, 1(1), 91–105.

163 Tangri, N. (2023). Waste incinerators undermine clean energy goals. *PLOS Climate,* 2(6).

164 Hogg, D. (2023). *Debunking efficient recovery: The performance of EU incineration facilities.* Equanimator Ltd for Zero Waste Europe. Available at: https://zerowasteeurope.eu/library/debunking-efficient-recovery/.

165 Alao, M.A., O.M. Popoola and T.R. Ayodele (2022). Waste-to-energy nexus: An overview of technologies and implementation for sustainable development. *Cleaner Energy Systems*, 3, 100034.

166 Kaza, S., *et al.* (2018). *What a waste 2.0: A global snapshot of solid waste management to 2050.* Washington, DC: World Bank. Available at: https://openknowledge.worldbank.org/entities/publication/d3f9d45e-115f-559b-b14f-28552410e90a.

167 Schaart, E. (2020). Denmark's 'devilish' waste dilemma. Politico. Available at: https://www.politico.eu/article/denmark-devilish-waste-trash-energy-incineration-recycling-dilemma/ [accessed July 2023].

168 Kaza, S., *et al.* (2018). *What a waste 2.0: A global snapshot of solid waste management to 2050.* Washington, DC: World Bank. Available at: https://openknowledge.worldbank.org/entities/publication/d3f9d45e-115f-559b-b14f-28552410e90a.

169 Maasakkers, J.D., *et al.* (2022). Using satellites to uncover large methane emissions from landfills. *Science Advances*, 8(32), eabn9683.

170 Kaza, S., *et al.* (2018). *What a waste 2.0: A global snapshot of solid waste management to 2050.* Washington, DC: World Bank. Available at: https://openknowledge.worldbank.org/entities/publication/d3f9d45e-115f-559b-b14f-28552410e90a.

171 UNEP (2023). *Topic sheet: Just transition.* United Nations Environment Programme (UNEP). Available at: https://wedocs.unep.org/20.500.11822/42231.

172 United Nations (2019). *The Sustainable Development Goals report 2019.* New York, NY: UN Department of Economic and Social Affairs (DESA). Available at: https://unstats.un.org/sdgs/report/2019/.

173 United Nations (2022). *The Sustainable Development Goals report 2022.* New York, NY: UN Department of Economic and Social Affairs (DESA). Available at: https://unstats.un.org/sdgs/report/2022/.

174 United Nations (2022). *The Sustainable Development Goals report 2022.* New York, NY: UN Department of Economic and Social Affairs (DESA). Available at: https://unstats.un.org/sdgs/report/2022/.

175 C40 (2018). *Consumption-based GHG emissions of C40 cities.* C40 Cities. Available at: https://www.c40knowledgehub.

org/s/article/Consumption-based-GHG-emissions-of-C40-cities?language=en_US.

176 WIPO (2022). *Global innovation index 2022: What is the future of innovation-driven growth?* Geneva: World Intellectual Property Organization (WIPO). Available at: https://www.wipo.int/global_innovation_index/en/.

177 Lacy, P. and J. Rutqvist (2015). *Waste to wealth: The circular economy advantage*. Accenture Strategy.

178 IPCC (2022). *Climate change 2022: Mitigation of climate change. Technical summary. Working Group III contribution to IPCC sixth assessment report.*, Cambridge: Intergovernmental Panel on Climate Change (IPCC). Available at: https://www.ipcc.ch/report/sixth-assessment-report-working-group-3/.

179 WRI (2023). *The global land squeeze: Managing the growing competition for land*. World Resources Institute (WRI). Available at: https://www.wri.org/research/global-land-squeeze-managing-growing-competition-land.

180 Zernicke, C., *et al.* (2023). *WEB-GIS-TOOL: Estimation of greenhouse gas savings due timber use in the urban built environment*. Oslo, Norway: World Conference on Timber Engineering 2023.

181 Zero Waste Scotland (2018). A scheme for Scotland. Available at: https://depositreturnscheme.zerowastescotland.org.uk/benefits#:~:text=Tackling%20climate%20change&text=The%20scheme%20will%20cut%20emissions,one%20year%20in%20the%20UK [accessed July 2023].

3 / Agriculture and land use

Photos: Getty Images

Technological developments and trends

Emissions from major areas of agriculture

Human-created carbon dioxide (CO_2) emissions come from two main sources – fossil fuels and land use change and management. While fossil fuel is the dominant source, generating around 10 gigatons CO_2eq/yr, land use and land use change are estimated to account for between 1 and 2 GtCO2eq/yr or around 11 percent of annual global CO_2 emissions.[1] This figure includes loss of biomass and soil carbon, peat drainage and burning, etc. However, when the global warming effect of other greenhouse gases (GHGs), such as methane emitted by agricultural practices, is taken into account this sector's contribution to annual global GHG emissions doubles to 22 percent, although this estimate should be treated with caution due to the complex nature of the sector.[2] A recent study indicates that global food consumption alone risks adding close to 1 degree Celsius to the planet's temperature by 2100, with three-quarters of this increase attributable to high methane emission sources, such as livestock. It also indicates that up to 55 percent of this warming effect can be avoided through better farming practices, changes in people's dietary habits and reduced food waste.[3]

Global food consumption alone risks adding close to 1 degree Celsius to the planet's temperature by 2100

One reason why agriculture is considered responsible for such a large contribution to global GHG emissions relates to the high proportion of methane emitted from agricultural activities. Methane has a stronger atmospheric warming effect than CO_2 but it also breaks down much faster with a half-life of around 12 years compared to 120 years for CO_2. This means that the atmospheric heating effect of methane is around 84 times higher than CO_2 during the first 20 years after its release, and around 28 times higher over a 100-year period. Agriculture is also a major emitter of nitrous oxide (N_2O), another potent greenhouse gas, but in smaller quantities with a correspondingly lower contribution to global warming than methane and CO_2. Therefore, reducing emissions from agriculture is vital for achieving the goals of the 2015 United Nations (UN) Paris Agreement. In the words of the Intergovernmental Panel on Climate Change (IPCC): "Agriculture provides the second largest share of the mitigation potential, with 4.1 (1.7–6.7) $GtCO_2$eq/yr ... from cropland and grassland soil carbon management, agroforestry, use of biochar, improved rice cultivation, and livestock and nutrient management."[4] Add to this that agriculture occupies around five billion hectares of land or 38 percent of the global land surface[5] and is responsible for 70 percent of global freshwater withdrawals,[6] making its environmental footprint enormous. So too is its vulnerability to the impact of climate change (see WIPO's *Green Technology Book: Solutions for Climate Change Adaptation*). Figure 3.1 illustrates the composition of the sector's various emissions. Enteric fermentation is methane emitted from the digestive process of ruminants.

Figure 3.1 Relative emissions from selected agricultural activities, world average CO_2eq, 1990–2020

Source: FAOSTAT, 2023.

Reducing emissions from agriculture is vital for achieving the goals of the 2015 United Nations (UN) Paris Agreement

Agriculture is a major GHG emitter and has an enormous environmental footprint but it is also a sector with thriving innovation and new solutions that are being embraced by farmers, as this chapter will show. Farming is hard labor and farmers have always been dependent on tools that help them grow more with less risk. Clearly, agriculture is also extremely diverse and depends on many local factors, not least climate and soils. Therefore, the solutions are also highly diverse.

This chapter focuses on solutions for reducing emissions from agriculture, highlighting specific sectors that represent some of the main GHG emission sources, namely livestock, soils, land use and forestry, and rice cultivation. The role of data and advanced technology in agriculture more generally is also examined. Other sectors and large emission sources that could have been considered include energy use in agriculture, food waste or agricultural waste management, but to examine all these is beyond the scope of a single publication.

Farm animals

Technological trends relating to livestock are following several different paths. In terms of reducing methane emissions from the digestive processes of cattle, several feed supplements already on the market promise significant reductions. This field is seeing rapid developments and some companies are even marketing low-carbon meat produced by cattle treated with such supplements. Another approach is to increase the general productivity of livestock rearing and hereby reduce emissions per product produced. This approach encompasses a broad swath of technologies which have been refined over decades. Currently, much investment and media attention are focused on alternative meat products. Plant-based alternatives are the most widely developed and popular and also the easiest to bring to the market. Several brands are already available in many countries and competition is fierce. A more technically challenging alternative is cultured meat in various forms. Some companies are ready to scale up their production and products have already been approved on two major markets. However, the technical and economic feasibility, as well as the benefits for the climate, are still to be confirmed. At this stage, it appears most likely that the biggest emission reduction impact will come from the less visible meat replacements, such as the protein sources used in mass-produced food items by large food-industry players. The substitution of new plant-based products with a proven much lower carbon footprint could make a real difference, even given a short time horizon. However, the simplest solution to reducing GHG emissions from livestock is simply to eat less meat, especially beef. Changing meat consumption to favor, for example, pigs, poultry, rabbits and fish, whose digestive systems release significantly less methane, may also help.

The simplest solution to reducing GHG emissions from livestock is simply to eat less meat, especially beef

Improving range management and avoiding land conversion both have major potential to reduce livestock emissions. Several solutions for optimization of grazing patterns and crops are already on the market. Deforestation results in substantial emissions and livestock rearing is often the main driver. Better use of land that is already being cultivated will have major climate change benefits. This, again, underlines the importance of more efficient use of resources and land in agricultural systems. There is a plethora of technologies that can assist in achieving this goal, ranging from early warning systems to optimized use of inputs (fertilizers, pesticides, etc.) and water to advanced monitoring of soil and crop parameters. Effective policy and legal restrictions will be necessary to preserve the world's forests. The rapid developments in satellite and drone-based imaging and sensors - which produce vast amounts of data that is then made accessible on mobile platforms and other software systems - can provide the insight needed to implement such restrictions and monitor their effectiveness. The forests that remain, as well as those that are being restored, will need to be protected against disturbance, not least forest fires - another area that is receiving a lot of attention and where innovation is thriving.

Soils - the basis for everything

Soils play a major role in climate change due to the vast amount of carbon they already store in relatively stable form. Technologies that support regenerative agriculture are numerous and some, such as mechanical seed drills that enable minimum and no-till practices, have been around for decades. Most no-till agriculture still relies on utilization of pesticides, but new technologies such as autonomous and lightweight or even flying machines offer alternative mechanical weeding and precision spraying. New natural and organic pesticides and fertilizers may also help improve soil health and hence store soil carbon. Adding microbes and other additives to soil is shown to speed up that process and carbon can be added directly, for example in the form of biochar. Emphasis is currently also being placed on improved crop rotation and the use of nitrogen-fixating cover crops capable of extracting nitrogen from air in new combinations to improve soil carbon.

Soils of particular concern for climate change due to high methane emissions are waterlogged rice fields

One use of soils that is a particular concern for climate change due to high methane emissions is waterlogged rice fields (paddies), especially in Asia. Research is underway to better monitor and mitigate this source of GHG emissions but has not yet yielded easily implementable solutions. Temporarily draining paddies could have a major beneficial impact but is not feasible in all systems due to their intricate water management and sharing arrangements. Growing rice as a dry crop would be an efficient means of reducing methane emissions, but flooded rice still represents more than 75 percent of global rice production[7] and it may be necessary to develop new rice varieties to enable expansion of dry rice cultivation. Producing more with less, including reducing food loss and waste, therefore currently appears to be the most feasible mitigation action. However, the mitigation potential of this approach may be modest as most rice cultivation systems are already very intensive.

Data and IT-based technologies - the next big thing in agriculture?

This chapter considers advanced agricultural technologies, including technology sectors such as precision farming, which itself encompasses a vast range of technologies. This is an area of agricultural technology where innovation is happening at a fast pace.

So, is the world on the brink of a new agricultural revolution which will drastically transform the planet's agricultural systems? The answer is probably not. Agriculture in many countries is already highly advanced and intensive. New technologies can offer novel solutions to stubborn problems as well as further increases in resource and labor efficiency. Tools are becoming more effective and more capable, but their adoption is not taking place in a revolutionary way. Rather, farmers (who are generally risk averse) will invest in new tools when they can see a clear, primarily economic, advantage. They cannot afford to risk taking the plunge into a whole new setup. For example, the adoption of precision farming technologies is likely to start with step-wise improvements, such as precision global positioning system (GPS) guided machines rather than autonomous ones and adjustable spraying nozzles that can help reduce the use of inputs and other resources. To conquer the market, the advantages of using sensors on farm machines and in the fields, coupled with satellite and, to a lesser extent, drone images, still remain to be proved. Although market predictions for precision agriculture technologies are glowing, sales trends are positive and technology patents are rapidly increasing, their use is still far from mainstream.

Tools are becoming more effective and more capable, but their adoption is not taking place in a revolutionary way

Some advanced technologies, such as spraying drones and weeding robots, do seem to offer important potential advantages, but other agriculture tools are likely to be accepted by farmers only when they see a clear, and specifically economic, advantage coupled with limited risk. Rental or service packages for such new technologies may be required to persuade farmers, offering the potential to save the significant up-front costs of investments in new but traditional farm machinery. A shift toward more sustainable agriculture is already taking place in many countries. Organic farming is widespread, fueled by consumer demand and correspondingly higher product prices. The consumer demand mechanism has already proven powerful and, if coupled with legislation and policy-induced restrictions as well as financial support for climate change friendly practices, indicates that rapid and important changes can indeed be made. As usual, technology has an important enabling role to play. However, as with most things, much depends on the local context, both between countries and between regions within countries. The local context is highly diverse and so also is the appetite and the capability to embark on new solutions.

Patents and finance

The agricultural sector is experiencing high levels of innovation, expressed in terms of patents. Patent filings in agricultural engineering have increased by around 10 percent per year between 2000 and 2017, showing a sixfold increase during this period (see figure 3.2).[8] With patent filings for all technologies growing by 400 percent between 2001 and 2020,[9] technological innovation levels in the agricultural sector are well above the average, as evidenced by the number of agricultural patent filings.

Figure 3.2 Number of agricultural engineering patent filings, 2000 to 2017

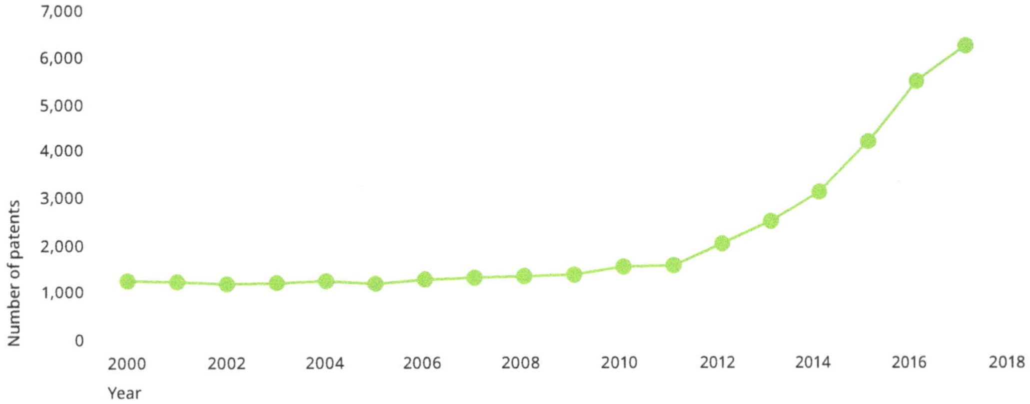

Source: Sozzi *et al.*, 2018.

Agricultural inputs such as pesticides and herbicides are among the fields showing most activity, with 40,000 patents granted within the last 10 years. As in many other technology areas, patenting in agriculture is concentrated geographically, with China leading in this case, followed by the United States, the Republic of Korea, the Russian Federation, Japan and Brazil.[10]

Innovation in agricultural drones and robots

Drones are often promoted as a new technology that offers many advantages for farmers, not least in relation to labor cost savings and reduced use of expensive chemicals. Patenting activities seem to confirm strong interest in the field. Research conducted in 2023 into patents in relation to agricultural drones found 23,501 relevant patents, dominated by patents in communication technology, sensing devices, sprayer technologies and power systems. Although patenting in this area only started within the last decade, for sprayer drones, for example, there are now around 600 patents annually, up from just a handful in 2013.[11]

A study from 2019 on the patenting of robot technology for agriculture identified the following major fields in patent filing, in order of volume:[12]

1. robotic arms (for handling, harvesting, etc.)
2. means of travel and specialized vehicles
3. mechatronics applied to fishing or fish farming
4. animal husbandry and analysis
5. image capture
6. cutting tools
7. radio frequency identification (RFID) tags applied to agriculture
8. plant growing systems
9. robotic supply of food
10. automated irrigation.

The study also revealed that China and the United States are the major filing countries.

Innovation in livestock and soil carbon

Methane emissions from cattle are a major climate change concern and patent analyses confirm that intensive innovation is being invested in finding solutions. Feed additives are a technology that is showing promising potential for reducing methane emissions and patent analyses indicate exponential growth in filings since the early 2000s. Plant-based additives have seen the strongest growth but a large variety of active compounds in methane-reducing feed additives have also been patented. European Union (EU) countries are taking the lead with private actors dominating the field.[13] Seaweed as a feed additive is an area of innovation with particular potential and a study identified 1,640 patents up to 2020, with almost half originating in the United States.[14]

One of the major challenges involved in addressing the issue of soil carbon in climate change is developing reliable and affordable methods for measuring soil carbon

One of the major challenges involved in addressing the issue of soil carbon in climate change is developing reliable and affordable methods for measuring soil carbon. Since at least 2015, this has been a highly active field of innovation, which seemed to peak in 2019 and then fell away somewhat, at least in terms of analyzing the 425 patent families that can be identified in this field. China is strongly dominant in patent filing in this field, with its universities predominating as primary actors.[15]

Innovation in environmental Earth observation

Much of the data required for precision farming to be effective is generated by remote sensing platforms, typically satellites but also drones. Satellites offer consistent multispectral image products with short revisit times but depend on cloud-free conditions. Multispectral images can be used for a broad suite of detailed analyses of vegetation and forest conditions and crop development during the growing season. The market for satellite images has developed rapidly over the past couple of decades with the combination of national public satellites and a highly active private sector resulting in a growth rate of around 10 percent per year.[16] After communication satellites, Earth observation (EO) satellites are the largest group of satellites with 1,192 units in orbit at the end of 2022. In 2022, 140 EO satellites were launched, corresponding to growth of 13 percent. The EO satellites are controlled by 237 organizations with around half owned by the 10 biggest operators. Almost half of the EO satellites in orbit have commercial uses and this is also where growth in satellite launches is strongest with close to 20 percent in 2022.[17]

The market for satellite images has developed rapidly over the past couple of decades with the combination of national public satellites and a highly active private sector

These strong trends are also reflected in patent filings. Filings for green applications of satellite-based sensing data increased by a massive 1,800 percent between 2001 and 2020. This includes a broad range of environmental applications such as climate change mitigation, weather prediction, pollution detection and environmental monitoring. A major part of these filings related to signal processing, but development and miniaturization of instruments and platforms, artificial intelligence (AI) processing and sensor development are also highly active fields. China is dominating the patent filings in this area with 71 percent in 2021, although these are mainly domestic filings. In terms of international filings, the United States dominated with a 43 percent share while the EU accounted for 25 percent of international filings.[18] The analysis also shows that these patents are filed primarily within the technical fields of crop productivity, land use, rivers and coastal zones, clouds and extreme events. These represent commercially important activities and the findings reflect the strong private sector engagement that was also observed in the data on satellite launches.

Financing the green transition in agriculture

Finance allocated to various sectors within agriculture and land use indicates the importance that policymakers and private funders attribute to the sector. The agriculture sector is particularly complex due to the huge number of widely different activities it encompasses, the various ways these are implemented and the local contexts. This also makes deployment of financial support diverse and sometimes complex. The following section details some overall pointers and gives examples of the type of investments that are happening in various agriculture subsectors.

On average in 2019 and 2020, climate finance for agriculture, forestry and related sectors received only 2.5 percent of total climate finance. As reported by major multilateral funding mechanisms and organizations. This highlights its underfunding compared to sectors such as renewable energy (51 percent) and low-carbon transport (26 percent).[19] While crop and livestock farming contributes almost 14 percent of global GHG emissions, it received only 0.35 percent (USD 2 billion) of total climate finance in 2019/20.[20]

The majority of agriculture climate finance originates from public sources, as private sector contributions are constrained by perceived risks prompting the need for scalable blended finance approaches.[21] Carbon accounting is particularly difficult for agricultural projects due to measurement uncertainties and therefore agricultural offsetting projects are rare, accounting for just 1 percent of all carbon credits issued.[22]

The East Asia and Pacific regions lead in terms of agricultural climate finance receipts, trailed by sub-Saharan Africa where agriculture constitutes 23 percent of the region's gross domestic product (GDP).[23] Yet, despite the fact that 95 percent of the world's farms are operated by small-scale farmers, only 40 percent of total committed funds cater to small-scale farming.[24]

Presently, agricultural climate finance falls short of Paris Agreement targets, requiring a 26-fold increase in funding (USD 423 billion annually by 2030) in contrast to the current average funding USD 16.3 billion annually.[25]

Alternative foods

During 2019/20, approximately USD 1.5 billion of company-level investments were dedicated to agrifood tech startups, primarily focusing on GHG mitigation. The food and diet sector received the largest share (68 percent), channeling support primarily toward startups involved in cultured meat, novel ingredients and plant-based proteins. The consistent year-on-year growth in venture capital investments, alongside the rise of these startups in smaller markets, reflects the escalating global demand for plant-based and alternative diets.[26]

Both developed and, increasingly, developing markets are witnessing heightened consumer awareness and interest in alternative proteins. This trend is predominantly attributed to concerns regarding the environment, health and animal welfare,[27] but as this is a novel sector, producers must find ways to reduce costs for consumers.[28] Investment in alternative proteins reached over USD 5 billion in 2021, fueled by an anticipated 11 percent share of protein consumption by 2035, potentially reducing emissions equivalent to global aviation.[29]

Alternative foods are currently excluded from carbon markets due to difficulties in developing reliable carbon accounting methods for these products. Policy changes, along with novel methodologies for carbon accounting, are recommended to align the alternative protein and fat industries with environmental goals and support sustainable consumption patterns.

Precision farming

Public funding for precision farming has been supported by major policy initiatives. Under the European Green Deal and Farm to Fork Strategy, funding comes through the Common Agricultural Policy eco-schemes.[30] In the United States, the Precision Agriculture Loan Act 2023 aims to unlock financing for precision agriculture technologies, offering loans for between three and 12 years of up to USD 500,000 at interest rates of less than 2 percent.[31]

The precision farming market is predicted to grow from USD 9.7 billion in 2023 to USD 21.9 billion by 2031. North America, Europe and the Asia Pacific region will see major growth, driven by GHG reduction goals, internet of things (IoT) integration and governmental support.[32]

However, in 2022 investors displayed a shift in preference compared to the previous year, with a notable decrease of 23 percent in investment in emerging agricultural technologies, a sector that held the top spot in 2020. Instead, they directed their investments toward hyper-local vertical farming. For example Infarm, a German vertical farming enterprise, secured a substantial 58 percent share of the total European investment capital allocated to the emerging agricultural technologies category in 2021.[33]

Sustainable rice farming

As discussed later in this chapter, reducing methane emissions from rice farming is technically challenging but nevertheless funding is finding its way toward this important goal.

This year, the World Bank approved a loan of USD 255 million for an initiative that aims to mitigate methane emissions from rice production in Hunan province, China's largest rice-producing region. Over a five-year period, financing for the program is set to reach USD 1.24 billion, with the Chinese Government contributing USD 988 million.[34]

The International Fund for Agricultural Development (IFAD) has launched an initiative to reduce methane emissions from small-scale farming in developing countries. The new program will receive USD 3 million in support from the Global Methane Hub and USD 1 million from the US State Department.[35]

Although the system of alternate wetting and drying (AWD) is recognized as an efficient practice for reducing methane emissions, the resulting emissions reduction is particularly difficult to measure and AWD projects have so far been excluded from carbon credits, effectively cutting off a potentially enabling source of funding.[36]

Regenerative agriculture

Efforts to restore soil carbon are complex and because measuring the effects of initiatives can be challenging, robust methods for verifying climate gains need to be developed. Nevertheless, the regenerative agriculture market is projected to increase from USD 975 million in 2022 to approximately USD 4.3 billion by 2032[37] with climate financing initiatives from both private and public bodies driving this trajectory.

As an example, PepsiCo introduced a USD 1.25 billion 10-year Green Bond initiative to support regenerative agriculture[38] and Danone North America, in collaboration with the National Fish and Wildlife Foundation, has raised USD 3 million of US Department of Agriculture (USDA) funding, with the aim of expanding their soil health program in tandem with farmers.[39]

EU-funded projects focus on carbon sequestration using crop diversification and organic fertilization through grants from the European Agricultural Fund for Rural Development.[40] Furthermore, the USDA has allocated over USD 3.1 billion across 141 projects via the Partnerships for Climate-Smart Commodities plan, with a specific emphasis on soil carbon measurement and monitoring.[41]

Photo: Getty Images / Umkehrer

Livestock

Livestock is responsible for most of the GHG emissions in the agricultural sector and accounts for almost 6 percent of all anthropogenic GHG emissions.[42]

Most of these emissions originate from digestive processes in ruminants and there are limits to what can be done to reduce this source. Therefore, it is likely that the largest abatement gains will have to come from changes in consumer patterns toward less or different meat consumption, as well as avoiding the conversion of natural land into livestock pastures.[43] Increased focus on recycling of nutrients in all stages of the livestock production process, including reducing food loss and waste, can also make significant contributions.[44]

It is likely that the largest abatement gains will have to come from changes in consumer patterns toward less or different meat consumption

Enteric fermentation

Ruminant livestock, such as cattle, buffalo, goats and sheep, produce large amounts of methane as a by-product of the activity of microbes processing cellulose in their digestive tracts, a process commonly referred to as enteric fermentation. It is estimated that up to 30 percent of all anthropogenic methane emissions originate with ruminants.[45] Livestock are found in a large variety of agricultural systems, from poor smallholders to large industrial farms, and in all climates. They are often an intrinsic part of cultural, economic and food security aspects of rural livelihoods. Livestock provide not only protein in the form of meat and milk, but also power for traction and transport, manure (for fuel and fertilizer), hides and fibers and a means of accumulating savings, especially for poor households. It is estimated that around 59 percent of the 729 million poor people living in rural and marginal areas are livestock farmers.[46]

The amount of methane that is released into the atmosphere by ruminants is determined by several factors, including level of intake, type and quality of feed, energy consumed, size and growth rate, production level and ambient temperature.[47] The way these factors influence the animals varies according to breed, and therefore animal genetics is an additional variable.

More productive systems emit less methane

The factors listed above also indicate that methane emissions vary with the productivity of systems, and high productivity systems have much lower emissions per product produced than less intensive systems, as illustrated in figure 3.3.[48, 49] Therefore, reducing poverty and increasing rural livelihood standards through productivity increases is also likely to have a positive effect on GHG emissions.[50] In that respect, means for reducing emissions from smallholder livestock may partly overlap with initiatives targeting adaptation, as adaptation is to a large degree about bolstering the resilience and robustness of the most vulnerable through improved livelihood conditions and food security (see also *Green Technology Book: Solutions for Climate Change Adaptation*).

Figure 3.3 **Correlation between national average of GHG emissions per kg milk produced and productivity (kg milk per cow per year)**

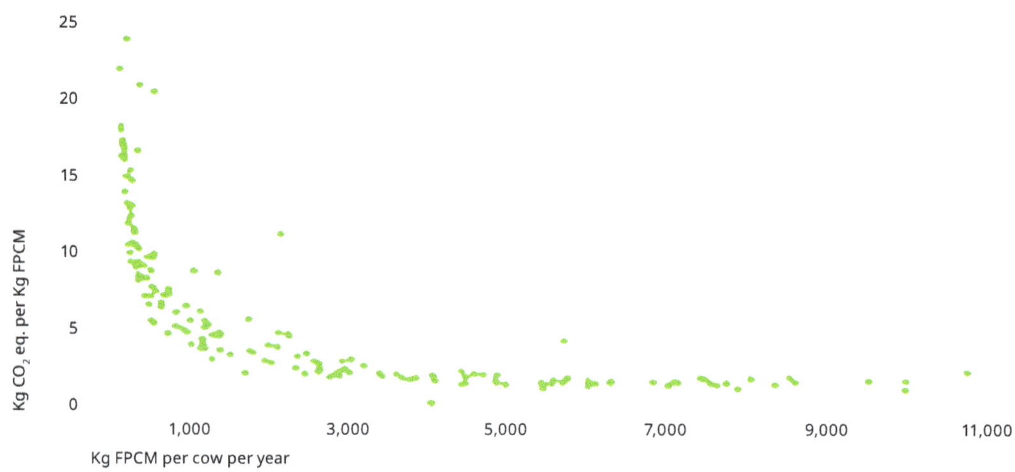

Notes: Green dots indicate countries. FPCM stands for fat- and protein-corrected milk, which is a standardization measure of milk production; GHG is greenhouse gas.
Source; FAO (2019).

Cattle are responsible for around 77 percent of enteric methane emissions, followed by buffalo at 14 percent and small ruminants at 9 percent.[51] Targeting cattle rearing is therefore a high priority mitigation strategy. With the aim of productivity increases in mind, the three main target areas for bringing down emissions from livestock are feeding, animal health and husbandry, and genetics and breeding.

Feeds and additives that reduce emissions

Not all feeds result in the same levels of methane emissions from enteric fermentation. Shifting to easily digestible grains and adding nitrates to livestock feed may help reduce methane production and also increase productivity though more efficient digestion.[52] Feed supplements may also help to reduce emissions. Some additives directly inhibit methane generation while others affect the availability of hydrogen and CO_2, resulting in less methane production.[53] The following section gives a few examples of methane-inhibiting feed additives but this is an innovation-intensive field and hundreds of relevant patents can be found in the WIPO GREEN Database of needs and green technologies.

Furthermore, the protein composition of fodder can be modified to reduce methane emissions. Some of these methane-reducing protein sources include synthetic amino acids, algal, fungal or microbial protein and insects.[54] Feed is one of the main determinators of animal productivity, and hence the emissions per product produced. Improved feed quality can produce the same amount of animal products with lower methane emissions. Therefore, improved pasture management, forage mix and species, ration balancing and targeted feed preparation and preservation are factors that can be addressed.

Cattle are responsible for around 77 percent of enteric methane emissions, followed by buffalo at 14 percent and small ruminants at 9 percent

Animal health and climate mitigation are complementary

Healthy animals are generally also more productive, so targeting factors that are detrimental to animal health and living conditions will also have a positive effect on methane emissions. This includes issues that influence the reproductive rate and productive lifespan of animals, live-weight, milk yield, fertility, etc.

Selective breeding and conservation of indigenous breeds with specific tolerances can optimize the adaptability of livestock to local conditions, again increasing productivity and thereby reducing methane emissions. Having access to a wide genetic pool through artificial insemination can allow farmers to modify their herds' ability to thrive in local environments and on locally available feeds, and increase their resilience to climate change.[55] New breeds developed through genetic modification may have special abilities to optimize digestion of feed resulting in lower emissions, improved resistance to common diseases and stronger resilience to environmental factors such as heat and water stress with associated changes in feed. For more on livestock adaptation options, see the *Green Technology Book: Solutions for Climate Change Adaptation*.

Replacement of meat and dietary shifts

Changing consumption patterns for meat and other animal-derived products may well be one of the most important factors for limiting emissions from livestock, simply by having fewer of them. And innovation and technology are providing abundant solutions at a rapid pace. However, meat consumption overall is following a growing trend, although in the short term growth is expected to be modest due to high consumer prices and weak income growth.[56]

Meat consumption grows with income level

Consumption of meat is correlated with household wealth, meaning that generally, the better off a household is, the more meat it consumes - up to a certain point. Even though poverty and malnutrition are still prevalent in many parts of the world, several very large emerging economies are developing rapidly and raising living standards for substantial parts of their populations. Middle-income countries are therefore the main driver behind increased meat demand. In higher-income countries, disposable income is no longer a main factor determining meat consumption, but people in those countries still consume about seven times more meat than people in low-income countries.[57] Meat consumption is therefore likely to continue increasing. Add to this global population growth and increased longevity. Currently standing at 8 billion people, the world population is projected to reach 9.7 billion in 2050 with more people added to that total until at least 2100, although with large regional variations and some countries already experiencing shrinking populations.[58] The population growth factor alone is likely to result in increased meat and dairy product consumption.

From ruminants to alternative proteins

Shifting more meat consumption from ruminants to monogastric species, such as pigs, rabbits, poultry and fish, whose digestive processes produce much less methane, can be one pathway toward reducing the climate change footprint of livestock. However, this approach may be offset by some of these animals being more reliant on grain and pulses as fodder, giving rise to other potential environmental impacts.

In some countries, especially the wealthier ones, there are tendencies for stronger consumer awareness of the environmental and climate change footprint of the meat and dairy industry, of animal welfare and of personal health costs, and many consumer groups are motivated to reduce consumption of such products. In India, for example, religion plays a central role in many people's preference for a vegetarian diet.[59] For many, such a change in diet will be achieved by the replacement of meat with other protein sources, especially plant-derived ones. Such a shift in dietary habits will also have environmental benefits as meat is resource inefficient due to the nutrient conversion process that animals represent. The carbon footprint argument is gaining importance in the increasingly competitive market for meat and dairy alternatives,[60] but as these products, and in particular cultivated meat, are highly processed and thus may themselves have substantial carbon footprints, it is uncertain how much this trend will contribute to mitigating livestock emissions.

> Alternative proteins, and in particular cultivated meat, are highly processed and thus may themselves have substantial carbon footprints

Replacing meat with plant- or fungi-based alternatives and producing meat in ways other than raising and killing animals, has gained considerable media attention and capital investments in recent years (figure 3.4).[61] The Protein Directory, a web-based database of alternative protein companies, contains more than 1,800 listings and is growing fast, although not all companies directly target replacing meat and animal protein.[62] Replacing live animal-based protein can be achieved in several ways. Cutting-edge technologies include cellular agriculture (or cultivated meat) where meat cells are produced in bioreactors or by in vitro cultivation based on original live animal cells, processing of plant-derived proteins into milk- and meat-like products, precision fermentation, 3D printing, fungi fermentation and microbe cultivation. It is also possible to genetically modify plants and microflora (yeast) to produce animal proteins which can improve the texture, taste and nutritional value of meat alternatives. The alternative protein technologies experiencing the fastest growth and those companies that have received the greatest amount of investment are the plant-based processes, probably because these are relatively well tested and can enter the market more quickly.[63] Selling cultivated meat is, to date (mid-2023), only permitted in Singapore and the United States. Nevertheless, there are already more than 150 companies working on developing and scaling up this technology.[64] Insect-based meat alternatives offer another line of development, which has the advantage of ease of farming and a wide variety of feeding options. Still in development, this option has so far mainly targeted the animal feed and pet food sectors.[65]

Figure 3.4 **Alternative meat products on offer in a supermarket in Geneva, Switzerland, July 2023**

Photo 3: Peter Oksen

Alternative meat products do exist on the market already, but scaling up to mass production with significant resultant effects on livestock numbers is still some way off. However, replacing meat and milk protein in industrial food products, such as powdered milk, egg and minced beef, may be a more feasible route toward emission reduction impacts, as this would not significantly affect taste or texture. It may therefore be mainstreamed within large food producers and supply chains more easily than replica meat products that must satisfy individual consumers' preference for color, texture, aroma, taste and even sound, which are hard to reproduce in processes alternative to live animals.

Range management and avoided land use change

Most livestock are reared in mixed crop–livestock systems, often including trees and occupying vast swathes of land area. Livestock is the largest driver of deforestation globally, not least in Latin America where it is dominant.[66] This process of converting forest and other land cover types into rangelands and mixed forestry and grazing (silvo-pastoral) systems leads to the release of carbon from burning trees and undergrowth that are not being replaced (replanted). Reducing livestock-related deforestation is one of the largest potential mitigation measures to combat livestock GHG emissions. However, grazing areas and rangelands also contain large amounts of sequestered carbon and maintaining healthy and well-managed grazing lands can increase the soil carbon content still further.

Range management in non-equilibrium

In regions of high rainfall variability, such as the arid to semi-arid Sudanian and Sahelian climate zones where livestock grazing is typically based on commons management, the interplay of grazing pressure, rainfall and land degradation has been debated for decades.[67] The discussion has been fueled not least by ideas inspired by political ideology such as the tragedy of the commons, first published in 1968,[68, 69] and land tenure in general. The basic notion of non-equilibrium rangeland theory is that high rainfall variability is a more important factor for determining soil and vegetation health than livestock grazing pressure. Rangelands have been found to be able to regenerate quickly when abundant rain arrives.[70] This view opposed often popularized images of advancing deserts and sand dunes and permanent conversion of a given number of hectares annually into irreversibly degraded land.[71, 72] Actually, land cover types such as forests in more stable rainfall regimes can to some degree also be characterized as not being in an equilibrium or climax vegetation state as they are often made up of a patchwork of areas in various stages of regeneration from some kind of disturbance.

The non-equilibrium ideas are important for a clear understanding of range management. For example, a term such as carrying capacity (a non-static measure of the population size that can be sustained in a given land area) becomes much less useful in areas of high rainfall variability as it is based on more stable and predictable environments. This again has implications for rangeland management, as grazing patterns are required that provide more flexibility than can be achieved by rotation between fixed and fenced pastures. This favors traditional seasonal and opportunistic systems of cattle migrations, transhumance, etc.[73, 74]

Regenerating the rangelands

Regenerative grazing is a term that covers various initiatives aiming to maintain productive grazing lands without the use of artificial fertilizers and preserve or increase their soil carbon content.[75] The practice The system can include improved grazing management such as grazing rotation to ensure optimal regrowth (for example, through sensor and information technology (IT)-based range management tools and solar-powered electric fences), using specific plant species, providing protection against soil erosion and integrating trees into rangelands.[76] Restoring degraded rangelands through regenerative grazing promotes soil carbon accumulation and can even qualify for carbon credits, thus adding a further economic incentive. However, regenerating degraded rangelands takes time and the permanence of the measures must be continuously verified. Considering the vast areas of land involved, the potential is large.

Land used for cultivating livestock fodder can also sequester carbon if managed well. This means that technologies for optimizing grazing and rangeland management can not only reduce loss of soil carbon on degraded lands but can also allow those lands to act as carbon sinks by increasing soil carbon sequestration.

With increased access to satellite-based internet coverage at close to normal consumer prices, the possibility of connecting various sensors becomes more relevant, providing farmers with real-time data on temperature in sheds, herd movements, water quality, feed silo status, etc. Radio frequency identification (RFID) tags have been in widespread use for years and allow for closer monitoring of the health and condition of individual animals.

As discussed above, general livestock productivity improvements are likely to also reduce GHG emissions per product produced, and all technologies that contribute to productivity increases would therefore be relevant. The focus in this chapter is on technologies that are capable of targeting GHG emissions reduction more or less directly, but it should be kept in mind that the field of productivity-improving solutions is much larger and broader than can be covered here. Another technological field is the capture of methane gas from manure. This can range from simple farm-level installations, basically consisting of large rubber bags or coatings, to

Restoring degraded rangelands through regenerative grazing promotes soil carbon accumulation and can even qualify for carbon credits

industrial-scale bioreactors possibly including equipment for gas purification and compression. Collection of manure from individual farms (for example in scaled-up installations) has turned out to be a challenge in certain settings.

It should also be noted that many solutions address both adaptation and mitigation simultaneously. The Green Technology Book collection in the WIPO GREEN Database of needs and technologies contains many more examples of technologies that are relevant for both adaptation and mitigation.

Innovation examples

Photo: Getty Images /© Rudimencial

Fewer emissions and higher productivity of cattle in Uruguay

Uruguay is a small country with a highly important agricultural sector, especially livestock. The 12 million cattle in Uruguay, more than triple the number of its people, cause 75 percent of the country's GHG emissions and 91 percent of its methane emissions. Supported by the Climate and Clean Air Coalition (CCAC) of the United Nations Environment Programme (UNEP) and several other partners, the "Ganadería y Clima" project worked with 60 farms to identify practical ways of reducing methane emissions from the cattle. The focus was on optimizing animal conditions and included improved grass and feed as well as managing cattle body fat reserves. By carefully monitoring and recording emissions, the project aimed to increase productivity and income for participating farmers and at the same time reduce emissions. Results were almost immediate. In the first year, methane emissions were reduced by 6 percent per kg meat produced and in the second year by 23.5 percent. After only two years, farmers had increased their meat production by 9 percent and their income by 32 percent - an impressive result considering that the country endured severe drought during this period. The results confirm the link between productivity and methane emissions discussed in this chapter.[77]

Photo: Getty Images /© Smederevac

Global Livestock Environmental Assessment Model (GLEAM)

Developed by the United Nations Food and Agriculture Organization (FAO), GLEAM is a modeling tool that allows analysts to identify GHG emissions and other environmental dimensions at various stages along the livestock supply chains. Although designed as a global model, national and sub-national parameters are included, down to a resolution of around 10 × 10 km. The model can be used to simulate various livestock, feed and management practices and thereby provide scenarios for different adaptation and mitigation options, including methane emissions. Additional modules are being added to the model so that it can also assess aspects such as nutrients, water and biodiversity.

The model has been used in a wide variety of regional and geophysical contexts. For example, in Uruguay it helped identify the combination of herd and health management, nutrition and feeding management strategies and genetics that would reduce methane emissions from the beef cattle sector. In Kenya it was used to identify changes in feed composition and practices, and improvements to the energy efficiency of equipment and manure management that could reduce GHG emissions. These data were also used by the Gold Standard to issue carbon credit certifications.[78, 79]

- Contact: WIPO GREEN Database

Technology solutions

Proven technologies

Range management: mobile solar-powered electric livestock fences

Africa Power Fencing

Photo: Getty Images / © Stephen Barnes

Solar-powered electric fences may provide a cheap and flexible way for implementing a grazing rotation plan, for example as part of a regenerative grazing program. This South African company provides a large selection of solar-powered electric fence systems. Several flexible and portable systems provide fencing for between 1 and 16 hectares and have an inbuilt battery for continuous operation. The units can operate for several weeks without sun and without requiring attendance. The units are easy to move and attach to existing fences. Larger fixed solar and battery-based systems can cover up to 400 hectares.

- Contracting type: For sale/service
- Technology level: Low
- Country of origin: South Africa
- Availability: Botswana, Kenya, Malawi, Mozambique, Namibia, South Africa, United Republic of Tanzania, Zambia, Zimbabwe
- Contact: WIPO GREEN Database

Range management: livestock software management

AgriWebb

Photo: Getty Images / © Manhattan001

AgriWebb's software platform tracks and records livestock on the farm and through the supply chain. The company creates a virtual map of the entire farm and the application allows farmers to digitally track livestock movement, weight gain, grazing days left in a paddock and other performance indicators. The software then calculates input costs of production for each area of the farm, allowing farmers to gain insights on where to reduce spending and how to maximize output.

- Contracting type: For sale/service
- Technology level: Medium
- Country of origin: Australia
- Availability: Australia, Canada, Ireland, New Zealand, United Kingdom, United States
- Contact: WIPO GREEN Database

Range management: advanced RFID ear tags for herd monitoring

Herdwhistle

Photo: Getty Images/© lucknoadisbrador

Radio frequency identification (RFID) is a well-proven and widely used technology that allows monitoring of individual animals. Typically in the form of an ear tag, the RFID tag sends a signal to a receiver which can be placed in various places of interest for data collection, such as feeding troughs, water stations, etc. In this way, detailed information on the behavior, feeding and drinking patterns of each animal can be gathered, facilitating early alerts of potential health issues and overall condition of the animals. Extra-long range tags are available. The system allows for data-driven decision-making for herd management and can be connected to mobile phones.

- Contracting type: For sale
- Technology level: Medium
- Country of origin: Canada
- Availability: Canada, United States
- Contact: WIPO GREEN Database

Range management: climate-smart Brachiaria grass for improved livestock productivity

Consultative Group on International Agricultural Research (CGIAR)

Photo: © CGIAR

Low livestock productivity has plagued sub-Saharan Africa for a long time and is a factor in creating a severe food shortage for one of the fastest growing human populations in the world. Some of the drivers that contribute to this low productivity are feeds shortage and low-quality feeds. Brachiaria grass offers a solution because it produces large amounts of high-quality biomass, thus improving quality feed availability, and its high nutrient value increases livestock productivity, reducing the overall carbon footprint of the livestock production system. Brachiaria also tolerates extreme climatic conditions and grows well in low fertility soils. It is an important complement to other forage grasses, such as Napier grass, widely cultivated in sub-Saharan Africa.

- Contracting type: For sale
- Technology level: Low
- Country of origin: Kenya
- Availability: Burundi, Cameroon, Democratic Republic of the Congo, Ethiopia, Gambia, Ghana, Kenya, Malawi, Mali, Mozambique, Nigeria, Rwanda, Senegal, Somalia, South Africa, South Sudan, Sudan, Swaziland, Uganda, United Republic of Tanzania, Zambia, Zimbabwe
- Contact: WIPO GREEN Database

Methane reduction: Bovaer cattle feed supplement for methane reduction

DSM-Firmenich

Photo: Getty Images / © J Brarymi

The Bovaer cattle feed supplement works by suppressing the enzyme involved in producing methane in the enteric fermentation process. Just a few grams in a cow's daily feed can result in a significant reduction in methane emissions of up to 30 percent and takes effect after only 30 minutes. The product has been thoroughly tested and is being piloted by Arla Foods, the biggest dairy company in Denmark.

- Contracting type: For sale
- Technology level: Low
- Country of origin: Switzerland
- Availability: Worldwide
- Contact: WIPO GREEN Database

Methane reduction: biodigester – high resistance flexible PVC material

Coplast Group

Photo: Getty Images / © Suparirk

The biodigester is made of a flexible high-resistance PVC material and is available in a range of sizes to suit different needs. The system also includes installation accessories. It is a solution for making profitable use of solid organic waste from cattle and pigs. The system in operation efficiently produces biogas (methane) for use as fuel. In addition, it generates high-quality biofertilizer, which stimulates the germination of seeds and the development and growth of plants. The biodigester comprises a hermetic chamber that stores the gas and a lagoon for the drainage of the biofertilizer.

- Contracting type: For sale
- Technology level: Medium
- Country of origin: Peru
- Availability: Peru
- Contact: WIPO GREEN Database

Frontier technologies

Range management: grazing management with virtual fences

Nofence

Photo: Getty Images/© Clara Bastian

Nofence aims to revolutionize livestock management with its virtual fencing solution. The animals are equipped with a GPS-enabled collar that emits audio signals when the predefined grazing boundary is transgressed. Grazing areas can be defined in real time using a mobile phone app, thus reducing the need for physical fences. Grazing events are meticulously recorded, ensuring optimal plant recovery periods for sustainable land management. By practising effective grazing techniques, such as high-density grazing, grazing for shorter periods and promoting grass regrowth, farmers can enhance profitability while prioritizing soil health and water, nutrient and light access. Nofence's innovative approach enables farmers to track their animals in real time and receive notifications about their movements, thereby promoting animal welfare and safety.

- Contracting type: For sale/service
- Technology level: Medium
- Country of origin: Norway
- Availability: Ireland, Norway, Spain, United Kingdom, United States
- Contact: WIPO GREEN Database

Range management: turning food waste into animal feed through insects

Better Origin

Photo: Getty Images/© Joko Suryanta

Better Origin offers an innovative solution that transforms food waste into sustainable animal feed. By harnessing the power of black soldier fly larvae, the technology enables the conversion of food waste into nutrient-rich insect products. This approach addresses the significant environmental impact of food waste, which contributes up to 10 percent of GHG emissions. Better Origin's technology helps to mitigate CO_2 emissions locally, tackles on-farm food waste and reduces the need for soy as a feedstock, thereby avoiding deforestation. Their insect-based ingredients, such as insect puree, insect meal and insect oil, provide a sustainable source of protein for poultry, aquaculture and pet food while facilitating waste management. The automated insect farming systems, housed in standard shipping containers, are driven by AI which optimizes yields, while the chitin and chitosan produced in the process offer versatile applications in various industries.

- Contracting type: For sale
- Technology level: Low
- Country of origin: United Kingdom
- Availability: European Union, United Kingdom, United States
- Contact: WIPO GREEN Database

Methane reduction: NP Rumen – a natural feed additive reducing livestock methane

LIAV (Industrial Laboratory for Veterinary Alternatives)

Photo: © LIPAV

Moroccan company LIAV has developed a feed additive based on natural ingredients that both reduces methane emissions and improves livestock health. NP Rumen is a solution that claims to reduce methane emissions from dairy cows, beef cattle and other ruminant herds by more than 30 percent. NP Rumen promotes improved animal health and zootechnical performance to deliver high-quality end-products.

- Contracting type: For sale
- Technology level: Low
- Country of origin: Morocco
- Availability: Morocco, Saudi Arabia, United Arab Emirates
- Contact: WIPO GREEN Database

Methane reduction: seaweed as a feed ingredient for livestock

FutureFeed

Photo: Getty Images / © spiderment

FutureFeed is working on the use of seaweed, more specifically Asparagopsis, as a feed ingredient to reduce methane emissions and improve feed efficiency. The seaweed contains bromoform, a bioactive compound which acts as an inhibitor in methanogenesis. The company holds the intellectual property rights for the use of Asparagopsis as a livestock feed ingredient and licenses the technology to companies worldwide, in compliance with industry standards. For example, in Sweden the company Volta Greentech markets climate-friendly meat based on the use of the feed supplement.

- Contracting type: License
- Technology level: Low
- Country of origin: United States
- Availability: Australia, Canada, Europe, New Zealand, United States
- Contact: WIPO GREEN Database

Meat and dairy alternative: dairy protein from precision fermentation
Perfect Day

Photo: Getty Images/© S_Bachstroem

Milk protein (whey) can be produced by using microflora to ferment a mixture of water, nutrients and sugar. The microflora used in Perfect Day's technology is equipped with the DNA for producing a pure animal protein. The whey protein can replace animal-based dairy protein in products such as ice cream, bread, cookies, cream and milk, thereby eliminating the need for methane-emitting dairy cows. Since the protein product is close to the animal-based protein in taste and food qualities, it can be incorporated into the production processes of a large range of products without changing their taste or texture or affecting consumer preferences. The impact of such an innovation could therefore be significant.

- Contracting type: For sale
- Technology level: Medium
- Country of origin: United States
- Availability: Worldwide
- Contact: WIPO GREEN Database

Meat and dairy alternative: meat cultivated from animal cells
Upside Foods

Photo: © Upside Foods

Based on live animal cells to create cell lines, the meat is grown in cultivators in a nutrient-rich solution. The growth process takes two to three weeks, after which the meat is molded into the form of the meat it is to resemble. It can then be prepared and cooked as normal meat. Because it is based on actual animal cell derived cell lines, many of the meat characteristics are preserved in the final product. Its new production facilities are enabling the company to rapidly scale up production to more than 100 tons of meat per year.

- Contracting type: For sale
- Technology level: Low
- Country of origin: United States
- Availability: United States
- Contact: WIPO GREEN Database

Meat and dairy alternative: plant-based meat developed using AI

NotCo

Photo: Getty Images /© nerudol

The company has developed an AI model that compares the known molecular composition of animal-based meat products with similar components in edible plants. This can speed up the process of defining combinations of plant-based components which can emulate the taste, texture, aroma and other properties of animal-based meat and dairy products. Several patents have been granted for the AI model. Products include burger meat, chicken substitutes and milk.

- Contracting type: For sale
- Technology level: Low
- Country of origin: United States
- Availability: Argentina, Brazil, Canada, Chile, Mexico, United States
- Contact: WIPO GREEN Database

Meat and dairy alternative: 3D printed plant-based meat

Redefine Meat

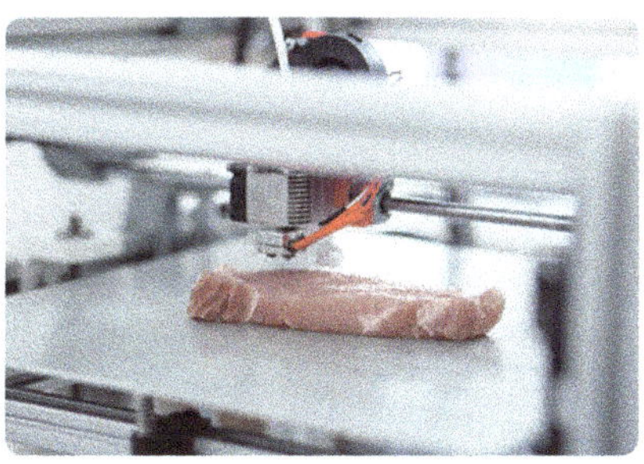

Photo: Getty Images /© Zinkevych

The company specializes in replicated whole meat cuts by using sophisticated additional manufacturing technology, also known as 3D printing. This allows the fully plant-based product (composed mainly of soy and wheat protein) to emulate the structure and texture of animal-based meat, including plant-based fats and other components which add smell and taste to the cooked meat.

- Contracting type: For sale
- Technology level: Low
- Country of origin: Israel
- Availability: Israel, most of the EU
- Contact: WIPO GREEN Database

Meat and dairy alternative: alternative protein food sourced from spirulina algae

SimpliiGood

Photo: Getty Images /© Rocky89

The technology produces an alternative protein derived from spirulina. Spirulina is a type of blue-green algae known for its rich nutritional profile and minimal environmental footprint. The cultivation of spirulina requires significantly less land, water and other resources compared to traditional livestock farming. It has a high protein content, making it an excellent alternative to animal-based protein sources. Spirulina cultivation has the potential to capture and sequester CO_2 from the atmosphere.

- Contracting type: For sale
- Technology level: Medium
- Country of origin: Israel
- Availability: Israel, United Kingdom
- Contact: WIPO GREEN Database

Horizon technologies

Methane reduction: wearable device for capturing enteric fermentation emissions from cattle

ZELP

Photo: © ZELP

A British company is developing wearable technology for cows that can collect methane from cow burps and convert it into CO_2. The wearable contains a solar-powered pump that collects the methane from the cow's nostrils leading it into a chamber where it is oxidized to CO_2 in a chemical process. Almost all burp-related methane is released through the cow's nose. The wearable can also be used for collecting detailed data on methane emission and animal health and conditions. Several patents have been obtained for the technology.

- Contracting type: N/A
- Technology level: Medium
- Country of origin: United Kingdom
- Availability: N/A
- Contact: WIPO GREEN Database

Methane reduction: garlic and citrus-based feed additive for reducing enteric methane emissions

Mootral

Photo: Getty Images/© DewaldKirsten

UK-based Swiss-British company Mootral is working on testing and perfecting a new feed additive which has been shown to reduce methane emissions by 38 percent in field trials. The additive is based on a combination of active compounds derived from garlic and bioflavonoids from citrus. The additive is being designed to fit well into feed chains of a variety of farming systems. Several patents have been obtained for the technology.

- Contracting type: N/A
- Technology level: Low
- Country of origin: United Kingdom
- Availability: N/A
- Contact: WIPO GREEN Database

Methane reduction: methane-reducing feed supplement based on seaweed

Rumin8

Photo: Getty Images / © Damocean

Rumin8 offers technology-driven solutions to reduce methane emissions from livestock and create a secure, climate-friendly food system. Their feed supplements replicate nature's compounds, effectively reducing enteric methane production in cattle. By stabilizing and replicating anti-methanogenic compounds found in rangeland plants and red seaweed, Rumin8's patented technology provides scalable and effective methane-reducing supplements. Ongoing trials demonstrate over 85 percent methane reduction, equating to the removal of two tons of carbon emissions per cow per year.

- Contracting type: N/A
- Technology level: Low
- Country of origin: Australia
- Availability: N/A
- Contact: WIPO GREEN Database

Methane reduction: innovative technology for effective use of methane

Osaka University

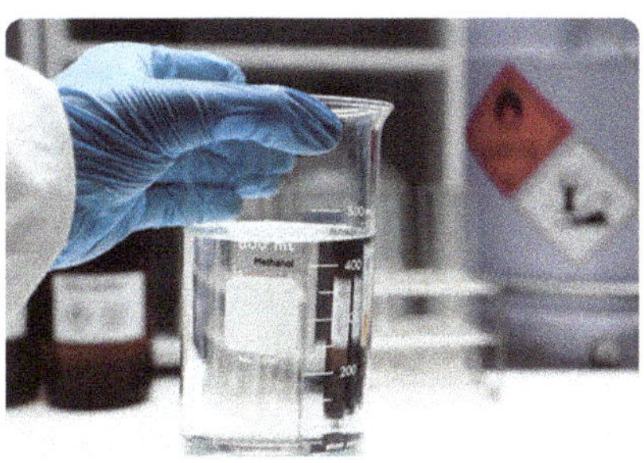

Photo: Getty Images / © Kittisak Kaewchalun

By synthesizing methanol from methane gas and air at room temperature and atmospheric pressure, methane gas, a greenhouse gas generated in dairy farming and other industries, can be reduced and methanol (which has several industrial uses) can be synthesized with low levels of energy consumption. Using this technology, methanol and formic acid can be produced with relatively low energy requirements while reducing the methane gas generated in the dairy farming industry. In addition, unlike conventional production methods, a higher yield of methanol can be produced and CO_2 emissions can be reduced to zero, thereby contributing to energy saving and carbon neutrality.

- Contracting type: N/A
- Technology level: High
- Country of origin: Japan
- Availability: N/A
- Contact: WIPO GREEN Database

Meat and dairy alternative: plant-grown animal protein – molecular farming

Moolec

Photo: © MOOLEC

The company takes an alternative approach to making meat without animal cruelty. Here plants are modified to become small bioreactors producing animal proteins. The technology enables the incorporation of genetic DNA codes of animal proteins into the genomes of food crops such as soybean. Each protein is carefully chosen to enhance the desired attributes such as flavor, consistency and nutritional composition. The protein can enter the food value chain in a wide range of products without the need for live animals.

- Contracting type: N/A
- Technology level: Medium
- Country of origin: Luxembourg
- Availability: N/A
- Contact: WIPO GREEN Database

Meat and dairy alternative: cultured meat creation technology

Joes Future Foods, STET

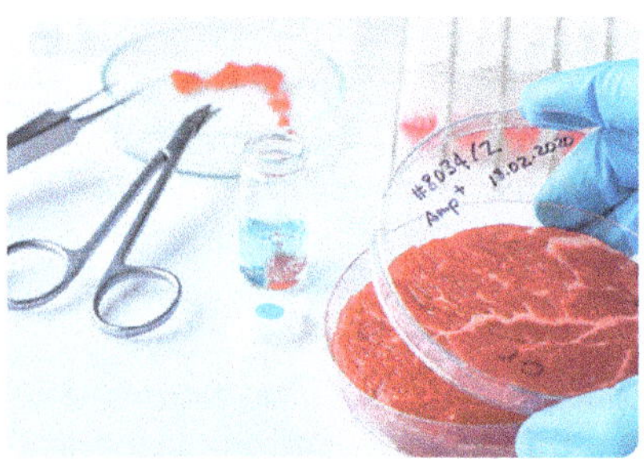
Photo: Getty Images / © anyaivanova

Cultured meat is an emerging method of meat production based on the growth pattern of meat in animal bodies. It uses in vitro cultivation and biomanufacturing techniques to grow animal cells and produce edible meat. The production process follows these basic steps: (1) cell tissue is extracted from the animal and the stem cells are isolated; (2) large-scale cultivation and proliferation is carried out in bioreactors; (3) molds, bioreactors or 3D printing are used to produce muscle tissues on a large scale; (4) finally, food-processing techniques are applied to make cell-cultured meat products.

- Contracting type: N/A
- Technology level: Low
- Country of origin: China
- Availability: N/A
- Contact: WIPO GREEN Database

Photo: Getty Images / Robert_Ford

Soils, land use change and forestry

A growing world population means increasing demand for food and resources. Even if population growth halted overnight, the fact that a significant part of the global population has insufficient or poor quality food would necessitate substantial growth in food production. This necessarily comes primarily from agriculture and agriculture offers two ways of accommodating growth – through expansion (cultivating more land) or intensification (producing more from the same land). Of course, expansion can take place without using more land – for example, in vertical farming, urban agriculture, rooftop farming, etc. While such systems can contribute significantly to the production of crops such as vegetables and legumes, most systems (including greenhouses, etc. in peri-urban areas) still require land.[80] Emissions from land use are complex and go both ways – release and sequestration. Land use change also leads to changes in albedo (a measure of energy reflectance), evapotranspiration and release of various volatile compounds.[81]

From ancient times right up to today, new land is continually being brought under the plough. Very often this is forest land. Around 10,000 years ago, some 57 percent of the Earth's landmass was covered in forest (the rest was wild shrub and grassland). Today, forest covers only 38 percent of Earth's landmass[82]. Forests represent a significant carbon reservoir and help to build up soil carbon as well as providing several other environmental services. However, forests are vulnerable to destruction and can therefore be considered as temporary storage, as the accumulated carbon is likely to be released when the trees die and decompose, unless they are replaced by new vegetation. This process of regeneration would be the normal course of events in a stable forest ecosystem, which therefore would effectively constitute long-term carbon storage.

Agriculture offers two ways of accommodating growth – through expansion (cultivating more land) or intensification (producing more from the same land)

The global rate at which forest is being converted to other land use, such as agriculture or infrastructure development, etc. (that is, deforestation), is currently around 5 million hectares per year, with 95 percent taking place in the tropics, estimated to contribute 6.6 percent of annual global CO_2 emissions.[83] The major drivers of deforestation are agriculture, wood extraction and infrastructure development.[84] In terms of agriculture, beef, soybean and palm oil are the major culprits. Beef is by far the largest driver of deforestation, especially in the Amazon rainforest.[85] Around half of global deforestation is countered by forest regrowth.[86] Much of Europe's forest was cleared centuries ago to provide land for agriculture, wood for fuel and timber for ship and house building. Temperate regions have, since 1990, generated more forest than they destroy. Since the peak deforestation rate in the 1980s, rates have slowly declined, although they still indicate net deforestation. China, India and Türkiye are currently the countries with the highest reforestation rates but it should be noted that the reforestation undertaken is often monoculture and sometimes uses invasive species – neither factor benefiting biodiversity. Forest loss also results from degradation of forest land without necessarily changing the land use completely and where regrowth would be able to occur. Forest and carbon storage loss therefore is a result of both deforestation and forest degradation. Around a quarter of global annual forest loss is from deforestation while the rest is from degradation, more or less equally distributed between wildfires, logging and shifting cultivation (temporary fields in forest areas).[87]

China, India and Türkiye are currently the countries with the highest reforestation rates

Other land cover types, such as wetlands, peatlands, steppe and grasslands, are also converted to agricultural land. Peatlands are of particular concern as they store vast amounts of carbon, accumulated over centuries, which is released through drainage, drying out and burning. Carbon emissions from land use, land-use change and forestry (LULUCF) make up as much as 21 percent of global anthropogenic GHG emissions but due to the complexity of the processes involving both emissions and sinks, the estimates are rather uncertain. Deforestation is estimated to account for around 45 percent of these emissions.[88] The Amazon rainforest covers 6.7 million km^2 (twice the area of India), but already between 18 and 20 percent has been deforested and another 38 percent degraded, with the risk of reaching a 25 percent tipping point, after which the Amazon ecosystem is at risk of breakdown.[89]

As mentioned in the introduction, agriculture and land use have the second largest mitigation potential after energy supply. Within this group, the biggest mitigation potential lies in "reduced conversion of natural ecosystems" (4.1 $GtCO_2eq/yr$) and another 2.8 $GtCO_2eq/yr$ from "ecosystem restoration, afforestation, reforestation". It is estimated that 30-50 percent of the Earth's land, freshwater and ocean areas must be conserved in order to maintain the resilience of biodiversity and ecosystem services.[90]

There is therefore a strong imperative for reversing the carbon emissions from LULUCF, and innovation and technology can provide some of the solutions.

Limiting conversion of natural ecosystems

In relation to reducing land conversion - which offers the greatest mitigation potential - policy and economics play crucial roles. However, technology can help policymakers and businesses understand the current state of forests and other high-carbon areas, visualize losses from land conversion and pave the way for efficient monitoring, which may trigger carbon financing. With the increasing availability of accurate and frequently updated data, it will be harder for decision-makers to act against climate pledges and other commitments. Satellites, drones, in-situ sensors and advanced software platforms make all this data available at low cost and often even free of charge. Furthermore, data can cross national borders, enabling a complete ecosystem or watershed approach rather than focusing only on national resources.

The demand side can also be supported with innovation and technology. All the technologies that allow farmers to be more productive by intensifying their production and by producing more with less land, can reduce the need to convert forests into new agricultural fields. However, for this to be effective, strong policy measures are also required to limit expansion of agriculture into new areas and to limit negative impacts of a more intensified agricultural system. Agricultural intensification has already had an enormous impact, clearly illustrated by the 7 percent increase in agricultural land since 1961, while global population has expanded by 147 percent.[91] This result was brought about not least by the green revolution and associated technological advancements, and innovation and technology continue to support this trend. This chapter has already touched on several relevant technologies and the list of options and possibilities is long indeed. The more advanced technologies associated with precision farming support this objective, as do new plant varieties, better agricultural inputs and more efficient irrigation. But simpler tools and technologies, which can provide that extra yield and security for the farmer, also make a contribution.

Ecosystem restoration, afforestation and reforestation

The protection of existing forests and ecosystems, and restoration of those that have been disturbed or destroyed, is crucial for achieving the Paris Agreement goals. In order to act as carbon sinks, forests must be monitored and protected against destructive events such as forest fires, which are already exacerbated by climate change. Here, technologies such as new tree varieties that are more resistant to fire and better adapted to variable growing conditions are important, as is forest health monitoring. Due to the vast and often relatively inaccessible areas covered by forests, drones and satellite multispectral images are particularly useful. Multispectral images can reveal detailed information on the condition of the forest, identify pest attacks and monitor several other growth parameters. This information can be treated in GIS and other advanced software systems for improved management and planning and is also a prerequisite for issuance and verification of carbon credits. Some of these technologies are described in Chapter 3 of the *Green Technology Book: Solutions for Climate Change Adaptation*.

What is on the land not only determines the actual storage of carbon in vegetation, but also has a direct influence on the carbon that is stored underground. As such, land use change will often directly influence the carbon content of soils.

Soil carbon restoration

Soils contain large reservoirs of carbon. Globally, soils hold three times more carbon than the atmosphere contains.[92, 93] This vast amount of carbon is stored in soil organic matter, typically in the form of humus (dark organic part of soil), in the top 30-40 cm, and can be released through land use change and soil degradation. Alternatively, it can be increased through land restoration and appropriate cultivation practices.

GHG emissions from soils are mostly in the form of CO_2 and are complex to estimate, not least because of the many different forms of land use. For example, in the EU in 2019, member states reported net emissions of 108 million tons of CO_2 ($MtCO_2$) from organic soil and net removals of 44 $MtCO_2$ from mineral soil.[94] The symbiosis between plants and mycorrhizal fungi in the soil also affects the mechanism of soil carbon accumulation and loss.[95] Although soil carbon can remain stable for millennia, global warming is expected to increase the atmospheric release of soil carbon through increased microbial decomposition, potentially creating a feedback loop that will exacerbate the effects of climate change.[96, 97] Soils also contain and release nitrogen oxides (NOx) and here also emissions take place through microbial activity that is sensitive to temperature, precipitation and other factors. However, the net emission of NOx from soils in various climate change scenarios is uncertain and is only partly understood.[98] The soil carbon budget has been negative for decades, meaning that more soil carbon is released than is being sequestered, but this can be reversed.

Globally, soils hold three times more carbon than the atmosphere

The mitigation potential of soil carbon is debated, but there is general agreement that the potential is highly significant.[99] At the 2015 United Nations Climate Change Conference (COP 21) in Paris, the "4 per 1,000 – Soils for Food Security and Climate" initiative was launched, based on the idea that increasing soil carbon by 0.4 percent per year (4 per 1,000) in the top 30–40 cm of soils, is enough to stop the increase of CO_2 in the atmosphere.[100] However, realizing this goal will require significant permanent changes to the ways millions of farmers cultivate their lands, which effectively reduces the realistic mitigation potential significantly.

Restoring soil carbon and soil organic content not only acts as a CO_2 sink but has important co-benefits. These include improved soil fertility, and hence crop yields, increased climate change resilience and reduced soil erosion and water runoff. If soil regeneration is done through restoration of ecosystems and avoided conversion to agriculture or built-up areas, etc. it has associated benefits such as natural habitat and biodiversity gains. Restoring soil carbon therefore has intrinsic climate change adaptation benefits, and biodiversity gains may open up new income streams for farmers, such as from tourism and hunting.

One of the major challenges facing soil carbon restoration is that it requires large areas to be monitored and verified consistently over a long period. Restoration works take place over a period of 20–30 years and must be maintained permanently through proper land management to avoid reversion. However, if well maintained, soil carbon is generally less vulnerable to sudden disturbances such as fires, wind and pests than are aboveground biomass such as shrubs and trees.

Soils, with the exception of some wetlands, have a saturation point beyond which they can no longer absorb soil organic matter. However, this generally occurs only after decades of restoration, depending on the state of soil carbon depletion, and therefore does not diminish the potential of soil carbon to play an important role in the urgently needed removal of atmospheric carbon.[101]

Biological and mineral products that help to build up soil carbon and improve soil health can be added to the soil. These can be in the form of microbes, which help to fixate carbon in the soil, pulverized minerals that speed up carbon sequestration and specific microbes that can help increase the transport of carbon from plant roots into the soil, such as rhizobacteria and mycorrhizal fungi.[102] Carbon, in the form of biochar (see box 3.1), can be incorporated directly into the soil and is likely to remain there for millennia, thus effectively taking that carbon out of circulation.

Box 3.1 Biochar

Biochar is a charcoal-like stable form of carbon made from pyrolysis (burning without oxygen) of organic material such as farm waste and by-products (for example, rice husks, peanut- and coconut shells). As it is highly porous, lightweight, fine-grained and has a large surface area, biochar adds desirable physical properties to soil and increases soil fertility. Depending on its origin, it consists of around 70 percent carbon. Biochar production has several advantages, such as recycling organic waste, renewable energy production, removing carbon from circulation and increasing soil carbon.[103] Biochar's efficiency in generating these benefits depends on climate, context, methods, etc. and the mitigation potential therefore also varies considerably.

Despite all these advantages, there are still relatively few soil carbon projects compared to forest projects, for example, that can be supported by verified Emission Reduction Credits (ERCs). This is partly due to the limited experience with such projects as they were excluded from the Kyoto Protocol's Clean Development Mechanism. However, this situation is changing rapidly and new services for registering, marketing and monitoring ERCs from regenerative agriculture are gaining popularity. By injecting carbon funding into regenerative farming and other soil carbon-positive activities, farmers may obtain the financial encouragement that makes the difference and reduces risks when deciding whether to change their practices. Incentives that make transitions economically viable for farmers are crucial for widespread adoption of new practices and include carbon-removal marketplaces, transition finance, ecosystem service payments, transition loans, crop insurance, etc. and here too innovation and technology have contributions to make.

Many ways to restore soil carbon

Several approaches and agriculture practices exist for restoring soil carbon using both simple and more advanced technologies.

Regenerative agriculture is one of the terms that often surfaces in relation to restoration of soil carbon. The term is broad and covers many technologies, techniques and practices that may have a positive impact on land and agricultural systems, and thereby soil carbon. Most often it comprises alternative land preparation practices, such as no-tillage, planting and ploughing down cover plants to protect soils from erosion and accumulate organic matter within the soil, use of nitrogen-fixating trees, legumes and cover plants, combined agriculture, forestry and also livestock in carefully managed systems, legumes in pastures, perennial crops with deep roots, peatland restoration, avoidance of pesticides, insecticides and synthetic fertilizers, and use of bio-based fertilizers, manure, compost and soil improvement additives, such as biochar. It also comprises technologies in relation to soil sampling, analyses, monitoring and validation.

Zero- and low-tillage technologies

Zero-till, no-tillage or conservation agriculture is an approach in which the soil is disturbed as little as possible and bare soil exposure is avoided. It entails leaving crop residue from the previous harvest intact and avoiding soil preparation, such as plowing and harrowing, combined with the use of cover crops. Promoted since the 1960s, the practice originally mostly targets avoiding soil erosion and is widespread, especially in the United States and Latin America, where, in Brazil and Argentina, for example, more than half of all food is grown under the no-tillage system. Other benefits are reduced use of fuel, avoidance of soil compaction, increased water infiltration, reduced pollution of waterways from runoff and improved air quality due to reduced wind erosion of bare soil.[104] How great an effect no-tillage can have on soil carbon sequestration is debated and will depend on various factors such as the soil characteristics, crops, practices, climate, etc.[105] Sowing and other processes require specialized equipment, typically a disc seeder which opens a slit in the soil and deposes the seed and chemical fertilizer simultaneously underground. Many adaptations to such seed drills already exist and recent advances in GPS-controlled precision agriculture machines are enabling soil disturbance and compaction to be minimized.[106]

In practice, adoption of the no-tillage approach often goes through three steps when transforming agricultural practices into full conservation agriculture systems, namely: no-burning, no ploughing and growing a cover crop. Experience shows that reaching the last stage can be difficult for many farmers and the process can take several years.[107] The costs related to the acquisition of new equipment are also a common barrier to adoption.[108]

More sustainable weeding technologies

One of the major environmental drawbacks of the no-tillage approach is widespread reliance on herbicides for weeding, such as glyphosate or similar compounds under trademarks such as Roundup, Touchdown and Buster. Development of herbicide resistance in weeds is a related serious concern. Alternatives to herbicides are being developed and several bio-based products certified for biological agriculture are available, which could provide an option with fewer health risks for both soils and consumers. Especially in South America, the use of crop rotation and cover crops, some with allelopathic benefits (producing biochemicals that hamper growth of others), and mechanical weeding have been able to reduce dependency on herbicides and synthetic fertilizers.[109] Integrated weed management and careful use of crop rotation and cover crops may reduce the amount of herbicide used, but whether herbicides can be fully eliminated is still a focus of agronomic research.[110]

Many forms of mechanical weeding exist but most have in common the fact that they must be pulled by a tractor or similar heavy machinery, in direct opposition to the principle of no-till. But here also innovation and technology may offer alternatives. Weeding robots, being smaller and lighter, may provide a feasible option for mechanical weeding in no-till systems. Swarms of lightweight weeding robots could potentially eliminate the need for herbicides. Other solutions opt for single units with solar panels and/or swappable batteries that allow for extended periods of operation, which makes up for their sometimes-slow operating speed. Some solutions use optical sensors to identify weeds and accurately apply small doses of herbicide thus greatly reducing the use of chemicals. If spraying is done by drones guided by images of the field that identify areas where spraying is needed, the amount of herbicide used can be reduced with fewer wheels on the ground. Business models based on robot rental are helping to make them more economically attractive to farmers.

More ways to recover soil carbon

Other forms of regenerative agriculture, such as organic farming, agroecology, silvopasture (integration of trees and grazing), climate-smart agriculture, agroforestry and permaculture are all complex and not mutually exclusive agricultural systems that can have substantial positive impacts on soil carbon in specific geographies. It is often a matter of rethinking existing practices – for example, planting livestock fodder such as nitrogen-fixating alfalfa as a cover crop between rows of other crops where livestock can graze and deposit manure. Land taken out of cultivation and used for solar panels may also accumulate soil carbon. If the land with solar panels is cultivated, it has the potential to both increase soil carbon and replace fossil fuel. New agrivoltaic arrays allow more sunlight to reach the plants beneath, while some crops, such as cauliflower and cabbage, are shade tolerant. Tomatoes, berries, grapes and fruit trees have also been shown to perform well in agrivoltaic scenarios. For some crops, the protection against extreme heat makes up for the reduced direct sunlight exposure.[111] Implementing agrivoltaics on rooftops in urban areas is also gaining attention.[112]

In summary, increasing soil carbon can be achieved based on readily available measures that do not require large investments or more land, have a small water footprint and trigger important co-benefits.

Increasing soil carbon can be achieved based on readily available measures that do not require large investments or more land, have a small water footprint and trigger important co-benefits

Innovation examples

Photo: Getty Images / © phuttaphat tipsana

COMET-Farm – a whole farm and ranch carbon and GHG accounting system

The online platform allows farmers to enter details about their land and practices and, based on this information, calculate their carbon emissions. Data required include field and soil characteristics, previous crops, management practices and use of inputs and fuel. Fields can be identified and demarcated in satellite images and the system can be used with no prior training. Once the farm data are entered, a carbon footprint report is issued and the farmer can simulate various options for reducing emissions and sequestering carbon. A stand-alone tool, COMET-Energy can be used to assess emission reductions based on planned fuel savings. COMET-Farm is an initiative from the United States Department of Agriculture Natural Resources Conservation Service and Colorado State University. It is available in the United States.

- Contact: WIPO GREEN Database

Photo: Getty Images / © Madalin Olariu

Farmer Managed Natural Regeneration

Farmer Managed Natural Regeneration (FMNR) is a cost-effective land restoration technique aimed at alleviating poverty and hunger among subsistence farmers by enhancing food and timber production while increasing climate resilience. Through FMNR, trees and shrubs are systematically regrown and managed from felled stumps, sprouting root systems or seeds, contributing to improved soil fertility, reduced erosion and increased biodiversity. Integrated with crops and grazing pastures, regrown trees also provide additional benefits, such as doubling crop yields, providing timber, firewood, fodder and shade for livestock, and offering wild foods for nutrition and medication. The FMNR Hub, backed by World Vision Australia's Natural Resources Management unit, has coordinated global development projects, providing technical support, building scientific credibility, advocating for FMNR and raising project funds. FMNR is now implemented in several countries worldwide, including Ethiopia, Ghana, Indonesia, Kenya, Mali, Rwanda, Senegal, Somalia, Timor Leste, Uganda and the United Republic of Tanzania.

- Contact: WIPO GREEN Database

Technology solutions

Proven technologies

Soil carbon: biochar from oil palm empty fruit bunches (EFB)

Agricultural Environmental Research Institute

Photo: © Agricultural Environmental Research Institute

BPSI Agricultural Environment, Indonesia, has developed a simple technology for producing biochar from agricultural waste, such as corncobs, rice husks and EFB. Biogas produced from cow dung is used for the pyrolysis process at 500°C for biochar production. After pyrolysis, the biochar is sprayed with water (to avoid complete combustion), sun-dried, then milled using a grinder. The smoke from the pyrolysis process is liquefied through a condensation process. The resulting liquid smoke or wood vinegar can be used for producing antiseptic soap, food preservatives (for meat or fish), cosmetics and vegetable pesticide ingredients. Activated carbon can also be produced in a pyrolysis process at higher temperatures (800–900°C).

- Contracting type: For sale
- Technology level: Low
- Country of origin: Indonesia
- Availability: Indonesia
- Contact: WIPO GREEN Database

Soil carbon: quantifying on-farm GHG emissions and soil carbon sequestration

The Cool Farm Alliance

Photo: Getty Images/© Rifka Hayati

The Cool Farm Alliance offers the Cool Farm Tool, an online calculator that allows farmers to measure and manage their environmental impacts. In development for more than 10 years, the technology tracks GHG emissions, water usage, biodiversity, and food loss and waste. It helps farmers manage supply chains, communicate environmental benefits and engage suppliers. The tool provides quick estimations, stimulates thinking about management practices and tailors results to specific fields. It encourages good agricultural practices and has been adopted by multinational companies.

- Contracting type: Free or with membership
- Technology level: Medium
- Country of origin: United Kingdom
- Availability: Worldwide
- Contact: WIPO GREEN Database

Climate-smart agriculture: agrivoltaics – solar panels on farmland

SolarEdge

Photo: Getty Images/© Miropa

SolarEdge offers agrivoltaics solutions, combining solar energy and farming on the same farmland. This innovative approach promotes sustainable farming practices while generating additional revenue and offsetting electricity costs. By elevating the solar panels, the system minimizes the impact of severe weather on the crops beneath and provides shade that keeps the soil moist, reducing irrigation expenses. The optimized solution incorporates an AI-powered tracker control system that automatically adjusts solar panel angles based on sunlight, weather and agricultural seasonal patterns. SolarEdge's Monitoring Platform ensures efficient dual-use farming by tracking system performance data, enabling immediate fault detection and facilitating remote maintenance, thus maximizing solar production and uptime.

- Contracting type: For sale/service
- Technology level: Medium
- Country of origin: Israel
- Availability: Worldwide
- Contact: WIPO GREEN Database

Soil management: mobile soil analyzer

Pronova

Photo: Getty Images/© Viktoriia Oleinichenko

The AMOLA® Agrar mobile laboratory allows quick, easy and reliable soil evaluation to be carried out in the laboratory or in the field. The mobile lab contains all necessary reagents and equipment for determining the presence of the main readily soluble nutrients available to plants: nitrogen, phosphorus and potassium. The analyses are based on the extraction of soil nutrients into liquids, which are treated with color reagents. The AMOLA® base unit performs an accurate measurement of the color of the reagents and provides the measurement results. It is useful for applications in agriculture, horticulture, tree nurseries and composting plants. AMOLA® is also used by consultants and plant production specialists.

- Contracting type: For sale
- Technology level: Medium
- Country of origin: Germany
- Availability: Worldwide
- Contact: WIPO GREEN Database

Soil management: mobile compost-turning machine

Shunzhi Machinery

Photo: Getty Images/ © Sergio Cervera Moreno

The Shunzhi fertilizer compost machine is a complete set of mobile equipment for the production of bio-organic fertilizer. It uses a rotary cutter shaft to mix, raise and stack the fertilizer base raw materials. The advanced fermentation process is designed according to the principle of high-quality fermentation so the fermentation bacteria have space to function optimally. This allows for production of better-quality organic fertilizers. The operation can take place in the open field or in a shed or greenhouse.

- Contracting type: For sale
- Technology level: Medium
- Country of origin: China
- Availability: Worldwide
- Contact: WIPO GREEN Database

Soil management: agricultural hydrogel

Plantagel

Photo: © Plantagel

Plantagel is a plant hydrogel, also known as potassium polyacrylate or hydroabsorbent crystals. It is a superabsorbent potassium polymer that retains up to 300 times its weight in water. Its use in agriculture retains nutrient-rich water at the roots of the plant, preventing it from draining into the subsoil and keeping it available to the plant rhizome, thus saving up to 85 percent of water, fertilizers and irrigation. It fulfills a very similar function to sodium hydrogel (used in diapers and sanitary napkins), but sodium is harmful to plants and soil. Potassium is also a fertilizer that enhances the quality of both plant and soil. Plantagel has a useful life in the soil for up to five years.

- Contracting type: For sale
- Technology level: Low
- Country of origin: Peru
- Availability: South America
- Contact: WIPO GREEN Database

Frontier technologies

Soil carbon: soil carbon platform for farmers
Agreena

Photo: Getty Images / izzetugutmen

Fintech company Agreena's software platform allows farmers to plan, track and validate their transitions to regenerative agriculture. The company helps farmers build a revenue stream and overcome technical barriers. It offers a simple way for farmers to plan and implement carbon emission reducing processes in their agriculture, and based on which the company verify and issue carbon credits making conversion to climate-smart agriculture economically beneficial for farmers. Agricultural practices include crop rotation, no-till, use of cover crops, etc. By using satellite images, advanced modeling and other techniques, the company can assess emission reductions or soil carbon gains.

- Contracting type: For service
- Technology level: Medium
- Country of origin: Denmark
- Availability: Worldwide
- Contact: WIPO GREEN Database

Soil carbon: microbial products that fixate carbon and other plant nutrients in the soil
Andes

Photo: Getty Images / VR19

Andes offers a product that utilizes microorganisms to remove CO_2 from the atmosphere effectively and permanently. These beneficial microorganisms are applied to the soil alongside agricultural seeds, such as corn and wheat. The microorganisms work symbiotically with plant roots, accelerating the conversion of CO_2 into minerals. By integrating seamlessly with existing farm operations, Andes' microorganism technology transforms agricultural fields into carbon sinks while also supporting food production. The build-up of minerals in agricultural fields yields several benefits, including improved water drainage, increased soil nutrient content, reduction in plant diseases and stabilized soil organic matter.

- Contracting type: For sale
- Technology level: Low
- Country of origin: United States
- Availability: United States
- Contact: WIPO GREEN Database

Soil carbon: soil microbiome – soil genetic analysis
GoSolos Ltda

GoSolos performs soil microbiome analyzes by DNA sequencing to assess microbial diversity and soil biological activity. From a soil sample collected by the customer and sent to the company's laboratory, the technology can identify the microbial species present in the soil and provide information on the microbial composition, the risk of soil disease, soil health and biological activity. To help interpret the results, GoSolos offers a technical delivery that allows the customer to clearly understand the data obtained and make decisions about soil management. The analysis offered by the technology is important for identifying beneficial and pathogenic species present in the soil, enabling preventive measures to maintain soil health and promote better plant growth.

- Contracting type: For service
- Technology level: Medium
- Country of origin: Brazil
- Availability: Brazil
- Contact: WIPO GREEN Database

Soil management: peptide-empowered insecticides
Vestaron

Vestaron specializes in peptide-based crop protection for fruits, vegetables, ornamentals and other specialty crops, offering novel, effective chemical solutions that target neuromuscular systems in insects. Their peptides overcome resistance issues and offer a safe profile for workers, beneficial organisms and the environment. Vestaron's approach combines synthetic pesticides with the safety and sustainability of biologicals. Their insecticides can be used independently or in rotation with conventional insecticides, making them valuable tools for integrated pest management and resistance management programs. Their range of products includes Spear RC for row crops, Spear LEP for fruits and vegetables, Spear-T for greenhouse pests, and Leprotec for caterpillars in various crops. Naturally occurring peptides are screened for efficacy and safety and the genes for the peptide are inserted into yeast strains used in the fermentation production process.

- Contracting type: For sale
- Technology level: Low
- Country of origin: United States
- Availability: Mexico, United States
- Contact: WIPO GREEN Database

Soil management: large drones for precision crop spraying
Hylio

Photo: Getty Images/© Kimwun

Hylio offers precision crop care through its autonomous AgroDrones. The drone systems provide user-friendly, reliable crop-spraying solutions, optimizing crop treatments and transforming traditional agricultural practices. The comprehensive system includes precision application, intelligent spray with digital flowmeters, real-time kinematic (RTK) compatibility for centimetre-level accuracy and autonomous operation with swarm control. The AgroDrones are designed for reliability and safety, equipped with millimetre-wave radar to avoid obstacles and redundant systems to handle component failures. Hylio's Agrosol ground control software platform streamlines crop protection, allowing farmers to plan treatments, command their drone fleet and analyze application data.

- Contracting type: For sale/service
- Technology level: Medium
- Country of origin: United States
- Availability: Canada, Colombia, Costa Rica, Dominican Republic, El Salvador, Ghana, Guatamala, Honduras, United States
- Contact: WIPO GREEN Database

Soil management: fleet of small weeding robots
Greenfield Weedbot

Photo: Getty Images/© piranka

The company develops small robots that can do several agricultural tasks, such as preparing a mulch layer for seeding, weeding and planting cover crops. Some of the robots are still in development. The Weedbot performs simple non-selective weeding between rows of crops. It repeatedly cuts the weed close to the ground. Working in swarms, the robots can replace herbicides and combat herbicide-resistant weeds. The robots can be rented, making the technology more economically accessible for farmers.

- Contracting type: For rent
- Technology level: Medium
- Country of origin: United States
- Availability: United States
- Contact: WIPO GREEN Database

Soil carbon: implementation service for regenerative agriculture

LandPrint Soluções Tecnologicas Ltda

Photo: Getty Images/© andreswd

LandPrint scales regenerative agriculture in the agri-food value chain through certified digital measurements and environmental data, which are used by farmers, corporations and financial institutions to implement, monitor and finance the regenerative transition. Digital tools measure and assess the adoption of regenerative practices and the environmental quality of a farm or group of farms, issuing certified environmental data. Financial institutions and corporations utilize LandPrint's measurement and scoring system to develop financial incentives that assist farmers in adopting regenerative agriculture and nature-based solutions profitably and at a large scale, while demonstrating compliance with environmental, social and governance (ESG) and Sustainable Development Goal (SDG) objectives. Farmers use LandPrint's measurement system to monitor the environmental quality of their farms and plan future actions based on incentives promoted by the financial and corporate sectors.

- Contracting type: For service
- Technology level: Medium
- Country of origin: Brazil
- Availability: Brazil
- Contact: WIPO GREEN Database

Soil carbon: plants for enhanced carbon capture

Living Carbon

Photo: Getty Images/© skynesher

Living Carbon is a company dedicated to responsibly rebalancing the planet's carbon cycle by harnessing the power of plants. The company views the challenge of climate instability as a significant opportunity for global mobilization and technological advancements that restore ecosystems and enhance biodiversity. Living Carbon utilizes advanced biotechnology to develop solutions for efficiently removing carbon from the atmosphere. The technology focuses on generating high-quality carbon removal projects with unique co-benefits. The company's biotech seedlings can capture more carbon on less land using abandoned or degraded land for reforestation. Living Carbon's expertise spans various areas, including tissue culture, gene discovery, gene editing, enzymology and tree growth, enabling the company to enhance natural traits in plants to stabilize the climate. It has planted over 170,000 trees in Pennsylvania, Georgia and Ohio, including around 8,900 photosynthesis-enhanced poplars.

- Contracting type: For service
- Technology level: Low
- Country of origin: United States
- Availability: United States
- Contact: WIPO GREEN Database

Forest management: drone-based aerial ignition for wildfire suppression

Drone Amplified

Photo: Getty Images / © photos

IGNIS is a patented technology and fire control system that enables aerial ignition during wildfires using drones. Aerial ignition involves burning up existing fuels ahead of a wildfire in order to starve the fire and create a fuel break – so called prescribed fires. The technology allows for aerial ignition from a distance during conditions that are unsafe for humans, for example at night or during large and smoky fires. The drones carry "dragon eggs" or fireballs that ignite when they land on the ground. The fireballs contain potassium permanganate which, when mixed with glycol, starts a chemical reaction resulting in a fire. Some 400 of these fireballs can be secured to one drone. The company Drone Amplified pioneered the technology using unmanned aerial system fire ignition. The drones are controlled using an app designed for firefighters. The IGNIS drone system can cover 1,600 acres in a day.

- Contracting type: For sale
- Technology level: Medium
- Country of origin: United States
- Availability: United States
- Contact: WIPO GREEN Database

Horizon technologies

Soil carbon: basalt for carbon sequestration and improved soil health

Lithos

Photo: Getty Images / © Tashka2000

Lithos' technology offers a solution to accelerate mineral weathering using basalt application on croplands. By spreading basalt, they increase the amount of dissolved inorganic carbon, leading to eventual storage as ocean carbonates. This process effectively removes CO_2 from the atmosphere while simultaneously promoting crop growth. The technology utilizes novel soil models and machine learning to optimize CO_2 removal, ensuring maximum efficiency. Basalt reacts with rainwater, converting atmospheric CO_2 to dissolved bicarbonate and releasing essential nutrients into the soil. The dissolved bicarbonate is transported via rivers and streams to the coastal ocean, where it remains stable for millennia. Lithos closely monitors river networks to prevent leakage and tracks the carbon's life cycle from application to permanent deposition as calcium carbonate minerals on the ocean floor.

- Contracting type: N/A
- Technology level: Low
- Country of origin: United States
- Availability: N/A
- Contact: WIPO GREEN Database

Climate-smart agriculture: vertical agrivoltaics

TotalEnergies

Photo: Getty Images / C. pixabay

TotalEnergies and its partners have developed three pilot vertical agrivoltaic demonstration plots in France to study the impact of solar panels on crops and compile a repository of agronomic benefits for its agrivoltaic projects. Solar panels on fields may influence crop yields in several ways, both positive and negative. After implementation of the pilots, it was found that a yield increase was observed across all plots – 100 kg per hectare increase for wheat compared to previous harvests and 200 kg for lentils. Wheat protein levels also increased by 2 percent. This may be the result of the wind protection that installed panels provide for plants. The company is now looking to confirm these results with its other 140 agrivoltaic projects in various stages of development.

- Contracting type: N/A
- Technology level: Medium
- Country of origin: France
- Availability: N/A
- Contact: WIPO GREEN Database

Soil management: autonomous weeding robot using a high-precision microwave gun

Robotec

Photo: Getty Images / Sterras59

Robotec is a Ukrainian company that develops different types of autonomous robots. The first of these, "Agrotec", is used to automatically detect weeds by analyzing images received through its stereo camera using proprietary AI algorithms. After detecting the weeds, the robot kills them using a focused microwave beam. The speed of the robot can be adjusted depending on the density of weeds detected so that no weeds are missed. The images can also be used to determine whether the crops themselves have been infected by any pathogens. The company is also investigating the use of an ultrasonic hydrogen peroxide fog generator to eradicate fungi and viruses.

- Contracting type: N/A
- Technology level: Medium
- Country of origin: Ukraine
- Availability: N/A
- Contact: WIPO GREEN Database

Soil management: advanced smart agricultural robots supporting biodiverse farming

Pixelfarming Robotics

Photo: Getty Images / © Igor Borisenko

Robot One is one of the smart agricultural robots designed by Pixelfarming Robotics to control weeds without the use of artificial chemicals. It is designed to control plants and weeds autonomously, based on computer vision and can be equipped with tools for specific crop treatment. It works on the principle of "Scan and Act". High-resolution cameras make a scan of the field and AI trains the robot to recognize the crop. By choosing a tool such as a strimmer or laser, the user can decide what action the robot must take to remove the weeds.

- Contracting type: N/A
- Technology level: Medium
- Country of origin: Netherlands (Kingdom of the)
- Availability: N/A
- Contact: WIPO GREEN Database

Soil management: high-precision smart sprayer

Ecorobotix

Photo: Getty Images / © PhotoTalk

The Swiss company Ecorobotix has developed ARA, a high-precision smart sprayer which is mounted to a traditional tractor. This spraying module is "smart" in that it collects 10 images per second and then uses AI to determine what is the crop and what is a weed. Different types of treatments can be applied either to the weed or to the crop depending on the time of the season. For instance, a herbicide could be applied to weeds while an insecticide or fungicide can be applied to the crop only. The data generated are saved in the cloud and can be used to improve subsequent treatment methods based on long-term trends. The sprayer itself is 6 m in length and is comprised of 156 nozzles, which are adjustable in height. A tablet is provided as part of the system so that the driver can monitor the rate of use of each particular chemical from within the tractor cabin.

- Contracting type: N/A
- Technology level: Medium
- Country of origin: Switzerland
- Availability: N/A
- Contact: WIPO GREEN Database

Forest management: AI-based real-time fire identification

EXINN Technology Center and Think Bank Albania Foundation

Photo: Getty Images / E+ Cristian Martin

The technology is a system of real-time fire identification using drone technology and AI. Through a combination of existing tools, satellite technology and products, the inventors aim to develop real-time maps with information about fires. A specifically developed AI model would then be able to use the real-time map feed to detect fires, without the need for human supervision, after which it would automatically notify a drone or a fleet of drones of the relevant coordinates. The drones would be fitted with image-recognition technology specifically trained to detect the sources of fire, as well as fire-extinguishing balls which could be dropped into the source of fire. This automated system could enable fast, cost-effective and safe firefighting.

- Contracting type: N/A
- Technology level: High
- Country of origin: Albania
- Availability: N/A
- Contact: WIPO GREEN Database

Photo: Getty Images / beemore

Rice cultivation

Rice is the staple food of some 3.5 billion people, predominantly in Asia. It accounts for around 8 percent in weight of the world's crop production with the biggest producers being China, India, Bangladesh and Indonesia[113] in order of production. Rice is cultivated on more than 169 million hectares globally.

Flooded rice fields are major GHG emitters

Almost all rice is cultivated as wet rice in fields that are covered in water for most of the growing season. Rice can also be planted on dry soils, also called upland rice, but one of the big advantages of wet rice is that weeds pose much less of a problem in waterlogged fields. Wet rice systems are often labor intensive. Manual transplanting of rice plants, where seedlings are grown in nurseries for 15–40 days, requires up to 30 labor-days per hectare.[114] Transplanting gives the rice a competitive advantage over weeds and reduces the time the rice is in the field, which can allow for two or three crops in a season. The transplanting of seedlings can also be done using machines, which further shortens the cultivation time and saves water, hence reducing GHG emissions.[115]

The practice of using waterlogged rice fields (paddies) also makes rice production one of the major GHG emitters. The anaerobic conditions in the waterlogged paddies lead to emissions of methane when organic matter, mostly straw, is decomposed by microorganisms. Globally, wet rice production accounts for 10–12 percent of the world's methane emissions, which translates into 1.3–1.5 percent of global GHG emissions. In terms of methane and nitrous oxide (N_2O) alone, studies indicate that rice has a global warming potential between four and six times that of other major crops per ton of grain produced.[116] This figure includes wheat and maize but does not take into consideration direct CO_2 emissions. In Southeast Asia, rice is the origin of 25–33 percent of regional methane emissions.[117, 118, 119] Rice cultivation also emits N_2O from excess fertilizers and CO_2, partly from the more than 80 percent of rice straw that is burned in the fields postharvest globally. Rice straw has short fibers which potentially make it useful for the pulp board and paper industry and it can also be used in cattle feed and bedding.[120] Postharvest crop losses in the drying and milling process are between 10 and 12 percent in Indonesia and Viet Nam. If these losses could be avoided, fewer crops would be needed, with corresponding emission reductions.

As figure 3.5 shows, there are significant variations in methane emissions between the major rice-producing economies. This finding alone indicates that there are indeed ways to reduce the emissions generated by rice production.

Globally, wet rice production accounts for 10–12 percent of the world's methane emissions, which translates into 1.3–1.5 percent of global GHG emissions

Figure 3.5 Methane emissions in rice farming, 2018

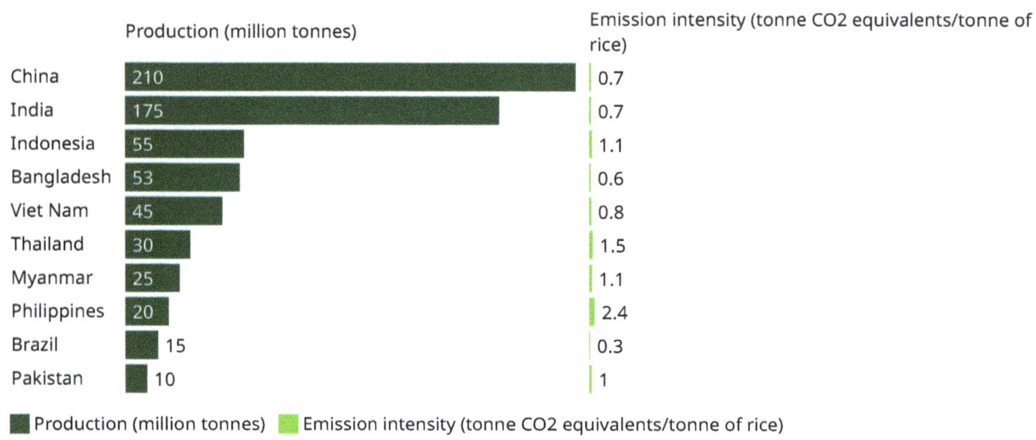

Source: Umali-Deininger, 2022.

Rice cultivation provides a livelihood for at least 150 million smallholder farmers with less than one hectare of land and most of them are poor.[121] China, the world's largest producer, cultivates 20 percent of the paddy fields globally, producing 29 percent of the world's rice and also 29 percent of global paddy field methane emissions. Smallholders dominate Chinese agriculture, cultivating 98 percent of the country's cropland. However, associated as it is with low salaries and hard work, rice cultivation is often unable to compete with better paid industrial jobs in the major cities of the south.[122] In the longer term, this could pave the way for larger farms with more advanced technology to replace labor and optimize systems for lower methane emissions while increasing productivity. Such systems include connected sensors that facilitate optimal water management, insecticidal lights, low-carbon digital twin systems, precision farming and autonomous farming machines. Potentially, deployment of such technologies could be supported by carbon credit schemes.[123] A study from Thailand indicated that larger and more productive farms had 11 percent lower GHG emissions than individual smallholdings as well as lower costs and higher profits.[124] How such findings can be translated into practical applications is, however, uncertain. Restructuring the entire rice sector may prove socially and economically impossible, and promoting tools and practices used in more productive systems among smallholders may therefore be more realistic.

System changes reduce emissions

Wet rice cultivation is an intricate and tightly controlled process, but due to the strong dominance of smallholder farmers, who are often poor, the degree of mechanization is low. Therefore, in order to reduce emissions from rice production on a larger scale, any changes introduced must have minimal risk and capital requirements, and also lead to increased productivity and income. Rice cultivation has already seen dramatic changes. The green revolution that started in the 1960s introduced improved rice varieties, fertilizer and water management, which led to very significant increases in productivity. In China, the adoption of hybrid rice varieties led to rice production increases of 44 percent on 14 percent less land, feeding an extra 60 million people annually.[125] The development of hybrid or improved rice varieties continues with the widespread adoption of new dwarf varieties while other improvements target shortening the growing period from 160–200 days to 110–130 days. In certain areas this could allow a third rainy season crop to be cultivated.

One of the nuclei of the green revolution, the International Rice Research Institute (IRRI) in the Philippines, is now promoting the System of Rice Intensification (SRI), which is a set of techniques that can significantly increase yields. It is based on four main principles: (1) early, quick and healthy plant establishment; (2) reduced plant density for optimized utilization of nutrients, water and sunlight; (3) soil enrichment with organic matter; and (4) temporary drainage by alternate wetting and drying rather than continuous flooding.[126] Combined with selection of seeds that are well adapted to local conditions, SRI can increase plant productivity and reduce water use through temporary drainage. SRI is not necessarily an organic farming system and often incorporates synthetic fertilizers and other chemical inputs. However, SRI methods advocate for an optimized use of external synthetic inputs which should reduce over time as the soil organic matter is increased and the soil biota become more abundant and diverse. It can increase resilience and can contribute to mitigation by reducing fertilizer and pesticide use and reduce methane emissions by up to a third when fields are drained at least once in a growing season.[127, 128] However, SRI can be labor intensive, which may prove to be a limiting factor.

In order to reduce emissions from rice production on a larger scale, any changes introduced must have minimal risk and capital requirements, and also lead to increased productivity and income

SRI is part of the suite of climate-smart agriculture (CSA) practices which seek to increase agricultural productivity while reducing emissions and increasing resilience. Applying a holistic approach to agricultural development, CSA can target improvements in land and soil fertility management, water use and improved irrigation, crop and livestock variety development and choice, cropping pattern and calendar, and combination of production systems, such as forests, cropping, aquaculture, animal husbandry, etc. Implementation of CSA is highly context dependent and will require research for local adaptation as well as efficient extension services. The approach is strongly promoted by the FAO, the World Bank, the Consultative Group on International Agricultural Research (CGIAR) research program on Climate Change, Agriculture and Food Security and several other organizations. Private agribusiness companies are also increasingly promoting CSA among their smallholder suppliers.

Less water in rice fields reduces methane emissions

Cultivation of wet rice demands a lot of water. In Asia, between 1,300 and 1,500 mm of water is typically required, depending on soil composition. To produce 1 kg of rice, an average of 1,432 liters are used, and 35–43 percent of global irrigation water is allocated to wet rice production.[129] This also makes rice production vulnerable to changes in rainfall due to climate change. For example, in 2022 the area planted with rice in India was 13 percent less than normal due to lack of rainfall.[130] The precise control of irrigation water demands cooperation and coordination among farmers, adherence to specific rules and the construction of intricate irrigation canals, weirs, etc.

One good example of a technique that embraces both SRI and CSA practices and that can reduce both dependency on irrigation water and methane emissions is the practice of alternate wetting and drying (AWD). This simple practice only requires a perforated plastic tube in the ground and good control of the irrigation water. Research has shown that wet rice does not need to be flooded during the whole growing season but can alternate between dry and wet conditions. The tube reveals the level of water in the soil during the dry phase, and when a predetermined level is reached the field is flooded again for a period of time. This practice can reduce methane emission by up to 70 percent (with an average 48 percent reduction) and save up to 30 percent water.[131] However, the control over irrigation required to drain a rice field during the growing season may not be possible in all systems. In some areas it rains so much that draining the paddies is difficult, and in other regions it may require coordination with other rice farmers and upgrading of water management, especially in gravity-fed irrigation systems. Policy issues, water-pricing schemes and lack of extension services may also act as barriers to AWD implementation.[132] Adoption of AWD is more feasible in pump-based irrigation systems than in systems that rely on surface water and irrigation canals. AWD also works best with accurately levelled fields that avoid high points drying out too much. Using lasers for precise field levelling is a technology that can help reduce cultivation time, as crops mature more evenly, save water and make fertilizer use more efficient.[133] An unleveled field requires 80–100 mm more water than a level one to cover completely.[134]

To produce 1 kg of rice, an average of 1,432 liters are used, and 35–43 percent of global irrigation water is allocated to wet rice production

In China and several other countries, some farmers cultivate rice on raised beds of soil and flood only the furrows in-between the beds, thus reducing water use as well as methane emissions, reportedly by up to 80 percent. The furrows can remain flooded all year round, which further eases irrigation management requirements.[135]

Another option for reducing the waterlogging of rice crops is dry seeded rice, where the grains are sown onto dry fields as are most other crops. This can be done manually or using machines and requires much less labor than the transplanting of rice seedlings. It also saves water and, because the soils are in an aerobic condition throughout most of the growing season, it reduces methane emissions.[136]

The potential of upland rice and technology

Upland rice, growing rice on rain-fed (dry) soils, is a common practice in the highlands of Southeast Asia which avoids the methane emissions associated with wet rice. When waterlogging no longer protects against most weeds, weeding must be carried out, mostly manually. However, planting rice in dry fields combined with weeding robots and other technologies could possibly be a pathway to almost methane-free rice production. Yields for upland rice can be as high as for wet rice, but following current practices on more marginal sloping fields in relatively low-input systems, they are normally lower. Development of short-duration improved varieties that are resistant to the common rice blast fungus, to drought and to cold mountainous climates, could increase the potential of upland rice.[137] To what extent it could replace wet rice and thus eliminate most of the methane emissions is still an open question.

An alternative option of growing wet rice on upland fields using a film of mulch to maintain anaerobic conditions and hence reducing the risk of rice blast disease has also been tried. Yields obtained in trials were comparable with wet rice yields and had better nutrient composition. The potential methane emission reduction gains are still unknown.[138]

Monitoring and collecting methane

Methane emission reductions can also be achieved through collection of methane from paddy soils in biogas reactors. These can be simple rubber coatings over an in-field gas collection bed of soil mixed with rice straw. In a Japanese system (production of biomethane gas (G) as renewable energy (E) from a tanbo (T), which means "paddy field" in Japanese) the sampling beds are connected to gas collection bags with claims that the system is able to produce up to 100 liters/day per m^2.[139] However, the process requires investment in both materials and collection bed preparation and may therefore be beyond the reach of most farmers.

Measurement of methane from paddy fields can be challenging. The most common method is the use of measurement boxes on the ground to capture the methane. Another common method is eddy covariance, which can register gas flux. Recent research has established parameters for correlation of eddy measurements with instrument height, allowing for more precise measurement of methane from paddy fields.[140] Monitoring and verification are necessary to unlock funding that supports sustainable rice farming. For example, in Thailand green loans, improved crop insurance, socially responsible contract farming, multi-donor funds, carbon credits and green bonds for sustainable rice are available.[141]

Innovation examples

Photo: Getty Images / © bluesky85

Sustainable agriculture transformation project in Viet Nam

Farmers in Viet Nam's Mekong Delta have demonstrated that methane emissions can be significantly reduced by combining several CSA practices. As part of a project supported by the World Bank, farmers adopted practices such as AWD, improved irrigation management, field leveling, use of high-yield and drought-, pest- and flood-resistant rice varieties, improved tillage practices, and soil analyses and targeted fertilizer use. The project supported the Vietnamese Government's 1M-5R program (one "Must", stipulating the use of improved seeds, and five "Reductions" – in irrigation water, seeding rate, nitrogen fertilizer, pesticides and postharvest losses during drying and milling) covering almost a quarter of a million rice farmers. Farmers' yields were increased by 10–18 percent and profits by about 29 percent, while GHG emissions were reduced by 7.3 tons CO_2eq/yr per hectare and water use was reduced by 15–40 percent.[142, 143]

Photo: Getty Images / © phanasitti

Liberian farmers use solar-powered irrigation to enable a second rice crop

In Liberia's Bong County, farmers are implementing solar-powered irrigation and SRI to increase productivity in the face of climate change. Affordable and reliable irrigation coupled with improved water management are therefore important measures which may help farmers obtain a stable and sufficient harvest. Implemented as part of a UN Climate Technology Centre and Network (CTCN) pilot project involving several local partners, the current rice cultivation practices in the county were analyzed and new technological solutions designed and implemented as a pilot alongside development of local capacities. The solar-powered irrigation system made water management more affordable and, in combination with AWD, water is applied intermittently which reduces pressure on local water sources. SRI practices, such as optimal spacing of seedlings, is also increasing productivity. The initiative enables the farmers to grow a second rice crop in the rainy season, potentially followed by a crop of vegetables.[144]

Technology solutions

Proven technologies

Improved cultivation: direct seeded rice
KS Agrotech

Photo: Getty Images/© Rio Prastyo

Direct seeded rice has emerged as an economically viable and environmentally promising alternative to Asia's most dominant method, known as puddled transplanted rice. It addresses several major drivers of rural change in the region, such as rising labor and water scarcity and increased profitability by reducing cultivation costs. The Indian company KS Agrotech produces a range of farm machines, including the direct seeder. It can plant seeds directly in the field without preparation or flooding and saves time and labor. The dry seed is drilled into the ground at a depth of 2-3 cm.

- Contracting type: For sale
- Technology level: Low
- Country of origin: India
- Availability: India
- Contact: WIPO GREEN Database

Improved cultivation: rice transplanter machine
Yancheng Shunyu Agricultural Machinery Co., Ltd.

Photo: Getty Images/© fz750

Rice transplanting is a slow and laborious process, typically done by hand, one plant at a time. Transplanter machines can speed up the process significantly, saving labor costs and reducing the time the crop is in the field, thereby also potentially reducing water use and methane emissions. The company provides a wide variety of machines, ranging from small, two-row hand-operated machines to eight-row self-driving units, which can dispense fertilizer at the same time.

- Contracting type: For sale
- Technology level: Medium
- Country of origin: China
- Availability: China
- Contact: WIPO GREEN Database

Improved cultivation: sturdy lasers for accurate levelling of paddy fields

Spectra

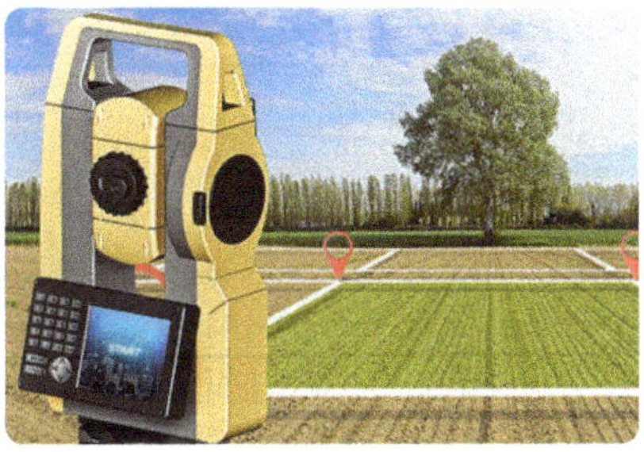

Photo: Getty Images / © Francesco Scatena

Spectra offers a range of cutting-edge grade lasers which can be used for levelling paddy fields and thereby optimizing water use and facilitating efficient periodic drainage. Designed for precision performance, these lasers are highly accurate over long distances. One model features automatic self-levelling, grade matching for unknown grades and a digital readout receiver. The company's grade lasers contribute to reducing errors and time consumption, aligning with environmental sustainability and precision needs.

- Contracting type: For sale
- Technology level: Medium
- Country of origin: United States
- Availability: Worldwide
- Contact: WIPO GREEN Database

Improved cultivation: alternate wetting and drying (AWD)

IRRI

Photo © IRRI

AWD is a water-saving technology that allows farmers to reduce irrigation water consumption in rice fields by 30 percent without yield penalty. AWD has been proven to effectively mitigate GHG emissions, specifically methane, from rice production by between 30 and 70 percent. During the dry phases, the methane-producing bacteria are inhibited, thus reducing GHG emissions. AWD entails periodic draining of the field to a predetermined threshold and re-flooding. A practical way to implement AWD safely is by using a "field water tube" ("pani pipe") to monitor the water depth on the field. After irrigation, the water depth will gradually decrease. When the water level has dropped to about 15 cm below the surface of the soil, irrigation should be applied to re-flood the field to a depth of about 5 cm. From one week before to one week after flowering, the field should be kept flooded, topping up to a depth of 5 cm as needed. After flowering, during grain filling and ripening, the water level can be allowed to drop again to 15 cm below the soil surface before re-irrigation. AWD can be started a few weeks (1–2 weeks) after transplanting. When many weeds are present, AWD should be postponed for 2–3 weeks to assist weed suppression by the ponded water.

- Contracting type: N/A
- Technology level: Medium
- Country of origin: Philippines
- Availability: Worldwide
- Contact: WIPO GREEN Database

Reducing loss: rice husk briquette machines, livestock bedding and water purifiers
TROMSO Co. Ltd

Photo: © Tromso

The company offers briquette machines that convert rice husks into biofuel (briquettes), biochar machines to add value to crop residues and water purifiers which incorporate rice husk activated carbon. The briquette machines add value to rice husks by producing environmentally friendly biofuels. The biochar machines convert crop residues into organic soil conditioners by carbonizing the crop residues under specific temperatures and times.

- Contracting type: For sale/service
- Technology level: Medium
- Country of origin: Japan
- Availability: Japan, Nigeria, Senegal, United Republic of Tanzania, Viet Nam
- Contact: WIPO GREEN Database

Reducing loss: rice harvest dryers
Mecmar

Photo: Getty Images / ©jchamp

Drying rice is a necessary but delicate process. In many regions the grains are simply spread out on the ground to dry in the sunshine, which results in significant harvest loss. Harvested rice typically has more than 20 percent moisture, which must be reduced to 12–14 percent for prolonged shelf life. Drying must be done within 12–24 hours of harvest to avoid quality loss. The Italian company Mecmar produces both large, fixed tower dryer installations and small mobile units. Offering reduced drying times and uniform drying, the solutions ensure that the grain is dried with minimal loss. Avoiding food loss is part of productivity improvements which contribute to reducing GHG emissions.

- Contracting type: For sale
- Technology level: Low
- Country of origin: Italy
- Availability: Australia, Bangladesh, EU, Iran, Kazakhstan, Kyrgyzstan, Philippines, Türkiye, Uganda, United States
- Contact: WIPO GREEN Database

Improved cultivation: air-powered rice seeding technology

Brooklyn Bridge to Cambodia, Inc.

Photo: © Brooklyn Bridge to Cambodia, Inc.

The Eli Seeder 3.0 is an inexpensive mechanized seeder designed to improve the efficiency of rice seeding. The company focused initially on dissemination in Cambodia. The machine can split rice seeds into 12 even rows and uses airflow to feed a burst of seed to one row at a time. The device shoots the seed into the ground at high pressure while creating sufficiently wide gaps between each deposit to allow for growth and sunlight. The seeder can be connected to two- or four-wheel tractors.

- Contracting type: For sale
- Technology level: Low
- Country of origin: Cambodia
- Availability: Cambodia
- Contact: WIPO GREEN Database

Improved cultivation: seed film cultivation (SFC)

Green and Seed Corp.

Photo: © Green and Seed

SFC is a new sowing method using a biodegradable film to which seeds are attached. The film is spread out on the field and covered by mulch. A special tractor attachment (the mulcher), pulled by a tractor, spreads out the seed film on the field and covers it with a thin layer of soil to ensure seed–soil contact, while simultaneously installing the drip irrigation tapes under the seed film. SFC eliminates the labor-intensive stages of sowing, seedling transplanting and weeding in crop cultivation, and prevents loss of water, fertilizer and soil temperature, providing an optimal environment for crop growth and thereby enabling higher yields. SFC is suitable for growing large-area row crops, such as rice and wheat, as a food security solution for water-stressed countries.

- Contracting type: For sale
- Technology level: Medium
- Country of origin: South Korea
- Availability: South Korea, Viet Nam, China, United Arab Emirates (UEA)
- Contact: WIPO GREEN Database

Improved cultivation: software platform that provides optimal irrigation schedule

IrriPasture

Photo: Getty Images/© Sinhyu

IrriPasture is an irrigation optimization tool originally designed for dairy farming, but now finding applications in rice paddies. Created for Australian dairy pastures, it improves irrigation processes by accurately calculating and recommending the daily water requirements. This is achieved by analyzing weather data to forecast the specific water needs of the crops. IrriPasture's analysis of local weather information enables farmers to make informed decisions about irrigation, ultimately leading to more efficient water usage. The platform is easy to use and is provided free of charge, providing an accessible solution for farmers to improve their irrigation practices and maximize crop yield while minimizing water consumption.

- Contracting type: Free
- Technology level: Medium
- Country of origin: Philippines
- Availability: Worldwide
- Contact: WIPO GREEN Database

Reducing loss: rice husks as raw material for biopolymers

Biopolymer

Photo: © Biopolymer

Biopolymer focuses on the research and manufacturing of natural-based raw materials, including coffee grounds, starch, rice husks, bagasse and seaweed. These materials are harnessed to develop sustainable products that cater to human needs. By utilizing abundant natural resources, Biopolymer not only offers a cost-effective solution that reduces reliance on fossil fuels but also actively addresses the global issue of environmental pollution. The bio-based materials can be employed in various production techniques, such as blow molding, injection molding and extrusion molding, offering flexibility in manufacturing processes.

- Contracting type: For sale
- Technology level: Medium
- Country of origin: Viet Nam
- Availability: Viet Nam
- Contact: WIPO GREEN Database

Measuring GHGs: advanced in-field methane gas measurement for research

Li-Cor

Photo: Getty Images/© CaoChunhai

The company offers a broad range of scientific gas measurement devices. The Trace Gas Analyzer is a lightweight, portable unit in patented portable, rugged and weather-resistant casing with hot-swappable batteries and on-board display. Capable of operating in harsh environments, its makers claim that it can offer in-field performance comparable to laboratory conditions. It can measure CO_2, CO_2 isotopologues, ammonia, methane and nitrous oxide.

- Contracting type: For sale
- Technology level: High
- Country of origin: United States
- Availability: Worldwide
- Contact: WIPO GREEN Database

Horizon technologies

Improved rice varieties: SUSIBA2 rice for reduced methane emission

Fujian Academy of Agriculture Sciences, Swedish University of Agricultural Sciences

Photo: Getty Images/© jxfzsy

Researchers from Fujian Academy of Agriculture Sciences and Swedish University of Agricultural Sciences have developed a new rice variety which is claimed to be able to cut methane emission from wet rice production by up to 50 percent, especially during the warm seasons. By inserting a gene from barley into the rice, the plant redirects more starch into the grains and less into the roots. This provides fewer nutrients for decomposition by microbes in the anaerobic environment of flooded rice fields, a process that is generally a major source of methane emissions. The genetically modified rice was created in 2015 and is still being researched and tested.

- Contracting type: N/A
- Technology level: Low
- Country of origin: China
- Availability: N/A
- Contact: WIPO GREEN Database

Improved rice varieties: development of high-yielding rice varieties for smallholder farmers

University of Oxford

Photo: Getty Images/© kudou

The C4 Rice Project is a scientific initiative aimed at developing high-yielding rice varieties for smallholder farmers. Collaborating across seven institutions in five countries, researchers are seeking to apply innovative scientific approaches to address the global challenge of feeding over 3 billion people who depend on rice for survival. Traditional rice breeding programs have hit a yield barrier, making it essential to explore new possibilities. The project's goal is to introduce "C4" traits into rice, which are predicted to enhance photosynthetic efficiency by 50 percent, improve nitrogen and water use efficiency, and increase resilience to reduced land area, decreased fertilizer use and unpredictable water supplies.

- Contracting type: N/A
- Technology level: Low
- Country of origin: United Kingdom
- Availability: N/A
- Contact: WIPO GREEN Database

Improved rice varieties: development of rice resistant to iron deficiency in calcareous soil

Ishikawa Prefectural University, Akita Prefectural University

Photo: Getty Images/© kudou

If plants do not get enough iron they cannot synthesize the chlorophyll necessary for photosynthesis, and therefore cannot grow. In alkaline soil, such as calcareous soil, which is found worldwide, iron does not dissolve into the soil and therefore cannot be absorbed by plants, so iron deficiency is especially pronounced. Iron deficiency presents a critical agricultural problem. The universities' technology has produced rice with better resistance to iron deficiency by gene manipulation and enhancing the factors governing the rice's iron absorption capacity. The rice's ability to absorb iron from the soil is enhanced and various cultivation conditions are improved.

- Contracting type: N/A
- Technology level: Medium
- Country of origin: Japan
- Availability: N/A
- Contact: WIPO GREEN Database

Improved cultivation: Pheromone-based insecticide for Indonesian rice farmers

Provivi

Photo: Getty Images / © zulpian_capture

The US-based agricultural input company Provivi specializes in developing pheromone-based pesticides. In cooperation with Syngenta, the company has developed a new pheromone-based pesticide, Nelvium, targeting pests in rice in Indonesia. The pheromone acts as a mating disruption agent thereby reducing the spread of the insects without actually killing them. It works by saturating the pheromone signals that female insects use to attract males, and hence disrupts the mating process of the insects. The pesticide is species specific and non-toxic to other insects. By protecting the crop and increasing yield, the technology also reduces emissions per crop produced. Nelvium was officially launched in 2022 and should be available in Indonesia in the near future.

- Contracting type: N/A
- Technology level: Low
- Country of origin: Switzerland, United States
- Availability: N/A
- Contact: WIPO GREEN Database

Improved cultivation: fertigation with treated municipal wastewater in paddy rice cultivation

Yamagata University

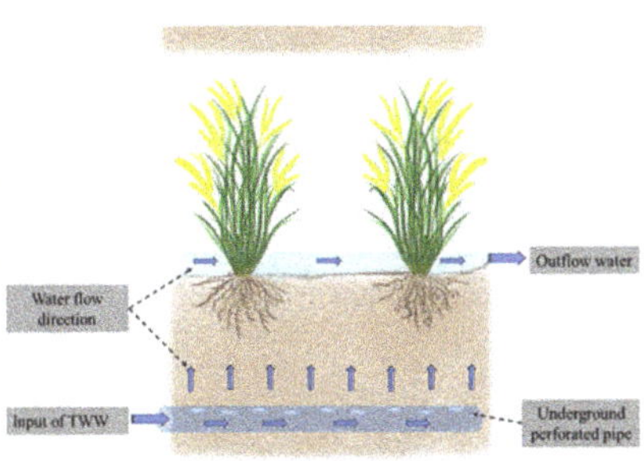

Photo: © Yamagata University

Continuous fertigation systems can produce high yields of protein-rich rice without the use of mineral fertilizers, while also significantly reducing GHG emissions from rice paddy fields. Recycling treated municipal wastewater for crop irrigation contributes to the conservation of freshwater resources for other uses, while nutrients in the wastewater can be effectively recycled in soil, making farming soil more fertile. These irrigation systems produced comparable yields with significantly higher protein contents in rice grains when compared to conventional rice fields supplemented with high doses of mineral fertilizers and irrigated with channel water. In addition, the continuous sub-irrigation system has been optimized for appropriate irrigation flow rates and timings to vastly reduce methane and nitrous oxide emissions by at least 80 and 60 percent, respectively.

- Contracting type: N/A
- Technology level: Medium
- Country of origin: Japan
- Availability: N/A
- Contact: WIPO GREEN Database

Improved cultivation: rice paddy weeding robot
Moondino

Photo: Getty Images / © Remi Lasseigne

The MOONDINO is an autonomous weeding robot which supports the dry sowing of rice by weeding and tilling the soil between the rice seedlings. It is powered by solar panels. The robot records a spatial map of the location of each seed when it is sown and uses GPS to navigate. By supporting dry sowing, the robot reduces both the amount of water used and the amount of methane released during rice production. The weeding robot eliminates the need for chemical herbicides.

- Contracting type: N/A
- Technology level: Medium
- Country of origin: Switzerland
- Availability: N/A
- Contact: WIPO GREEN Database

Photo: Getty Images / kinwun

Data and precision farming

Agriculture has always been dependent on tools. Working the soil and transporting crops, manure and water is hard labor. Finding solutions that can ease the farmer's workload has therefore always been a strong driver of innovation, as are efforts to ensure a reliable and plentiful harvest in the face of uncertain weather and water supply. And innovations abound. From simple hand tools to large, animal-drawn tools for preparing the soil, all the way up to sophisticated irrigation systems, complex agricultural inputs, new plant varieties, self-driving or flying machines and systems for monitoring crop development from space. History has shown that farmers are acutely aware of the value of efficient tools.

Climate change is exacerbating the vulnerability of farming and farmers all over the world as they have to adapt to both slow onset and abrupt changes. The contributions that innovation and technology can make are described in the *Green Technology Book: Solutions for Climate Change Adaptation*.

Due to the large environmental footprint of farming in terms of land conversion and deforestation, soil degradation, water use, nutrient runoff, energy use and effects on biodiversity, farmers in many countries must comply with various restrictions and laws. GHG emissions are a consequence of several of these issues and restrictions related to emissions are some of the latest imposed on farmers. However, reducing emissions is not only a matter of complying with new rules and demands, it also represents an opportunity to change farming systems, tools and people's approach to farming. This brings with it the opportunity to transition to something better, often with several co-benefits including economic ones. Sometimes, markets drive these changes through new consumer demands and this can open the way for new opportunities, making new approaches to agriculture good business. Innovation and technology have several solutions ready or in development which can make the necessary changes attractive to farmers, and not least younger farmers, who are often well-accustomed to technology and data handling.

Ag tech to attract youth to farming

In many countries today, the farming sector is struggling to attract the next generation. Many young people shy away from its hard manual labor, often with attendant risks and meager outcomes. City-based stable incomes in industry and other sectors often prove more attractive. The children of farmers find it financially difficult to take over the family farm in certain countries. In some ways, this bleak image of agriculture and youth contradicts the projected positive trends of the sector. There will be an increased demand for farm products and prices are expected to rise in the longer term. Demand for various types of food is changing and the sector is therefore in a highly dynamic situation and must respond to both new consumer

Demand for various types of food is changing and the sector is therefore in a highly dynamic situation and must respond to both new consumer trends and changing climatic conditions

trends and changing climatic conditions. Therefore, the economic future of agriculture should be bright, although the process of translating these prospects into higher farm-gate prices and income for farmers may be complex and opaque.

Innovation and technology may play an important role in this process as youth are accustomed to and tend to favor advanced IT and complex machinery, so this may therefore be an important factor in rendering farm work more attractive to the next generation. Technology may also help to counter labor shortages, which already pose a major problem in many regions. The diversity of solutions that are, or are close to being, available is simply staggering. And they cover a vast range of technological fields, such as biotechnology, chemistry, biology, zoology, hydrology, mechanics, IT, sensors, cameras, AI-algorithms, cloud computing and energy, to name just a few. This section details some examples for inspiration, especially for young farmers, to help persuade them to stay in the trade in spite of its inherent risks and embrace the new ways of doing things that are developing at an extremely rapid pace.

Advanced ag tech and its contribution to mitigation

Many of the advanced technologies in agriculture target efficiency in terms of labor, energy and resources. Only some of these also have direct benefits for climate change mitigation. Gains in energy efficiency are generally beneficial for mitigation, and even more so if fossil fuel-based machines are replaced by electric ones.

Technologies that facilitate precision application of inputs such as fertilizers and pesticides will have mitigation benefits through reduced use of such products, which give rise to emissions during their production, particularly inorganic fertilizers. Reducing the use of pesticides may also benefit soil health and hence soil carbon sequestration. Weeding robots could make it possible to shift to no-till agriculture with less dependence on pesticides and direct benefits for soil carbon sequestration.

Use of in-field and drone- or satellite-based sensors enhances farmers' knowledge of the state of their crops. This facilitates optimization and has the potential to enhance yields, thus producing more with less which is likely also to reduce emissions (for example, by avoiding the conversion of forest and other land use types to agricultural use). The same applies to monitoring of forest health and forest fires with the aim of preserving carbon sinks. New plant varieties, genetically modified or developed through targeted breeding, can directly promote traits that lead to fewer emissions, reduce crop losses and limit food loss and waste.

In general, data sharing and detailed monitoring of sustainable agricultural practices, such as systematic crop rotation and the use of nitrogen-fixating cover crops, can facilitate the widespread adoption of such practices. Monitoring and advanced soil sampling and, even genetic, analyses are prerequisites for the verification of climate benefits, thus unlocking the door to climate financing. Technology-based real-time monitoring of livestock movements and animal health can increase efficiency, which has a direct impact on reducing methane emissions from enteric fermentation in ruminants.

While the advanced ag tech market is still dominated by developed countries, it does not mean that farmers, food businesses and consumers in developing countries are not embracing data and digital technologies. For example, African agrifoodtech companies, predominantly in Egypt, Kenya, Nigeria and South Africa, are receiving significant venture capital investments. Especially attractive to investors are companies that are implementing digital solutions to support the exchange of food and other goods between farmers and consumers, for example through business-to-business platforms and tools.[145] There are, however, risks that digital and other

New plant varieties, genetically modified or developed through targeted breeding, can directly promote traits that lead to fewer emissions, reduce crop losses and limit food loss and waste

advanced new ag tech may further deepen the digital divide and allow the already better-off to prosper while poorer smallholders are left behind.[146] Some of the new technologies are primarily targeting larger farmers in richer countries, but at the same time the wide diversity in mobile phone-based and other digital technologies highlights their usefulness in diverse contexts. As also mentioned in other sections of this chapter, new ownership structures and agricultural service companies using advanced machines or renting them out may bring the technological frontier within reach also of the smallholder farmers in a variety of contexts.

Is advanced ag tech actually being used?

Clearly there are many advanced and elaborate solutions available. We hear a lot about drones and self-driving farm machines, satellite monitoring and precision farming. But is this new hard- and software worthwhile? Is it actually being used, or is it mostly promotional material from startups and companies looking for investments?

In a webinar for young farmers organized by the World Farmers' Organization in mid-2023, we had the occasion to ask the participants about their use of such technologies. Young farmers from Australia, Brazil, Finland and New Zealand could all readily give examples of how they use drones for herding livestock, crop monitoring and other technologies from the suite of precision agriculture technologies. These anecdotal observations are backed by numbers, as detailed below.

In biotechnology, Syngenta, a major crop variety seed and chemical input producer, reported a 19 percent growth in sales in 2023, generated by high demand for products and services targeting yield increases and sustainable farming methods. The company also claims that its digital solutions have been adopted on some 88 million hectares. In China, sales of the company's new digital Modern Agriculture Platform (MAP) for sustainable agriculture guidance, crop traceability and market connection to premium buyers, grew by 76 percent and currently has 2 million registered users.[147]

The market for agricultural robots currently totals USD 13.5 billion, dominated by the United States, Europe and Asia. It is projected to grow to USD 40 billion in the next five years – but that, of course, is just a projection.[148] The agricultural drone market shows similar dominance, currently standing at USD 4.6 billion and with an even stronger projected growth of 31 percent by 2028.[149] In China, in 2021, there were already 120,000 agricultural drones in use on 71 million hectares, a steep rise from the 13,000 units in use in 2017, in a market heavily dominated by the two Chinese drone companies DJI and XAG.[150, 151]

Probably the most efficient way to get new agricultural technologies into the field is through long-established dealer networks. John Deere, an American agricultural machinery manufacturer, is the largest of these, accounting for around a fifth of the agriculture equipment market, and is an example of one of the companies competing to be at the technological cutting edge. By 2012, John Deere had already installed a telematics gateway into all its large farm machines, which allows remote monitoring of each machine's condition, and in recent years the company has made several large acquisitions of robots and computer vision companies. The self-driving tractor R8 went on sale in 2022 and the "See & Spray" precision spraying system is already in use.[152] The company's sales from its prediction and precision agriculture division stood at USD 22 billion in 2022, up from USD 16.6 billion the year before.

Denmark has a large and well-developed agricultural sector where concentration on larger and highly efficient farms has been the development trend for decades. It would therefore be expected that Danish farmers would be early adopters of precision farming technologies.

An analysis from the Danish statistical services in 2022 indicates that precision farming technologies are used by 37 percent of farmers, up from 23 percent in 2018. However, as large farms are the most eager adopters, it also means that precision agriculture in some form is used on 76 percent of agricultural land in Denmark (up from 57 percent in 2018).

The most commonly used precision farming technology is precision steering with RTK-GPS (a highly accurate form of GPS tracking), in use on 66 percent of farm areas, followed by individual control of spray nozzles to avoid overlap spraying on 57 percent of farm areas. Use of software for planning fertilizer requirements and satellite and drone images are both employed on 26 percent of Danish farmland (drones much less commonly than satellites), while crop sensors on machines are used on only 5 percent of farmland. The analysis also shows that cost is the major limiting factor for farmers, that fields often show too little variation to justify such investments, and that there is a general lack of knowledge. Difficulties in getting the equipment to work was reported as the second highest obstacle in 2018 but was only reported by 11 percent of farms in 2022. It is common for the equipment used to be owned by professional operators, with the exception of very large farms.[153, 154]

These findings are also supported by a local farm machine service and sales company that we interviewed in Brøns, in the Southern part of Denmark. Local farmers are increasingly using spot-spraying technologies based on controllable spray nozzles, RTK-GPS and satellite or drone images indicating areas to be sprayed. The use of drone and satellite images as guidance for precision spraying is one of the fastest growing technology deployments and most modern sprayers are already compatible with the technology. Rapid delivery services for repeated image capture and analyses during the growing season, semi-automatic data upload to farm machines and favorable per-area prices compared to manual procedures offer strong incentives to farmers. The company aims to achieve, on average, a 40 percent reduction in the use of chemical inputs through the deployment of such technologies. Some extension services also offer drone images of fields for uploading to enabled equipment. Spraying drones are not yet in common use partly as they are hampered by legislation, which requires human supervision at all times and forbids drones to cross roads, among other use restrictions. Autonomous tractors and other autonomous machines are not yet in use and may not offer a particular advantage in the relatively small fields most commonly found in Denmark. Electric farm vehicles are also not in common use except for smaller specialized units, such as loaders.[155]

There are also indications that these technologies are already being put to good use by farmers

So, although there is probably an element of window dressing and fanciful promises relating to the merits of new technologies, there are also indications that these technologies are already being put to good use by farmers. They may not be mainstreamed yet, and some of the more advanced technologies still have to prove their worth, but the trend is upward and the markets have big expectations.

Innovation examples

Photo: Getty Images / © ozgurdonmaz

Using drones for pesticide treatment of pepper trees in China
Sichuan pepper is a popular Chinese chili spice often grown on irregular terrain and slopes. In Jiangjin district, DJI Agras MG-1 drones were used to apply pesticides against the highly damaging spider mite. The trees grow between 2 and 7 m tall and are typically sprayed manually using backpack sprayers which can cover around 0.5 hectare per day. The drones can spray around 4 hectares per day, thus dramatically increasing efficiency and improving crop protection, with the latter

having potential climate change mitigation benefits. The deployment of drones was supported by a nationwide pilot subsidy program.[156]

Photo: Getty Images /© Jitti Narksompong

Satellite images for forage index assurance

Livestock farmers are dependent on good pastures, but the yield and quality vary from one year to another and are being influenced by climate change. Having the right pasture and feed is also crucial for the health and productivity of the animals, which again influences the amount of GHG emitted, not least methane. A targeted insurance product can help provide farmers with the quality feed they need when their own pastures fail and is therefore a solution with both climate change adaptation and mitigation qualities. The French insurance companies Crédit Agricole Assurances and Pacifica Assurances Dommages have developed a forage insurance product that relies on multispectral satellite images supplied by Airbus. The satellite observations allow the companies to monitor pasture development in real time and generate maps showing the percentage of green vegetation cover which are used to create a yearly grassland production index. Scientific in-field observations over several years have established a solid correlation between the index produced and real growth. This allows farmers to receive insurance payouts on time without the need for time-consuming in-field inspections, etc. Such index-based crop insurance products are also increasingly becoming available to farmers in developing countries and can provide an important livelihood safeguard against climate change impacts. Crédit Agricole has commercialized index-based pasture insurance since 2015.[157]

Photo: Getty Images /© Kinwun

Agricultural drones in Türkiye

Farmers in Türkiye are using sprayer drones to save labor costs and reduce chemical and water use in crop spraying. Reduced chemical use lowers emissions from crop production and is beneficial for soil health and soil carbon. As crops mature, conventional tractors with spraying equipment destroy plants and struggle with access in muddy fields. Daytime spraying is hindered by the country's high temperatures and strong sunlight, while nighttime spraying often results in excessive use of chemicals. To address these challenges, farmers are turning to GPS-guided sprayer drones. Drones are much faster than tractor-based spraying and, as they do not touch the field, they neither damage plants, get stuck in mud nor require irrigation hoses to be removed to allow access. In the city of Konya, farmers have drastically reduced the use of chemicals and therefore also water for spraying, which is becoming an increasingly critical resource. In the Trakya region, an insect attack on sunflower crops in 2022 caused severe damage and led to a trial spraying of affected areas using drones. The positive results led to the purchase of two spraying drones. The Chamber of Agriculture of Aksaray is now actively promoting agricultural drones, with plans to extend drone services to all farmers in the region in 2023.[158]

Technology solutions

Proven technologies

Precision farming: precision positioning for advanced farming solutions

Trimble

Photo: © Trimble

The company has a long track record in satellite-based positioning systems. Based on high-precision GPS location systems such as real-time kinematics, the company offers a range of precision agriculture solutions. In partnership with other companies, Trimble has developed spot spraying and autonomous farm machines. The company's position technology portfolio is a basis for many precision farming systems and enables farmers to increase efficiencies, enhance productivity and reduce costs while optimizing inputs. These measures result in increased yield, water efficiency, cost savings and enhanced worker safety, as well as reduced carbon emissions and waste.

- Contracting type: For sale
- Technology level: Medium
- Country of origin: United States
- Availability: Worldwide
- Contact: WIPO GREEN Database

Precision farming: telemetry and automation

Corvus

Photo: Getty Images/@S-S-S

AGDP (Precision Agro-Livestock) is a web-based system capable of receiving data from remote stations (scales, hoppers, harvesters, etc.), organizing it and then processing the data using complex software. Sensors and cameras on various farm machines feed data to the system, allowing for detailed monitoring and automation.

- Contracting type: For sale/service
- Technology level: Medium
- Country of origin: Argentina
- Availability: Argentina
- Contact: WIPO GREEN Database

Precision farming: agricultural drones and autonomous ground vehicles
XAG

Photo: Getty Images / © Andrey Popov

The company offers a range of cutting-edge agricultural drones that are designed to modernize farming practices. Central to the company's portfolio are drones, including the XAG P100, V40, P40, P Series 2020 and P Series 2019 models. This comprehensive suite of drones, robots, AI and IoT applications offer the tools needed for transitioning to a smart agriculture ecosystem.

- Contracting type: For sale
- Technology level: Medium
- Country of origin: China
- Availability: Worldwide
- Contact: WIPO GREEN Database

Monitoring: imaging for fruit yield estimation
FruitSpec Ltd.

Photo: Getty Images / © andreswd

FruitSpec has developed an innovative technology based on hyper-spectral imaging and deep learning algorithms. FruitSpec's approach allows the analysis of fruit tree images and distinguishes between green leaves and green fruits. Until now, one of the main technological challenges in providing early season fruit yield estimates has been the inability to distinguish green fruit from green leaves in an image. FruitSpec's technology solves this problem, enabling companies to count the number of fruits and estimate fruit sizes for accurate early season fruit yield estimation. The company claims to be able to generate yield estimates with more than 90 percent accuracy at the start of the growing season when fruits are still green. After analyzing the images uploaded to the cloud, the company provides the customer with a yield estimation report detailing figures such as fruit count, size and weight distribution and heatmaps. This information helps to reduce food loss and optimize production, helping to reduce emissions per fruit harvested.

- Contracting type: For service
- Technology level: Medium
- Country of origin: Israel
- Availability: Argentina, Australia, Chile, Israel, Morocco, South Africa, Spain, United States
- Contact: WIPO GREEN Database

Food waste: IoT-enabled cold storage services

Akofresh

Photo: Getty Images / © Baloncici

The company's IoT-enabled mobile off-grid cold storage preservation technology comprises cold room panels, solar panels, sensors, a compressor and an air cooler. The unit extends the shelf life of perishable crops from the usual five-day period to 21 days. Farmers appreciate the technology because it helps them to extend the shelf life of their crops and reduce wastage. The extended storage period allows farmers more time to find buyers or agents to sell their crops to and ensure that the buyer is offering them a fair price.

- Contracting type: For sale/service
- Technology level: Medium
- Country of origin: Ghana
- Availability: Ghana
- Contact: WIPO GREEN Database

Frontier technologies

Precision farming: automated use of remote sensing for precision spraying

Skymaps

Photo: Getty Images / © AndreyPopov

Skymaps' technology, CultiWise, uses remote sensing to enable farmers to gather and analyze real-time data to inform their decision-making. Using aerial imagery from satellites or drones and spectroscopy, CultiWise can operate at a level as granular as the individual plant, enabling targeted chemical application rather than blanket field spraying. This precision reduces chemical usage and enhances yields, leading to cost savings for farmers. The platform is aligned with the rapid transformation of the agriculture industry, providing an accessible and user-friendly tool for farmers to optimize their practices through data-driven insights.

- Contracting type: For sale/service
- Technology level: Medium
- Country of origin: Czech Republic
- Availability: Europe
- Contact: WIPO GREEN Database

Precision farming: laser weeding module using computer vision to detect weeds

Carbon Robotics

Photo: Getty Images / © JJ Gouin

LaserWeeder is a module that attaches to a tractor and uses an AI-powered algorithm to differentiate between weeds and a series of recognized crops. High-powered, precise lasers are used to kill any weeds detected. The module includes a series of 42 different cameras which form part of a feedback-loop, allowing the deep learning algorithm to identify crops and differentiate them from weeds. There are 30 different lasers that can fire every 50 milliseconds and are effective in different lighting conditions.

- Contracting type: For sale
- Technology level: Medium
- Country of origin: United States
- Availability: United States
- Contact: WIPO GREEN Database

Precision farming: drones, autonomous farm machines and precision sprayers for precision agriculture

John Deere

Photo: Getty Images / © baranozdemir

The company offers a range of technologically advanced products for farming and agriculture. Their electrification solutions replace traditional engines and hydraulics with electric drives, resulting in greater efficiency and lower emissions. The zero emission compact utility tractor is designed for sustainable farming, with high power output and low maintenance costs. The eAutoPowr transmission is a wear-free and efficient continuously variable transmission that provides electrical power for external consumption. John Deere also collaborates on innovative projects, such as the large spraying drone (VoloDrone) for crop protection and autonomous electric tractors for reduced soil compaction. AI is integrated into the company's "See & Spray" technology, recognizing and treating weeds precisely and thereby reducing pesticide usage. The Command Cab is an AI-powered farm machinery control and operations system.

- Contracting type: For sale
- Technology level: Medium
- Country of origin: United States
- Availability: Worldwide
- Contact: WIPO GREEN Database

Precision farming: fixed-wing drone for field mapping

AgEagle

Photo: Getty Images/Loilo

The eBee Ag is a fixed-wing drone which maps fields to a high degree of accuracy. The device is fully portable, folds up into a waterproof backpack and is launched by hand. The underside of the drone is constructed of polypropylene mesh to ensure that it is shock-absorbent. The construction is modular so broken parts can be easily replaced. Use cases include land surveying, water and soil management, weed control and yield prediction for crops. Users map out an area that they would like to survey and the flight plan is generated automatically by the software. The drone has a flight time of up to 55 minutes, which allows it to map 160 hectares in a single flight. It also includes real-time kinematics within its camera, which allows it to map to an accuracy of 2.5 cm.

- Contracting type: For sale
- Technology level: Medium
- Country of origin: United States
- Availability: Switzerland, United States
- Contact: WIPO GREEN Database

Monitoring: crop monitoring using advanced satellite data and analytics

EOS Data Analytics

Photo: Getty Images/© PjPhoto69

Based on their own constellation of seven specialized agriculture monitoring satellites and publicly available satellites, the company provides detailed field and forest mapping for a range of crop development variables. The system can monitor crop growth as a function of weather and input use, detect changes and allow for resource-efficient planning of the growing season. The data provided can provide a basis for precision farming systems.

- Contracting type: For sale/service
- Technology level: Medium
- Country of origin: Ukraine
- Availability: Worldwide
- Contact: WIPO GREEN Database

Data in farming: IoT, business intelligence and blockchain technology for smart agriculture

Libelium

Photo: Getty Images / © B4LLS

Libelium provides IoT solutions for water management and environmental monitoring across sectors such as agriculture, industry and smart cities. The company's Plug & Sense Smart Environment PRO enables real-time monitoring of temperature, humidity, particulate matter and various gases. In response to the growing concern over meat consumption's environmental impact, livestock producers are using Libelium's technology to reduce emissions. By using IoT solutions, intensive cattle farming projects can optimize livestock production by monitoring animal feeding, behavior and environmental conditions. Collected data is analyzed on a web platform, enabling stakeholders to make informed decisions and mitigate greenhouse gas emissions. Libelium's web platform employs business intelligence techniques, generating models and simulations to define optimal configurations and improve farm performance.

- Contracting type: For sale/service
- Technology level: Medium
- Country of origin: Spain
- Availability: European Union
- Contact: WIPO GREEN Database

Data in farming: digital agriculture platform in China

Syngenta

Photo: Getty Images / © structuresxx

The Modern Agriculture Platform (MAP) by Syngenta establishes a transformative network of MAP Centers designed to facilitate sustainable farm modernization. This platform guides farmers toward modern practices that enhance crop quality and profitability, while reducing environmental impact. An integral aspect of MAP is the MAP beSide program, a strategic initiative aimed at assisting farmers in cultivating premium, traceable crops using environmentally conscious methods. Collaboration with Alibaba's Hema fresh grocery chain (a prominent player in China's online retail landscape) amplifies the platform's impact by channeling high-quality crops to consumers through a respected retail channel.

- Contracting type: For sale
- Technology level: Medium
- Country of origin: China
- Availability: China
- Contact: WIPO GREEN Database

Precision farming: precision crop-spraying systems

Greeneye Technology

Photo: Getty Images/© moiseXVII

The company aims to reduce chemical usage while increasing productivity and profitability for farmers through the application of AI and deep learning. By transitioning from broadcast spraying to precise and selective spraying of pesticides, the company's products streamline the pest control process in agriculture. Greeneye's proprietary Selective Spraying system seamlessly integrates with existing agricultural sprayers, allowing real-time and species-specific spraying of chemicals only where needed. With modular design and compatibility with the Agricultural Industry Electronics Foundation (AEF) ISOBUS Database, Greeneye's system can be easily integrated into any sprayer. This innovative approach offers seamless integration, affordability and the ability to simultaneously perform contact and residual herbicide spraying, maximizing profitability for farmers.

- Contracting type: N/A
- Technology level: High
- Country of origin: Canada
- Availability: N/A
- Contact: WIPO GREEN Database

Precision farming: Per Plant farming – using robotics for precision farming

Small Robot Company

Photo: Getty Images/© fotokostic

The company aims to revolutionize agriculture through the use of robotics and AI, creating a sustainable and profitable farming model known as Per Plant farming. Traditional farming methods are facing challenges such as stagnating yields, rising machinery costs and environmental crises caused by heavy machinery and chemical use. Per Plant precision agriculture offers a solution that is kinder to the soil, the environment and farmers' profitability. By leveraging autonomous data collection and processing, the company provides Per Plant Intelligence as a service, enabling farmers, seed companies and nutrient companies to make informed decisions based on detailed crop health insights. Their robots, Tom and Wilma, autonomously map fields, digitize plant locations and provide AI-driven advice for optimal crop management, reducing herbicide usage and improving fertilizer application timing. The company's technology empowers farmers to achieve increased yields, environmental sustainability and financial success.

- Contracting type: N/A
- Technology level: Medium
- Country of origin: United Kingdom
- Availability: N/A
- Contact: WIPO GREEN Database

Precision farming: Bug Vacuum - autonomous insect removal robot

Agrobot

The Bug Vacuum is an autonomous robot that navigates a predetermined path, turning at the end of each row and aspirating lygus bugs which are present in crops. The fan height is adjustable to optimize the fan's ability to aspirate the bugs. The technology has a number of inbuilt safety mechanisms, including sensors to detect obstacles and a safety bumper that engages the brakes in the event of a collision.

- Contracting type: N/A
- Technology level: High
- Country of origin: Spain
- Availability: N/A
- Contact: WIPO GREEN Database

Precision farming: automated artichoke cultivation

Universidad Privada Antenor Orrego

The technology is a robotic system that automates the quality control of artichoke seedling growth, providing three levels of quality: good, regular and bad. The system complements the work of specialized operators, increasing the productive capacity of a nursery and therefore increasing the customer portfolio and decreasing instances of final customers returning stock. The robotic system comprises the following modules: a standard artichoke germination tray feeder, a computer vision component, a seedling elevator and a multi-articulated gripper. Each element is efficiently integrated allowing the system to perform continuous, stable and robust quality control of seedling growth in industrial nurseries. Currently the system's transplant success rate (pick, transfer and drop) is over 98 percent.

- Contracting type: N/A
- Technology level: High
- Country of origin: Peru
- Availability: N/A
- Contact: WIPO GREEN Database

Precision farming: autonomous agricultural robot for weeding, seeding, spraying and planting

XMachines

Photo: Getty Images © JJ Gouin

The company is an Indian robotics and AI company based in Hyderabad that specializes in designing and manufacturing autonomous agricultural robots for precision farming. XMachines' miniature tractor-like robotic device utilizes AI and robotics to function as a reliable farm hand, offering precision in various farm activities. The robot can be used for seed and sapling planting, micro spraying, fertilizer spraying and other tasks with accuracy and efficiency. Through their AI-enabled robotic machines, XMachines seeks to provide cost-effective solutions for small-scale farmers with small land holdings and empower them with the benefits of mechanization. The robots can operate autonomously or be controlled manually through a joystick. The devices bring much-needed precision and efficiency to farm operations, helping farmers save on costs and enhance productivity.

- Contracting type: N/A
- Technology level: Medium
- Country of origin: India
- Availability: N/A
- Contact: WIPO GREEN Database

Notes

1 IPCC (2021). *Working Group I sixth assessment report: The physical science basis – Full report.* Geneva: Intergovernmental Panel on Climate Change (IPCC). Available at: https://www.ipcc.ch/report/ar6/wg1/#SPM.

2 IPCC (2023). *Synthesis report (SYR) of the IPCC sixth assessment report (AR6): Summary for policymakers.* Geneva: Intergovernmental Panel on Climate Change (IPCC). Available at: https://www.ipcc.ch/report/ar6/syr/.

3 Ivanovich, C.C., *et al.* (2023). Future warming from global food consumption. *Nature Climate Change*, 13(3), 297–302.

4 IPCC (2022). *Climate change 2022: Mitigation of climate change – Technical summary, Working Group III contribution to IPCC sixth assessment report.* Cambridge, UK: Intergovernmental Panel on Climate Change (IPCC). Available at: https://www.ipcc.ch/report/sixth-assessment-report-working-group-3/.

5 FAO (2023). Land use in agriculture by the numbers. Food and Agriculture Organization of the United Nations (FAO). Available at: http://www.fao.org/sustainability/news/detail/en/c/1274219/ [accessed May 2023].

6 World Bank (2023). Water in agriculture. World Bank. Available at: https://www.worldbank.org/en/topic/water-in-agriculture [accessed May 2023].

7 Nawaz, A., *et al.* (2022). Increasing sustainability for rice production systems. *Journal of Cereal Science*, 103, 103400.

8 Sozzi, M., *et al.* (2018). *Patent trends in agricultural engineering.* Jelgava, Latvia: Engineering for rural development and University of Padova, Italy. Available at: https://www.tf.llu.lv/conference/proceedings2018/Papers/N329.pdf.

9 EPO (2022). *Space-borne sensing and green applications*, Patent insight report. Munich, Germany: European Patent Office. Available at: https://link.epo.org/web/Space-borne%20sensing%20and%20green%20applications%20report.pdf.

10 Caner, D., J. Claes, D. De Clercq and M. Taksyak (2023). Needle in a haystack: Patents that inspire agricultural innovation. McKinsey & Company. Available at: https://www.mckinsey.com/industries/agriculture/our-insights/needle-in-a-haystack-patents-that-inspire-agricultural-innovation [accessed October 2023].

11 Trappey, A.J.C., *et al.* (2023). A comprehensive analysis of global patent landscape for recent R&D in agricultural drone technologies. *World Patent Information*, 74, 102216.

12 Chapelier, E., Hanaf, A. and Gourragne A. (2020). Patent mapping analysis in the field of agricultural robotics. Global Organization For Agricultural Robotics (GOFAR). Available at: https://www.agricultural-robotics.com/news/patent-mapping-analysis-in-the-field-of-agricultural-robotics [accessed October 2023].

13 Caprarulo, V., *et al.* (2022). Innovations for reducing methane emissions in livestock toward a sustainable system: Analysis of feed additive patents in ruminants. *Animals*, 12(20), 2760.

14 Fatimi, A. (2021). The use of seaweeds in the formulation of feeds for livestock: Patent analysis. In *2nd International Electronic Conference on Animals – Global Sustainability and Animals: Welfare, Policies and Technologie.* Basel, Switzerland: MDPI.

15 IP Australia (2023). Patent analytics on low emission technologies. Intellectual Property Office of Australia. Available at: https://www.ipaustralia.gov.au/tools-and-research/professional-resources/data-research-and-reports/publications-and-reports/2022/11/30/03/16/patent-analytics-on-low-emission-technologies [accessed October 2022].

16 ESA (2023). A closer look at the latest earth observation services industry trends. The European Space Agency (ESA). Available at: https://space-economy.esa.int/article/72/a-closer-look-at-the-latest-earth-observation-services-industry-trends [accessed October 2023].

17 Pixalytics (2023). How many earth observation satellites orbiting in 2023? Pixalytics. Available at: https://www.pixalytics.com/earth-observation-satellites-2023/ [accessed October 2023].

18 EPO (2022). *Space-borne sensing and green applications.* Patent insight report, Munich, Germany: European Patent Office. Available at: https://link.epo.org/web/Space-borne%20sensing%20and%20green%20applications%20report.pdf.

19 CPI (2022). *Landscape of climate finance for agriculture, forestry, other land use and fisheries: Preliminary findings.* Climate Policy Initiative (CPI). Available at: https://www.climatepolicyinitiative.org/publication/landscape-of-climate-finance-for-agriculture-forestry-other-land-uses-and-fisheries/.

20 CPI (2023). *Landscape of climate finance for agrifood systems.* Climate Policy Initiative (CPI). Available at: https://www.climatepolicyinitiative.org/wp-content/uploads/2023/07/Landscape-of-Climate-Finance-for-Agrifood-Systems.pdf.

21 CPI (2022). *Landscape of climate finance for agriculture, forestry, other land use and fisheries: Preliminary findings.* Climate Policy Initiative (CPI). Available at: https://www.climatepolicyinitiative.org/publication/landscape-of-climate-finance-for-agriculture-forestry-other-land-uses-and-fisheries/.

22 Berkeley (2023). Berkeley carbon trading project: Voluntary registry offsets database. Center for Environmental Public Policy (CEPP) and Goldman School of Public Policy, University of California, Berkeley. Available at: https://gspp.berkeley.edu/research-and-impact/centers/cepp/projects/berkeley-carbon-trading-project/offsets-database [accessed October 2023].

23 CPI (2022). *Landscape of climate finance for agriculture, forestry, other land use and fisheries: Preliminary findings.* Climate Policy Initiative (CPI). Available at: https://www.climatepolicyinitiative.org/publication/landscape-of-climate-finance-for-agriculture-forestry-other-land-uses-and-fisheries/.

24 CPI (2020). *Examining the climate finance gap for small-scale agriculture.* Climate Policy Initiative (CPI). Available at: https://www.ifad.org/documents/38714170/42157470/climate-finance-gap_smallscale_agr.pdf/34b2e25b-7572-b31d-6d0c-d5ea5ea8f96f.

25 CPI (2022). *Landscape of climate finance for agriculture, forestry, other land use and fisheries: Preliminary findings.* Climate Policy Initiative (CPI). Available at: https://www.climatepolicyinitiative.org/publication/landscape-of-climate-finance-for-agriculture-forestry-other-land-uses-and-fisheries/.

26 AgFunder (2022). *2022 AgFunder AgriFoodTech Investment Report.* San Francisco, CA: AgFunder. Available at: https://agfunder.com/research/2022-agfunder-agrifoodtech-investment-report/.

27 Bashi, Z., *et al.* (2019). *Alternative proteins: The race for market share is on.* McKinsey & Company. Available at: https://www.mckinsey.com/industries/agriculture/our-insights/alternative-proteins-the-race-for-market-share-is-on.

28 McKinsey (2022). *Make room for alternative proteins: What it takes to build a new sector.* McKinsey & Company. Available at: https://www.mckinsey.com/capabilities/mckinsey-digital/our-insights/make-room-for-alternative-proteins-what-it-takes-to-build-a-new-sector.

29 BCG (2022). *The untapped climate opportunity in alternative proteins.* Boston Consulting Group (BCG). Available at: https://www.bcg.com/publications/2022/combating-climate-crisis-with-alternative-protein.

30 Climate ADAPT (2023). Precision Agriculture. The European Climate Adaptation Platform Climate-ADAPT. Available at: https://climate-adapt.eea.europa.eu/en/metadata/adaptation-options/precision-agriculture [accessed October 2023].

31 EDF (2023). 'Precision Agriculture Loan Act' unlocks new financing for climate solutions. Environmental Defense Fund (EDF). Available at: https://www.edf.org/media/precision-agriculture-loan-act-unlocks-new-financing-climate-

solutions [accessed October 2023].

32 MarketsandMarkets (2023). Precision farming market size, share, industry report, revenue trends and growth drivers. MarketsandMarkets. Available at: https://www.marketsandmarkets.com/Market-Reports/precision-farming-market-1243.html [accessed October 2023].

33 AgFunder (2022). *AgFunder European investment report*. San Fransisco, CA: AgFunder. Available at: https://research.agfunder.com/europe-2022-agrifoodtech-report-investnl.pdf.

34 World Bank (2023). World bank loan will support reducing methane, saving water in Hunan's rice paddies. World Bank Group. Available at: https://www.worldbank.org/en/news/press-release/2023/05/31/world-bank-loan-will-support-reducing-methane-saving-water-in-hunan-s-rice-paddies [accessed October 2023].

35 IFAD (2023). New IFAD initiative will help reduce global warming by lowering methane emissions from small-scale farming. International Fund for Agricultural Development (IFAD). Available at: https://www.ifad.org/en/web/latest/-/new-ifad-initiative-will-help-reduce-global-warming-by-lowering-methane-emissions-from-small-scale-farming.

36 Berkeley (2023). Berkeley carbon trading project. Voluntary registry offsets database. Center for Environmental Public Policy (CEPP), Goldman School of Public Policy, University of California, Berkeley. Available at: https://gspp.berkeley.edu/research-and-impact/centers/cepp/projects/berkeley-carbon-trading-project/offsets-database [accessed October 2023].

37 Precedence Research (2023). Regenerative agriculture market. Precedence Research. Available at: https://www.precedenceresearch.com/regenerative-agriculture-market [accessed October 2023].

38 PepsiCo (2023). Pepsico issues new $1.25 billion 10-year green bond as company accelerates pep+ transformation. PepsiCo. Available at: https://www.pepsico.com/our-stories/press-release/pepsico-issues-new-125-billion-10-year-green-bond-as-company-accelerates-pep-tra07202022 [accessed October 2023].

39 Danone (2020). Danone North America and the National Fish and Wildlife Foundation join forces. Danone North America. Available at: https://www.danonenorthamerica.com/news/danone-north-america-and-the-national-fish-and-wildlife-foundation-join-forces-to-leverage-3-million-in-federal-funding-for-shared-commitment-to-regenerative-agriculture/ [accessed October 2023].

40 European Commission (2021). Evaluation of the impact of the Common Agricultural Policy on climate change and greenhouse gas emissions. *Commission staff working document*, Directorate-General for Agriculture and Rural Development. Brussels: Publications Office of the European Union. Available at: http://op.europa.eu/en/publication-detail/-/publication/7307349a-ba1a-11eb-8aca-01aa75ed71a1 [accessed October 2023].

41 USDA (2022). *Partnerships for climate-smart commodities*. United States Department for Agriculture (USDA). Available at: www.usda.gov/climate-solutions/climate-smart-commodities.

42 Climatewatch (2023). Climatewatch. Available at: https://www.climatewatchdata.org/ [accessed May 2023].

43 Havlík, P., *et al.* (2014). Climate change mitigation through livestock system transitions. *Proceedings of the National Academy of Sciences*, 111(10), 3709–14.

44 FAO (2019). *Five practical actions towards low-carbon livestock*. Rome: Food and Agriculture Organization of the United Nations (FAO). Available at: https://www.fao.org/3/ca7089en/ca7089en.pdf.

45 FAO (2016). *Reducing enteric methane for improving food security and livelihoods*. New Zealand: Food and Agriculture Organization of the United Nations (FAO). Available at: https://www.ccacoalition.org/en/resources/reducing-enteric-methane-improving-food-security-and-livelihoods.

46 FAO (2016). *Reducing enteric methane for improving food security and livelihoods*. New Zealand: Food and Agriculture Organization of the United Nations (FAO) , New Zealand. Available at: https://www.ccacoalition.org/en/resources/reducing-enteric-methane-improving-food-security-and-livelihoods.

47 FAO (2016). *Reducing enteric methane for improving food security and livelihoods*. New Zealand: Food and Agriculture Organization of the United Nations (FAO) , New Zealand. Available at: https://www.ccacoalition.org/en/resources/reducing-enteric-methane-improving-food-security-and-livelihoods.

48 CCAC (2023). Enteric fermentation. Climate & Clean Air Coalition (CCAC) and United Nations Environment Programme (UNEP). Available at: https://www.ccacoalition.org/eN/Activity/enteric-fermentation [accessed May 2023].

49 IPCC (2022). *Climate change 2022: Mitigation of climate change – Full report, Working Group III contribution to IPCC sixth assessment report*. Cambridge, UK: Intergovernmental Panel on Climate Change (IPCC). Available at: https://www.ipcc.ch/report/sixth-assessment-report-working-group-3/.

50 FAO (2016). *Reducing enteric methane for improving food security and livelihoods*. New Zealand: Food and Agriculture Organization of the United Nations (FAO) , New Zealand. Available at: https://www.ccacoalition.org/en/resources/reducing-enteric-methane-improving-food-security-and-livelihoods.

51 FAO (2016). *Reducing enteric methane for improving food security and livelihoods*. New Zealand: Food and Agriculture Organization of the United Nations (FAO) , New Zealand. Available at: https://www.ccacoalition.org/en/resources/reducing-enteric-methane-improving-food-security-and-livelihoods.

52 Pasture.io (2023). Scientists are breeding climate-friendly cows & soon they'll be on your farm. Pasture.io. Available at: https://pasture.io/dairy-industry/breeding-climate-friendly-cows [accessed July 2023].

53 Cargill (2023). How feed impacts your farm's methane output. Cargill. Available at: http://dx.doi.org/ [accessed June 2023].

54 FAO (2019). *Five practical actions towards low-carbon livestock*. Rome: Food and Agriculture Organization of the United Nations (FAO). Available at: https://www.fao.org/3/ca7089en/ca7089en.pdf.

55 FAO (2017). *Livestock solutions for climate change*. Rome: Food and Agriculture Organization of the United Nations (FAO). Available at: https://www.fao.org/3/i8098e/i8098e.pdf.

56 OECD and FAO (2023). *OECD–FAO Agricultural Outlook 2023–2032*. Paris: Organisation for Economic Co-operation and Development (OECD). Available at: https://www.fao.org/documents/card/en/c/cc6361en.

57 OECD and FAO (2023). *OECD–FAO Agricultural Outlook 2023–2032*. Paris: Organisation for Economic Co-operation and Development (OECD). Available at: https://www.fao.org/documents/card/en/c/cc6361en.

58 UN (2023). Peace, dignity and equality on a heathy planet. United Nations (UN). Available at: https://www.un.org/en/global-issues/population [accessed May 2023].

59 Corichi, M. (2021). Eight-in-ten Indians limit meat in their diets, and four-in-ten consider themselves vegetarian. Pew Research Center. Available at: https://www.pewresearch.org/short-reads/2021/07/08/eight-in-ten-indians-limit-meat-in-their-diets-and-four-in-ten-consider-themselves-vegetarian/ [accessed August 2023].

60 Leveau, M. (2022). The FoodTech Innovation 'blind spots' of the last decade – Going beyond the hype – Part 1. Forward Fooding. Available at: https://forwardfooding.com/blog/foodtech-trends-and-insights/the-foodtech-innovation-blind-spots-go-beyond-the-hype-part-1/ [accessed 2023 June].

61 Leveau, M. (2022). The FoodTech Innovation 'blind spots' of the last decade – Going beyond the hype - Part 1. Forward Fooding. Available at: https://forwardfooding.com/blog/foodtech-trends-and-insights/the-foodtech-innovation-blind-spots-go-beyond-the-hype-part-1/ [accessed 2023 June].

62 Protein Directory (2023). Protein Directory – The largest alt protein database globally. Available at: https://

proteindirectory.com/ [accessed June 2023].

63 Leveau, M. (2022). The FoodTech Innovation 'blind spots' of the last decade - Going beyond the hype - Part 1. Forward Fooding. Available at: https://forwardfooding.com/blog/foodtech-trends-and-insights/the-foodtech-innovation-blind-spots-go-beyond-the-hype-part-1/ [accessed 2023 June].

64 Crownhart, C. (2023). Here's what we know about lab-grown meat and climate change. *MIT Technology Review Explains*. Massachusetts Institute of Technology (MIT). Available at: https://www.technologyreview.com/2023/07/03/1075809/lab-grown-meat-climate-change/ [accessed July 2023].

65 Paradisi, L. (2021). Understanding the future of protein. Forward Fooding. Available at: https://forwardfooding.com/blog/foodtech-trends-and-insights/understanding-the-future-of-protein/ [accessed July 2023].

66 FAO (2019). *Five practical actions towards low-carbon livestock*. Rome: Food and Agriculture Organization of the United Nations (FAO). Available at: https://www.fao.org/3/ca7089en/ca7089en.pdf.

67 Engler, J.-O. and H. von Wehrden (2018). Global assessment of the non-equilibrium theory of rangelands: Revisited and refined. *Land Use Policy*, 70, 479–84.

68 Hardin, G. (1968). The tragedy of the commons. *Science*, 162(3859), 1243–48.

69 Ross, E.B. (1998). *The Malthus factor: Population, poverty, and politics in capitalist development*, London and New York: Zed Books.

70 Helldén, U. (1991). Desertification – Time for an assessment. *Ambio*, 20(8), 372–83.

71 Fairhead, J. and M. Leach (1996). Colonial science & its relics in West Africa. In M. Leach and R. Mearns (eds) *The lie of the land, challenging received wisdom on the African Environment*. Oxford, UK: The International African Institute with James Currey, 105–21.

72 Fairhead, J. and M. Leach (1996). *Misreading the African landscape: Society and ecology in a forest-savanna mosaic, African Studies*. Cambridge, UK: Cambridge University Press.

73 Oksen, P. (2001). *Cattle, conflict and change: Animal husbandry and Fulani – Farmer interactions in Boulgou province, Burkina Faso*. Unpublished thesis (Ph.D.), Roskilde University.

74 Ellis, J.E., M.B. Coughenour and D.M. Swift (1993). Climate variability, ecosystem stability, and the implications for range and livestock development. In R.H. Behnke, I. Scoones and C. Kerven (eds), *Range ecology at disequilibrium*. London: Overseas Development Institute, 31–41.

75 Smith, S. (2023). 10 things you should do to get started with regenerative grazing. Noble Research Institute. Available at: https://www.noble.org/regenerative-agriculture/10-things-you-should-do-to-get-started-with-regenerative-grazing/ [accessed July 2023].

76 FAO (2017). *Livestock solutions for climate change*. Rome: Food and Agriculture Organization of the United Nations (FAO). Available at: https://www.fao.org/3/i8098e/i8098e.pdf.

77 CCAC (2023). Uruguay reduces livestock emissions while increasing productivity in a ccac-supported pilot project. Climate & Clean Air Coalition (CCAC) and United Nations Environment Programme (UNEP). Available at: https://www.ccacoalition.org/news/uruguay-reduces-livestock-emissions-while-increasing-productivity-ccac-supported-pilot-project [accessed October 2023].

78 CCAC (2023). Enteric fermentation. Climate & Clean Air Coalition (CCAC). United Nations Environment Programme (UNEP). Available at: https://www.ccacoalition.org/eN/Activity/enteric-fermentation [accessed May 2023].

79 FAO (2023). Global Livestock Environmental Assessment Model (GLEAM). Food and Agriculture Organization of the United Nations (FAO). Available at: https://www.fao.org/gleam/en/ [accessed May 2023].

80 O'Sullivan, A., *et al.* (2019). Strategies to improve the productivity, product diversity and profitability of urban agriculture. *Agricultural Systems*, 174, 133–44.

81 UNFCCC (2023). Land use, land-use change and forestry (LULUCF). United Nations Framework Convention on Climate Change (UNFCCC). Available at: https://unfccc.int/topics/land-use/workstreams/land-use--land-use-change-and-forestry-lulucf [accessed July 2023].

82 Ritchie, H., F. Spooner and M. Roser (2021). Deforestation and forest loss. OurWorldInData.org. Available at: https://ourworldindata.org/forests-and-deforestation [accessed August 2023].

83 Ritchie, H. (2021). Cutting down forests: What are the drivers of deforestation? OurWorldinData.org. Available at: https://ourworldindata.org/what-are-drivers-deforestation [accessed August 2023].

84 Geist, H.J. and E.F. Lambin (2002). Proximate causes and underlying driving forces of tropical deforestation: Tropical forests are disappearing as the result of many pressures, both local and regional, acting in various combinations in different geographical locations. *BioScience*, 52(2), 143–50.

85 Ritchie, H. (2021). Cutting down forests: What are the drivers of deforestation? OurWorldinData.org. Available at: https://ourworldindata.org/what-are-drivers-deforestation [accessed August 2023].

86 Ritchie, H., F. Spooner, and M. Roser (2021). Deforestation and forest loss. OurWorldInData.org. Available at: https://ourworldindata.org/forests-and-deforestation [accessed August 2023].

87 Ritchie, H., F. Spooner, and M. Roser (2021). Deforestation and forest loss. OurWorldInData.org. Available at: https://ourworldindata.org/forests-and-deforestation [accessed August 2023].

88 UNFCCC (2023). Land use, land-use change and forestry (LULUCF). United Nations Framework Convention on Climate Change (UNFCCC). Available at: https://unfccc.int/topics/land-use/workstreams/land-use--land-use-change-and-forestry-lulucf [accessed August 2023].

89 World Bank (2023). Eight Amazonian countries with the power to save the planet. The World Bank. Available at: https://www.worldbank.org/en/news/feature/2023/07/05/ocho-paises-de-la-amazonia-con-el-poder-de-salvar-el-planeta-america-latina [accessed July 2023].

90 IPCC (2021). *Working Group I Sixth Assessment Report: The Physical Science Basis – Summary for policymakers*. Geneva: Intergovernmental Panel on Climate Change (IPCC). Available at: https://www.ipcc.ch/report/ar6/wg1/#SPM.

91 Ritchie, H., F. Spooner, and M. Roser (2021). Deforestation and forest loss. OurWorldInData.org. Available at: https://ourworldindata.org/forests-and-deforestation [accessed August 2023].

92 Bossio, D.A., *et al.* (2020). The role of soil carbon in natural climate solutions. *Nature Sustainability*, 3(5), 391–98.

93 Hicks Pries, C.E., *et al.* (2017). The whole-soil carbon flux in response to warming. *Science*, 355(6332), 1420–23.

94 EEA (2022). Briefing: Soil carbon. European Environment Agency (EEA). Available at: https://www.eea.europa.eu/publications/soil-carbon [accessed June 2023].

95 Hawkins, H.-J., *et al.* (2023). Mycorrhizal mycelium as a global carbon pool. *Current Biology*, 33(11), R560–R73.

96 Hicks Pries, C.E., *et al.* (2017). The whole-soil carbon flux in response to warming. *Science*, 355(6332), 1420-23.

97 MIT (2023). Soil-based carbon sequestration. Massachusetts Institute of Technology (MIT). Available at: https://climate.mit.edu/explainers/soil-based-carbon-sequestration [accessed June 2023].

98 IPCC (2021). *Working Group I sixth assessment report: The physical science basis. Full report*. Geneva: Intergovernmental Panel on Climate Change (IPCC). Available at: https://www.ipcc.ch/report/ar6/wg1/#SPM.

99 Bossio, D.A., *et al.* (2020). The role of soil carbon in natural climate solutions. *Nature Sustainability*, 3(5), 391–98.

100 4 per 1000 (2023). The international "4 per 1000" initiative – Soils for food security and climate. Agricultural Research Centre for International Development (CIRAD). Available at: https://4p1000.org/?lang=en [accessed June 2023].

101 Bossio, D.A., *et al.* (2020). The role of soil carbon in natural climate solutions. *Nature Sustainability*, 3(5), 391–98.

102 Ellis, J. (2023). Reversing agriculture's emissions with carbon-fixing soil inputs. Cleantech Group. Available at: https://www.cleantech.com/reversing-agricultures-emissions-with-carbon-fixing-soil-inputs/ [accessed July 2022].

103 Spears, S. (2018). What is biochar? Regeneration International. Available at: https://regenerationinternational.org/2018/05/16/what-is-biochar/ [accessed June 2023].

104 Baker, J.C. and K.E. Saxton (2007). The 'what' and 'why' of no-tillage farming. In C.J. Baker and K.E. Saxton (eds), *No-tillage seeding in conservation agriculture, 2nd edn*. Rome: Food and Agriculture Organization of the United Nations (FAO) and Commonwealth Agricultural Bureau (CAB) International, 1–10.

105 Powlson, D.S., *et al.* (2014). Limited potential of no-till agriculture for climate change mitigation. *Nature Climate Change*, 4(8), 678–83.

106 Rainbow, R. and R. Derpsch (2011). Advances in no-till farming technologies and soil compaction management in rainfed farming systems. In P. Tow, et al. (eds), *Rainfed farming systems*. Dordrecht: Springer Netherlands, 991–1014.

107 FAO (2021). A step-by-step approach toward a gradual adoption of the full conservation agriculture technology: An example from Timor-Leste. *TECA – Technologies and Practices for Small Agricultural Producers*. Food and Agriculture Organization of the United Nations (FAO). Available at: www.fao.org/in-action/kore/good-practices/good-practices-details/en/c/1413322 [accessed July 2023].

108 Rainbow, R. and R. Derpsch (2011). Advances in no-till farming technologies and soil compaction management in rainfed farming systems. In P. Tow, et al., eds., *Rainfed farming systems*, Dordrecht: Springer Netherlands, 991–1014.

109 Rainbow, R. and R. Derpsch (2011). Advances in no-till farming technologies and soil compaction management in rainfed farming systems. In P. Tow, et al., eds., *Rainfed farming systems*, Dordrecht: Springer Netherlands, 991–1014.

110 Colbach, N. and S. Cordeau (2022). Are no-till herbicide-free systems possible? A simulation study. *Frontiers in Agronomy*, 4.

111 Hanley, S. (2022). Agrivoltaics – Solar panels & tomatoes may be perfect for each other. Cleantechnica. Available at: https://cleantechnica.com/2022/12/01/agrivoltaics-solar-panels-tomatoes-may-be-perfect-for-each-other/ [accessed July 2023].

112 Casey, T. (2023). More bad news for fossil fuels: Rooftop solar meets agrivoltaics. Cleantechnica. Available at: https://cleantechnica.com/2023/04/07/more-bad-news-for-fossil-fuels-rooftop-solar-meets-agrivoltaics/ [accessed July 2023].

113 FAO (2022). *World food and agriculture: Statistical yearbook 2022*. Rome: Food and Agriculture Organization of the United Nations (FAO). Available at: https://www.fao.org/documents/card/en/c/cc2211en.

114 IRRI (2023). Manual transplanting. International Rice Research Institute (IRRI). Available at: http://www.knowledgebank.irri.org/training/fact-sheets/crop-establishment/manual-transplanting#:~:text=Why%20transplant%20rice%3F,and%20has%20variable%20water%20levels. [accessed July 2023].

115 IRRI (2019). Machine transplanting. International Rice Research Institute (IRRI). Available at: https://ghgmitigation.irri.org/mitigation-technologies/machine-transplanting [accessed July 2023].

116 Linquist, B., *et al.* (2012). An agronomic assessment of greenhouse gas emissions from major cereal crops. *Global Change Biology*, 18(1), 194–209.

117 Umali-Deininger, D. (2022). *Greening the rice we eat*. Washington, DC: World Bank. available: https://blogs.worldbank.org/eastasiapacific/greening-rice-we-eat?cid=SHR_BlogSiteEmail_EN_EXT.

118 Kurnik, J. and K. Devine (2022). Innovation in reducing methane emissions from the food sector: Side of rice, hold the methane. World Wildlife Fund. Available at: https://www.worldwildlife.org/blogs/sustainability-works/posts/innovation-in-reducing-methane-emissions-from-the-food-sector-side-of-rice-hold-the-methane [accessed July 2023].

119 WRI (2023). Our world in data: Emissions by sector. World Reesources Institute (WRI). Available at: *https://ourworldindata.org/emissions-by-sector* [accessed June 2023].

120 Kurnik, J. and K. Devine (2022). Innovation in reducing methane emissions from the food sector: Side of rice, hold the methane. World Wildlife Fund. Available at: https://www.worldwildlife.org/blogs/sustainability-works/posts/innovation-in-reducing-methane-emissions-from-the-food-sector-side-of-rice-hold-the-methane [accessed July 2023].

121 Umali-Deininger, D. (2022). *Greening the rice we eat*. Washington, DC: World Bank. available: https://blogs.worldbank.org/eastasiapacific/greening-rice-we-eat?cid=SHR_BlogSiteEmail_EN_EXT.

122 Zhijiang, X. (2023). Chinese rice farming trials cut methane emissions. China Dialogue. Available at: https://chinadialogue.net/en/food/chinas-rice-farming-trials-cut-methane-emissions-and-increase-yields/ [accessed July 2023].

123 Xiaodan, Y. (2022). Rice can also reduce carbon emissions! A low-carbon experiment in the field: How to build a closed loop of technology, cost, and carbon trading? Daily Economic News newspaper. Available at: https://www.nbd.com.cN/Articles/2022-10-21/2505684.html [accessed July 2023].

124 Arunrat, N., *et al.* (2021). Comparison of GHG emissions and farmers' profit of large-scale and individual farming in rice production across four regions of Thailand. *Journal of Cleaner Production*, 278, 123945.

125 Li, J., Y. Xin and L. Yuan (2009). *Hybrid rice technology development: Ensuring China's food security*, IFPRI discussion paper. Washington, D.C: International Food Policy Research Institute (IFPRI). Available at: http://www.ifpri.org/publication/hybrid-rice-technology-development.

126 Cornell University (2017). System of rice intensification – SRI methodologies. Cornell University, College of Agriculture and Life Sciences. Available at: http://sri.ciifad.cornell.edu/aboutsri/methods/index.html [accessed July 2017].

127 Lai, C. (2022). System of rice intensification: A solution to methane emissions and food insecurity. Earth.org. Available at: https://earth.org/system-of-rice-intensification/ [accessed July 2023].

128 Oksen, P. (2023). Climate smart technologies in adaptation – Agriculture – Sustainable Success Stories. Available at: https://sustainablesuccessstories.org/technologies/climate-smart-technolgies-adaptation-agriculture/ [accessed July 2023].

129 IRRI (2021). How to manage water. *Rice knowledge bank*, International Rice Research Institute (IRRI). Available at: http://www.knowledgebank.irri.org/step-by-step-production/growth/water-management [accessed July 2023].

130 Anand, S. (2023). Rice acreage down 13% till Aug 5 due to rain shortfall. India Times. Available at: https://economictimes.indiatimes.com/news/economy/agriculture/rice-acreage-down-13-till-aug-5-due-to-rain-shortfall/articleshow/93439236.cms [accessed July 2023].

131 IRRI (2019). Alternate wetting and drying. International Rice Research Institute (IRRI). Available at: https://ghgmitigation.irri.org/mitigation-technologies/alternate-wetting-and-drying [accessed July 2023].

132 Alauddin, M., *et al.* (2020). Adoption of alternate wetting and drying (AWD) irrigation as a water-saving technology in Bangladesh: Economic and environmental considerations. *Land Use Policy*, 91, 104430.

133 IRRI (2019). Laser land levelling. International Rice Research Institute (IRRI). Available at: https://ghgmitigation.irri.org/mitigation-technologies/laser-land-leveling [accessed July 2023].

134 IRRI (2021). How to manage water. *Rice knowledge bank*, International Rice Research Institute (IRRI). Available at: http://www.knowledgebank.irri.org/step-by-step-production/growth/water-management [accessed July 2023].

135 Zhijiang, X. (2023). Chinese rice farming trials cut methane emissions. China Dialogue. Available at: https://chinadialogue.net/en/food/chinas-rice-farming-trials-cut-methane-emissions-and-increase-yields/ [accessed July 2023].

136 IRRI (2019). Dry seeded rice. International Rice Research Institute (IRRI). Available at: https://ghgmitigation.irri.org/mitigation-technologies/dry-seeded-rice [accessed July 2023].

137 Ahmadi, N., *et al.* (2004). Upland rice for highlands: New varieties and sustainable cropping systems for food security promising prospects for the global challenges of rice production the world will face in the coming years?' in I. T. A. FAO (ed), *Rice in Global Markets and Sustainable Production Systems Conference*, Rome, Italy, 12–13 February 2004. Rome: Food and Agriculture Organization of the United Nations (FAO), 14 p.

138 Xu, H.-l., *et al.* (2012). Paddy rice can be cultivated in upland conditions by film mulching to create anaerobic soil conditions. *Journal of Food Agriculture and Environment*, 10(2), 695–702.

139 Shaohua, C., *et al.* (2020). Establishment of a novel technology permitting self-sufficient, renewable energy from rice straw in paddy fields. *Journal of Cleaner Production*, 272, 122721.

140 Kang, M., *et al.* (2023). On securing continuity of eddy covariance flux time-series after changing the measurement height: Correction for flux differences due to the footprint difference. *Agricultural and Forest Meteorology*, 331, 109339.

141 Checherina, P. (2022). Using climate-smart rice to reduce methane emissions from agriculture. Climate & Clean Air Coalition (CCAC) and United Nations Environment Programme (UNEP). Available at: https://www.ccacoalition.org/en/news/using-climate-smart-rice-reduce-methane-emissions-agriculture [accessed July 2023].

142 Umali-Deininger, D. (2022). *Greening the rice we eat*. Washington, DC: World Bank. available: https://blogs.worldbank.org/eastasiapacific/greening-rice-we-eat?cid=SHR_BlogSiteEmail_EN_EXT.

143 World Bank (2023). Sustainable agriculture transformation project. World Bank. Available at: https://projects.worldbank.org/en/projects-operations/project-detail/P145055 [accessed August 2023].

144 CTCN (2023). From solar farm to table, in Liberia improved solar powered irrigation practices are securing lowland rice production. UN Climate Technology Centre & Network (CTCN). Available at: https://www.ctc-n.org/news/solar-farm-table-liberia-improved-solar-powered-irrigation-practices-are-securing-lowland-rice [accessed October 2023].

145 Ngige, L. (2022). Africa agrifoodtech startups raise $1bn in 5 years, but just 1% of global investment. Agfunder Network. Available at: https://agfundernews.com/africa-agrifoodtech-startups-raise-1bn-in-5-years [accessed October 2023].

146 Trendov, N.M., S. Varas and M. Zeng (2019). *Digital technologies in agriculture and rural areas: Status report.* Rome: Food and Agriculture Organization of the United Nations (FAO). Available at: https://www.fao.org/3/ca4985en/ca4985en.pdf.

147 Syngenta (2023). Syngenta Group reports record $33.4 billion sales and $5.6 billion EBITDA in 2022. Syngenta Group. Available at: https://www.syngentagroup.com/en/media/syngenta-news/year/2023/syngenta-group-reports-record-334-billion-sales-and-56-billion-ebitda [accessed July 2023].

148 MarketsandMarkets (2023). Agricultural robots market industry analysis: Types, advantages, and forecast. MarketsandMarkets. Available at: https://www.marketsandmarkets.com/Market-Reports/agricultural-robot-market-173601759.html [accessed July 2023].

149 MarketsandMarkets (2023). Agriculture drones market share, industry size and growth forecast – 2030. MarketsandMarkets. Available at: https://www.marketsandmarkets.com/Market-Reports/agriculture-drones-market-23709764.html [accessed July 2023].

150 Claver, H. (2023). Agricultural drones market to hit revenue of USD 14,237.6 million by 2033. Future Farming. Available at: https://www.futurefarming.com/tech-in-focus/drones/agricultural-drones-market-to-hit-revenue-of-us-14237-6-million-by-2033/ [accessed August 2023].

151 Ipsos (2019). *China's agriculture drone revolution*. Hong Kong: Ipsos Business Consulting. Available at: https://www.ipsos.com/sites/default/files/ct/publication/documents/2020-10/china-agriculture-drones.pdf.

152 Citywire (2023). Deere bets the farm on $150bn 'precision agriculture' opportunity. Citywire. Available at: https://citywire.com/pro-buyer/news/deere-bets-the-farm-on-150bn-precision-agriculture-opportunity/a2408316 [accessed August 2023].

153 Statistics Denmark (2018). *Precision agriculture*. Nyt fra Danmarks Statistik, Copenhagen: Statistics Denmark. Available at: https://www.dst.dk/Site/Dst/SingleFiles/GetArchiveFile.aspx?fi=formid&fo=agriculture-2018--pdf&ext.

154 Danmarks Statistik (2022). Stigning i areal med præcisionslandbrug. *Nyt fra Danmarks Statistik*. Available at: https://www.dst.dk/da/Statistik/nyheder-analyser-publ/nyt/NytHtml?cid=42525 [accessed August 2023].

155 Brons Group (2023). Local use of precision farming equipment. [Interview], 16 August 2023. Available at: https://bronsgroup.com/.

156 Ipsos (2019). *China's agriculture drone revolution*. Hong Kong: Ipsos Business Consulting. Available at: https://www.ipsos.com/sites/default/files/ct/publication/documents/2020-10/china-agriculture-drones.pdf.

157 Airbus (2023). To insure grasslands against climate risks, Crédit Agricole Bank uses Airbus' satellite imagery. Airbus Intelligence. Available at: https://www.intelligence-airbusds.com/newsroom/case-studies/agriculture/credit-agricole-uses-satellite-imagery-to-insure-grasslands/#solution [accessed October 2023].

158 DJI Agriculture (2023). Saving up to 95% water, improving efficiency, while saving chemicals: DJI Agras drones benefit farmers in Turkey during drought. DJI Global. Available at: https://ag.dji.com/case-studies/ag-case-en-t30-tr-drought [accessed October 2023].

4 / Industry

Photos: Getty Images

Technological developments and trends

Steel and cement are responsible for around half of all industrial greenhouse gas emissions[1] and nearly 14 percent of emissions worldwide.[2, 3] Growing global population and urbanization trends are key drivers increasing demand for steel and cement in the construction industry and transport industry. Advancements in technology have a pivotal role to play in mitigating the effects of climate change by optimizing material use, improving production processes and adopting alternative fuels.

Demand-side interventions crucial for emissions reduction

A key take-away regarding steel and cement's climate impact is this: many construction projects use 30 to 50 percent more cement and steel than required when these materials are used more efficiently.[4] Reducing demand for materials is increasingly recognized as necessary for emissions reduction. Such an intervention for steel and cement requires smarter design, education and changes to building codes.

Technology to mitigate climate change has an important role to play. Modern, lightweight and low-carbon materials, plus computer modeling for climate-smart design, all help reduce over-engineering and waste of resources.[5] Reuse and recycling technologies further limit demand for primary production. The growing use of electric arc furnaces (EAFs), which are furnaces that produce steel using electricity instead of fossil fuels, is increasing the scrap recycling rate as they can be fed almost exclusively with recycled steel. But this must be supported through better sorting and better availability of quality scrap metals. According to Bataille *et al.*,[6] the main route toward decarbonizing steel is by increasing scrap use from 26 to 46 percent of global production by 2050.

Many construction projects use 30 to 50 percent more cement and steel than required when these materials are used more efficiently

The promise of green hydrogen

The single most high-impact climate change mitigation strategy for industry is to switch to cleaner fuels.[7] Improving energy efficiency is also crucial, but views differ on the extent of its untapped potential within the mature steel and cement sectors. Direct reduced iron (DRI) as an alternative to traditional ironmaking for the steel industry means iron can be produced directly through a solid-state process. The DRI process currently constitutes five percent of global steel production – and has opened the door to replacing fossil fuels as a fuel source. While DRI mainly inputs natural gas, green hydrogen is an emerging and lower carbon alternative whose emission-reduction potential is up to 97 percent.[8, 9]

The downside is that green hydrogen steel and cement plant production and application is not expected to scale this decade. Moreover, it is dependent on an abundance of renewable energy sources. Most steel and cement plants are located in countries whose electric grid systems are fossil-fuel heavy.[10] This highlights the importance of a dual focus on a general greening of electricity grids.

Alternative fuels and electrification in steel and cement

In the cement sector, a majority of plants already burn alternative fuels – such as used oils, biomass or other waste types – to some extent. However, there is a lack of a consensus on the climate impact of biomass and waste incineration, with environmental organizations working toward limiting their use in cement plants.[11] Despite this, their use is growing, with countries such as Germany having achieved nearly 70 percent alternative fuel use within its cement sector, mainly by burning plastic, sewage sludge and other waste fractions.[12]

In terms of electrification technologies, maturity level differs between the steel and cement sectors. Although there are companies in Finland and Sweden developing electric kilns for the cement industry, they have not been piloted at a cement plant. Challenges relate to high cost, stability and the capacity to generate high temperatures. Electric-arc steelmaking has by contrast come significantly further, accounting for almost 29 percent of all steel produced in 2018.[13]

Managing demand for materials with a large carbon footprint such as steel and cement is crucial as cities, economies and populations continue to grow

Leapfrogging with breakthrough technologies

Booming demand for construction materials has stagnated climate change mitigation progress.[14] Managing demand for materials with a large carbon footprint such as steel and cement is crucial as cities, economies and populations continue to grow. Emerging economies and developing countries face a dual challenge of development, on the one hand, and decarbonization, on the other. An integrated approach is therefore necessary if carbon lock-in and a costly transition are to be avoided.

Slow progress on decarbonization calls for innovative and transformative solutions. The steel and cement sectors continue to explore breakthrough technologies to reach climate goals. These include carbon capture and storage, green hydrogen and alternative methods for cement production. On the horizon are Industry 4.0 revolution technologies for interconnected and "smart" plants. Such technologies allow components of steel and cement manufacturing to interact better through process monitoring and energy and material use optimization. They include technologies such as digital twins, internet of things (IoT) sensors and artificial intelligence (AI)-supported diagnostics for operations monitoring.

Breakthrough technologies could bring leapfrogging opportunities. A number of studies have shown them to be instrumental for the fundamental changes needed to achieve global climate targets.[15] Yet, although these technologies may be promising, their development and deployment requires high capital investment and progress has so far been slow.

Proven solutions require urgent implementation

Out of 29 active carbon capture and storage (CCS) projects worldwide, only one has been developed commercially at an iron and steel plant. For cement, two projects are under construction and four in early development.[16, 17] Globally, just 0.1 percent of the world's emissions are currently captured and stored.[18] Meanwhile, the climate change mitigation potential of emerging technologies is unclear from a life-cycle perspective, for example, for digital technologies. The information and communications technology (ICT) sector can offer tools for industry to monitor and lower its energy usage and emissions. But the ICT sector itself accounts for between 1.8–2.8 percent of global GHG emissions – and by some estimates even up to 3.9 percent.[19]

Moreover, a heavy reliance on breakthrough and emerging solutions risks overlooking proven technologies and thus missing the window of opportunity to act on climate change. Considering the long lifespan of industrial plants, the steel and cement sectors must adopt and implement new low-carbon technologies this decade. This reduces the risk of stranded assets such as steel furnaces which could become inoperable or devalued as countries seek to reduce their carbon emissions.[20] While innovation is needed, a first priority must be to implement and scale those technologies proven to be effective for material efficiency and circularity, fuel switching and process efficiency. This chapter presents an array of examples, from proven to horizon technologies.

Patents and finance

A range of models and forecasts indicate that existing technologies will not take us all the way to net-zero emissions.[21] Continued innovation and development of technology to mitigate climate change is therefore crucial. Examining trends in the patenting of new solutions points to where innovation is most active. The examples below focus particularly on breakthrough technologies, such as hydrogen and CCS, where significant innovation and scale-up is called for.

Patent trends for decarbonizing steel and cement

A 2022 patent analysis of low-emission steel and iron ore found 4,246 patent families have been filed since 2015 - and the number is growing. While most patents filed related to iron ore processing and transport, production methods for low-emission steel have seen the fastest growth. Patents included CCS incorporation into blast furnaces, substitution of coke with alternative fuels, electric arc furnaces and direct reduced iron (DRI) technologies. This is also where the majority of emissions occur. China had the most patent applicants in this field, accounting for 88 percent of patents filed.[22]

For cement, the number of low-carbon technology patents have also grown steadily since 2000, with China as a major innovation hub. Research has focused most on substituting clinker - an integral but energy-intensive component of cement production - and less on radical changes to the raw material mix. However, while clinker-substitution technologies and chemical admixtures have twice as many patent families compared to novel cement technologies, few are yet commercialized.[23] Better performance-based standards could help drive the development of alternative materials within the cement industry.[24]

Patent trends for carbon capture and storage

As noted by the International Energy Agency (IEA), global patent applications for CCS technologies have lost momentum in recent years. Patents in the CCS sector have declined by almost 7 percent since 2013, after witnessing near 10 percent growth over the previous decade.[25] This is contrary to the general technology patent application trend. One explanation could be exaggerated expectations in the early 2000s regarding CCS technology scale-up, followed by its financial viability coming into question. That said, the total number of patents is significant. Nearly 42,000 patent families have been filed in relation to CCS since 2015. A majority are in an active state, meaning the patent has been granted and can be used by the owner. Among the top filers are applicants from China, primarily companies, followed by universities.[26]

Patent trends for hydrogen technologies

Hydrogen technologies and patents are steadily increasing, largely driven by government policies. As of early 2021, more than 30 countries had produced hydrogen roadmaps.[27] Since 2010, more than 32,000 patent families have been filed globally. Of those, 77 percent are active, potentially indicating a high level of commercial interest. China, the United States and Japan dominate in terms of number of patent filings across hydrogen technology areas. More than half of patents focus on hydrogen production, mainly related to electrolysis, the rest focus on storage, distribution and utilization.[28]

In terms of hydrogen utilization, a majority of patent filings relate to its application in industrial processes and electricity generation (figure 4.1). This is promising for the steel and cement sectors[29]

Figure 4.1 Global patent filings for hydrogen utilization, 2010–2020

Source: IP Australia, 2021.

Patent trends for Industry 4.0 technologies

Patent applications for Industry 4.0 technologies – defined in the Industry 4.0 chapter – have seen a remarkable development in the past decades. Their growth is five times the baseline growth rate for technologies overall, and accounted for 11 percent of global patenting activity in 2018 (figure 4.2).[30]

This massive growth in applications is dramatically bigger in the United States compared to Europe, Japan, China and the Republic of Korea, respectively. Patenting activity is also highly concentrated. The United States and China have the largest digital platforms, host half the world's biggest data centers and have the highest 5G adoption rates. In terms of research and development, the United States and China account for 70 percent of the world's top AI researchers and 94 percent of AI start-up funding in the past five years.[31]

Certain technologies have seen an even more explosive patent growth. Blockchain patent filings have grown by between 140–230 percent annually since 2013.[32] Artificial intelligence and machine learning filings increased four-fold globally between 2012–2016, 92 percent of which were active in 2019.[33]

Figure 4.2 Global growth in patents for Industry 4.0 technologies (dark green) compared to all technology fields (green), 2000–2018

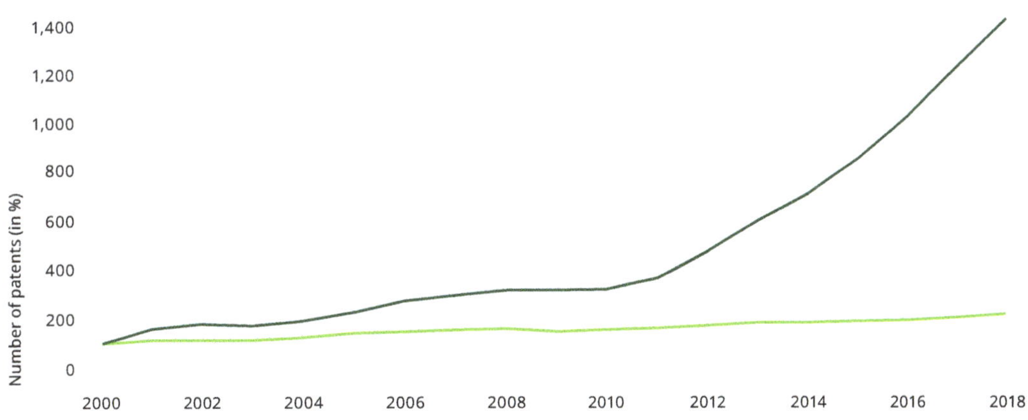

Source: EPO, 2020.

However, by no means do all the patent applications in question relate to the manufacturing industry. For blockchain, applications mainly relate to payments and transaction systems, financial services and e-commerce.[34] For machine learning, of the 36,740 patents filed since 2012, only 1,549 relate to industry and physical manufacturing applications, but instead include sensors for optimizing performance and monitoring, supply chain optimization and the use of machine learning for better product design.[35]

ICT technologies in the manufacturing industry have the potential to reduce GHG emissions. They can do so by enabling better energy monitoring and management. Yet, the rate of innovation within the energy-saving ICT sector slowed over the past decade. On a more positive note, the slow-down in energy-saving ICT innovation has been less marked than for other climate change mitigation technologies.[36]

Significant investment gap for steel and cement decarbonization

Mitigation technologies in the steel and cement sectors have to contend with complex and long-term investment cycles. This means that only significant and urgent upfront investment can help avoid a carbon lock-in effect. For steel, adopting low-carbon solutions will require close to USD 200 billion globally until 2050. In addition, USD 2 trillion is needed for necessary infrastructure such as CO_2 pipelines and storage facilities.[37] According to a report by research and consultancy company Wood Mackenzie, decarbonizing steel will require a USD 1.4 trillion investment by 2050, together with "nothing less than a revolution at every stage of the value chain" in order to get us there.[38]

Despite a growing number of announced investments, a concert of interventions is needed if low-carbon technologies are to be significantly accelerated. For steel, there is a 855-metric tonne capacity gap between what is planned for low-carbon steel production and potential investment in high-carbon steel production this decade.[39] For decarbonizing cement, a cost assessment of low-carbon technologies per tonne of CO_2 reduced serves to highlight the range of costs associated with the various options. Interestingly, certain technologies such as clinker substitutes show a negative abatement cost, indicating their high-impact potential if scaled and promoted.[40]

Mitigation technologies in the steel and cement sectors have to contend with complex and long-term investment cycles. This means that only significant and urgent upfront investment can help avoid a carbon lock-in effect

Governments play a key role

Major steel and cement producers are simultaneously investing in proven technologies while funding research and development into breakthrough technologies. Government grants play a key role in these sectors' climate transition. In March 2023, the US Government announced USD 6 billion funding directed at decarbonizing heavy industries, such as steel, cement and aluminum, through competitive grants to cover projects led by technology providers, industry and universities.[41] Countries including France, Germany and the United Kingdom (UK) have likewise pledged significant funds to these same sectors. In 2022, Germany provided more than USD 700 million to fund steel producer Salzgitter's low-carbon initiative to build two direct reduction plants and three electric arc furnaces. Earlier that year, the French Government announced a USD 1.7 billion investment pledge by 2030 in support of ArcelorMittal's low-carbon program.[42] The European Union's (EU) Green Deal and the United States' Inflation Reduction Act are likely to incentivize further support, while the EU's new Carbon Border Adjustment Mechanism putting a carbon price on imported goods is expected to incentivize emission reduction in internationally-traded commodities like steel and cement.

High-income countries and China are responsible for most low-carbon steel projects (for primary production).[43] At the same time, China relies on high-emitting blast furnaces that are still relatively new. Much will depend on China, producer of more than 54 percent of the world's steel.[44]

Avoiding conventional primary production may be even more important in India, the second largest steel producer and the country with the biggest estimated growth in steel demand.[45] While a number of large high-carbon steel plants are planned[46], certain companies are leading the transition. For example, Indian steel company JSW Steel recently raised USD 1 billion in sustainability-linked bonds.[47]

Innovative funding mechanisms at exploration stage

New initiatives are arising to innovate the deployment of low-carbon technologies. Many are still in the exploration phase. Financing Steel Decarbonization is a USD 1 billion funding mechanism proposed by company Smartex and the National Renewable Energy Laboratory (NREL) in the United States to promote the adoption of a wide range of technologies within the Indian steel sector. Funds must first be pooled from donor grants, private investors and other sources; half will cover the implementation of commercial technologies, and half will go toward piloting breakthrough technologies.[48] This is key considering breakthrough technologies, such as green hydrogen and carbon capture technologies, are still at the pre-commercial development stage.

Other innovative initiatives to finance industrial decarbonization include carbon contracts for difference (CCfD) - a financial instrument in which a fixed carbon price is set over a given period of time, to be shared between a public and private entity with the aim of reducing investment risk for companies. Green public procurement is also growing in relevance. For instance, the Industrial Deep Decarbonisation Initiative (IDDI) is a global coalition of private and public sector organizations whose aim is to encourage at least 10 governments to commit to the public procurement of low-carbon steel and cement within the next three years.

A large proportion of international climate finance goes toward climate change mitigation projects. However, few of these have benefitted the steel and cement sectors

Green steel assurances are yet another approach pioneered by a few large steelmaking companies in Europe. This involves issuing CO_2-saving certificates for low-carbon initiatives. These can then be traded as premiums to customers who are eventually able to claim the equivalent reductions in their Scope 3 emissions (see box 4.6) according to GHG protocol standards. A yet unsolved challenge is third-party verification and the risk of double-selling certificates in the downstream value chain.[49]

Meanwhile, the interest of venture capital firms and banks in steel and cement decarbonization startups has increased, with more than USD 7 billion raised within the past two years. Swedish startup H2 Green Steel alone has secured nearly USD 5 billion in debt financing from public and private banks.[50]

More international collaboration needed

To avoid carbon lock-in, developing countries need to adopt climate technologies alongside the rest of the world. International cooperation through technical assistance, technology transfer, grants and loans has an important role to play, but has fallen short so far.

A large proportion of international climate finance goes toward climate change mitigation projects. However, few of these have benefitted the steel and cement sectors. In fact, international finance institutions have limited exposure to either sector and their green industrial strategies are at an early stage.[51] However, they have a key role to play in emerging and developing nations in terms of de-risking investments for early adopters, stimulating demand, strengthening value chains and investing in enabling technologies.

Carbon credits and pricing schemes

In terms of carbon credits, the steel and cement sectors are both included in major schemes. These include the EU emission trading system, as well as China's carbon market, which became operational in 2021 and is three times the size of the EU emissions market. Furthermore, India has now announced its plan to start a carbon trading market for major emitters within the energy, steel and cement industries.[52] We are already seeing the impact of carbon credits. Following the Canadian Government's declared intention to increase the carbon price from USD 30/tCO_2 to USD 130/tCO_2 by 2030, Algoma Steel announced a USD 529 million investment into converting its high-emitting blast furnace into an electric arc furnace - a move that could reduce the company's emissions by 70 percent. More than half of the funds needed to cover the transition were provided by the government in this case.[53]

Carbon markets are, however, riddled with free allowances and exemptions for key emitters. In reality, they cover no more than 20 percent of global steelmaking capacity. Moreover, current pricing levels are not sufficient to achieve 2050 net-zero targets. International cooperation is central to creating a level playing field within these industries and ensuring that a loss of competitiveness does not continue to be a barrier to more ambitious carbon pricing.[54]

Rules to govern the international carbon market proposed under Article 6 of the Paris Agreement have now been agreed upon. It is envisaged that countries' carbon markets will be linked together and a central United Nations (UN) mechanism created for emissions trading through the implementation of specific projects. When in place, such funding mechanisms are expected to help implement low-carbon projects within the steel and cement industries in the medium to long term.[55]

Photo: Getty Images / Phyrart Studio

Iron and steel

Although production efficiency has improved significantly over the past 100 years, total CO_2 emissions from the steel sector are increasing, mainly driven by steel demand. A technological pathway toward decarbonizing steel does exist combining both current and emerging technologies.

Key areas for steel decarbonization

More than half of the steel sector's initiative announcements regarding low-carbon steelmaking relate to replacing the high-emitting blast furnace method of making iron. These often involve combining direct-reduced iron (DRI), electric arc furnace (EAF) and hydrogen technologies. Other initiatives mainly relate to scrap steel recycling.[56] However, there is no single solution to steel decarbonization. Technologies such as heat recovery and biomass integration could offer a transitional pathway, until breakthrough technologies reach maturity - and low-carbon ambitions match investment. This Industry chapter presents an array of key technologies focused on the high-emitting stages within steelmaking (box 4.1).

Box 4.1 Steel sector emissions

The iron and steel industry is responsible for at least 7-9 percent of global greenhouse gas (GHG) emissions.[57] GHG emissions occur at every stage of the steelmaking process, from the mining of iron ore to shaping the final product. While more efficient direct reduced iron (DRI) plants are growing in number, most emissions come from the blast-furnace preparation of iron for steel production (figure 4.3). Globally, the demand for steel is expected to have grown by more than a quarter by 2050, using 2019 as a baseline.[58] Asia remains the largest steel-consuming region. But demand from Africa - the world's fastest-growing region with a population projected to grow 220 percent by 2100 - is rising quickly (albeit from a relatively low level). It is projected that come 2050, 80 percent of buildings in Africa will have been constructed after 2015.[59] At the same time, steel - a key component of wind turbines, e-vehicles and railways - continues to be essential for decarbonization itself.

Figure 4.3 Emissions from various stages within the steelmaking process

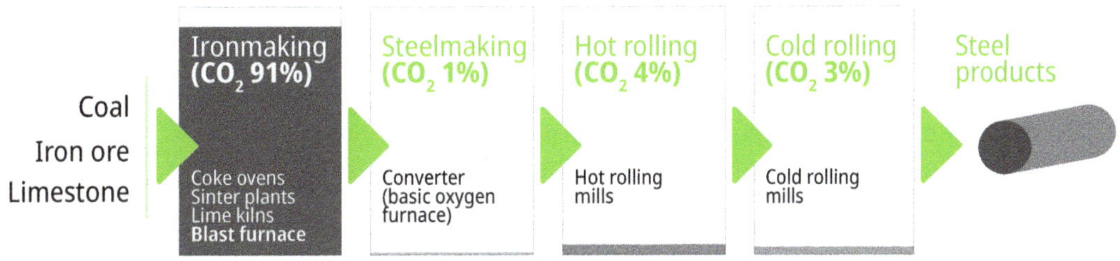

Source: ECN, 2015.

Retrofitting or phasing out blast furnaces

Traditionally, pig iron (see box 4.2) is made in blast furnaces. This is the most carbon-intensive part of steelmaking (see box 4.1). Blast furnaces have been around for hundreds of years and the potential for further efficiency improvement is limited. Any low-carbon scenario that includes blast furnaces would probably need to rely on emerging technologies such as carbon capture and storage (CCS) to reach its climate goals.[60] However, CCS is not a mature technology - and time is short.

Around 71 percent of current global blast furnace capacity will come to the end of its operational life before 2030.[61] Considering the 20-year lifespan of such facilities, the sector needs urgent investment into new solutions to avoid a decade-long lock-in to old technologies. Researchers have estimated that a decade of delay in replacing blast furnaces could consume 12 percent of the remaining carbon budget.[62]

Today's pace of blast furnace replacement is too slow to achieve the Paris Agreement's 1.5-degree Celsius target.[63] Blast furnace retrofitting is therefore an alternative measure. This involves measures such as lining blast furnaces, recovering gas for electricity generation and integrating biomass into blast furnace fuel in regions where there is a high sustainable biomass availability.[64]

Researchers have estimated that a decade of delay in replacing blast furnaces could consume 12 percent of the remaining carbon budget

Box 4.2 Two steelmaking routes

Steel is an alloy of iron and carbon that is both stronger and more fracture-resistant than iron. It can be either recycled from scrap steel or produced through processing iron ore. Steel is produced via two main routes: the blast furnace-basic oxygen furnace (BF-BOF) route and electric arc furnace (EAF) route, with variations and combinations in between.

The key difference between the two routes is the raw materials consumed. For the BF-BOF route, these are predominantly iron ore, coal and recycled steel. The EAF route mainly uses recycled steel and electricity. Depending on plant configuration and recycled steel availability, other sources of metallic iron such as direct-reduced iron (DRI) or hot metal can also be directed to the EAF route. Iron manufactured in a blast furnace is typically known as "pig iron" or "hot metal" and produced and processed in a liquid state.

Melting scrap in an EAF generates significantly less GHG emissions than the integrated BF-BOF route. But limited scrap availability constrains use.

Direct reduced iron (DRI) opens up for fuel switching

The biggest climate change mitigation potential to be found within the steel sector relates to fuel switching and electrification.[65] Conventionally, coal in the form of coke is used as feedstock for iron production. Specifically, it helps separate oxygen from iron ore within the blast furnace. Carbon monoxide's reaction with oxygen at high temperatures yields a purer iron material suitable for steelmaking. But this process also produces large amounts of CO_2.

A more low-carbon option is to produce iron through direct reduced iron (DRI) plants. Currently, most commercial DRI plants use natural gas instead of coal as the reducing agent for removing oxygen from iron ore. Because natural gas is still a fossil fuel, hydrogen - specifically green hydrogen - is being touted as a breakthrough alternative for direct reduction of iron ore. But the technology is not expected to achieve significant scale-up by the major steel-producing nations within the next decade (read more below).

Electrification of steelmaking

An alternative ironmaking horizon technology is iron reduction through applying electricity (electrolysis) at a high or low temperature.[66] This requires iron to be dissolved in a solvent.[67] One benefit is that electrolysis technologies could be more modular, requiring smaller facilities and offering greater flexibility. To date, only a few hundred kilograms of steel has been produced in a laboratory or at small pilot scale using this technology.

Electrification of the steelmaking process through EAFs opens up a further route away from fossil fuels. Direct reduced iron and EAFs are considered a cornerstone of steel decarbonization. While their deployment varies greatly between countries, a combination of the two technologies currently accounts for 5 percent of global steel production - and is growing.[68] This represents a significant emissions mitigation potential compared to the blast furnace and BF-BOF route.

Notably, an EAF's mitigation potential depends on key factors such as a country's energy mix and the percentage of scrap steel used as feedstock (box 4.3). For instance, the CO_2 intensity per tonne of steel produced by an EAF in India and China appears to be higher than for conventional steel production in Canada. Mainly, this is due to lower scrap recycling levels and higher fossil fuel rates within the grid.

Obviously, the choice of energy sources powering a country's electric grid is not in the hands of steel producers. Some steel producers are therefore developing their own renewable energy or entering into power purchase agreements with low emission generators.

Box 4.3 Steel recycling

Scrap steel can be sourced from cars, bridges and buildings. Every tonne of scrap that goes into steel production avoids 1.5 tonnes of CO_2 emission and 1.4 tonnes of iron ore consumption.[69] About one-third of steel production already uses scrap steel, and it is estimated that around 85 percent of steel is recycled. Expansion of scrap-based steel production and higher recycling rates depend in part on the availability of high-grade scrap, to which there is a limit. Measures such as improved separation of high-copper steel from other scrap streams can boost the availability of scrap corresponding to end-product requirements. In this regard, technologies such as laser-induced breakdown spectroscopy technologies to determine the content of alloys are under rapid development.[70, 71]

Material efficiency for reduced steel demand

A crucial but sometimes overlooked steel decarbonization strategy is material efficiency, wherein fewer resources are used to achieve the same result.[72] The EAF does more than just enable steelmaking electrification. It can also handle higher amounts of scrap steel than a basic oxygen furnace (up to 97 percent) and is an efficient way of melting scrap. Traditional steelmaking recycles no more than 25 percent of scrap steel in the process before having to increase energy input. The remaining 75 percent or more is virgin material (see box 4.3). Measures to keep steel flows clean (especially from copper) and ensure high-quality secondary steel are key. But for the steel sector material sustainability means going beyond scrap recycling.

Using steel more efficiently, for example by using less steel in construction, together with reusing and recycling, could cut steel demand by 20 percent by 2050[73] – or even 40 percent according to the IPCC.[74] Indeed, it is possible to cut steel use in buildings by almost a half while still meeting design specifications.[75] However, the single largest contributor to material efficiency would be to extend the lifespan of buildings. Reinforcing concrete with engineering steel combined with stainless steel, for example, can eliminate repairs and replacements resulting from steel degradation within concrete.

Material substitution for existing steel products, or design and quality improvements to avoid material degradation, are other options for reducing steel sector emissions. High-strength steel has the potential to cut material use by 30 to 40 percent in a range of cases.[76]

Avoiding steel loss: smart manufacturing and short lead times

Avoiding material loss in the steelmaking process can further contribute to GHG emission reduction. Up to half of steel supplied to the automotive industry currently ends up as scrap at the fabrication or forming stages and does not make it through to the final product.[77] Technologies that support material efficiency and circular material flows, such as near-net-shape casting (NNSC), 3D printing and powder metallurgy, could reduce waste by producing the desired shape with fewer processing stages. That said, they may only have a marginal positive impact. Avoiding material loss requires fundamental operational efficiency improvements and reduced lead times to better align the supply and demand sides of steel products.

The shortage of high-quality iron ore represents a significant bottleneck in steelmakers' efforts to reduce emissions. Therefore, expanding DRI use is dependent on upgrading lower-quality iron ore

At present, a network of steel stockholders separates steel producers from users. While standard-sized steel products suit producers and stockholders, these are not aligned to consumer need from a material use perspective. Enabling more end-use adapted steel production while maintaining short lead times could reduce material loss, owing to fewer steel products having to be cut to size at the user stage. Digital technologies that enable efficient supply chains could play an important role in this.

A limiting of steel demand and supply may raise concerns regarding a just transition, as the industry currently employs over six million people worldwide.[78] On the other hand, without targeted measures to reduce steel demand, CO_2 emissions are projected to continue rising.[79]

Access to raw materials a barrier

Material efficiency also means making the best use of available raw materials. One challenge with direct reduced iron (DRI) is that it makes iron ore impurities more difficult to remove. This is mainly due to the iron ore remaining solid throughout the production process. DRI requires iron ore with a higher iron content, of which there is an insufficient supply globally.

The shortage of high-quality iron ore represents a significant bottleneck in steelmakers' efforts to reduce emissions.[80] Therefore, expanding DRI use is dependent on upgrading

Recent innovation may allow seawater to be used instead of freshwater for hydrogen electrolysis, thus saving another increasingly critical resource – freshwater

lower-quality iron ore. This happens through a process known as beneficiation. Concentrated innovation efforts are focusing on improving beneficiation technologies through electrochemical processes.

Hydrogen innovation progressing slowly

Hydrogen is receiving much attention as an alternative fuel in ironmaking. When reducing iron ore using hydrogen instead of carbon, oxygen atoms no longer react with carbon atoms to produce CO_2. Instead, they react with hydrogen atoms, leaving water as a by-product. However, there is an important distinction between the ways in which hydrogen is produced, and in what type of furnace it can be used.

Today, almost all hydrogen is derived from natural gas in a process involving steam with high-energy requirements (also called gray hydrogen).[81] When gray hydrogen is used as a supplementary fuel in conventional blast furnaces, emission reduction is only around 2 percent. However, hydrogen can also be produced through the electrolysis of water. Hydrogen is considered green when the electrolysis is powered by renewable energy. If green hydrogen is used for direct reduction of iron (DRI), in the best-case scenario the CO_2 emitted is only 2.8 percent of what is emitted by a conventional blast furnace.[82]

Green hydrogen production is advancing – but only slowly. Today, primary steel production with electrolysis-derived hydrogen has the same CO_2 footprint as the most energy-efficient conventional blast furnace. This is because most current grid electricity is not green, but instead a mix of fossil fuel and renewable energy sources.[83] But with growing access to affordable renewable energy, green hydrogen could become a game-changer for lower-carbon steelmaking, both as a reducing agent and for powering steel electrification.

Sweden has already demonstrated green hydrogen-based DRI through its HYBRIT project (see innovation examples). And recent innovation may allow seawater to be used instead of freshwater for hydrogen electrolysis, thus saving another increasingly critical resource – freshwater.[84]

End-of-pipe carbon capture

Technological innovation is offering several breakthrough technologies. In reality, the transition toward steel sector decarbonization is slow paced. History has shown the industry to traditionally opt for gradual improvements over large-scale plant substitutions.[85] Exceptions include technology improvements such as continuous casting, or EAF penetration in certain regions with high scrap availability.

In place of phasing out carbon-intensive blast furnaces, the industry often emphasizes the potential of CCS technologies. Such technologies could reduce CO_2 emissions by up to 65 percent for a conventional steelmaking process, with captured CO_2 turned into useful products such as ethanol and methanol.[86]

However, the technological maturity of CCS is not advanced. Currently, only one of the 26 commercial CCS facilities in operation globally has been developed at an iron and steel plant.[87] Moreover, only a few major investments into CCS technologies appear to be planned.[88] On the other hand, the International Energy Agency envisages 15 percent of steel production processes to have been equipped with technologies that capture and store (or utilize) carbon by 2050 to meet Paris Agreement goals.[89]

Energy efficiency at its limit

Steel sector energy efficiency measures seem to have reached their limit in terms of emissions reduction. The best available technologies in this area are unable to provide more than around a 10 to 15 percent emission reduction – far below global targets.[90] A majority of steel producers already employ some form of energy management system to track and optimize energy usage.[91] However, another study suggests that, in the short term, retrofitting existing systems with the best efficiency technologies available today could have the greatest abatement potential.[92] Companies often invest in increasing the efficiency of auxiliary systems such as compressors and motors.[93]

Continuing the transition toward making proven technologies such as electric furnaces, preheaters and precalciners the industry norm is crucial. However, several other technologies – ranging from proven to horizon – deserve further research, investment and scaling in order to meet the steel sector's net-zero requirements.

Innovation examples

Photo: Getty Images / © audioundwerbung

Green hydrogen in Sweden
In 2021, Swedish company SSAB delivered the world's first batch of fossil-free steel to carmaker Volvo. This so-called green steel was delivered as part of HYBRIT, a project in collaboration with mining company LKAB and energy producer Vattenfall. It has been described as fossil free for two reasons. The iron ore is reduced (as in reduced from iron ore to iron) using green hydrogen instead of coke and the steel made in an electric arc furnace powered by renewable energy. Unlike coke, which emits carbon, hydrogen produces water vapor as a by-product. Now that the technology has been demonstrated at pilot scale, the company is working toward commercializing their low-carbon steel by 2026. Also in Sweden, H2 Green Steel is moving toward producing steel through a similar low-carbon process. That company is aiming for commercialization by 2025, and to be producing five million tonnes of steel a year by 2030.

Photo: Getty Images / © sdlgzps

Energy efficiency measures at Saldanha Works in South Africa
Steel producer ArcelorMittal Saldanha in South Africa has managed to save 80 GWh of energy and mitigate more than 77,000 tonnes of CO_2 in a single year. It did so by implementing an energy management system. The plant is no longer in service because of financial instability, but its earlier investments into energy efficiency measures have demonstrated they can lead to cost savings. The company saved roughly South African rand (R) 90 million in 2011 (equivalent to USD 35 million at the time) through a minimal capital investment of R500,000 (USD 197 million). Its adoption of an energy management system, together with energy system optimization measures to reduce the plant's production energy intensity, was supported by the United Nations Industrial Development Organization (UNIDO). Examples of technical interventions include reduced liquefied petroleum gas (LPG) use and the installation of solar lights and efficient water heating systems, as well as optimization of (i) post-combustion cooling fans, (ii) water-cooling systems and (iii) ladle stations for transporting molten metal.[94]

Photo: Getty Images / © Sander Stock

On-site solar power for steel production
Although it eliminates coke use, a switch to an electric arc furnace only brings with it significant mitigation benefits if the electricity used is fossil-free. Grid energy mix varies significantly from country to country. Some steel producers have opted for on-site renewable energy production to guarantee a cleaner electricity stream. In Kenya, the Devki Group is host to several steel factories around the country. Its aim is to generate

more than 6 GWh of power a year from solar panels installed on factory rooftops. The same goes for EVRAZ North America's Rocky Mountain steel mill in Colorado, United States. The mill - currently under construction - will be powered by a 300-MW solar farm comprising more than 750,000 solar panels.

Photo: Getty Images/© AvigatorPhotographer

Heat exchange in a Slovenian steel plant

A steel plant in Slovenia has used a heat exchanger to improve a production unit's energy efficiency by more than 40 percent. The resultant reduction in CO_2 equivalents is estimated to be around 425 tonnes a year. The steel plant SIJ Metal Ravne - part of the EU's ETEKINA innovation initiative - has demonstrated a heat-pipe heat exchanger prototype by installing it above a gas-powered furnace. The heat exchanger consisted of two parts: an air-to-air section and an air-to-water section. This is to maximize heat recovery. Exhaust gases are captured at a high temperature (about 450°C) and channeled to the first part of the heat exchanger where air to the furnace is heated. The exhaust flue gases (now at a lower temperature of around 220°C) continue onward toward the second part of the heat exchanger, where they heat water to warm the plant's office buildings. Only then are the flue gases (now at around 150°C) released into the atmosphere. The energy savings that came from the heat-pipe exchanger made it financially viable, the steel plant recouping the exchanger's market value within nine months of installation.[95]

Technology solutions

Proven technologies

Mining and pre-treatment: lower-carbon iron pelletizing

Metso Outotec

Photo: Getty Images/© Ihor Martsenyuk

Life-cycle assessments of iron ore mining and processing for steelmaking show that a majority of emissions happen during the agglomeration stage. This is when iron ore is massed into larger components in the form of sinter or pellets. These are then input into blast furnaces to make steel. The sintering process produces higher emissions than pelletizing.[96] Pellets are more expensive, but the iron content is typically higher as they undergo a beneficiation process to improve the quality. Inputting pellets into furnaces instead of sinter results in lower overall fuel consumption, as well as carbon mitigation. This is mainly owing to lower coke use.[97] Metso Outotec is a company designing and suppling iron ore pelletizing plants. The company is working toward lower-carbon producing pellet plants by looking at gas schemes, advanced combustion and burner technology and process optimization. Its Ferroflame™ LowNO_x burner can reduce nitrogen oxide (NO_x) emissions from pelletizing by up to 80 percent compared to traditional burners.

- Contracting type: For sale/service
- Technology level: Medium
- Country of origin: Finland
- Availability: Worldwide
- Contact: WIPO GREEN Database

Iron production: natural gas-based direct reduced iron (DRI)

Midrex Technologies Inc.

Photo: © Midrex Technologies

Unlike blast furnaces, DRI plants do not use coke to prepare iron for steelmaking. Instead, natural gas is converted into a reducing gas that flows through the iron ore, reducing its oxygen content and producing sponge-like iron. This can then be pressed into briquettes or discharged hot or cold in pellet or lump form. A majority of global DRI is produced in MIDREX® plants using natural gas as the reducing gas source. Midrex Technologies has patented a number of associated products and processes supporting DRI with natural gas. They include the MIDREX® Reformer (which turns natural gas into the reducing gases hydrogen and carbon monoxide) and the MIDREX® Shaft Furnace in which the iron is reduced.

- Contracting type: For sale/service
- Technology level: High
- Country of origin: Japan
- Availability: Worldwide
- Contact: WIPO GREEN Database

Iron production: iron ore smelting reduction

Primetals Technologies

Photo: Getty Images /© zhaojiankang

Unlike the conventional blast furnace route, the smelting reduction process does not need coke or sinter. Iron ore is reduced in either one or two stages. In the two-stage process, the ore is partially reduced before being further reduced and melted in a separate process reactor. The technology is suitable for medium-scale integrated plants. COREX is a commercially successful smelting reduction process developed by Voest-Alpine Industries (VAI). First installed in 1988, it is now offered by companies such as Primetals Technologies. A benefit of the COREX process is that it uses oxygen instead of a hot nitrogen blast, thereby reducing NO_x emissions. Nonetheless, the process remains energy-intensive and it is likely to need to be coupled with carbon capture technologies to contribute adequately to sector carbon efficiency.

- Contracting type: For sale/service
- Technology level: High
- Country of origin: United Kingdom
- Availability: Worldwide
- Contact: WIPO GREEN Database

Iron production: blast furnace energy monitoring
Fluke Corporation

Photo: Getty Images / © sdlgzps

Monitoring temperature, as well as pressure and other blast furnace factors, provides a good energy consumption overview. This helps avoid blockages and errors in the process. The data provided allows production schedule adjustments to be made that take into account electricity peaks and supply limitations. Fluke's series of Endurance pyrometers determine stove temperature in order to control both stove heat and cold blast. Temperatures are measured by a sensor and observed from the safety of a control room.

- Contracting type: For sale
- Technology level: High
- Country of origin: United States
- Availability: Worldwide
- Contact: WIPO GREEN Database

Iron production/steel production: hot-charging iron into a steelmaking furnace
Midrex Technologies Inc.

Photo: © Midrex Technologies

When direct reduced iron (DRI) is combined with an electric arc furnace (EAF) to produce steel, energy can be saved by not having to cool and store iron between two stages. If the DRI plant and EAF are located next to each other, hot-charging technology allows iron to instead be fed continuously into the furnace, thereby minimizing heat loss. Midrex has developed just such a hot-charging solution called the HOTLINK® SYSTEM. It delivers iron to the EAF at a temperature of up to 700°C by positioning the shaft furnace above or adjacent to the EAF and discharging hot iron directly.

- Contracting type: For sale/service
- Technology level: High
- Country of origin: Japan
- Availability: Worldwide
- Contact: WIPO GREEN Database

Steel production: electric arc furnace (EAF) with scrap preheating

JP Steel Plantech Co.

Photo: Getty Images / © georgeclerk

An EAF uses electrodes to generate the heat required to melt steel. EAFs are widely used in steelmaking in countries like the United States as an alternative to conventional blast and basic oxygen furnaces (BF-BOFs). They are becoming increasingly popular in Europe and other parts of the world. EAFs contribute to electrification of the steelmaking process and reduce coke-dependency. They can also be fed with almost 100 percent recycled scrap, compared to about 25 percent for conventional furnaces. Nonetheless, they still require a lot of energy. Steel Plantech has developed the ECOARC™ – an EAF focused on energy recovery and efficiency. The ECOARC™ preheats scrap inside a shaft attached directly to the furnace shell using exhaust gas. This exhaust gas is then used to treat unwanted chemicals from waste gas in a combustion chamber without requiring extra fuel.

- Contracting type: For sale/service
- Technology level: High
- Country of origin: Japan
- Availability: Asia
- Contact: WIPO GREEN Database

Steel production: electric arc furnace (EAF) post combustion

Nippon Sanso Holdings Corporation

Photo: Getty Images / © scanrail

EAF productivity can be increased by making use of the chemical energy embedded in carbon monoxide. Carbon monoxide is released during the melting and refining of steel scrap. Further heat can be released by injecting oxygen to post-combust the carbon monoxide. The heat generated can then be returned to the process. Nippon Sanso Holdings Corporation has developed SCOPE-JET, a post-combustion technology that uses unburned exhaust gas in EAFs. Carbon monoxide, fuel and other carbon material within the furnace is burned by releasing oxygen from a lance installed in the furnace wall. The company has also developed a control system for monitoring the composition of unburned gas at any given moment, enabling secondary combustion process optimization.

- Contracting type: For sale/service
- Technology level: High
- Country of origin: Japan
- Availability: Worldwide
- Contact: WIPO GREEN Database

Steel production: a reheating furnace with a regenerative burner
Nippon Steel Engineering Corporation

Photo: Getty Images / © jordachelr

Reheating furnaces heat up steel such as slabs and billets to a temperature of about 1,200°C. At this temperature steel becomes suitable for rolling in a mill. Nippon Steel Engineering has developed a reheating furnace equipped with two burners that recover heat from waste gas. An energy saving of more than 30 percent can be achieved by continuously recovering heat for reuse in the preheating of combustion air. Contracting type: For sale/service

- Technology level: High
- Country of origin: Japan
- Availability: Worldwide
- Contact: WIPO GREEN Database

Steel production: jet process to maximize scrap use
Primetals Technologies

Photo: Getty Images / © Andrei Merzlov

In most steelmaking processes, different proportions of hot metal and metal scrap can be used as input. However, there is a limit of about 20 to 30 percent to how much scrap steel can be input into a conventional basic oxygen furnace (BOF). Because scrap comes in solid form, adding more than that would require additional heating and melting. Ordinarily this would require too much energy for the cost to be viable. However, the Jet Process technology developed by Primetals Technologies increases the efficiency of this process with the potential for a higher rate of scrap use. At the core of the technology is a converter blowing a hot blast thus ensuring that injected coal is fully combusted and more heat transferred.

- Contracting type: Service
- Technology level: High
- Country of origin: United Kingdom
- Availability: Worldwide
- Contact: WIPO GREEN Database

Iron production: hydrogen-based direct-reduced iron (DRI)

Midrex Technologies Inc.

Photo: © Midrex Technologies

Midrex has developed MIDREX H2™. This uses hydrogen as a reducing gas in a shaft furnace to produce direct reduced iron (DRI). The company has signed a contract with Sweden-based H2 Green Steel to supply the technology for a commercial DRI plant in Boden, Sweden, based on 100 percent hydrogen. Plants can operate at 2.5 Mt/year with between 55–75 percent hydrogen in the reducing gas.

- Contracting type: For sale/service
- Technology level: High
- Country of origin: Japan
- Availability: Worldwide
- Contact: WIPO GREEN Database

Iron production: biomass integration and microwave energy for iron ore reduction

Rio Tinto

Photo: Getty Images /© imantsu

BioIron™ is a technology that uses biomass (instead of coal) and microwave energy to reduce iron ore to iron. Mining company Rio Tinto aims to scale up this process – which has so far been tested at pilot level – through the use of sustainable biomass combined with carbon capture technologies. The biomass is derived from non-food sources, such as agricultural by-products like wheat straw, canola stalks, barley straw and sugar cane bagasse. By combining biomass with microwave technology, heat is generated for the reduction of iron ore into iron.

- Contracting type: For collaboration
- Technology level: High
- Country of origin: Australia
- Availability: Germany
- Contact: WIPO GREEN Database

Iron and steel production: real-time temperature monitoring using laser technology

OnPoint Solutions/Koch Engineered Solutions (KES)

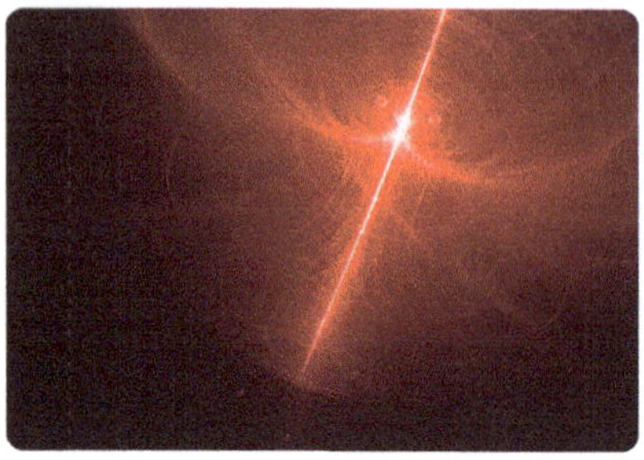

Photo: Getty Images / © Bara7

Monitoring the temperature of hot metal during the steelmaking process can be difficult. It often requires a break in production and manual temperature checking using costly disposable probes. OnPoint Solutions provides various laser-based services for measuring temperature, CO_2 and other iron and steelmaking process indicators. Beams of light are passed through the furnace and absorbed by the carbon monoxide, water vapor and oxygen present. Light loss is then analyzed in order to infer the furnace's combustion efficiency. Being able to control energy and gas use enables adjustments to be made that enhance carbon mitigation. Laser sensors provide visual data in real-time and allow for such adjustments to be made quickly.

- Contracting type: For collaboration
- Technology level: High
- Country of origin: United States
- Availability: Worldwide
- Contact: WIPO GREEN Database

Iron and steel production: HIsarna ironmaking process

Tata Steel

Photo: Getty Images / © Bim

HIsarna is a two-stage direct reduced iron technique that has been developed by several stakeholders, beginning in 1986. Recent developments have been led by Tata Steel and the Rio Tinto Group. Iron ore is directly reduced into liquid iron without having to first produce iron ore pellets or sinter. The technique allows the raw material to be input in powder form, increasing energy efficiency and reducing the carbon footprint. Currently at the pilot stage, Tata Steel is considering scaling HIsarna technology with a focus on India.

- Contracting type: For collaboration
- Technology level: High
- Country of origin: India
- Availability: India
- Contact: WIPO GREEN Database

Carbon capture: carbon capture and utilization at a steel plant

LanzaTech

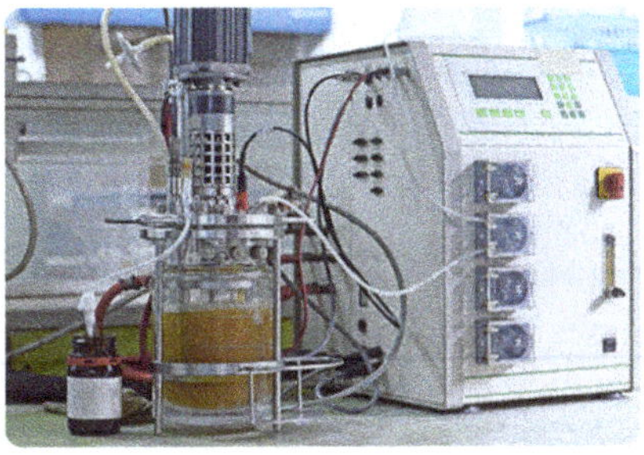

Photo: Getty Images / © Kallayanee Naloka

LanzaTech has developed a carbon capture and utilization (CCU) technology that produces ethanol from carbon-rich industrial waste gases. The technology uses biocatalysts to transform gases from steel mills and other sources into ethanol through a microbial fermentation process. The ethanol can then be used in chemical processes producing jet fuels, paints and plastics. Several companies, including in Belgium and China, are currently developing large-scale commercial and demonstration plants. The Steelanol project is a CCU plant being developed at an ArcelorMittal steel plant in Belgium. In China, the Beijing Shougang LanzaTech New Energy Technology company is using this technology to convert waste gas into fuel and chemicals.

- Contracting type: For collaboration
- Technology level: High
- Country of origin: United States
- Availability: Belgium, China, United States
- Contact: WIPO GREEN Database

Horizon technologies

Mining and pre-treatment: fossil-free iron ore pellets using bioenergy

LKAB

Photo: Getty Images / ©David Ziegler

Biomass could be considered a candidate fuel in steelmaking. For example, in the form of biocoal (torrefied waste wood) or biochar it can replace some of the pulverized coal currently injected into a blast furnace. It is commercially viable primarily for smaller furnaces, owing to biomass's lower calorific value compared to coal. Biomass can also be used in the first stages of steelmaking. In early November 2022, the mining company LKAB announced it had created the world's first "fossil-free" iron ore pellets, with biofuel taking the place of oil and coal during the heating process. Biofuel requires a change to the heating technology for producing the pellets, and full-scale tests are currently underway.

- Contracting type: For collaboration
- Technology level: Medium
- Country of origin: Sweden
- Availability: N/A
- Contact: WIPO GREEN Database

Mining and pre-treatment: beneficiation of lower-grade iron ore
Electra

Photo: Getty Images /© Valter Cunha

Several lower-carbon steelmaking processes require iron ore with an iron content above 67 percent. Unfortunately, such high-quality iron ore only makes up a fraction of global iron ore supply. Start-up Electra aims to address this bottleneck for greener steelmaking. By dissolving low-grade iron ore in a solution, the company aims to extract refined iron. Electra's approach involves an electrochemical process that lowers the process temperature from 1,600 to 60°C. Improving the quality of iron ore means it can be used in an electric arc furnace, reducing the overall carbon footprint of the steel produced compared to traditional furnaces.

- Contracting type: For collaboration/investment
- Technology level: High
- Country of origin: United States
- Availability: N/A
- Contact: WIPO GREEN Database

Iron production: iron ore production by electrolysis at low temperature
ArcelorMittal

Photo: Getty Images /© Yelizaveta Tomashevska

ArcelorMittal is exploring electrolysis for steel production using the ULCOWIN electrowinning technology developed in 2004. To date, the technology has only been demonstrated at pilot level, producing just a few kilograms of steel. A larger pilot is now planned at a research center in France. Electrolysis is a low-temperature electrochemical process that produces solid iron from iron ore without the need for coke. Iron ore is suspended in an alkaline electrolyte solution at about 100°C. As an electrical current passes through the solution, oxygen and iron are separated. The iron is then fed into an electric arc furnace, where it can also be combined with scrap steel. Using renewable energy as the energy source could reduce direct CO_2 emissions from steelmaking by 87 percent.[98]

- Contracting type: For collaboration
- Technology level: High
- Country of origin: Luxembourg
- Availability: N/A
- Contact: WIPO GREEN Database

Iron production: molten oxide electrolysis (MOE)
Boston Metal

Photo: © Boston Metal

Boston Metal's MOE technology was originally developed at the Massachusetts Institute of Technology (MIT). The technology removes the need for coal in steel production and an electrolytic cell replaces traditional blast furnaces for making iron. In the MOE cell, an inert anode is immersed in an electrolyte containing iron ore and then electrified. When the cell heats to 1,600°C, the electrolyte splits the iron oxide bonds within the ore to produce pure liquid metal. Powering the MOE cells with renewable electricity reduces carbon emissions to close to zero. MOE technology can also be applied to the extraction of critical metals from low-concentration materials currently considered waste, thereby reducing the financial and environmental liabilities of slag for mining companies.

- Contracting type: For collaboration
- Technology level: High
- Country of origin: United States
- Availability: N/A
- Contact: WIPO GREEN Database

Iron production: direct reduction of lower-grade iron ore
BlueScope

Photo: Getty Images / © Katherine O'Brien

Direct reduced iron (DRI) is considered a key decarbonization technology for the steel sector. However, the process relies on higher quality iron ore with an iron content of above 67 percent, the availability of which is limited. BlueScope – in partnership with Rio Tinto – is now investigating a technique that could potentially work with lower-grade iron ore for DRI. This technique combines DRI with a conventional basic oxygen furnace (BOF). However, a melting stage is added in between where the DRI is melted to remove impurities such as slag before being charged into the BOF. The two companies intend to use green hydrogen from renewable electricity to fuel the DRI process.

- Contracting type: For collaboration
- Technology level: High
- Country of origin: Australia
- Availability: N/A
- Contact: WIPO GREEN Database

Iron production: sodium as reducing agent in ironmaking

Helios Project Ltd

Photo: Getty Images/© Elena Bionysheva-Abramova

Helios – originally a space company – develops processes for separating oxygen from metals. This has led to discoveries relevant for low-carbon ironmaking, their method aiming to produce iron from iron ore while emitting oxygen instead of CO_2. The technology is based on using sodium instead of conventional coke as the iron-reducing agent in a two-stage process. First, sodium reduces iron ore to iron. Then the sodium oxides produced as a by-product are dissociated, so as to reclaim the sodium in metal form and keep it within a closed loop.

- Contracting type: For collaboration
- Technology level: High
- Country of origin: Israel
- Availability: N/A
- Contact: WIPO GREEN Database

Steel production: high-strength steel for mass production

University of Sheffield

Photo: Getty Images/© gerenme

Reducing steel in cars and buildings is essential for mitigating the steel sector's climate impact. Using higher quality high-strength steels, can reduce the weight of components and extend their life. While high-strength steel has been available for a long time, recent advances have improved its strength even further. However, higher costs are a barrier to mass production. Researchers at the University of Sheffield believe they have now developed a new way of making an ultra-fine-grained, high-strength steel suitable for mass production which may be of particular interest to the automobile industry. Copper – an ingredient usually considered a contaminant – is incorporated to increase steel strength. When the steel is heated during processing, the added copper restricts grain growth, leaving a very fine microstructure that is highly strong, ductile and thermally stable.

- Contracting type: For collaboration
- Technology level: High
- Country of origin: United Kingdom
- Availability: N/A
- Contact: WIPO GREEN Database

Photo: Getty Images/Kuriele...007

Cement

Key players are racing toward the commercialization of breakthrough technologies for cement kiln electrification, novel cement types and carbon capture. Yet, faced by major trends in urbanization and population growth, decarbonizing cement will not be possible, unless we take a hard look at how cement and concrete are used and consumed. Across the value chain, technology will need to play a crucial role.

Demand for cement outpacing cement decarbonization

Technological advancements have already significantly reduced cement production's overall climate impact. Since the 1970s, energy intensity in the sector has dropped by more than

30 percent.[99] Cement manufacturers have largely adopted the more energy-efficient dry process for producing clinker – the intermediary product when making the most common cement type Portland cement (box 4.4). Dry kilns equipped with preheaters and precalciners are proven best available technologies that serve to elevate and optimize temperatures of raw material and fuel before entering the kiln.

Box 4.4 Wet versus dry cement-making

Traditionally, cement plants fed limestone to the kiln by producing a slurry using water. While this mixes the materials more evenly, the evaporation of water is very energy-intensive. In most regions, these so-called wet kilns have been almost completely phased out in favor of more advanced dry processes for making clinker.[100]

Despite progress in reducing process emissions, global cement demand for construction has more than doubled since the early 2000s.[101] Projected to rise further by up to 23 percent by 2050, cement demand will far outweigh efficiency gains based on current levels of climate ambition.[102] More than half of GHG emissions from cement originate from China alone, followed by India. While cement production within China is likely to decline in the long term as urban growth levels out, it will continue to grow in rapidly expanding cities in Asia and Africa.[103] The hardest emissions to tackle are those stemming from the chemical process for making clinker. To address this requires technological adoption targeting both fuel and process emissions (box 4.5).

Optimizing building design to avoid cement overuse

Building codes and standards with overly cautious requirements often result in cement overuse. Without this overdesign, one-fifth of the carbon that currently goes into cement-making could be saved.[104] Despite their climate mitigation potential, demand-side management and material efficiency have been largely overlooked in favor of energy efficiency measures.[105]

Engineering software and modelling tools can enable a leaner design requiring less concrete. But bespoke approaches are often considered expensive. However, advancements in automated design software are expected to make material-saving designs more competitive.[106] Furthermore, building information modeling (BIM) and digital material passports enable "design for disassembly" ensuring more materials are reused or recycled at the end of a building's life.

Building codes and standards with overly cautious requirements often result in cement overuse. Without this overdesign, one-fifth of the carbon that currently goes into cement-making could be saved

Building longevity and waste upcycling

Concrete from construction and demolition waste is difficult to recycle. But innovators are exploring up-cycling as an alternative to down-cycling as gravel or aggregate. One example is turning concrete into a paste for use as a raw material for products with identical properties to clinker. Another is using recycled concrete paste to capture CO_2 through enforced carbonation.

Demand for concrete can also be reduced by extending its life-span. Solutions such as self-healing concrete and biomineralization products help mend cracks in concrete, meaning bridges and buildings can survive wear-and-tear for longer. At the factory level, novel technologies and methods like additive manufacturing, 3D-printing and prefabrication can help avoid production stage wastage.

Box 4.5 Cement sector emissions

Cement - the binding agent for concrete - is the most widely used building block in our cities and infrastructure. Although it accounts for around 8 percent of global GHG emissions,[107] the sector is notoriously difficult to decarbonize. This is partly due to emissions being integral to the chemical process for making clinker - a key ingredient in cement. Clinker is responsible for most of the GHG emissions from cement (figure 4.4). To make clinker, limestone is heated to form lime through a calcination process. Each kg of lime produced releases up to 1.8 kg of CO_2.[108] The second greatest source of emissions is the burning of fossil fuels to reach the high temperatures needed by the cement kiln. This accounts for 40 percent of total cement production emissions.[109, 110]

Figure 4.4 Emissions at each stage of a typical cement manufacturing process, CO_2 kg/tonne

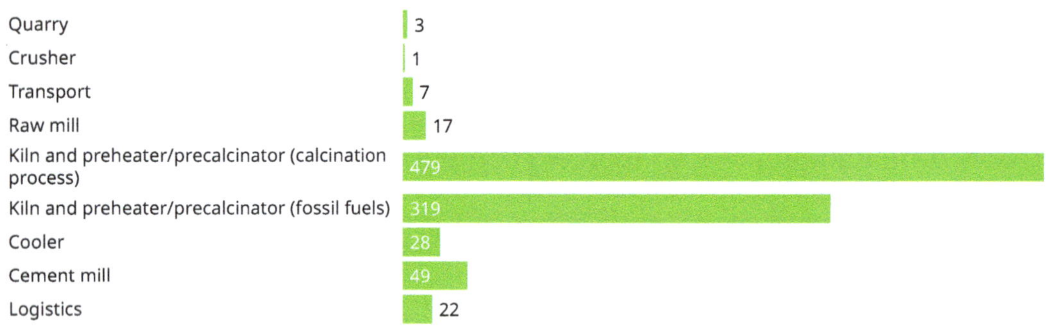

Source: McKinsey, 2020.

Challenges in reducing clinker content in cement

Decarbonizing cement often comes down to managing the components of cement itself. The most common cement - Portland cement - has a clinker content of over 95 percent.[111] Reducing the clinker-to-cement ratio is a key mitigation measure, as most emissions occur during clinker production. Replacing clinker with supplementary cementitious materials such as fly ash, natural pozzolans, ground limestone and calcined clay can help significantly reduce energy intensity for each tonne of cement produced. Yet, the IEA reports the global cement-to-clinker ratio having increased by an average of 1.6 percent a year between 2015 and 2020. This is reportedly the main reason for increased emissions within the sector.[112] While technological innovation is important, outdated standards for the low-carbon concrete and cement used in construction are a significant barrier.

Blended cement and clinker substitutes are already available on the market. Increasing the amount of calcined clay in cement, using readily available materials, may reduce the clinker ratio by around 30 percent.[113] Alternatives such as calcined clay, pozzolans and more limestone in cement are gaining attention. This is driven in part by the need for alternative clinker substitutes to fly ash and slag, both by-products of carbon-intensive industrial processes.

Energy efficiency technologies already implemented

The cement sector consumes over 6 percent of global energy. Over 60 percent of the electrical energy consumed is during the crushing and milling of raw materials and clinker.[114] Vertical roller mills – with an energy-saving potential of up to 30 percent[115] – are long established in the industry[116], with even more efficient alternatives available on the market.

Adding a preheater and precalciner stage between mill and main kiln is another state-of-the-art technology adopted in almost all new plants in major cement producing nations. This technology can reduce cement kiln energy usage by almost half.[117] Furthermore, almost all new plants already use dry-process kilns instead of the high-emitting wet process.[118]

The cement sector is evidently a mature industry. Because of this, efficiency improvements may have plateaued, with only smaller incremental gains made in recent years

Efficiency gains possible in ancillary equipment

The cement sector is evidently a mature industry. Because of this, efficiency improvements may have plateaued, with only smaller incremental gains made in recent years. Today, the most efficient cement plants are only able to achieve an energy saving of less than 1 percent a year through technology upgrade.[119] The scope for further efficiency gains is most limited in countries with the youngest cement plants, such as China, India and Viet Nam.[120]

However, although key energy efficiency technologies have already been implemented worldwide, further energy savings can be made. This can be done by equipping mills and kilns with more efficient separators and grate coolers. High-efficiency separators improve grain size distribution for better grinding performance, thus reducing a mill's grinding power requirements. Reciprocating grate coolers are movable grate plates that push clinker forward horizontally as it is cooled by cold air blown from beneath. In so doing, hot air is supplied to the kiln and preheater system. Over time, grate cooler efficiency has improved with more recent developments enabling better targeted cooling.

Harnessing heat loss

Globally, up to half of industry's energy consumption is wasted in lost heat.[121] Insulating against heat loss and leakage is one solution. Recovery of heat lost from kiln flue gases is another, and one that presents an important opportunity to reduce the cement sector's overall climate impact.

When not being reused on-site to preheat raw materials or generate steam, the exhaust gas given off by modern cement plants is typically hot enough to be reused by power producers for their heat and steam needs. Often this reused heat is fed into a larger grid, an on-site powerplant or to other nearby industries. It can also be taken directly by local consumers for heating and cooling purposes. For example, in the Danish city of Aalborg, where 15 percent of the city is heated by the local cement plant.[122]

For example, in the Danish city of Aalborg, where 15 percent of the city is heated by the local cement plant

Waste used as fuel risks lock-in

Many cement manufacturers have switched from oil to natural gas over recent years. But a switch to alternative lower-carbon cement kiln energy sources is challenging for several reasons. From the burning of worn tires in the 1950s to hazardous waste fuels in the late 1980s and early 1990s, many scrap options have had detrimental environmental and health-related side-effects.[123]

Several types of waste streams are used in cement kilns, including from industrial by-products, the agricultural sector and municipal solid waste. While the availability of homogenous waste streams is a limiting factor, new types of technologies could enable low-calorific waste to be used as a future fuel.

On the other hand, cement kiln incineration may lock-in waste streams that could otherwise have been reused or recycled. Today, the practice of burning plastic in cement kilns is growing, along with its associated air pollution concerns and risk of undercutting plastic recycling efforts.[124]

Biomass use growing but not a silver bullet

Despite the challenges faced, alternative fuels meet an average 18 percent of the global cement industry's thermal energy need, though far less in emerging and developing economies.[125] There are current examples of cement kilns operating entirely on alternative fuels,[126] underlining the potential of this approach. Fuel alternatives that avoid waste incineration dependency include hydrogen and biomass integration. And on the horizon is heat generation via plasma generators and microwave energy technology.[127]

An advantage of biomass as a fuel is that it is easily integrated into existing processes. For cement, biofuels could replace up to 30 percent of fossil fuel use without significant capital investment.[128] The EU's cement industry has increased biomass use to 16 percent of the fuel mix.[129] However, the future of biomass as an alternative fuel is uncertain. This is because of competing demand from other sectors, conflicting agricultural land needs and the lower calorific value of most organic materials. Overall, overcoming the barriers to scaling alternative fuels within the cement sector will require a breakthrough in cement kiln electrification.

Cement kiln electrification at pilot stage

Technological options for the direct electrification of cement are limited and unavailable in the near term. A significant investment scale-up would be required in order to advance technologies such as electrolysis beyond the pilot stage. The cement sector has the lowest electrification potential of any industrial sector, with many technologies at the early stages of technological maturity.[130] The challenge stems partly from having to achieve the high temperatures needed by the cement kiln in the absence of highly energy-dense fossil fuels. While electrification could hold future promise, it relies on cheap renewable electricity to make it both commercially viable and sustainable.

Advancements in carbon capture technology

Given the current dominance of clinker and fossil fuel use within the cement sector, carbon capture and storage (CSS) is considered unavoidable if emission reduction targets are to be met.[131] No industrial-scale CSS solution has yet been deployed at a cement plant. But recently the EU put EUR 16 million of funding toward implementing direct-separation CSS technology at a German cement plant. Moreover, Heidelberg Materials are integrating CCS at a cement plant in Norway planned for completion in 2024.[132]

In terms of proven technologies, amine scrubbing – a chemical process to remove CO_2 – is a more established solution with high carbon recovery rates. Smaller cement plants in countries like China and India are already applying the technology. This captures CO_2 from flue gases post-combustion and dissolves the CO_2 in amines – an organic compound – to produce a carbon-free gas stream. The solvent can then be regenerated through heating to obtain pure CO_2 gas. But the technology is expensive. Decarbonization through amine scrubbing could double the cost of today's cement.[133]

No industrial-scale CSS solution has yet been deployed at a cement plant

The industry is exploring other innovative ideas for capturing CO_2 emissions from cement, with varying results. Direct air capture (DAC), for instance, entails capturing CO_2 directly from the atmosphere instead of from flue gases. However, CO_2 capture from flue gases directly after combustion is cheaper and less energy-intensive owing to the higher concentration of CO_2.[134] An even higher concentration of CO_2 in flue gas could be achieved by oxyfuel combustion, which is when coal is burned in oxygen rather than air.[135] Oxyfuel combustion can be combined with post-combustion CO_2 capture from flue gases and is considered to have high potential for retrofitting to existing lime plants.[136, 137] Calcium looping, in which limestone is created through a reversible reaction between CO_2 and lime, could also hold potential. However, no large-scale demonstration of the technology is yet available.[138]

Utilizing captured carbon

Once captured, CO_2 can be stored or treated in a number of ways through carbon capture utilization and storage (CCUS). Carbon mineralization entails injecting CO_2 into wet concrete. Curing concrete (to improve strength and durability) in the presence of CO_2 has been shown to improve performance.[139] Innovation is thriving in this space. But such technologies are reliant on a significant expansion of infrastructure in order to capture and transport CO_2. Furthermore, limited efficiency and high costs present significant barriers to industrial-scale application.[140] Yet, the Intergovernmental Panel on Climate Change (IPCC) views CCUS as an inevitable part of decarbonizing the industry sector and achieving net-zero emissions by 2050.[141]

Innovation examples

Photo: Getty Images/© AlbertPego

Industrial-scale cement plant carbon capture and storage
Cement manufacturer HeidelbergCement (now Heidelberg Materials) is working toward delivering low-carbon cement by developing the world's first industrial-scale carbon capture and storage (CCS) project at a cement production facility. The plant in question is being constructed in Brevik, Norway, and scheduled to be fully operational by 2024. The plan is to capture 400,000 tonnes of CO_2 annually by using a mixture of water and organic amine solvents to absorb the CO_2. It will then be compressed and shipped for storage in reservoirs below the seabed. In addition to these CCS efforts, the company is making greater use of alternative fuels and alternative secondary cementitious materials. It is also developing technologies for recycling concrete paste for use in capturing CO_2 through enforced carbonation.

Photo: Getty Images/© ewg3D

District heating using local cement plant surplus heat
Aalborg Portland, a large cement manufacturer in Denmark, is recovering flue gas to provide heating for the local population. Heated gas – that would otherwise go to waste – is collected at the kiln and treated through a combined gas cleaning and heat recovery system. Impurities such as sulphur are removed before the heat is forwarded for district heating use. The company has supplied surplus heat to the local grid since the 1990s. Today, this recovered heat provides 25 percent of district heating in the Aalborg municipality of Denmark.

Photo: Getty Images / © alex_skp

Low-carbon cement use in major construction projects

What have the Olympic Village in Paris and the United Kingdom's new HS2 high-speed railway line got in common? They are both large-scale construction projects under development using low-carbon cement with reduced clinker content supplied by Ecocem. A completed project using the same low-carbon cement is the Aviva Stadium, the Republic of Ireland's national rugby and football stadium. Covering 6.4 hectares and having a 50 m tall façade, the company estimates the project to have saved approximately 4,000 tonnes of CO_2. During the stadium's construction, 8,000 precast concrete units were produced off-site and 72,000 tonnes of concrete made at the location. While details on the composition and method are sparse, the Ecocem company has delivered 20 million tonnes of its low-carbon cement to various projects.

Technology solutions

Proven technologies

Grinding and crushing: vertical roller mills for locally-produced cement

LOESCHE GmbH

Photo: Getty Images / © Bilanol

Raw materials and cement clinker have traditionally been grinded in ball mills with poor energy efficiency. Vertical roller mills reduce cement grinding energy consumption and are suitable for very fine cements and aggregates. These mills have existed for several decades and are in operation around the world, but have undergone various innovations over the years. In the 1960s, the LOESCHE company introduced rotary kilns with heat exchangers. In the 1990s, they introduced vertical roller mills able to grind both cement clinker and granulated slag (a by-product of ironmaking) in a single process and use kiln exhaust gases for dry grinding. LOESCHE currently supplies a compact cement grinding plant with a vertical roller mill suitable for small-scale cement plants within small but growing markets.

- Contracting type: For sale
- Technology level: Medium
- Country of origin: Germany
- Availability: Worldwide
- Contact: WIPO GREEN Database

Grinding and crushing: energy-saving raw material and clinker grinding
Fives Group

Photo: © Peter Oksen

FCB Horomill® is a ring roller mill originally developed by French plant manufacturer FCB-Ciment and Italian cement producer Buzzi Unicem Group. The mill can grind raw materials, clinker and cement additive materials, such as limestone and slag, without requiring injected water to control temperature. An integrated gas circuit enables efficient drying and processing of wet raw materials. Today, the Fives Group company provides the mills. According to the provider, they enable up to a 65 percent energy saving compared to ball mills and 10 to 20 percent compared to vertical roll mills.

- Contracting type: For sale/service
- Technology level: Medium
- Country of origin: France
- Availability: Worldwide
- Contact: WIPO GREEN Database

Grinding and crushing: high-pressure grinding roll
Takraf

Photo: © Takraf

High-pressure grinding roll technology for crushing feed materials in cement-making consume less energy than conventional mills and crushers. The technology involves two counter-rotating grinding rolls subjecting a column of material to high pressure. This results in micro-cracks in the material's particles, leading to mineral liberation and smaller-sized particles. These micro-cracks increase the particle contact surface leading to improved leaching performance and flotation efficiency. High-pressue grinding roll technology is more cost-efficient than traditional mills and crushers. The technology also consumes less power than alternatives and the large amount of fine cracks created in the material reduces the power needed for the ball mill downstream.

- Contracting type: For sale
- Technology level: High
- Country of origin: Germany
- Availability: Worldwide
- Contact: WIPO GREEN Database

Waste heat recovery: boilers for cement on-site power generation

Thermax Ltd.

Photo: © Thermax

Cement plants can recover waste heat at different stages of the cement-making process. This strengthens a plant's energy security while also lowering its CO_2 emissions. Thermax's waste heat recovery system is based on the Rankine Cycle. The company provides waste heat recovery boilers that leverage hot waste gases to generate steam for power-producing turbines, or for heating feedwater for the on-site powerplant. Waste heat is recovered at two points in the cement process: pre-heaters/calciners and clinker coolers. The company also collaborates with external partners to provide full heat recovery systems, including boilers, turbines and generators.

- Contracting type: For sale/service
- Technology level: Medium
- Country of origin: India
- Availability: Worldwide
- Contact: WIPO GREEN Database

Waste heat recovery: turbines for cement on-site power generation

Triveni Turbines

Photo: Getty Images/iStock/industryview

In cement plants, small-scale powerplants can be installed that run on waste heat from various processes. Recovered hot gases are passed through boilers to generate steam to drive electricity-producing turbines and generators. This can meet up to 30 percent of a cement plant's power requirements. Electricity generated through such a heat recovery practice also reduces CO_2 emissions, especially in countries with a high level of fossil fuel use. Waste heat recovery in cement power plants is based on thermodynamic cycles such as the Organic Rankine Cycle, the Kalina Cycle or the Steam Rankine Cycle. Triveni Turbines supplies and installs turbines based on SRC systems across India.

- Contracting type: For sale/service
- Technology level: Medium
- Country of origin: India
- Availability: India
- Contact: WIPO GREEN Database

Energy efficiency: cement kiln insulation and lining material

Morgan Advanced Materials

Photo: Getty Images/© jmsilva

In cement production, most emissions originate from the cement kiln. Ensuring kilns operate as efficiently as possible means making good use of the high temperatures achieved and avoiding unnecessary heat lost to the environment. Morgan Advanced Materials supplies a range of products for thermal management of the cement kiln and related components. These include insulators and materials for the pre-calciners, retainer ring, dropout area and so on. Among the company's products is the WDS Microporous back-up insulation material. This material extends kiln lining life-span and has a very low thermal conductivity coefficient which enhances thermal efficiency.

- Contracting type: For sale
- Technology level: Medium
- Country of origin: United Kingdom
- Availability: Worldwide
- Contact: WIPO GREEN Database

Energy efficiency: pre-drying alternative fuels using waste heat

stela Laxhuber GmbH

Photo: Getty Images/© CasarsaGuru

Pre-drying fuel for the cement kiln can enable better energy usage and a more homogenous input. Company stela Laxhuber provides customized solutions for a range of alternative fuels, including refuse derived fuel and solid shredded waste. The pre-drying belts run on waste heat from upstream production processes, which enhances energy efficiency further. The company provides two types of belt dryer, one more compact than the other. Belt widths vary between 2 and 8.4 m. Both are modular plant systems with top-down ventilation and low heat and electricity consumption.

- Contracting type: For sale
- Technology level: Medium
- Country of origin: Germany
- Availability: Worldwide
- Contact: WIPO GREEN Database

Clinker substitute: Portland limestone cement

Cemex

Photo: Getty Images/E alvarez

Clinker production is responsible for the majority of cement emissions. Replacing some of the clinker in cement can have a big impact on emission reduction. Portland limestone cement is a type of cement that has a higher limestone content, which partly replaces clinker. This blended cement can consist of up to 35 percent limestone (although this is not yet standard in many countries). In Mexico, the Cemex company supplies Cem II B-L 32.5N cement containing nearly 33 percent limestone. Although this type of limestone-blended cement was developed in the 1960s, it has gained popularity in recent years owing to its emissions-lowering ability.

- Contracting type: For sale
- Technology level: Medium
- Country of origin: Mexico
- Availability: Worldwide
- Contact: WIPO GREEN Database

Clinker substitute: calcined clay cement

FLSmidth

Photo: Getty Images/© JJFarquitectos

While replacing some of the clinker in cement with limestone can help reduce CO_2 emissions, limestone itself has a relatively large carbon footprint. FLSmidth has therefore adopted alternative clinker substitutes with a smaller carbon footprint. They include calcined clay and recycled cement. Calcined clay can be particularly useful for high-strength, lightweight concretes and in the pre-casting sector. The company claims their clay calciner system can reduce emissions by up to 40 percent by replacing up to 40 percent of the clinker. Clay is a naturally-occurring material. Dried and crushed clay is fed into a preheater/calciner system where it is treated thermally. The company supplies a calciner system for this process that can be retrofitted onto existing kilns and use various fuels, including waste fuel.

- Contracting type: For sale/service
- Technology level: Medium
- Country of origin: Denmark
- Availability: Worldwide
- Contact: WIPO GREEN Database

Alternative cement: hempcrete construction material

IsoHemp

Photo: Getty Images /©. Rick Thompson

Hempcrete is made by taking hemp and limestone and mixing them together with water. IsoHemp supplies a non-load-bearing glued masonry product in the form of blocks made from hemp. The product has a number of applications, for example, as an insulating envelope or for building partition walls. While hempcrete's carbon footprint is significantly smaller than for cement or concrete, application is limited owing to its lower compressive strength.

- Contracting type: For sale
- Technology level: Medium
- Country of origin: Belgium
- Availability: Worldwide
- Contact: WIPO GREEN Database

Frontier technologies

Clinker substitute: limestone calcined clay cement (LC_3)

LC_3

Photo: © LC3 project

A combination of limestone and calcined clay has produced a new type of cement – LC_3. The team behind LC_3 is focused on the research and testing of Portland cement blend consisting of limestone (15 percent), calcined clay (30 percent), clinker (50 percent) and gypsum. The innovation is in using low-grade clays available in abundance. The most suitable are those available in areas where cement demand is expected to increase the most, that is, tropical and sub-tropical regions. Low-grade clay use would avoid competition for resources with other industries such as ceramics or paper. Pilot projects and testing sites have used LC_3 cement in buildings, roads, a check dam and pavements. The company is focusing on bringing the product to market.

- Contracting type: For sale
- Technology level: Medium
- Country of origin: Switzerland, Cuba
- Availability: Worldwide
- Contact: WIPO GREEN Database

Alternative cement: biotech-based cement
Biomason

Photo: © Biomason

Biomason has developed a biological cement technology inspired by marine ecosystems. By mimicking how corals grow, their Biocement® uses carbon and calcium as building blocks to create structural cement. These cement bricks are grown in ambient temperatures with the aid of naturally-occurring living microorganisms (Sporosarcina pasteurii). When adding Biocement to various applications, it takes the product under 72 hours to set, cure and reach full strength, compared to 28 days for conventional concrete. The final product's size does not change. Rather, its "growing" refers to a strengthening in density due to biologically-produced calcium carbonate forming bridges between the aggregate grains. Biolith - Biomason's first commercially available product - is a precast product that can, for example, be used as tiling. It consists of 85 percent natural aggregate (e.g., loose sand and rocks) and 15 percent biocement material.

- Contracting type: For sale
- Technology level: Medium
- Country of origin: United States
- Availability: Worldwide
- Contact: WIPO GREEN Database

Alternative cement: bonded sand particles as cement substitute
University of Tokyo

Photo: © University of Tokyo

Researchers at the University of Tokyo have invented a novel production method for producing an alternative construction material to cement that uses readily available materials such as sand and gravel. The method relies on the bonding particles of silica (SiO_2) contained within the natural materials used. The method comprises several stages. First, the raw material containing silica is mixed together with an alcohol compound plus either an alkali metal compound or an alkaline earth metal compound. The mixture is then heated to produce a hardened body that can be used as a cement substitute in construction.

- Contracting type: For collaboration
- Technology level: Low
- Country of origin: Japan
- Availability: Japan
- Contact: WIPO GREEN Database

Alternative cement plus material efficiency: ceramic waste regeneration
Yi Design Company Limited

Photo: Getty Images / © Dinesh Ahir

Yi Design has developed a binding material plus a process for recycling large volumes of ceramic waste material and other industrial solid waste, such as glass and blast furnace slag. Materials are reprocessed into porous ceramic bricks and tiles by mixing crushed waste with a binder before sintering. Final product consists of 90 percent recycled material and intended to replace cement in construction. The bricks are absorbent therefore suitable for pavements to alleviate flooding.

- Contracting type: For sale
- Technology level: Medium
- Country of origin: China
- Availability: China
- Contact: WIPO GREEN Database

Material efficiency: geopolymer concrete
Polycare

Photo: © Polycare

Polycare is developing and manufacturing a circular micro-modular masonry system. These cement-free hollow blocks consist of up to 95 percent secondary raw materials. They are not glued or mortared, but joined together by inserted connecting elements. This masonry system allows construction professionals to meet regulatory requirements and achieve a 70 percent CO_2 reduction. Polycare considers buildings to be temporary "storage" for materials that can be reused in the future. The aim is cost savings, asset preservation and the avoidance of secondary costs like demolition and disposal. The company's research and development center is located in central Germany and production due to be piloted in Germany in 2024.

- Contracting type: For collaboration
- Technology level: Medium
- Country of origin: Germany
- Availability: Namibia
- Contact: WIPO GREEN Database

Material efficiency: biocement for concrete restoration
Basilisk

Photo © Basilisk

Extending the life of existing concrete infrastructure instead of demolishing and building from scratch avoids greenhouse gas emissions. Small cracks in concrete, for example, can be avoided or repaired using bio-based self-healing techniques. Biomineralization is a method that uses a bacterial calcium carbonate deposit to fill microcracks and which can also be used as binder. The technology was first applied in the 1990s. Basilisk supplies a product which, when blended into any concrete mix, exhibits self-healing properties.

- Contracting type: For sale
- Technology level: High
- Country of origin: Netherlands (Kingdom of the)
- Availability: Worldwide
- Contact: WIPO GREEN Database

Carbon capture: carbon mineralization in concrete
CarbonCure

Photo © CarbonCure

CarbonCure provides technology that injects CO_2 into fresh concrete as a way of storing emissions and thereby reducing the cement sector's overall climate impact. Once injected along with water, the CO_2 undergoes a mineralization process that embeds it within the concrete. This has the added benefit of improving compressive strength and reducing cement use in designs. The company acquires CO_2 from local industrial gas supply companies that have CO_2 recovery plants. These companies in turn access, capture and purify flue gas streams from other industries (refineries, ethanol plants etc.) whereby the captured gases are distributed for reuse via road, rail or direct pipeline.

- Contracting type: For sale/service
- Technology level: Medium
- Country of origin: Canada
- Availability: Worldwide
- Contact: WIPO GREEN Database

Carbon capture: alkaline carbonate-based adsorbent for carbon dioxide removal

Korea Institute of Energy Research

Photo: Getty Images/© Pro2sound

The KIERSOL process is based on an alkaline carbonate-based adsorbent for removing CO_2 from industrial processes. This differs from other commercial carbon capture processes that use, for example, an amine solution. The KIERSOL technology innovators claim the process uses 20 percent less energy than other carbon capture alternatives. Furthermore, owing to the adsorbent being strongly resistant to damaging substances in the exhaust gas, it does not need frequent replacement, making it more economical. The KIERSOL process can be applied to a wide range of industrial facilities, including steel and cement facilities.

- Contracting type: For collaboration
- Technology level: High
- Country of origin: Republic of Korea
- Availability: N/A
- Contact: WIPO GREEN Database

Electrification: electrochemical calcination

Sublime Systems

Photo: Getty Images/© Temir Shintemirov

Sublime Systems is working on a method of cement manufacturing that avoids kilns entirely. The kiln is the most energy- and fossil-intensive element of the cement-making process. Sublime Systems' technology builds on an electrochemical calcination process for extracting calcium from minerals at a low or ambient temperature. Instead of heat from a kiln, the company proposes to use an electrolyzer to split water in a pH gradient between two electrodes. In terms of input, many calcium-bearing mineral types are suitable for the process. They include low-grade limestone or minerals not embedded with CO_2. The technology can benefit from inventions already on the market by using commercial, off-the-shelf electrolyzer hardware. However, the level of decarbonization achieved by the technology depends on the energy source for the electrolyzer. Current production is on the scale of 100 tonnes per year in Sublime's pilot plant. The company is working toward building its first commercial plant.

- Contracting type: For collaboration
- Technology level: High
- Country of origin: United States
- Availability: N/A
- Contact: WIPO GREEN Database

Alternative cement: carbon-negative Portland cement
Brimstone

Photo: Getty Images / © Coprid

The Brimstone Process™ is described as a carbon-negative process for making Portland cement. Instead of using limestone, the company makes cement with lime from calcium silicate rocks. Because limestone calcination is responsible for more than 60 percent of cement emissions, eliminating limestone has significant climate benefits. Furthermore, the process generates a magnesium-based waste product able to absorb atmospheric CO_2 from fuel combustion. The cement itself is physically identical to conventional Portland cement. The technology is at an early stage of development. But this startup is planning toward advancing the process from laboratory to a demonstration plant.

- Contracting type: For collaboration
- Technology level: High
- Country of origin: United States
- Availability: N/A
- Contact: WIPO GREEN Database

Electrification: electrified hot gas production for the cement industry
Coolbrook

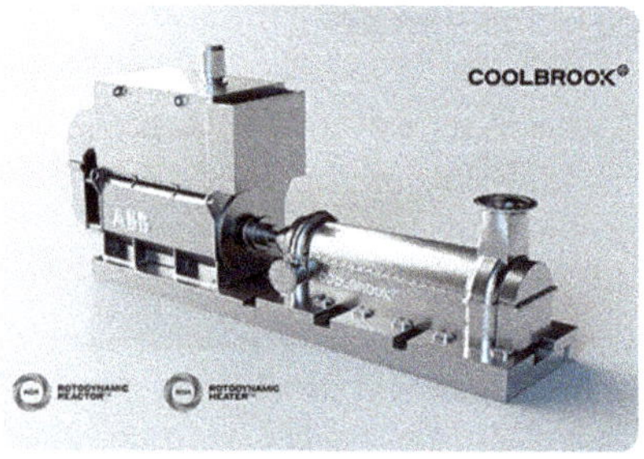

Photo: © Coolbrook

Coolbrook has developed a RotoDynamic Heater (RDH™). This technology electrifies high-temperature process heating across industry, including the steel and cement sectors. RDH™ is capable of producing temperatures of up to 1,700°C. Air, nitrogen and process gases are heated to a high temperature inside the heater. This replaces the traditional fossil fuel burning to reach the temperatures required by furnaces and kilns. Powered by renewable electricity, this is likely to result in a 30 percent reduction in production process CO_2 emissions, once implemented at scale. RDH™ is designed for retrofitting into existing facilities, as well as for new greenfield projects. The technology is being tested at a large-scale pilot plant in the Netherlands. The aim is for commercial demonstration projects to take place in 2024 and full commercial deployment to start around 2025.

- Contracting type: For collaboration
- Technology level: High
- Country of origin: Finland
- Availability: N/A
- Contact: WIPO GREEN Database

Carbon capture: calcium looping carbon capture technology
Sumitomo Corporation

Photo: Getty Images / © chinaphotographer

Calcium looping uses calcium oxide to remove carbon from flue gases. At the same time, heat can be recirculated in the process. With calcium looping, flue gas is mixed with calcium oxide in a fluidized bed. The gas is then mineralized into calcium carbonate and clean flue gas exits the unit. The calcium carbonate is then regenerated back to calcium oxide in the presence of fuel and oxygen, which is then circulated back to the carbonator. By-products such as calcined lime with ash and minerals are used as feedstock for the cement and lime industry.

- Contracting type: For sale/service
- Technology level: High
- Country of origin: Japan
- Availability: N/A
- Contact: WIPO GREEN Database

Industry 4.0

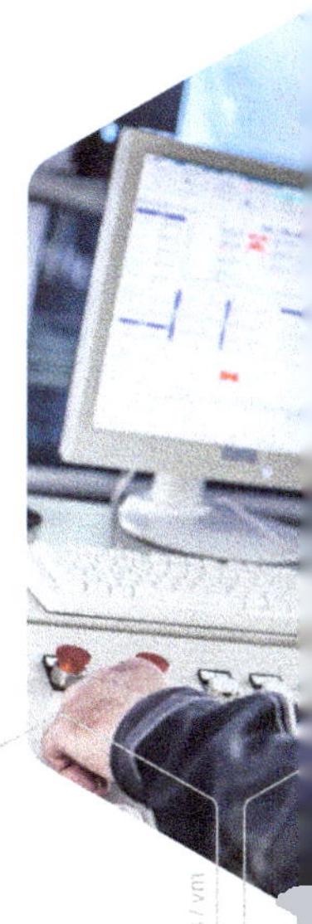

Photo: Getty Images / vm

International organizations are increasingly recognizing Industry 4.0 technologies for their potential role in industrial decarbonization. Yet, their contribution to climate change mitigation within manufacturing industry is uncertain and access highly uneven globally. This section seeks to shed light on Industry 4.0 progress, beyond the superlatives. The focus is on highlighting existing and emerging technologies and pointing to examples for improving energy and material efficiency, specifically in the high-emitting steel and cement sectors.

What is Industry 4.0?

Industry 4.0 – or the fourth industrial revolution – is a recently introduced term for the current digital transformation of the industrial sector. It is a continuation of the first industrial revolution that brought steam, the second, electricity, and the third of the early 1970s that brought digital technologies, electronics and factory floor automation. Today's technologies have evolved into so-called cyber-physical systems centered on connectivity. Thanks to its active promotion by organizations such as the World Economic Forum, Industry 4.0 as a term has gained popularity and is typically associated with anything linking industrial processes to advanced computing and modeling, internet of things (IoT), artificial intelligence (AI), robots, additive manufacturing, blockchain and so on.

Transforming sustainable manufacturing through technology integration

The technologies enable communication between industrial machines and systems (the physical world) and external systems (the cyber world). This means industrial parts can perform tasks with little human intervention, thereby increasing efficiency. The integration of such connections has so far been expensive and complex, but new standards and a rapid price drop for technologies such as sensors now enables smaller companies to access "plug and play" integration for their IT systems.[142] In short, Industry 4.0 has the ability to enable predictive and preventive maintenance, optimize supply chains, enhance customization and personalization, and can adapt quickly to changing market demands.

Some technologies have seen a higher rate of uptake among manufacturing industries. They include cloud computing, horizontal and vertical data integration, IoT and big data analytics. Others – among them additive manufacturing, virtual/augmented reality and AI – are being adopted at a slower rate, particularly among small and medium-sized enterprises.[143] Of course, the picture varies from sector to sector, and applications for technologies such as AI are developing rapidly.

Does Industry 4.0 contribute to industrial decarbonization today?

The narrative around Industry 4.0 and its contribution to decarbonizing manufacturing industries lacks consensus. The contribution of digital technologies to climate change mitigation in relation to sectors such as transport, buildings, media and agriculture is better understood. Empirical assessment of the manufacturing industry has been less comprehensive in comparison, other than in relation to smart grids. This may be owing to the relatively low digital penetration in this sector. Research also tends to focus on measuring Industry 4.0's impact on a firm's productivity rather than its decarbonization potential.

In general, gray literature dominates current research with sparse empirical data on implementation.[144] For instance, Fritzsche, Niehoff[145] analyzed documents from various intergovernmental organizations (IGOs) such as the International Energy Agency (IEA) and the United Nations Industrial Development Organization (UNIDO) on Industry 4.0's role in climate change. They all strongly associated Industry 4.0 with climate change mitigation. Moreover, the technologies were viewed as enablers for increasing energy and resource efficiency within industrial production. They note that:

> *Modern digital technologies are viewed – by IGOs – as enablers for clean industrial development, but again concrete figures or case studies regarding Industry 4.0 and climate change mitigation are lacking.*[146]

Industry reports also provide a positive outlook on the mitigation potential of digital technologies. A lot of data are emerging from companies themselves, such as Ericsson and Swisscom, on the enabling impact of digital technologies in relation to climate change.[147] However, assessment of their impact on industrial decarbonization has been less systematic than for other sectors.

Furthermore, research on possible negative environmental impacts from improving manufacturing productivity through digitalization is missing.[148, 149] Data on the net climate impact of digital technologies is also sparse. This is important considering the substantial energy demand of digital technologies themselves. In total, the information and communications technology (ICT) sector's carbon footprint has been estimated to be anything between 1.5–4 percent of the global total. But similar sector-wide data on Industry 4.0's GHG emissions abatement potential are less robust and there is no internationally agreed method of measurement.[150]

Research also tends to focus on measuring Industry 4.0's impact on a firm's productivity rather than its decarbonization potential

Positive view of Industry 4.0 often based on predictions of the future

More work is required to gather empirical evidence on Industry 4.0's GHG abatement impact. Meanwhile, countries' industrial decarbonization plans increasingly include digital transformation elements. Furthermore, there is no shortage of reports linking Industry 4.0 and climate change based on scenarios and assumptions about potential future impact on carbon, energy and materials savings. The IEA estimates digitalization of industrial processes could produce energy savings of up to 30 percent globally.[151] Consultancy company Accenture and World Economic Forum analyses estimate that digital technologies – if scaled across all of heavy industry – could reduce emissions by 20 percent by 2050.[152] For the material manufacturing sector specifically, they estimate that technologies like big data analytics and cloud or edge computing (i.e., distributed computing frameworks) could reduce emissions by 7 percent by 2050. Furthermore, the Association of German Engineers states that digitalization might lead to a 25 percent greater resource efficiency and a 20 percent reduction in carbon emission.[153]

Meanwhile, organizations such as the Global e-Sustainability Initiative have explored digital case examples and assessed digital technologies' overall climate abatement potential for the manufacturing and construction sectors. Their prediction is that data-driven, AI-powered, networked smart factories and supply chains could save 171–495 MtCO_2eq across seven major country studies.[154] On a global level, they predict that smart manufacturing could abate 22 percent (or 2.71 GtCO_2eq) in these two sectors by 2030 (although that figure may require updating).[155] Again, these are predictive assessments and, as such, not based on empirical evidence.

90 percent of all data stored is never utilized. Industry 4.0's potential contribution to manufacturing industry decarbonization therefore also depends on the ability of users to translate data into action

Industry 4.0 does not guarantee climate mitigation

There are optimistic expectations for the digital transformation of the manufacturing industry. However, industry's willingness to collect data via Industry 4.0 technologies does not automatically translate into climate change mitigation efforts, or even productivity growth. A study by IBM suggests that 90 percent of all data stored is never utilized.[156] Industry 4.0's potential contribution to manufacturing industry decarbonization therefore also depends on the ability of users to translate data into action.

Environmental benefits from new technologies are not guaranteed. An example from the steel sector is additive manufacturing (AM). According to one claim by the IEA, steel sector material losses could be reduced through improved manufacturing techniques, including AM. In this scenario, AM would enable complex shape formation and high-added-value products to be made from recycled powders, potentially reducing emissions and minimizing material loss.[157] However, there is no consensus on the sustainability of AM in the academic literature.

At worst, Industry 4.0 technologies could increase emissions

Additive manufacturing has been shown to have a larger carbon footprint compared to conventional steel manufacturing for each kilogram of material processed. This is owing to its high electrical energy intensity and low productivity.[158, 159, 160] Moreover, Dusík *et al.*,[161] assessed the best and worst-case environmental impacts of technologies, such as IoT, AM and AI, and found they could all increase GHG emissions if not managed properly.

Potential risk factors include higher energy consumption and greater energy intensity, as well as over-consumption and a change in business models. Difficult to measure and subject to much uncertainty, rebound effects deserve more attention.[162] The productivity gains for manufacturing industries expected from Industry 4.0 may lower product prices and stimulate higher consumption.[163] Ultimately this could offset or even reverse any energy and material savings achieved by applying Industry 4.0 technologies in the first place. This underscores the need to better understand the impact of these technologies before integrating them into decarbonization plans.

Slow rate of adoption

Industry itself appears cautious with regard to seizing Industry 4.0's potential for climate change mitigation. Among energy-intensive industries in Sweden (steel, pulp-and-paper, chemicals) energy efficiency is considered a positive side-effect of digital technologies, but not the main driver.[164] Indeed, a survey conducted among manufacturing industries in Italy reveals potential economic gain to be the key driver, while few associated Industry 4.0 with beneficial environmental impacts.[165]

Barriers to adopting Industry 4.0 technologies within the manufacturing industry typically include poor value-chain integration, cyber-security challenges, uncertainty about economic benefits, the workforce lacking necessary skills, high up-front costs, a lack of infrastructure and so on.[166]

Many developing countries are exploring digital technologies. But their readiness for implementing Industry 4.0 technologies is modest and the sustainability adoption rate in the manufacturing industry low compared to developed nations.[167] A total of 2.7 billion people globally continue to be offline.[168] Therefore inadequate or lacking digital infrastructure is an important barrier to adoption. That said, the high level of investment required for manufacturing industries to adopt Industry 4.0 is likely to be the most critical hurdle for companies in the developing world, along with the lack of a qualified workforce.[169]

Cases of Industry 4.0 use in manufacturing industry

Despite a need for a better understanding of Industry 4.0 impacts, there are plenty of cases of existing and potential use. While adoption rates within manufacturing industry are lower than for other sectors, digital frontrunners have adopted several of the technologies. Table 4.1 lists prevailing Industry 4.0 technologies alongside their potential application for climate change mitigation within manufacturing industry. Industry 4.0 technologies may have high or higher mitigation potential in other sectors, particularly the energy sector, which have not been included in this review.

Table 4.1 Potential cases for Industry 4.0 technology use for industrial decarbonization within manufacturing industry[170, 171, 172, 173, 174]

Industry 4.0 technology	Applications for climate change mitigation within manufacturing industry
Additive manufacturing and 3D printing	- Producing lightweight parts and products to reduce material consumption - Reducing energy use through optimized design and lower production runs - Waste as raw material - Customizing production to reduce process waste - Enabling local and on-site production to reduce transportation emissions - Enabling manufacturing to use fewer combinations of materials for easier material collection, sorting and recycling into manufacturing process
Advanced robotics and automation	- Streamlining manufacturing processes and reducing material loss - Smart sorting of industrial waste fractions for enhanced reuse and recycling - Optimizing inventory management, warehouse operations and transportation in manufacturing facilities - Reducing energy consumption in logistics and decarbonizing supply chains
Artificial intelligence	- Predictive maintenance to replace only required parts in a timely manner so as to extend machinery lifespan - Optimizing energy use through smart grid integration and energy management systems - Improving supply chain efficiency to reduce waste and emissions and optimize transport routes
Augmented reality	- Providing remote assistance to reduce travel and transportation emissions - Training employees in sustainable practices
Big data analytics	- Identifying energy and resource efficiency opportunities - Optimizing system and supply chain management - Analyzing climate impact of products throughout their life-cycle
Distributed ledger technology/blockchain	- Ensuring transparency and accountability in supply chain management and for carbon tracking - Digital material passports for identifying different material types and grades during disassembly to allow reuse and recycling into manufacturing process - Internet of materials accessing information on quality, availability and location of secondary materials for reintegration into manufacturing process
Cloud computing	- Hosting and scaling energy management and other related software

Industry 4.0 technology	Applications for climate change mitigation within manufacturing industry
Cyber-physical systems	- Optimizing fuel consumption and material handling - Flexible design configuration - Making available reliable data and life cycle assessment data collection
Digital twin	- Simulating manufacturing processes in order to identify and optimize energy and resource use - Enabling predictive maintenance to replace only the required parts in a timely manner so as to extend machinery lifespan
Drone technology	- Monitoring machinery and production line temperature using infrared and thermal technology - Detecting gas leaks
Internet of things	- Real-time monitoring and control of energy usage and emissions - Monitoring of waste generated during remanufacturing - Transparency and tracking of resource consumption in manufacturing processes and supply chains - Optimizing transport routes and logistics
Radio-frequency identification (RFID) and real-time locating system (RTLS)	- Optimizing material flow and the supply chain - Optimizing production inventory and storage space to avoid overstocking - Optimizing transport route

In addition to optimizing processes to reduce material and energy usage, digital technologies can be applied to monitoring emissions, such as those through leaks, or supply chain carbon tracking. This is particularly important in the context of Scope 3 emissions (box 4.6) for which manufacturing industry is increasingly accountable in terms of measuring and then addressing. Scope 3 emissions are those beyond a plant's immediate control, but which may cause significant climate impact. One example is the shipping or transportation of a final product from plant to consumer.

In this regard, digital technologies such as IoT and distributed ledger technology may enable better supply chain control and carbon tracking to optimize shipping routes. While cement sector emissions fall mainly within Scopes 1 and 2, 29 percent of steel sector emissions originate from Scope 3 supply chain emissions.[175]

Box 4.6 Greenhouse gas Scope 3 emissions

Digital technologies can play a key role in improving the monitoring of emissions from the manufacturing industry. This may be particularly relevant for tracking and reporting according to emission standards such as the GHG Protocol Corporate Accounting and Reporting Standard. This standard classifies a company's GHG emissions according to three "scopes." Scope 1 emissions are direct emissions from owned or controlled sources; for example, emissions associated with fuel combustion in boilers and furnaces. Scope 2 emissions are indirect emissions from the generation of purchased energy. Scope 3 emissions are all indirect emissions that occur within the reporting company's value chain, including both upstream and downstream emissions. Notably, digital technologies can help overcome the challenge of emissions double-counting by two or more organizations.[176]

Industry 4.0 in steel and cement sectors

This chapter of the *Green Technology Book* is focused on the steel and cement sectors. This section on Industry 4.0 explores the range of digital technologies relevant to these two sectors. Industry 4.0 implementation within the steel and cement sectors has been slow. The metal industry in general is lagging behind other industries when it comes to digital technology deployment.[177] However, there is some movement. A survey of the European steel sector reveals a majority of respondents strongly intend to invest in almost every Industry 4.0 technology, with a priority focus on cyber security and analytics, followed by IoT and virtual simulations. It is notable that the main expected benefit was reduced production costs (81 percent), whereas reduced CO_2 emissions were expected by little more than half (56 percent).[178]

Digital technologies are already used by the steel and cement sectors to monitor energy-related process parameters. Beyond that, such innovations can enable manufacturing plants to take a holistic look at fuel consumption and emissions from both upstream and downstream processes.

Steel and cement: from digital twins to material databases

The steel and cement sectors are now experimenting with the use of digital twins to simulate production processes and save on energy usage and resources, but it is still early days. Advanced diagnostics software is another key component. AI and machine learning tools are allowing real-time tracking in a way not previously possible. Material databases are another active field of research. Such databases are already common within the electronics manufacturing industry, with the EU and various standardization organizations working on developing Digital Product Passes.

The key economic driver behind these technologies is greater production flexibility.[179] But there are often clear dual benefits for cost and energy savings, for example for energy management systems or advanced automation processes. In related sectors, for example, the construction sector, connectivity, remote monitoring, 3D printing and predictive analysis are already transforming parts of traditional supply chains.[180] The technology solutions described provide an overview of the current state of Industry 4.0 technologies within the steel and cement sectors, ranging from proven to horizon stage.

The steel and cement sectors are now experimenting with the use of digital twins to simulate production processes and save on energy usage and resources, but it is still early days

Innovation examples

Photo: Getty Images / © xavierarnau

India's industrial lighthouse
Steel plants operators use a process known as superheating to bring molten steel to the correct temperature for casting. The ideal temperature range is narrow. And if the steel is either too hot or not hot enough, quality can be affected. To improve the process, plant managers at Tata Steel's Kalinganagar plant (one of the largest in India) have created an advanced analytics model that uses historical data to recommend process set points for higher strike rates (i.e., correct temperature predictions). The model is able to assess plant conditions and calculate how much heat to supply during superheating, in order for the molten steel to remain within target temperature range. This has resulted in a more effective process plus cost savings of USD 4 million a year. The plant has also invested in building the digital capacity of staff. It now employs over 30 analytics specialists who integrate the model into the company's plan to improve performance indicators such as energy consumption, throughput, quality and yield.[181]

Photo: Getty Images / © metamorworks

Digital twin and predictive maintenance within the cement sector
Holcim – a large multinational cement producer – has launched the world's first digital twin cement plant. The digital twin in question is a real-time 3D virtual model of a company site in Switzerland. Holcim's software and performance prediction algorithms are integrated into this 3D model, which uses sensors, data analytics and machine learning to prevent costly downtime and enable predictive maintenance. The project is part

of Holcim's Plants of Tomorrow program, using Industry 4.0 technologies across its sites to boost efficiency. The company plans to scale this digital twin technology across its operations, beginning in Europe. It expects this will save over 400,000 tonnes of CO_2 emissions, albeit over an undefined period of time.

Technology solutions

Proven technologies

Additive manufacturing (3D printing) of steel

SLM Solutions

Photo: Getty Images/© Marina Skoropadskaya

Continuous casting – the process whereby steel is shaped and solidified without interruption – has become the industry standard. Over 96 percent of steel is produced through this process which has reduced significantly the amount of liquid steel needed to produce steel sheets. Two more recent versions of this process are thin slab casting and near-net-shape casting (NNSC). Near-net-shape casting is a family of techniques where the production process is calibrated to make an object as close to its final shape as possible. Additive manufacturing (or 3D-printing) is one example. This reduces waste and removes several post-process stages, ultimately lowering energy consumption. SLM Solutions produces various machines for additive manufacturing. An example is the selective laser melting system SLM 280 2.0 suitable for medium-to-high volumes of metal additive manufacturing.

- Contracting type: For sale
- Technology level: High
- Country of origin: Germany
- Availability: Worldwide
- Contact: WIPO GREEN Database

Computer modelling for reduced resource use in construction

Autodesk

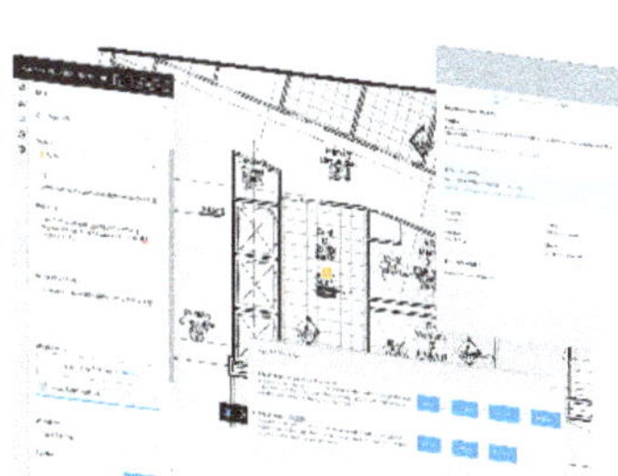

Photo: © Autodesk

Autodesk's BIM 360 is a cloud-based platform providing building information modeling (BIM) software for the construction industry. BIM is the foundation for digital transformation and allows architects to visualize and plan designs according to various scenarios and parameters. Moreover, it encourages building component reuse. It does so through better design and planning undertaken with a building's eventual deconstruction in mind. Autodesk's platform includes tools for 3D modeling, project management and collaboration. This helps reduce over-design and unnecessary use of high-carbon materials such as steel and cement.

- Contracting type: For sale/service
- Technology level: High
- Country of origin: United States
- Availability: Worldwide
- Contact: WIPO GREEN Database

Automated control system for electric arc furnaces

AMI Automation

Photo: Getty Images / © davit85

AMI Automation has developed an automated control system for steelmaking electric arc furnaces. The company's SmartFurnace™ technology is centered around artificial intelligence. Its different modules enable key parameters to be measured and controlled, including temperature, off-gas, slag level, arc stability, as well as gas, oxygen and carbon status. Laser technology and off-gas sensors allow best operating points and energy saving to be quickly identified. The system can also control the rate at which steel is input through continuous feeding systems so as to maintain optimal temperature.

- Contracting type: For sale/service
- Technology level: High
- Country of origin: Mexico
- Availability: Worldwide
- Contact: WIPO GREEN Database

Automation and control systems for steel and cement

Siemens AG

Photo: Getty Images / © WangAnQi

Siemens supplies a range of automation solutions for various industries, including steel and cement. Within the steel sector, Siemens offers solutions for automated material handling, such as the Siemens Mechatronic Solution for Material Handling (MSMH). This system uses advanced control algorithms and simulation tools to optimize material flow and reduce energy consumption. It incorportates a range of components - for example, cranes, conveyors and stackers - that can be configured to meet a steel plant's specific needs. Within the cement sector, Siemens provides the Simine Conveyors system. This uses advanced control algorithms and simulation tools to optimize conveyor belt operation and improve energy efficiency. Similarly, components such as drive systems, pulleys and belt cleaners can be tailored to a cement plant's specific requirements.

- Contracting type: For sale/service
- Technology level: High
- Country of origin: Germany
- Availability: Worldwide
- Contact: WIPO GREEN Database

Digital energy management system
Metron

Photo: Getty Images / © Terry J Alcorn

Metron's digital tool optimizes grinding mill efficiency, saving cement plants both cost and energy. The tool enables production planning according to energy market conditions by collecting data on production, consumption and operation parameters. Thereafter, sequencing rules are built to provide a holistic view of the plant, with personalized dashboards. Comparing data to baselines, real-time alerts are issued when ideal energy consumption is exceeded. Examples of data collected include mill intensity, furnace temperature, emission analysis and energy consumption.

- Contracting type: For sale/service
- Technology level: High
- Country of origin: France
- Availability: Worldwide
- Contact: WIPO GREEN Database

Frontier technologies

Digital twin in the steel sector: thermal management
Ansys/Tata Steel

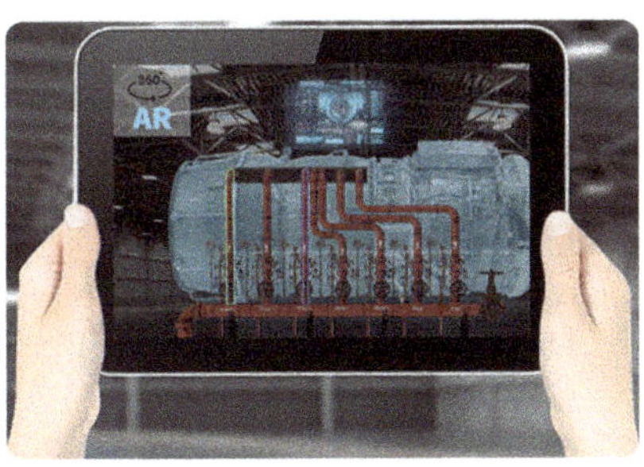

Photo: Getty Images / © Epstudio20

Tata Steel Nederland – one of Europe's top steel producers – has digitalized its thermal process management, working together with simulation company Ansys. Using digital twins, artificial intelligence and machine learning, the company aims to reduce energy consumption and maintenance costs. By analyzing past data and predicting future behavior, thermal simulations allow the company to explore variables like temperature, ladle number and refractory lining changes in an effort to optimize hot metal production.

- Contracting type: For sale/service
- Technology level: High
- Country of origin: United States
- Availability: Worldwide
- Contact: WIPO GREEN Database

Drones, cloud computing and machine learning: concrete infrastructure predictive maintenance

Sund & Bælt

Photo: © Sund & Bælt

Reinforced concrete deteriorates over time, exposing the embedded steel structure to rust. Company Sund & Bælt has deployed drones, cloud computing and machine learning algorithms to identify concrete damage to the seven kilometer-long Great Belt Bridge in Denmark. Thousands of aerial images taken by drones are stored on a digital platform then analyzed by algorithms to identify those bridge sections in need of repair. Such predictive maintenance extends the Bridge's service life and saves up to DKK 35 million a year (approximately USD 5 million) on operation and maintenance. Sund & Bælt now aim to share this solution with other bridge and infrastructure owners around the world.

- Contracting type: For collaboration
- Technology level: High
- Country of origin: Denmark
- Availability: Worldwide
- Contact: WIPO GREEN Database

Machine learning and Software as a Service in cement plants: optimizing fuel consumption

Petuum Inc.

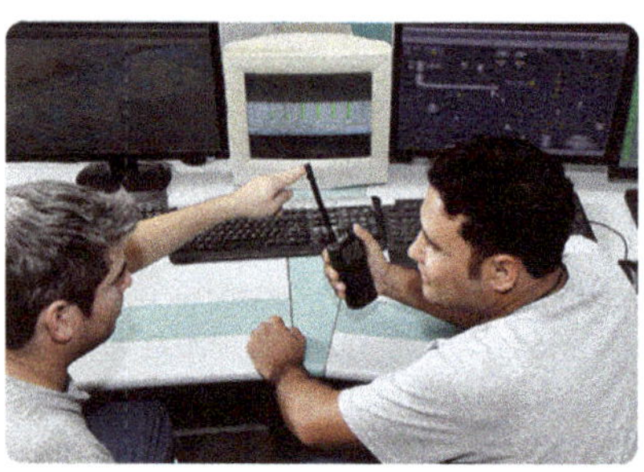

Photo: Getty Images/© Sykono

Researchers and software developers at Petuum Inc. have designed an autopilot system to optimize cement plant operation and reduce fuel consumption and emissions. The system is a machine learning-based Software as a Service (SaaS) able to learn manufacturing process dynamics. By analyzing these processes, the autopilot is able to increase the ratio of alternative fuels, from biowaste and worn tires to petroleum coke. It can also optimize cement production core processes, including the preheater, kiln and cooler. This lowers gases emissions, such as NO_x and SO_x, and reduces the heavy metals used, such as the mercury and lead released through burning petroleum coke. The system has been tested in a real-world environment. This resulted in energy savings and a decrease of up to 28,000 metric tonnes of CO_2 produced a year.

- Contracting type: For collaboration
- Technology level: High
- Country of origin: United States
- Availability: Worldwide
- Contact: WIPO GREEN Database

AI platform for control room operators: optimizing steel and cement energy usage
Carbon Re

Photo: © Carbon RE

Carbon Re's Delta Zero is a software platform that uses artificial intelligence (AI) to optimize steel and cement production processes. Analysis of real-time sensor data generates a high-resolution digital twin of the plant. This twin enables AI "agents" to learn process control through deep reinforcement learning - an AI area that has witnessed a significant breakthrough in recent years. Software then provides operators with clear, actionable recommendations for the various process stages and parameters. According to the company, up to 10 percent energy savings and 20 percent emission reductions can be achieved, while also keeping equipment within a safe operating space and controlling NO_x emission limits.

- Contracting type: For collaboration
- Technology level: High
- Country of origin: United Kingdom
- Availability: N/A
- Contact: WIPO GREEN Database

Distributed ledger technology for product tracking
Siemens AG

Photo: © Siemens AG

Siemens Insights Hub (former Mindsphere) digital IIoT platform tracks products transparently throughout their entire life-cycle. It is based on distributed ledger technology. The tool assesses all useful information before forwarding relevant data subsets to the distributed ledger. There the data are safely and transparently stored for relevant stakeholder access. This enables a better control of operations and the connection of assets such as products, plants, systems and machines to a central location where sustainability data can be collected, analyzed and acted upon.

- Contracting type: For sale/service
- Technology level: High
- Country of origin: Germany
- Availability: Worldwide
- Contact: WIPO GREEN Database

Mixed reality for manufacturing industries
Microsoft Corporation

Photo: © Microsoft Corporation

HoloLens2 is a Microsoft product that enables manufacturing plant and other industries staff to learn complex tasks and collaborate using mixed reality technology. Through mixed-reality applications, the technology aims to make manufacturing processes more lean and efficient, while reducing expert travel time. Hololens2 is a head-mounted device worn by staff on a needs basis.

- Contracting type: For sale/service
- Technology level: High
- Country of origin: United States
- Availability: Worldwide
- Contact: WIPO GREEN Database

Real-time cement plant optimization
TITAN Cement Group

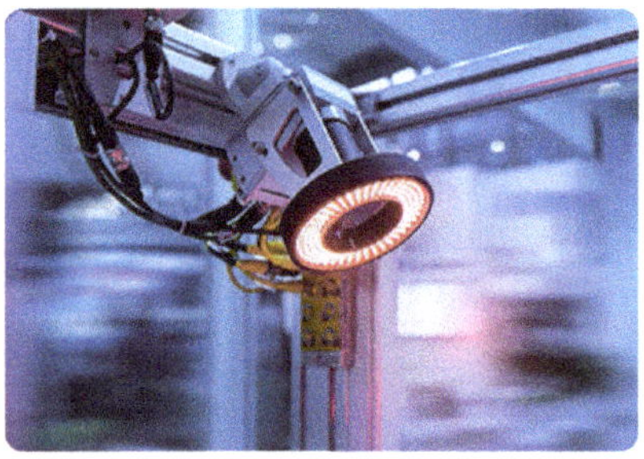
Photo: Getty Images/© kynny

TITAN Cement Group provides technology for optimizing cement plant production and energy efficiency. Sensors are integrated across plant equipment in order to record large volumes of operational data. Data is then transmitted, analyzed and used for the real-time optimization of production parameters, with the support of artificial intelligence technology.

- Contracting type: For sale/service
- Technology level: High
- Country of origin: Greece
- Availability: Worldwide
- Contact: WIPO GREEN Database

AI-based cement plant predictive maintenance
CemAI

Photo: Getty Images/© Goodvibes Photo

CemAI – part of TITAN Cement Group – supplies artificial intelligence-based predictive maintenance solutions for the cement sector. A specially developed algorithm, supported by sensors, helps predict plant failure. The technology simultaneously monitors the entire plant for anomalies, improving operational efficiency and reducing maintenance needs. Installation of the CemAI application takes approximately three months.

- Contracting type: For sale/service
- Technology level: High
- Country of origin: Greece
- Availability: Worldwide
- Contact: WIPO GREEN Database

Digital modeling for optimized transport routes

Western Digital

Photo: Getty Images/© ipopba

Western Digital develops digital models that optimize supply chains by automating transport and shipping routes. They have decreased supply chain transport transit time, thereby avoiding significant greenhouse gas emissions. The model builds on historical supply chain data and machine learning. It self-adjusts shipping routes based on changing requirements and customer purchase orders. This enables transport routes to be predicted more flexibly and accurately. The company has added carbon footprint as a metric to the model in order to track emission reductions, and a digital twin to run multiple model comparisons. The company is now working toward scaling and deploying the model.

- Contracting type: For collaboration
- Technology level: High
- Country of origin: United States
- Availability: N/A
- Contact: WIPO GREEN Database

Automated factories for mass production of buildings

ADMARES + KUKA

Photo: Getty Images/© JARAMA

ADMARES has been working with Siemens and KUKA on digitally transforming the construction industry via smart factories (including automation) and homes. KUKA – a supplier of intelligent automation systems – will be supporting the development of the world's first automated factory for off-site building production. Elements will include digital twins, robotized manufacturing and life-cycle digitalization. The technology aims to allow entire buildings to be mass produced at a factory by assembly-line workers.

- Contracting type: For collaboration
- Technology level: High
- Country of origin: Finland
- Availability: N/A
- Contact: WIPO GREEN Database

Notes

1 Ghoneim, R., G. Mete and A. Hobley (2022). Steel and cement can drive the decade of action on climate change: This is how. United Nations Industrial Development Organization (UNIDO), 'Industrial Analytics Platform'. Available at: https://iap.unido.org/articles/steel-and-cement-can-drive-decade-action-climate-change-how [accessed May 2023].

2 Lehne, J. and F. Preston (2018). *Making concrete change: Innovation in low-carbon cement and concrete*. London: Chatham House. Available at: https://www.chathamhouse.org/sites/default/files/publications/research/2018-06-13-making-concrete-change-cement-lehne-preston.pdf.

3 Kim, J., *et al.* (2022). Decarbonizing the iron and steel industry: A systematic review of sociotechnical systems, technological innovations, and policy options. *Energy Research & Social Science*, 89, 102565.

4 Material Economics (2019). *Industrial transformation 2050: Pathways to net-zero emissions from EU heavy industry (executive summary)*, Net Zero 2050 (Executive summary), Cambridge: University of Cambridge Institute for Sustainability Leadership (CISL). Available at: https://europeanclimate.org/wp-content/uploads/2019/11/25-04-2019-industrial-transformation-2050-executive-summary.pdf.

5 Brogan, C. (2022). 'Greening' cement and steel: 9 ways these industries can reach net zero. London: Imperial College. Available at: www.imperial.ac.uk/news/235134/greening-cement-steel-ways-these-industries [accessed May 2023].

6 Bataille, C., S. Stiebert and F.G.N. Li (2021). *Global facility level net-zero steel pathways.* Paris: The Institute for Sustainable Development and International Relations (IDDRI). Available at: http://netzerosteel.org/wp-content/uploads/pdf/net_zero_steel_report.pdf.

7 IPCC (2022). *Climate change 2022: Mitigation of climate change – Full report, Working Group III contribution to IPCC sixth assessment report.* Cambridge, UK: Intergovernmental Panel on Climate Change (IPCC). Available at: https://www.ipcc.ch/report/sixth-assessment-report-working-group-3/.

8 Arens, M., M. Åhman and V. Vogl (2021). Which countries are prepared to green their coal-based steel industry with electricity? – Reviewing climate and energy policy as well as the implementation of renewable electricity. *Renewable and Sustainable Energy Reviews*, 143, 110938.

9 Vogl, V., M. Åhman and L.J. Nilsson (2018). Assessment of hydrogen direct reduction for fossil-free steelmaking. *Journal of Cleaner Production*, 203, 736–45.

10 Arens, M., M. Åhman, and V. Vogl (2021). Which countries are prepared to green their coal-based steel industry with electricity? - Reviewing climate and energy policy as well as the implementation of renewable electricity. *Renewable and Sustainable Energy Reviews*, 143, 110938.

11 Zero Waste Europe (2020). *Why co-incineration of waste is not taxonomy-compliant and should be excluded*. Brussels: Zero Waste Europe. Available at: https://zerowasteeurope.eu/library/why-co-incineration-of-waste-is-not-taxonomy-compliant-and-should-be-excluded/.

12 VDZ (2021). *Environmental data of the German cement industry.* Düsseldorf: Verein Deutscher Zementwerke (VDZ). Available at: https://www.vdz-online.de/fileadmin/wissensportal/publikationen/umweltschutz/Umweltdaten/VDZ-Umweltdaten_Environmental_Data_2021.pdf.

13 Hites, B. (2020). The growth of EAF steelmaking. Recycling Today. Available at: https://www.recyclingtoday.com/article/the-growth-of-eaf-steelmaking/ [accessed May 2023].

14 Wang, P., *et al.* (2021). Efficiency stagnation in global steel production urges joint supply- and demand-side mitigation efforts. *Nature Communications*, 12(1), 2066.

15 Marmier, A. (2023). *Decarbonisation options for the cement industry.* Luxembourg: Publications Office of the European Union. Available at: https://publications.jrc.ec.europa.eu/repository/handle/JRC131246.

16 Hann, S. (2022). *Is net zero enough for the material production sector?* Bristol: Eunomia Research & Consulting Ltd. Available at: https://zerowasteeurope.eu/wp-content/uploads/2022/11/Is-Net-Zero-Enough-for-the-Materials-Sector-Report-1.pdf.

17 Global CCS Institute (2022). 2022 Status report: Appendices. Available at: https://status22.globalccsinstitute.com/2022-status-report/appendices/ [accessed May 2023].

18 Fennell, P., *et al.* (2022). Cement and steel – Nine steps to net zero. *Nature*, 603, 574–577. Available at: https://www.nature.com/articles/d41586-022-00758-4 [accessed May 2023].

19 Freitag, C., *et al.* (2021). The real climate and transformative impact of ICT: A critique of estimates, trends, and regulations. *Patterns*, 2(9), 100340.

20 Marmier, A. (2023). *Decarbonisation options for the cement industry.* Luxembourg. Available at: https://publications.jrc.ec.europa.eu/repository/handle/JRC131246.

21 Probst, B., *et al.* (2021). Global trends in the invention and diffusion of climate change mitigation technologies. *Nature Energy*, 6, 1077–86.

22 IP Australia (2022). Low emission steel, aluminium and iron ore. Available at: https://app.powerbi.com/view?r=eyJrIjoiNGMyYjE0NjItYzcxNy00NzViLWExYjEtZGE0YjZkYzIxOGUxIiwidCI6IjljMGNlZDQ5LTRlMzYtNGY4MS1iOGQ3LTEwYzRhMGNiZmYyZCJ9 [accessed May 2023].

23 Lehne, J. and F. Preston (2018). *Making concrete change: Innovation in low-carbon cement and concrete*. London: Chatham House. Available at: https://www.chathamhouse.org/sites/default/files/publications/research/2018-06-13-making-concrete-change-cement-lehne-preston.pdf.

24 ECOS (2023). *A performance-based standard for common cements*. ECOS Brief, Environmental Coalition on Standards (ECOS). Available at: https://ecostandard.org/publications/ecos-brief-a-performance-based-standard-for-common-cements/.

25 IEA (2019). *Global patent applications for climate change mitigation technologies – a key measure of innovation – are trending down*. Paris: International Energy Agency (IEA). Available at: https://www.iea.org/commentaries/global-patent-applications-for-climate-change-mitigation-technologies-a-key-measure-of-innovation-are-trending-down.

26 IP Australia (2022). Carbon capture and storage. Available at: https://app.powerbi.com/view?r=eyJrIjoiYjE1MDI2Y2ItY2Q0NC00NjUwLWE1NmYtODA4Njg0MTkzMjA4IiwidCI6IjljMGNlZDQ5LTRlMzYtNGY4MS1iOGQ3LTEwYzRhMGNiZmYyZCJ9 [accessed May 2023].

27 Xie, H., *et al.* (2022). *Progress in hydrogen fuel cell technology development and deployment in China*. Geneva: WIPO, Global Challenges Division. Available at: https://dx.doi.org/10.34667/tind.44764.

28 IP Australia (2021). *The power of hydrogen: Patent analytics on hydrogen technologies*. Available at: https://www.ipaustralia.gov.au/tools-and-research/professional-resources/data-research-and-reports/publications-and-reports/2022/09/30/hydrogen-technology-patent-analytics.

29 IP Australia (2021). *The power of hydrogen: Patent analytics on hydrogen technologies*. Available at: https://www.ipaustralia.gov.au/tools-and-research/professional-resources/data-research-and-reports/publications-and-reports/2022/09/30/hydrogen-technology-patent-analytics.

30 European Patent Office (2020). Fourth industrial revolution. Available at: https://www.epo.org/news-events/in-focus/

ict/fourth-industrial-revolution.html [accessed May 2023].

31 UNCTAD (2022). What is 'Industry 4.0' and what will it mean for developing countries? United Nations Conference on Trade and Development (UNCTAD). Available at: https://unctad.org/news/blog-what-industry-40-and-what-will-it-mean-developing-countries [accessed May 2023].

32 IP Australia (2018). *The blockchain innovation: A patent analytics report*. Available at: https://www.ipaustralia.gov.au/tools-and-research/professional-resources/data-research-and-reports/publications-and-reports/2022/09/30/02/59/the-blockchain-innovation-a-patent-analytics-report.

33 IP Australia (2019). *Machine learning innovation: A patent analytics report*. Available at: https://www.ipaustralia.gov.au/tools-and-research/professional-resources/data-research-and-reports/publications-and-reports/2022/09/30/03/31/machine-learning-innovation-a-patent-analytics-report.

34 IP Australia (2018). *The blockchain innovation: A patent analytics report*. Available at: https://www.ipaustralia.gov.au/tools-and-research/professional-resources/data-research-and-reports/publications-and-reports/2022/09/30/02/59/the-blockchain-innovation-a-patent-analytics-report.

35 IP Australia (2019). *Machine learning innovation: A patent analytics report*. Available at: https://www.ipaustralia.gov.au/tools-and-research/professional-resources/data-research-and-reports/publications-and-reports/2022/09/30/03/31/machine-learning-innovation-a-patent-analytics-report.

36 Probst, B., *et al.* (2021). Global trends in the invention and diffusion of climate change mitigation technologies. *Nature Energy*, 6, 1077-86.

37 CPI (2022). *Financing steel decarbonization*, Instrument Analysis. Climate Policy Initiative (CPI). Available at: https://www.climatepolicyinitiative.org/wp-content/uploads/2022/10/FSD-report.pdf.

38 Wood Mackenzie (2022). Pedal to the metal: Iron and steel's US$1.4 trillion shot at decarbonisation. *Horizons*. Available at: https://www.woodmac.com/horizons/pedal-to-the-metal-iron-and-steels-one-point-four-trillion-usd-shot-at-decarbonisation/ [accessed May 2023].

39 Maltais, A., *et al.* (2022). *The role of international finance institutions in the transition to low-carbon steel production*. Leadership Group for Industry Transition (LeadIT). Available at: https://www.sei.org/wp-content/uploads/2022/11/report-2209a-ifis-lhv2.pdf.

40 McKinsey (2020). *Laying the foundation for zero-carbon cement*, Chemicals Practice. McKinsey & Company. Available at: https://www.naiopmd.org/wp-content/uploads/2022/08/Cement-McKinsey-laying-the-foundation-for-zero-carbon-cement-v3.pdf.

41 Gardner, T. (2023). US announces $6 bln in grants to decarbonize heavy industry. *Reuters*. Available at: https://www.reuters.com/business/environment/us-announces-6-bln-grants-decarbonize-heavy-industry-2023-03-08/ [accessed May 2023].

42 UNEP FI (2023). *Climate risks in the industrials sector*, Sectoral Risk Briefings: Insights for Financial Institutions. UN Environment Programme Finance Initiative. Available at: https://www.unepfi.org/wordpress/wp-content/uploads/2023/04/Climate-Risks-in-the-Industrials-Sector.pdf.

43 Maltais, A., *et al.* (2022). *The role of international finance institutions in the transition to low-carbon steel production*. Leadership Group for Industry Transition (LeadIT). Available at: https://www.sei.org/wp-content/uploads/2022/11/report-2209a-ifis-lhv2.pdf.

44 Bataille, C., S. Stiebert, and F.G.N. Li (2021). *Global facility level net-zero steel pathways*. Paris: The Institute for Sustainable Development and International Relations (IDDRI). Available at: http://netzerosteel.org/wp-content/uploads/pdf/net_zero_steel_report.pdf.

45 Bataille, C., S. Stiebert, and F.G.N. Li (2021). *Global facility level net-zero steel pathways*. Paris: The Institute for Sustainable Development and International Relations (IDDRI). Available at: http://netzerosteel.org/wp-content/uploads/pdf/net_zero_steel_report.pdf.

46 OECD (2021). *Latest developments in steelmaking capacity*. Organisation for Economic Co-operation and Development (OECD). Available at: https://www.oecd.org/industry/ind/latest-developments-in-steelmaking-capacity-2021.pdf.

47 CPI (2022). *Financing steel decarbonization*. Instrument Analysis, Climate Policy Initiative (CPI). Available at: https://www.climatepolicyinitiative.org/wp-content/uploads/2022/10/FSD-report.pdf.

48 CPI (2022). *Financing steel decarbonization*. Instrument Analysis, Climate Policy Initiative (CPI). Available at: https://www.climatepolicyinitiative.org/wp-content/uploads/2022/10/FSD-report.pdf.

49 DNV (2023). Green steel assurance. Det Norske Veritas (DNV). Available at: https://www.dnv.com/services/green-steel-assurance-232895 [accessed May 2023].

50 Net Zero Insights (2023). An overview of the green steel startups and initiatives. Available at: https://netzeroinsights.com/resources/market-insights/green-steel-startups-funding-landscape/ [accessed May 2023].

51 Maltais, A., *et al.* (2022). *The role of international finance institutions in the transition to low-carbon steel production*. Leadership Group for Industry Transition (LeadIT). Available at: https://www.sei.org/wp-content/uploads/2022/11/report-2209a-ifis-lhv2.pdf.

52 Chaudhary, A. (2022). India planning carbon credit market for energy, steel and cement. The Economic Times. Available at: https://economictimes.indiatimes.com/industry/renewables/india-planning-carbon-credit-market-for-energy-steel-and-cement/articleshow/93297031.cms?from=mdr [accessed May 2023].

53 UNEP FI (2023). *Climate risks in the industrials sector*. Sectoral Risk Briefings: Insights for Financial Institutions, UN Environment Programme Finance Initiative. Available at: https://www.unepfi.org/wordpress/wp-content/uploads/2023/04/Climate-Risks-in-the-Industrials-Sector.pdf.

54 OECD (2022). *Assessing steel decarbonization progress: ready for the decade of delivery?* Organisation for Economic Co-operation and Development (OECD). Available at: https://www.oecd.org/industry/ind/assessing-steel-decarbonisation-progress.pdf.

55 GIZ (2021). *Potential of Article 6 and other financing instruments to promote Green Hydrogen in the Steel, Cement and Mining Industries*. Bonn, Germany: Deutsche Gesellschaft für Internationale Zusammenarbeit (GIZ) GmbH. Available at: https://www.carbon-mechanisms.de/fileadmin/media/dokumente/Publikationen/Bericht/Art.-6-Green-Hydrogen-Final-ENG.pdf.

56 Agora Energiewende (2023). Global steel transformation tracker. Available at: https://www.agora-energiewende.de/en/service/global-steel-transformation-tracker/ [accessed May 2023].

57 Kim, J., *et al.* (2022). Decarbonizing the iron and steel industry: A systematic review of sociotechnical systems, technological innovations, and policy options. *Energy Research & Social Science*, 89, 102565.

58 Blank, T.K. (2019). *The disruptive potential of green steel*, Insight brief. Rocky Mountain Institute (RMI). Available at: https://rmi.org/wp-content/uploads/2019/09/green-steel-insight-brief.pdf.

59 Westerholm, N. (2023). *Unlocking the potential of local circular construction materials in urbanising Africa*. United Nations One Planet Sustainable Buildings and Construction Programme. Available at: https://www.oneplanetnetwork.org/knowledge-centre/resources/

unlocking-potential-local-circular-construction-materials-urbanising.

60 Guevara Opinska, L., *et al.* (2021). *Moving towards zero-emission steel: Technologies available, prospects, timeline and costs*. Luxembourg: European Parliament. Available at: https://www.europarl.europa.eu/RegData/etudes/STUD/2021/695484/IPOL_STU(2021)695484_EN.pdf.

61 Nicholas, S. and S. Basirat (2022). *Iron ore quality a potential headwind to green steelmaking: Technology and mining options are available to hit net-zero steel targets*. Institute for Energy Economics and Financial Analysis (IEEFA). Available at: https://ieefa.org/resources/iron-ore-quality-potential-headwind-green-steelmaking-technology-and-mining-options-are.

62 Vogl, V., O. Olsson and B. Nykvist (2021). Phasing out the blast furnace to meet global climate targets. *Joule*, 5(10), 2646–62.

63 Ibid.

64 European Parliament (2021). *Carbon-free steel production: Cost reduction options and usage of existing gas infrastructure*. Brussels: European Parliamentary Research Service (EPRS). Available at: https://www.europarl.europa.eu/RegData/etudes/STUD/2021/690008/EPRS_STU(2021)690008_EN.pdf.

65 Kashyap, Y. (2022). Analysis: Costs and impacts of low-carbon technologies for steel and cement sectors in India. Climate Policy Initiative (CPI). Available at: https://www.climatepolicyinitiative.org/report-summary-costs-and-impacts-of-low-carbon-technologies-for-steel-and-cement-sectors-in-india/ [accessed May 2023].

66 Nicholas, S. and S. Basirat (2022). *Iron ore quality a potential headwind to green steelmaking: Technology and mining options are available to hit net-zero steel targets*. Institute for Energy Economics and Financial Analysis (IEEFA). Available at: https://ieefa.org/resources/iron-ore-quality-potential-headwind-green-steelmaking-technology-and-mining-options-are.

67 European Parliament (2021). *Carbon-free steel production: Cost reduction options and usage of existing gas infrastructure*. European Parliamentary Research Service (EPRS). Available at: https://www.europarl.europa.eu/RegData/etudes/STUD/2021/690008/EPRS_STU(2021)690008_EN.pdf.

68 Fan, Z. and J. Friedmann (2021). *Low-carbon production of iron & steel: Technology options, economic assessment, and policy*. Center on Global Energy Policy at Columbia University. Available at: https://www.energypolicy.columbia.edu/publications/low-carbon-production-iron-steel-technology-options-economic-assessment-and-policy.

69 World Steel Association (2021). Fact sheet: Scrap use in the steel industry. Available at: https://worldsteel.org/wp-content/uploads/Fact-sheet-on-scrap_2021.pdf [accessed May 2023].

70 Material Economics (2018). *The circular economy – A powerful force for climate mitigation*. Available at: https://circulareconomy.europa.eu/platform/en/knowledge/circular-economy-powerful-force-climate-mitigation.

71 World Steel Association (2021). Raw materials: Maximising scrap use helps reduce CO_2 emissions. Available at: https://worldsteel.org/steel-topics/raw-materials/ [accessed May 2023].

72 Kashyap, Y. (2022). Analysis: Costs and impacts of low-carbon technologies for steel and cement sectors in India. Climate Policy Initiative (CPI). Available at: https://www.climatepolicyinitiative.org/report-summary-costs-and-impacts-of-low-carbon-technologies-for-steel-and-cement-sectors-in-india/ [accessed May 2023].

73 IEA (2020). *Iron and steel technology roadmap*, Energy Technology Perspectives. Paris: International Energy Agency (IEA). Available at: https://iea.blob.core.windows.net/assets/eb0c8ec1-3665-4959-97d0-187ceca189a8/Iron_and_Steel_Technology_Roadmap.pdf.

74 IPCC (2022). *Climate change 2022: Mitigation of climate change. Full report. Working Group III contribution to IPCC sixth assessment report.*, Cambridge: Intergovernmental Panel on Climate Change (IPCC). Available at: https://www.ipcc.ch/report/sixth-assessment-report-working-group-3/.

75 Material Economics (2018). *The circular economy- a powerful force for climate mitigation*. Available at: https://circulareconomy.europa.eu/platform/en/knowledge/circular-economy-powerful-force-climate-mitigation.

76 Ibid.

77 Material Economics (2018). *The circular economy- a powerful force for climate mitigation*. Available at: https://circulareconomy.europa.eu/platform/en/knowledge/circular-economy-powerful-force-climate-mitigation.

78 World Steel Association (2021). Steel industry key facts. Available at: https://worldsteel.org/about-steel/steel-industry-facts/ [accessed May 2023].

79 IEA (2020). *Iron and steel technology roadmap*. Energy Technology Perspectives, Paris: International Energy Agency (IEA). Available at: https://iea.blob.core.windows.net/assets/eb0c8ec1-3665-4959-97d0-187ceca189a8/Iron_and_Steel_Technology_Roadmap.pdf.

80 Zeng, Y. and R. Cecil (2021). High-grade iron ore supply to struggle to meet demand as China decarbonizes: MI. S&P Global Market Intelligence. Available at: https://www.spglobal.com/commodityinsights/en/market-insights/latest-news/metals/060821-high-grade-iron-ore-supply-to-struggle-to-meet-demand-as-china-decarbonizes-mi [accessed May 2023].

81 Xie, H., *et al.* (2022). *Progress in hydrogen fuel cell technology development and deployment in China*. Available at: https://dx.doi.org/10.34667/tind.44764.

82 Vogl, V., M. Åhman, and L.J. Nilsson (2018). Assessment of hydrogen direct reduction for fossil-free steelmaking. *Journal of Cleaner Production*, 203, 736-45.

83 Blank, T.K. (2019). *The disruptive potential of green steel*. Insight brief, Rocky Mountain Institute (RMI). Available at: https://rmi.org/wp-content/uploads/2019/09/green-steel-insight-brief.pdf.

84 Sun, F., *et al.* (2021). Energy-saving hydrogen production by chlorine-free hybrid seawater splitting coupling hydrazine degradation. *Nature Communications*, 12(1), 4182.

85 Vogl, V., O. Olsson, and B. Nykvist (2021). Phasing out the blast furnace to meet global climate targets. *Joule*, 5(10), 2646-62.

86 European Parliament (2021). *Carbon-free steel production: Cost reduction options and usage of existing gas infrastructure*. European Parliamentary Research Service (EPRS). Available at: https://www.europarl.europa.eu/RegData/etudes/STUD/2021/690008/EPRS_STU(2021)690008_EN.pdf.

87 Hann, S. (2022). *Is net zero enough for the material production sector?*, Bristol: Eunomia Research & Consulting Ltd. Available at: https://zerowasteeurope.eu/wp-content/uploads/2022/11/Is-Net-Zero-Enough-for-the-Materials-Sector-Report-1.pdf.

88 LeadIT (2023). Green steel tracker. Leadership Group for Industry Transition (LeadIT). Available at: https://www.industrytransition.org/green-steel-tracker/ [accessed May 2023].

89 IEA (2020). *Iron and steel technology roadmap*. Energy Technology Perspectives, Paris: International Energy Agency (IEA). Available at: https://iea.blob.core.windows.net/assets/eb0c8ec1-3665-4959-97d0-187ceca189a8/Iron_and_Steel_Technology_Roadmap.pdf.

90 Conejo, A.N., J.-P. Birat and A. Dutta (2020). A review of the current environmental challenges of the steel industry and its value chain. *Journal of Environmental Management*, 259, 109782.

91 OECD (2015). *Energy efficiency in the steel sector: Why it works well, but not always*. Paris: Organisation for Economic Co-operation and Development (OECD). Available at: https://www.oecd.org/sti/ind/Energy-efficiency-steel-sector-1.pdf.

92 Stevens, I., *et al.* (2022). *Policy options for a net-zero emissions UK steel sector*, CREDS policy brief. Oxford, UK: Centre for Research into Energy Demand Solutions (CREDS). Available at: https://www.creds.ac.uk/publications/policy-options-for-a-net-zero-emissions-uk-steel-sector/.

93 Leoni, L., *et al.* (2021). Energy-saving technology opportunities and investments of the Italian foundry industry. *Energies*, 14(24), 8470.

94 UNIDO (2019). *Industrial energy efficiency improvement project in South Africa*. United Nations Industrial Development Organization (UNIDO). Available at: https://mkiee.ea.gov.mk/wp-content/uploads/2019/11/International-UNIDO-SA-IEE-Project-Arcelormittal-Saldanha-Works-Case-Study.pdf.

95 ESCI (2022). *Energy costs reduced by 40% in aluminium, steelworks and ceramics production*. European Science Communication Institute (ESCI). Available at: https://www.youtube.com/watch?v=VQwTogBhYz8.

96 Gan, Y. and W.M. Griffin (2018). Analysis of life-cycle GHG emissions for iron ore mining and processing in China – Uncertainty and trends. *Resources Policy*, 58, 90–96.

97 Mourão, J. M., *et al.* (2020). Comparison of sinter and pellet usage in an integrated steel plant' in *ABM BRAZIL – 2013 Annual Congress*. Belo Horizonte, Brazil.

98 European Commission (2017). Development of new methodologies for industrial CO_2-free steel production by electrowinning. Available at: https://cordis.europa.eu/project/id/768788 [accessed May 2023].

99 Atmaca, A. and M. Kanoglu (2012). Reducing energy consumption of a raw mill in cement industry. *Energy*, 42(1), 261–69.

100 Kahawalage, A.C., M.C. Melaaen and L.-A. Tokheim (2023). Opportunities and challenges of using SRF as an alternative fuel in the cement industry. *Cleaner Waste Systems*, 4, 100072.

101 Griffiths, S., *et al.* (2023). Decarbonizing the cement and concrete industry: A systematic review of socio-technical systems, technological innovations, and policy options. *Renewable and Sustainable Energy Reviews*, 180, 113291.

102 IEA (2018). *Technology roadmap: Low-carbon transition in the cement industry*. Paris: International Energy Agency (IEA). Available at: https://iea.blob.core.windows.net/assets/cbaa3da1-fd61-4c2a-8719-31538f59b54f/TechnologyRoadmapLowCarbonTransitionintheCementIndustry.pdf.

103 IEA (2022). *Cement*, Tracking report. Paris: International Energy Agency (IEA). Available at: https://www.iea.org/reports/cement.

104 The Concrete Centre (2020). *Remixed: How concrete is evolving for a net-zero built environment*. Concrete futures. Available at: https://www.concretecentre.com/TCC/media/TCCMediaLibrary/Publications/Promo%20Links/Concrete_Futures_Remixed_2020.pdf.

105 IRP (2020). *Resource efficiency and climate change: Material efficiency strategies for a low-carbon future*. Nairobi: International Resource Panel (IRP) and United Nations Environment Programme (UNEP). Available at: https://www.unep.org/resources/report/resource-efficiency-and-climate-change-material-efficiency-strategies-low-carbon.

106 Skinner, B. and R. Lalit (2023). With concrete, less is more. Rocky Mountain Institute (RMI). Available at: https://rmi.org/with-concrete-less-is-more/ [accessed May 2023].

107 Lehne, J. and F. Preston (2018). *Making concrete change: Innovation in low-carbon cement and concrete*. London: Chatham House. Available at: https://www.chathamhouse.org/sites/default/files/publications/research/2018-06-13-making-concrete-change-cement-lehne-preston.pdf.

108 Simoni, M., *et al.* (2022). Decarbonising the lime industry: State-of-the-art. *Renewable and Sustainable Energy Reviews*, 168, 112765.

109 Lehne, J. and F. Preston (2018). *Making concrete change: Innovation in low-carbon cement and concrete*. London: Chatham House. Available at: https://www.chathamhouse.org/sites/default/files/publications/research/2018-06-13-making-concrete-change-cement-lehne-preston.pdf.

110 JRC (2013). *Best Available Techniques (BAT) reference document for the production of cement, lime and magnesium oxide*. Geneva: Joint Research Centre (JRC). Available at: https://op.europa.eu/en/publication-detail/-/publication/12dbe9f3-28c6-44c9-8962-50a1359443d6.

111 JRC (2020). *Deep decarbonization of industry: The cement sector*. Brussels: European Commission Joint Research Centre (JRC). Available at: https://ee-ip.org/fileadmin/user_upload/IMAGES/Articles/JRC120570_decarbonisation_of_cement__fact_sheet.pdf.

112 IEA (2022). *Cement*. Tracking report, Paris: International Energy Agency (IEA). Available at: https://www.iea.org/reports/cement.

113 Sawyer, T. (2016). *The use of limestone as an extender and its effect on concrete properties*. Unpublished thesis.

114 Fatahi, R., *et al.* (2022). Modeling of energy consumption factors for an industrial cement vertical roller mill by SHAP-XGBoost: A "conscious lab" approach. *Scientific Reports*, 12(1), 7543.

115 Liu, C., *et al.* (2022). Analysis and optimization of grinding performance of vertical roller mill based on experimental method. *Minerals*, 12(2), 133.

116 Boehm, A., P. Meissner and T. Plochberger (2015). An energy based comparison of vertical roller mills and tumbling mills. *International Journal of Mineral Processing*, 136, 37–41.

117 Griffiths, S., *et al.* (2023). Decarbonizing the cement and concrete industry: A systematic review of socio-technical systems, technological innovations, and policy options. *Renewable and Sustainable Energy Reviews*, 180, 113291.

118 Kahawalage, A.C., M.C. Melaaen and L.-A. Tokheim (2023). Opportunities and challenges of using SRF as an alternative fuel in the cement industry. *Cleaner Waste Systems*, 4, 100072.

119 Fennell, P., *et al.* (2022). Cement and steel- nine steps to net zero. Nature. Available at: https://www.nature.com/articles/d41586-022-00758-4 [accessed May 2023].

120 Griffiths, S., *et al.* (2023). Decarbonizing the cement and concrete industry: A systematic review of socio-technical systems, technological innovations, and policy options. *Renewable and Sustainable Energy Reviews*, 180, 113291.

121 Woolley, E., Y. Luo, and A. Simeone (2018). Industrial waste heat recovery: A systematic approach. *Sustainable Energy Technologies and Assessments*, 29, 50–59.

122 WWF (2008). *How to turn around the trend of cement related emissions in the developing world*. Gland, Switzerland: WWF International. Available at: https://wwfint.awsassets.panda.org/downloads/english_report_lr_pdf.pdf.

123 Rahman, A., *et al.* (2015). Recent development on the uses of alternative fuels in cement manufacturing process. *Fuel*, 145, 84–99.

124 Brock, J., *et al.* (2021). 'Trash and burn: Big brands stoke cement kilns with plastic waste as recycling falters'. Available: at: https://www.reuters.com/investigates/special-report/environment-plastic-cement/ [accessed September 2023].

125 Kahawalage, A.C., M.C. Melaaen, and L.-A. Tokheim (2023). Opportunities and challenges of using SRF as an alternative fuel in the cement industry. *Cleaner Waste Systems*, 4, 100072.

126 GCCA (2021). *The GCCA 2050 cement and concrete industry roadmap for net zero concrete*. Global Cement and Concrete Association (GCCA). Available at: https://gccassociation.org/concretefuture/wp-content/uploads/2021/10/GCCA-Concrete-Future-Roadmap-Document-AW.pdf.

127 JRC (2020). *Deep decarbonization of industry: The cement sector*. Brussels: European Commission Joint Research Centre (JRC). Available at: https://ee-ip.org/fileadmin/user_upload/IMAGES/Articles/JRC120570_decarbonisation_of_cement__fact_sheet.pdf.

128 Kusuma, R.T., *et al*. (2022). Sustainable transition towards biomass-based cement industry: A review. *Renewable and Sustainable Energy Reviews*, 163, 112503.

129 JRC (2020). *Deep decarbonization of industry: The cement sector*. Brussels: European Commission Joint Research Centre (JRC). Available at: https://ee-ip.org/fileadmin/user_upload/IMAGES/Articles/JRC120570_decarbonisation_of_cement__fact_sheet.pdf.

130 Griffiths, S., *et al*. (2023). Decarbonizing the cement and concrete industry: A systematic review of socio-technical systems, technological innovations, and policy options. *Renewable and Sustainable Energy Reviews*, 180, 113291.

131 Simoni, M., *et al*. (2022). Decarbonising the lime industry: State-of-the-art. *Renewable and Sustainable Energy Reviews*, 168, 112765.

132 IEA (2022). *Direct air capture*. Paris: International Energy Agency (IEA). Available at: https://www.iea.org/reports/direct-air-capture

133 Hanifa, M., *et al*. (2023). A review on CO_2 capture and sequestration in the construction industry: Emerging approaches and commercialised technologies. *Journal of CO_2 Utilization*, 67, 102292.

134 IEA (2022). *Direct air capture*. Paris: International Energy Agency (IEA). Available at: https://www.iea.org/reports/direct-air-capture

135 JRC (2020). *Deep decarbonization of industry: The cement sector*. Brussels: European Commission Joint Research Centre (JRC). Available at: https://ee-ip.org/fileadmin/user_upload/IMAGES/Articles/JRC120570_decarbonisation_of_cement__fact_sheet.pdf.

136 Simoni, M., *et al*. (2022). Decarbonising the lime industry: State-of-the-art. *Renewable and Sustainable Energy Reviews*, 168, 112765.

137 Rahman, A., *et al*. (2015). Recent development on the uses of alternative fuels in cement manufacturing process. *Fuel*, 145, 84-99.

138 Hanifa, M., *et al*. (2023). A review on CO_2 capture and sequestration in the construction industry: Emerging approaches and commercialised technologies. *Journal of CO_2 Utilization*, 67, 102292.

139 Monkman, S., *et al*. (2018). Activation of cement hydration with carbon dioxide. *Journal of Sustainable Cement-Based Materials*, 7(3), 160–81.

140 Simoni, M., *et al*. (2022). Decarbonising the lime industry: State-of-the-art. *Renewable and Sustainable Energy Reviews*, 168, 112765.

141 IPCC (2023). *Synthesis report (SYR) of the IPCC sixth assessment report (AR6): Summary for policymakers*. Geneva: Intergovernmental Panel on Climate Change (IPCC). Available at: https://www.ipcc.ch/report/ar6/syr/.

142 Patsavellas, J. and K. Salonitis (2019). The carbon footprint of manufacturing digitalization: Critical literature review and future research agenda. *Procedia CIRP*, 81, 1354–59.

143 Rauch, E. and D.T. Matt (2021). Status of the implementation of Industry 4.0 in SMEs and framework for smart manufacturing. In D.T. Matt, V. Modrák and H. Zsifkovits (eds), *Implementing Industry 4.0 in SMEs: Concepts, examples and applications*. Cham: Springer International Publishing, 3–26.

144 Arlbjørn, J.S., *et al*. (2019). Drivers and barriers for Industry 4.0 readiness and practice: A SME perspective with empirical evidence. In *Hawaii International Conference on System Sciences*. Grand Wailea, Maui, HI.

145 Fritzsche, K., S. Niehoff and G. Beier (2018). Industry 4.0 and climate change – exploring the science – policy gap. *Sustainability*, 10(12). Available: at https://www.mdpi.com/2071-1050/10/12/4511 [accessed September 2023].

146 Fritzsche, K., S. Niehoff, and G. Beier (2018). Industry 4.0 and climate change – exploring the science – policy gap. *Sustainability*, 10(12). Available: at https://www.mdpi.com/2071-1050/10/12/4511 [accessed September 2023].

147 Bieser, J.C.T., *et al*. (2023). A review of assessments of the greenhouse gas footprint and abatement potential of information and communication technology. *Environmental Impact Assessment Review*, 99, 107033.

148 Fritzsche, K., S. Niehoff, and G. Beier (2018). 'Industry 4.0 and climate change—exploring the science-policy gap'. *Sustainability*, 10(12). Available: at https://www.mdpi.com/2071-1050/10/12/4511 [accessed

149 Bieser, J.C.T., *et al*. (2023). A review of assessments of the greenhouse gas footprint and abatement potential of information and communication technology. *Environmental Impact Assessment Review*, 99, 107033.

150 Bieser, J.C.T., *et al*. (2023). A review of assessments of the greenhouse gas footprint and abatement potential of information and communication technology. *Environmental Impact Assessment Review*, 99, 107033.

151 IEA (2019). *Energy efficiency 2019*. Paris: International Energy Agency (IEA). Available at: https://www.iea.org/reports/energy-efficiency-2019.

152 WEF (2022). Digital solutions can reduce global emissions by up to 20%: Here's how. World Economic Forum (WEF). Available at: https://www.weforum.org/agenda/2022/05/how-digital-solutions-can-reduce-global-emissions/ [accessed May 2023].

153 Chen, X., M. Despeisse and B. Johansson (2020). 'Environmental sustainability of digitalization in manufacturing: A review'. *Sustainability*, 12(24)Available: at [accessed

154 GeSI (2020). *Digital solutions for climate action*. Brussels, Belgium: Global e-Sustainability Initiative (GeSI). Available at: https://gesi.org/research/download/52.

155 GeSI (2015). ICT solutions for 21st century challenges. Global e-Sustainability Initiative (GeSI). Available at: https://smarter2030.gesi.org/ [accessed August 2023].

156 Chen, X., M. Despeisse, and B. Johansson (2020). Environmental sustainability of digitalization in manufacturing: A review. *Sustainability*, 12(24).

157 IEA (2020). *Iron and steel technology roadmap*. Energy Technology Perspectives, Paris: International Energy Agency (IEA). Available at: https://iea.blob.core.windows.net/assets/eb0c8ec1-3665-4959-97d0-187ceca189a8/Iron_and_Steel_Technology_Roadmap.pdf.

158 Haghdadi, N., *et al*. (2021). Additive manufacturing of steels: A review of achievements and challenges. *Journal of Materials Science*, 56(1), 64–107.

159 Peng, T., *et al*. (2018). Sustainability of additive manufacturing: An overview on its energy demand and environmental impact. *Additive Manufacturing*, 21, 694–704.

160 Sice, C. and J. Faludi (2021). Comparing environmental impacts of metal additive manufacturing to conventional manufacturing. *Proceedings of the Design Society*, 1, 671–80.

161 Dusík, J., *et al*. (2018). *Strategic environmental and social assessment of automation: Scoping working paper*.

Available at: https://www.researchgate.net/publication/326461326_Strategic_Environmental_and_Social_Assessment_of_Automation_Scoping_Working_Paper.

162 Bieser, J.C.T., *et al.* (2023). A review of assessments of the greenhouse gas footprint and abatement potential of information and communication technology. *Environmental Impact Assessment Review*, 99, 107033.

163 GeSI (2020). *Digital solutions for climate action*. Brussels, Belgium: Global e-Sustainability Initiative (GeSI). Available at: https://gesi.org/research/download/52.

164 Jasonarson, I. (2020). *Digitalization for energy efficiency in energy intensive industries*. Unpublished thesis (Independent thesis advanced level), KTH.

165 Brozzi, R., *et al.* (2020). The advantages of Industry 4.0 applications for sustainability: Results from a sample of manufacturing companies. *Sustainability*, 12(9), 3647.

166 Kumar, P., J. Bhamu and K.S. Sangwan (2021). Analysis of barriers to Industry 4.0 adoption in manufacturing organizations: An ISM approach. *Procedia CIRP*, 98, 85–90.

167 Nhamo, G., C. Nhemachena and S. Nhamo (2020). Using ICT indicators to measure readiness of countries to implement Industry 4.0 and the SDGs. *Environmental Economics and Policy Studies*, 22(2), 315–37.

168 ITU (2022). *Measuring digital development*. International Telecommunication Union (ITU). Available at: https://www.itu.int/itu-d/reports/statistics/facts-figures-2022/.

169 Sayem, A., *et al.* (2022). Critical barriers to Industry 4.0 adoption in manufacturing organizations and their mitigation strategies. *Journal of Manufacturing and Materials Processing*, 6(6), 136.

170 Chen, X., M. Despeisse, and B. Johansson (2020). 'Environmental sustainability of digitalization in manufacturing: A review'. *Sustainability*, 12(24). Available: at [accessed

171 Dusík, J., *et al.* (2018). *Strategic environmental and social assessment of automation: Scoping working paper.* Available at: https://www.researchgate.net/publication/326461326_Strategic_Environmental_and_Social_Assessment_of_Automation_Scoping_Working_Paper.

172 Barteková, E. and P. Börkey (2022). *Digitalisation for the transition to a resource efficient and circular economy*, OECD Environment Working Papers, No. 192. Paris: Organisation for Economic Co-operation and Development (OECD). Available at: https://www.oecd-ilibrary.org/content/paper/6f6d18e7-en.

173 de Sousa Jabbour, A.B.L., *et al.* (2018). When titans meet – Can industry 4.0 revolutionise the environmentally-sustainable manufacturing wave? The role of critical success factors. *Technological Forecasting and Social Change*, 132, 18–25.

174 Maghazei, O. and T. Netland (2020). Drones in manufacturing: Exploring opportunities for research and practice. *Journal of Manufacturing Technology Management*, 31(6), 1237–1259.

175 WEF (2021). *Net-zero challenge: The supply chain opportunity*, Insight report. World Economic Forum (WEF). Available at: https://www3.weforum.org/docs/WEF_Net_Zero_Challenge_The_Supply_Chain_Opportunity_2021.pdf.

176 GHG Protocol (2023). Greenhouse Gas Protocol FAQ. Available at: https://ghgprotocol.org/sites/default/files/standards_supporting/FAQ.pdf [accessed June 2023].

177 Gulda, M.P. (2021). *How digitalization will enable completely different ways of working in steelmaking.* H2 Green Steel. Available at: https://www.h2greensteel.com/stories/how-digitalization-will-enable-completely-different-ways-of-working-in-steelmaking.

178 EU (2021). *Digital transformation in European steel industry: State of art and future scenario.* European Union (EU). Available at: https://www.estep.eu/assets/Uploads/ESSA-D2.1-Technological-and-Economic-Development-in-the-Steel-Industry-Version-2.pdf.

179 Nguyen, L.D., *et al.* (2022). Analysis of distributed ledger technologies for industrial manufacturing. *Scientific Reports*, 12(1), 18055.

180 Lehne, J. and F. Preston (2018). *Making concrete change: Innovation in low-carbon cement and concrete.* London: Chatham House. Available at: https://www.chathamhouse.org/sites/default/files/publications/research/2018-06-13-making-concrete-change-cement-lehne-preston.pdf.

181 McKinsey (2022). How a steel plant in India tapped the value of data – and won global acclaim, *Impact story.* McKinsey & Company. Available at: https://www.mckinsey.com/industries/metals-and-mining/how-we-help-clients/how-a-steel-plant-in-india-tapped-the-value-of-data-and-won-global-acclaim [accessed May 2023].

Bibliography

4 per 1000 (2023). The international "4 per 1000" initiative – Soils for food security and climate. Agricultural Research Centre for International Development (CIRAD). Available at: https://4p1000.org/?lang=en [accessed June 2023].

Acebedo, B., M. C. Morant-Miñana, E. Gonzalo, I. Ruiz de Larramendi, A. Villaverde, J. Rikarte and L. Fallarino (2023). Current status and future perspective on lithium metal anode production methods. *Advanced Energy Materials,* 13(13), 2203744.

Aflaki, A., N. Mahyuddin, Z. Al-Cheikh Mahmoud and M. R. Baharum (2015). A review on natural ventilation applications through building façade components and ventilation openings in tropical climates. *Energy and Buildings,* 101, 153–62.

AgFunder (2022a). *2022 AgFunder AgriFoodTech Investment Report.* San Francisco, CA: AgFunder. Available at: https://agfunder.com/research/2022-agfunder-agrifoodtech-investment-report/.

AgFunder (2022b). *AgFunder European investment report.* San Fransisco, CA: AgFunder. Available at: https://research.agfunder.com/europe-2022-agrifoodtech-report-investnl.pdf.

Agora Energiewende (2023). Global steel transformation tracker. Available at: https://www.agora-energiewende.de/en/service/global-steel-transformation-tracker/ [accessed May 2023].

Ahmadi, N., J.-L. Dzido, M. Vales, J. Rakotoarisoa and A. Chabanne (2004). Upland rice for highlands: New varieties and sustainable cropping systems for food security promising prospects for the global challenges of rice production the world will face in the coming years? In I. T. A. FAO (ed.), *Rice in Global Markets and Sustainable Production Systems Conference*, Rome, Italy, 12–13 February 2004. Rome: Food and Agriculture Organization of the United Nations (FAO), 14 p.

Airbus (2023). To insure grasslands against climate risks, Crédit Agricole Bank uses Airbus' satellite imagery. Airbus Intelligence. Available at: https://www.intelligence-airbusds.com/newsroom/case-studies/agriculture/credit-agricole-uses-satellite-imagery-to-insure-grasslands/#solution [accessed October 2023].

Alao, M. A., O. M. Popoola and T. R. Ayodele (2022). Waste-to-energy nexus: An overview of technologies and implementation for sustainable development. *Cleaner Energy Systems,* 3, 100034.

Alauddin, M., M. A. Rashid Sarker, Z. Islam and C. Tisdell (2020). Adoption of alternate wetting and drying (AWD) irrigation as a water-saving technology in Bangladesh: Economic and environmental considerations. *Land use policy,* 91, 104430.

AlKheder, S. (2021). Promoting public transport as a strategy to reduce GHG emissions from private vehicles in Kuwait. *Environmental Challenges,* 3, 100075.

Almogbel, A., F. Alkasmoul, Z. Aldawsari, J. Alsulami and A. Alsuwailem (2020). Comparison of energy consumption between non-inverter and inverter-type air conditioner in Saudi Arabia. *Energy Transitions,* 4(2), 191–97.

Amoroso S., Aristodemou L., Criscuolo C., Dechezleprêtre A., Dernis H., Grassano N., Moussiegt L., Napolitano L., N. D., Squicciarini M. and T. A. (2021). *World corporate top R&D investors: Paving the way for climate neutrality – A joint JRC and OECD report.* Luxembourg: Publications Office of the European Union. Available at: https://www.oecd.org/sti/world-corporate-top-rd-investors-paving-the-way-for-climate-neutrality.pdf.

Anand, S. (2023). Rice acreage down 13% till Aug 5 due to rain shortfall. *India Times*. Available at: https://economictimes.indiatimes.com/news/economy/agriculture/rice-acreage-down-13-till-aug-5-due-to-rain-shortfall/articleshow/93439236.cms [accessed July 2023].

Anand, V., V. L. Kadiri and C. Putcha (2023). Passive buildings: A state-of-the-art review. *Journal of Infrastructure Preservation and Resilience,* 4(1), 3.

Andrijevic, M., C. F. Schleussner, M. J. Gidden, D. L. McCollum and J. Rogelj (2020). COVID-19 recovery funds dwarf clean energy investment needs. *Science,* 370(6514), 298–300.

Arens, M., M. Åhman and V. Vogl (2021). Which countries are prepared to green their coal-based steel industry with electricity? – Reviewing climate and energy policy as well as the implementation of renewable electricity. *Renewable and Sustainable Energy Reviews,* 143, 110938.

Arlbjørn, J. S., K. W. Jensen, K. Philipsen and A. Haug (2019). Drivers and barriers for Industry 4.0 readiness and practice: A SME perspective with empirical evidence'. In *Hawaii International Conference on System Sciences*. Grand Wailea, Maui, HI.

Arunrat, N., N. Pumijumnong, S. Sereenonchai, U. Chareonwong and C. Wang (2021). Comparison of GHG emissions and farmers' profit of large-scale and individual farming in rice production across four regions of Thailand. *Journal of Cleaner Production,* 278, 123945.

Atmaca, A. and M. Kanoglu (2012). Reducing energy consumption of a raw mill in cement industry. *Energy,* 42(1), 261-69.

Aziminezhad, M. and R. Taherkhani (2023). BIM for deconstruction: A review and bibliometric analysis. *Journal of Building Engineering,* 73, 106683.

Baker, J. C. and K. E. Saxton (2007). The 'what' and 'why' of no-tillage farming. In Baker, C. J. and K. E. Saxton (eds.) *No-tillage seeding in conservation agriculture, 2nd edn.*, Rome: Food and Agriculture Organization of the United Nations (FAO) and Commonwealth Agricultural Bureau (CAB) International, 1–10.

Barteková, E. and P. Börkey (2022). Digitalisation for the transition to a resource efficient and circular economy, *OECD Environment Working Papers, No. 192.* Paris: Organisation for Economic Co-operation and Development (OECD). Available at: https://www.oecd-ilibrary.org/content/paper/6f6d18e7-en.

Bashi, Z., R. McCullough, L. Ong and M. Ramirez (2019). *Alternative proteins: The race for market share is on.* McKinsey & Company. Available at: https://www.mckinsey.com/industries/agriculture/our-insights/alternative-proteins-the-race-for-market-share-is-on.

Bataille, C., S. Stiebert and F. G. N. Li (2021). *Global facility level net-zero steel pathways.* Paris: The Institute for Sustainable Development and International Relations (IDDRI). Available at: http://netzerosteel.org/wp-content/uploads/pdf/net_zero_steel_report.pdf.

BCG (2022). *The untapped climate opportunity in alternative proteins.* Boston Consulting Group (BCG). Available at: https://www.bcg.com/publications/2022/combating-climate-crisis-with-alternative-protein.

Berkeley (2023). Berkeley carbon trading project: Voluntary registry offsets database. Center for Environmental Public Policy (CEPP) and Goldman School of Public Policy, University of California, Berkeley. Available at: https://gspp.berkeley.edu/research-and-impact/centers/cepp/projects/berkeley-carbon-trading-project/offsets-database [accessed October 2023].

Bernhard, A. (2021). The great bicycle boom of 2020. BBC. Available at: https://www.bbc.com/future/bespoke/made-on-earth/the-great-bicycle-boom-of-2020.html [accessed July 2023].

Bharadwaj, S., S. Ballare, Rohit and M. K. Chandel (2017). Impact of congestion on greenhouse gas emissions for road transport in Mumbai metropolitan region. *Transportation Research Procedia,* 25, 3538–51.

Bieser, J. C. T., R. Hintemann, L. M. Hilty and S. Beucker (2023). A review of assessments of the greenhouse gas footprint and abatement potential of information and communication technology. *Environmental Impact Assessment Review,* 99, 107033.

Black, S., A. Liu, I. Parry and N. Vernon (2023). *IMF fossil fuel subsidies data: 2023 update,* Working paper. Washington DC: International Monetary Fund (IMF). Available at: https://www.imf.org/en/Publications/WP/Issues/2023/08/22/IMF-Fossil-Fuel-Subsidies-Data-2023-Update-537281 [accessed October 2023].

Blank, T. K. (2019). *The disruptive potential of green steel,* Insight brief. Rocky Mountain Institute (RMI). Available at: https://rmi.org/wp-content/uploads/2019/09/green-steel-insight-brief.pdf.

Boehm, A., P. Meissner and T. Plochberger (2015). An energy based comparison of vertical roller mills and tumbling mills. *International Journal of Mineral Processing,* 136, 37–41.

Bossio, D. A., S. C. Cook-Patton, P. W. Ellis, J. Fargione, J. Sanderman, P. Smith, S. Wood, R. J. Zomer, M. von Unger, I. M. Emmer and B. W. Griscom (2020). The role of soil carbon in natural climate solutions. *Nature Sustainability,* 3(5), 391–98.

Brand, C., E. Dons, E. Anaya-Boig, I. Avila-Palencia, A. Clark, A. de Nazelle, M. Gascon, M. Gaupp-Berghausen, R. Gerike, T. Götschi, F. Iacorossi, S. Kahlmeier, M. Laeremans, M. J. Nieuwenhuijsen, J. Pablo Orjuela, F. Racioppi, E. Raser, D. Rojas-Rueda, A. Standaert, E. Stigell, S. Sulikova, S. Wegener and L. Int Panis (2021). The climate change mitigation effects of daily active travel in cities. *Transportation Research Part D: Transport and Environment,* 93, 102764.

Brock, J., Y. C. Budiman, J. Geddie and V. Volcovici (2021). Trash and burn: Big brands stoke cement kilns with plastic waste as recycling falters. Available at: https://www.reuters.com/investigates/special-report/environment-plastic-cement/ [accessed October 2023].

Brogan, C. (2022). 'Greening' cement and steel: 9 ways these industries can reach net zero. London: Imperial College. Available at: www.imperial.ac.uk/news/235134/greening-cement-steel-ways-these-industries [accessed May 2023].

Brons Group (2023). *Local use of precision farming equipment.* [Interview], 16 August 2023. Available at: https://bronsgroup.com/.

Brozzi, R., D. Forti, E. Rauch and D. T. Matt (2020). The advantages of Industry 4.0 applications for sustainability: Results from a sample of manufacturing companies. *Sustainability,* 12(9), 3647.

Bruun, J. (2022). Breakthrough in separating plastic waste: Machines can distinguish 12 different types of plastic. Aarhus University. Available at: https://ingenioer.au.dk/en/current/news/view/artikel/gennembrud-i-plastsortering-maskiner-kan-nu-se-forskel-paa-12-forskellige-typer-plastik [accessed July 2023].

Buchanan, M. (2019). The benefits of public transport. *Nature Physics,* 15(9), 876–76.

C40 (2018). *Consumption-based GHG emissions of C40 cities.* C40 Cities. Available at: https://www.c40knowledgehub.org/s/article/Consumption-based-GHG-emissions-of-C40-cities?language=en_US.

Cabernard, L., S. Pfister, C. Oberschelp and S. Hellweg (2022). Growing environmental footprint of plastics driven by coal combustion. *Nature Sustainability,* 5.

Calaiaro, J. (2022). AI-guided robots are ready to sort your recyclables. Institute of Electrical and

Electronics Engineers (IEEE). Available at: https://spectrum.ieee.org/ai-guided-robots-are-ready-to-sort-your-recyclables [accessed July 2023].

Caner, D., J. Claes, D. De Clerq and M. Taksyak (2023). Needle in a haystack: Patents that inspire agricultural innovation. McKinsey & Company. Available at: https://www.mckinsey.com/industries/agriculture/our-insights/needle-in-a-haystack-patents-that-inspire-agricultural-innovation [accessed October 2023].

Caprarulo, V., V. Ventura, A. Amatucci, G. Ferronato and G. Gilioli (2022). Innovations for reducing methane emissions in livestock toward a sustainable system: Analysis of feed additive patents in ruminants. *Animals,* 12(20), 2760.

Cargill (2023). How feed impacts your farm's methane output. Cargill. Available at: http://dx.doi.org/ [accessed June 2023].

Casey, T. (2023). More bad news for fossil fuels: Rooftop solar meets agrivoltaics. Cleantechnica. Available at: https://cleantechnica.com/2023/04/07/more-bad-news-for-fossil-fuels-rooftop-solar-meets-agrivoltaics/ [accessed July 2023].

Castaldi, M. J. and N. J. Themelis (2010). The case for increasing the global capacity for waste to energy (WTE). *Waste and Biomass Valorization,* 1(1), 91–105.

CCAC (2023a). Enteric fermentation. Climate & Clean Air Coalition (CCAC) and United Nations Environment Programme (UNEP). Available at: https://www.ccacoalition.org/en/activity/enteric-fermentation [accessed May 2023].

CCAC (2023b). Promoting HFC alternative technology and standards. Climate & clean air coalition (CCAC). Available at: https://www.ccacoalition.org/fr/node/73 [accessed June 2023].

CCAC (2023c). Uruguay reduces livestock emissions while increasing productivity in a ccac-supported pilot project. Climate & Clean Air Coalition (CCAC) and United Nations Environment Programme (UNEP). Available at: https://www.ccacoalition.org/news/uruguay-reduces-livestock-emissions-while-increasing-productivity-ccac-supported-pilot-project [accessed October 2023].

CCFLA (2021). *The state of cities climate finance.* The Cities Climate Finance Leadership Alliance (CCFLA). Available at: https://www.climatepolicyinitiative.org/publication/the-state-of-cities-climate-finance/.

Chan, M., M. A. N. Masrom and S. S. Yasin (2022). Selection of low-carbon building materials in construction projects: construction professionals perspectives. *Buildings,* 12(4), 486.

Chapelier, E., Hanaf, A. and Gourragne A., (2020). Patent mapping analysis in the field of agricultural robotics. Global Organization For Agricultural Robotics (GOFAR). Available at: https://www.agricultural-robotics.com/news/patent-mapping-analysis-in-the-field-of-agricultural-robotics [accessed October 2023].

Chaudhary, A. (2022). India planning carbon credit market for energy, steel and cement. *The Economic Times*. Available at: https://economictimes.indiatimes.com/industry/renewables/india-planning-carbon-credit-market-for-energy-steel-and-cement/articleshow/93297031.cms?from=mdr [accessed May 2023].

Checherina, P. (2022). Using climate-smart rice to reduce methane emissions from agriculture. Climate & Clean Air Coalition (CCAC) and United Nations Environment Programme (UNEP). Available at: https://www.ccacoalition.org/en/news/using-climate-smart-rice-reduce-methane-emissions-agriculture [accessed July 2023].

Chen, X., M. Despeisse and B. Johansson (2020). Environmental sustainability of digitalization in manufacturing: A review. *Sustainability*, 12(24).

Churkina, G. and A. Organschi (2022). Will a transition to timber construction cool the climate? *Sustainability,* 14(7), 4271.

Citywire (2023). Deere bets the farm on $150bn 'precision agriculture' opportunity. Citywire. Available at: https://citywire.com/pro-buyer/news/deere-bets-the-farm-on-150bn-precision-agriculture-opportunity/a2408316 [accessed August 2023].

Claver, H. (2023). Agricultural drones market to hit revenue of USD 14,237.6 million by 2033. Future Farming. Available at: https://www.futurefarming.com/tech-in-focus/drones/agricultural-drones-market-to-hit-revenue-of-us-14237-6-million-by-2033/ [accessed August 2023].

Climate ADAPT (2023). Precision Agriculture. The European Climate Adaptation Platform Climate-ADAPT. Available at: https://climate-adapt.eea.europa.eu/en/metadata/adaptation-options/precision-agriculture [accessed October 2023].

Climatewatch (2023). Climatewatch. Available at: https://www.climatewatchdata.org/ [accessed May 2023].

Cojocaru, A. and D. Isopescu (2021). Passive strategies of vernacular architecture for energy efficiency. *Bulletin of the Polytechnic Institute of Iași. Construction. Architecture Section,* 67, 33–44.

Colbach, N. and S. Cordeau (2022). Are no-till herbicide-free systems possible? A simulation study. *Frontiers in Agronomy,* 4.

Conejo, A. N., J.-P. Birat and A. Dutta (2020). A review of the current environmental challenges of the steel industry and its value chain. *Journal of Environmental Management,* 259, 109782.

Corichi, M. (2021). Eight-in-ten Indians limit meat in their diets, and four-in-ten consider themselves vegetarian. Pew Research Center. Available at: https://www.pewresearch.org/short-reads/2021/07/08/eight-in-ten-indians-limit-meat-in-their-diets-and-four-in-ten-consider-themselves-vegetarian/ [accessed August 2023].

Cornell University (2017). System of rice intensification – SRI methodologies. Cornell University, College of Agriculture and Life Sciences. Available at: http://sri.ciifad.cornell.edu/aboutsri/methods/index.html [accessed July 2017].

Cozzi, L., A. Petropulos, L. Paoli, M. Huismans and A. Dasgupta (2023). As their sales continue to rise, SUVs' global CO_2 emissions are nearing 1 billion tonnes. International Energy Agency (IEA). Available at: https://www.iea.org/commentaries/as-their-sales-continue-to-rise-suvs-global-co2-emissions-are-nearing-1-billion-tonnes [accessed September 2023].

CPI (2020). *Examining the climate finance gap for small-scale agriculture.* Climate Policy Initiative (CPI). Available at: https://www.ifad.org/documents/38714170/42157470/climate-finance-gap_smallscale_agr.pdf/34b2e25b-7572-b31d-6d0c-d5ea5ea8f96f.

CPI (2021). *Global landscape of climate finance 2021.* Climate Policy Initiative (CPI). Available at: https://www.climatepolicyinitiative.org/publication/global-landscape-of-climate-finance-2021/.

CPI (2022a). *Financing steel decarbonization,* Instrument Analysis. Climate Policy Initiative (CPI). Available at: https://www.climatepolicyinitiative.org/wp-content/uploads/2022/10/FSD-report.pdf.

CPI (2022b). *Global landscape of climate finance: A decade of data.* Climate Policy Initiative (CPI). Available at: https://www.climatepolicyinitiative.org/publication/global-landscape-of-climate-finance-a-decade-of-data/.

CPI (2022c). *Landscape of climate finance for agriculture, forestry, other land use and fisheries: Preliminary findings.* Climate Policy Initiative (CPI). Available at: https://www.climatepolicyinitiative.org/publication/landscape-of-climate-finance-for-agriculture-forestry-other-land-uses-and-fisheries/.

CPI (2023). *Landscape of climate finance for agrifood systems.* Climate Policy Initiative (CPI). Available at: https://www.climatepolicyinitiative.org/wp-content/uploads/2023/07/Landscape-of-Climate-Finance-for-Agrifood-Systems.pdf.

Crownhart, C. (2023). Here's what we know about lab-grown meat and climate change. *MIT Technology Review Explains*, Massachusetts Institute of Technology (MIT). Available at: https://www.technologyreview.com/2023/07/03/1075809/lab-grown-meat-climate-change/ [accessed July 2023].

CTCN (2023). From solar farm to table, in Liberia improved solar powered irrigation practices are securing lowland rice production. UN Climate Technology Centre & Network (CTCN). Available at: https://www.ctc-n.org/news/solar-farm-table-liberia-improved-solar-powered-irrigation-practices-are-securing-lowland-rice [accessed October 2023].

Dabros, T. M. H., M. Z. Stummann, M. Høj, P. A. Jensen, J.-D. Grunwaldt, J. Gabrielsen, P. M. Mortensen and A. D. Jensen (2018). Transportation fuels from biomass via fast pyrolysis, catalytic hydrodeoxygenation, and catalytic fast hydropyrolysis. *Progress in Energy and Combustion Science,* 68, 268–309.

Danmarks Statistik (2022). Stigning i areal med præcisionslandbrug. *Nyt fra Danmarks Statistik.* Available at: https://www.dst.dk/da/Statistik/nyheder-analyser-publ/nyt/NytHtml?cid=42525 [accessed August 2023].

Danone (2020). Danone North America and the National Fish and Wildlife Foundation join forces. Danone North America. Available at: https://www.danonenorthamerica.com/news/danone-north-america-and-the-national-fish-and-wildlife-foundation-join-forces-to-leverage-3-million-in-federal-funding-for-shared-commitment-to-regenerative-agriculture/ [accessed October 2023].

Daziano, R. A. (2022). Willingness to delay charging of electric vehicles. *Research in Transportation Economics,* 94, 101177.

De Munck, C., G. Pigeon, V. Masson, C. Marchadier, F. Meunier, P. Bousquet, B. Tremeac, M. Merchat, P. Poeuf and A. Lemonsu (2013). How much air conditioning can increase air temperatures for a city like Paris (France)? *International Journal of Climatology,* 33, 210–27.

de Sousa Jabbour, A. B. L., C. J. C. Jabbour, C. Foropon and M. Godinho Filho (2018). When titans meet - Can industry 4.0 revolutionise the environmentally-sustainable manufacturing wave? The role of critical success factors. *Technological Forecasting and Social Change,* 132, 18–25.

DJI Agriculture (2023). Saving up to 95% water, improving efficiency, while saving chemicals: DJI Agras drones benefit farmers in Turkey during drought. DJI Global. Available at: https://ag.dji.com/case-studies/ag-case-en-t30-tr-drought [accessed October 2023].

DNV (2023). Green steel assurance. Det Norske Veritas (DNV). Available at: https://www.dnv.com/services/green-steel-assurance-232895 [accessed May 2023].

Dong, Y., M. Coleman and S. Miller (2021). Greenhouse gas emissions from air conditioning and refrigeration service expansion in developing countries. *Annual review of environment and resources,* 46.

dos Muchangos, L. S. and A. Tokai (2020). Greenhouse gas emission analysis of upgrading from an open dump to a semi-aerobic landfill in Mozambique - The case of Hulene dumpsite. *Scientific African,* 10, e00638.

Dosumu, O. and C. Aigbavboa (2019). An investigation of the barriers to the uptake of local materials in Africa: A literature review approach. African Journal of Science, Technology, Innovation and Development.

Dusík, J., T. Fischer, B. Sadler, R. Therivel and I. Saric (2018). *Strategic environmental and social assessment of automation: Scoping working paper.* Available at: https://www.researchgate.net/publication/326461326_Strategic_Environmental_and_Social_Assessment_of_Automation_Scoping_Working_Paper.

ECN (2015). Webinar: Introduction to technologies for energy efficiency in the industry sector. [Webinar online], available at: https://www.ctc-n.org/calendar/webinars/introduction-technologies-energy-efficiency-industry-sector [accessed October 2023].

ECOS (2023). *A performance-based standard for common cements,* ECOS Brief. Environmental Coalition on Standards (ECOS). Available at: https://ecostandard.org/publications/ecos-brief-a-performance-based-standard-for-common-cements/.

EDF (2023). 'Precision Agriculture Loan Act' unlocks new financing for climate solutions. Environmental Defense Fund (EDF). Available at: https://www.edf.org/media/precision-agriculture-loan-act-unlocks-new-financing-climate-solutions [accessed October 2023].

EEA (2018). *Electric vehicles from life cycle and circular economy perspectives.* European Environment Agency (EEA). Available at: https://www.eea.europa.eu/publications/electric-vehicles-from-life-cycle.

EEA (2022). Briefing: Soil carbon. European Environment Agency (EEA). Available at: https://www.eea.europa.eu/publications/soil-carbon [accessed June 2023].

EEA (2023a). *Decarbonising heating and cooling – A climate imperative.* Copenhagen, Denmark: European Environment Agency (EEA). Available at: https://www.eea.europa.eu/publications/decarbonisation-heating-and-cooling.

EEA (2023b). *Transport and environment report 2022.* European Environment Agency (EEA). Available at: https://www.eea.europa.eu//publications/transport-and-environment-report-2022.

EIT Urban Mobility (2022). *Urban mobility next 8: Expectations and success factors for urban air mobility in Europe.* Barcelona, Spain: EIT Urban Mobility. Available at: https://www.eiturbanmobility.eu/wp-content/uploads/2022/11/EIT-UrbanAirMobility.pdf.

Ellis, J. (2023). Reversing agriculture's emissions with carbon-fixing soil inputs. Cleantech Group. Available at: https://www.cleantech.com/reversing-agricultures-emissions-with-carbon-fixing-soil-inputs/ [accessed July 2022].

Ellis, J. E., M. B. Coughenour and D. M. Swift (1993). Climate variability, ecosystem stability, and the implications for range and livestock development. In Behnke, R. H., I. Scoones and C. Kerven (eds) *Range ecology at disequilibrium*. London: Overseas Development Institute, 31–41.

EMF (2020). *Financing the circular economy: Capturing the opportunity.* Ellen MacArthur Foundation (EMF). Available at: https://ellenmacarthurfoundation.org/financing-the-circular-economy-capturing-the-opportunity.

Engler, J.-O. and H. von Wehrden (2018). Global assessment of the non-equilibrium theory of rangelands: Revisited and refined. *Land use policy,* 70, 479–84.

EPO (2021). *Patents for tomorrow's plastics: Global innovation trends in recycling, circular design and alternative sources.* Munich, Germany: European Patent Office (EPO). Available at: https://www.ovtt.org/wp-content/uploads/2021/10/patents_for_tomorrows_plastics_study_en.pdf.

EPO (2022a). Insights into urban mobility. European Patent Office (EPO). Available at: https://www.epo.org/about-us/annual-reports-statistics/statistics/2021/insight-into-smart-urban-mobility.html [accessed August 2023].

EPO (2022b). *Space-borne sensing and green applications,* Patent insight report. Munich, Germany: European Patent Office. Available at: https://link.epo.org/web/Space-borne%20sensing%20and%20green%20applications%20report.pdf.

EPO and IEA (2020). *Innovation in batteries and electricity storage.* International Energy Agency (IEA) and European Patent Office (EPO). Available at: https://www.iea.org/reports/innovation-in-batteries-and-electricity-storage.

EPO and IEA (2021). *Patents and the energy transition.* European Patent Office (EPO). Available at: https://iea.blob.core.windows.net/assets/b327e6b8-9e5e-451d-b6f4-cbba6b1d90d8/Patents_and_the_energy_transition.pdf.

EPO and UNEP (2015). *Climate change mitigation technologies in Europe – evidence from patent and economic data.* Nairobi: United Nations Environment Programme (UNEP). European Patent Office (EPO). Available at: https://www.epo.org/news-events/in-focus/sustainable-technologies/clean-energy/europe.html.

ESA (2023). A closer look at the latest earth observation services industry trends. The European Space Agency (ESA). Available at: https://space-economy.esa.int/article/72/a-closer-look-at-the-latest-earth-observation-services-industry-trends [accessed October 2023].

ESCI (2022). Energy costs reduced by 40% in aluminium, steelworks and ceramics production. [online], Available at: https://www.youtube.com/watch?v=VQwTogBhYz8 [accessed].

Escobar, N., S. Haddad, J. Börner and W. Britz (2018). Land use mediated GHG emissions and spillovers from increased consumption of bioplastics. *Environmental Research Letters,* 13, 125005.

EU (2021). *Digital transformation in European steel industry: State of art and future scenario.* European Union (EU). Available at: https://www.estep.eu/assets/Uploads/ESSA-D2.1-Technological-and-Economic-Development-in-the-Steel-Industry-Version-2.pdf.

European Commission (2017). Development of new methodologies for industrial CO_2-free steel production by electrowinning. Available at: https://cordis.europa.eu/project/id/768788 [accessed May 2023].

European Commission (2021). Evaluation of the impact of the Common Agricultural Policy on climate change and greenhouse gas emissions. *Commission staff working document*, Directorate-General for Agriculture and Rural Development. Brussels: Publications Office of the European Union. Available at: http://op.europa.eu/en/publication-detail/-/publication/7307349a-ba1a-11eb-8aca-01aa75ed71a1 [accessed October 2023].

European Parliament (2021). *Carbon-free steel production: Cost reduction options and usage of existing gas infrastructure.* European Parliamentary Research Service (EPRS). Available at: https://www.europarl.europa.eu/RegData/etudes/STUD/2021/690008/EPRS_STU(2021)690008_EN.pdf.

European Patent Office (2020). Fourth industrial revolution. Available at: https://www.epo.org/news-events/in-focus/ict/fourth-industrial-revolution.html [accessed May 2023].

Fairhead, J. and M. Leach (1996a). Colonial science & its relics in West Africa. In Leach, M. and R. Mearns (eds) *The lie of the land, challenging received wisdom on the African Environment*. Oxford, UK: The International African Institute with James Currey, 105-21.

Fairhead, J. and M. Leach (1996b). *Misreading the African landscape: Society and ecology in a forest-savanna mosaic, African Studies.* Cambridge, UK: Cambridge University Press.

Fan, Z. and J. Friedmann (2021). *Low-carbon production of iron & steel: Technology options, economic assessment, and policy.* Center on Global Energy Policy at Columbia University. Available at: https://www.energypolicy.columbia.edu/publications/low-carbon-production-iron-steel-technology-options-economic-assessment-and-policy.

FAO (2016). *Reducing enteric methane for improving food security and livelihoods.* New Zealand: Food and Agriculture Organization of the United Nations (FAO). Available at: https://www.ccacoalition.org/en/resources/reducing-enteric-methane-improving-food-security-and-livelihoods.

FAO (2017). *Livestock solutions for climate change.* Rome: Food and Agriculture Organization of the United Nations (FAO). Available at: https://www.fao.org/3/i8098e/i8098e.pdf.

FAO (2019). *Five practical actions towards low-carbon livestock.* Rome: Food and Agriculture Organization of the United Nations (FAO). Available at: https://www.fao.org/3/ca7089en/ca7089en.pdf.

FAO (2021). A step-by-step approach toward a gradual adoption of the full conservation agriculture technology: An example from Timor-Leste. *TECA – Technologies and Practices for Small Agricultural Producers*, Food and Agriculture Organization of the United Nations (FAO). Available at: www.fao.org/in-action/kore/good-practices/good-practices-details/en/c/1413322 [accessed July 2023].

FAO (2022). *World food and agriculture: Statistical yearbook 2022.* Rome: Food and Agriculture Organization of the United Nations (FAO). Available at: https://www.fao.org/documents/card/en/c/cc2211en.

FAO (2023a). Global Livestock Environmental Assessment Model (GLEAM). Food and Agriculture Organization of the United Nations (FAO). Available at: https://www.fao.org/gleam/en/ [accessed May 2023].

FAO (2023b). Land use in agriculture by the numbers. Food and Agriculture Organization of the United Nations (FAO). Available at: http://www.fao.org/sustainability/news/detail/en/c/1274219/ [accessed May 2023].

FAOSTAT (2023). Food and agriculture data. Food and Agriculture Organization of the United Nations (FAO). Available at: https://www.fao.org/faostat/en/#home [accessed July 2023].

Fatahi, R., H. Nasiri, E. Dadfar and S. Chehreh Chelgani (2022). Modeling of energy consumption factors for an industrial cement vertical roller mill by SHAP-XGBoost: a "conscious lab" approach. *Scientific Reports,* 12(1), 7543.

Fatimi, A. (2021). The use of seaweeds in the formulation of feeds for livestock: Patent analysis. In *2nd International Electronic Conference on Animals – Global Sustainability and Animals: Welfare, Policies and Technologie*. Basel, Switzerland: MDPI.

Fennell, P., J. Driver, C. Bataille and S. J. Davis (2022). Cement and steel – Nine steps to net zero. *Nature*, 603, 574–577. Available at: https://www.nature.com/articles/d41586-022-00758-4 [accessed May 2023].

Frączek, B. and A. Urbanek (2021). Financial inclusion as an important factor influencing digital payments in passenger transport: A case study of EU countries. *Research in Transportation Business & Management,* 41, 100691.

Freitag, C., M. Berners-Lee, K. Widdicks, B. Knowles, G. S. Blair and A. Friday (2021). The real climate and transformative impact of ICT: A critique of estimates, trends, and regulations. *Patterns,* 2(9), 100340.

Fritzsche, K., S. Niehoff and G. Beier (2018). Industry 4.0 and climate change – exploring the science-policy gap. *Sustainability,* 10(12). Available at: https://www.mdpi.com/2071-1050/10/12/4511 [accessed September 2023].

Furfari, S. (2016). Energy efficiency of engines and appliances for transport on land, water, and in air. *Ambio,* 45(1), 63–68.

Gan, Y. and W. M. Griffin (2018). Analysis of life-cycle GHG emissions for iron ore mining and processing in China – Uncertainty and trends. *Resources Policy,* 58, 90–96.

Gardner, T. (2023). US announces $6 bln in grants to decarbonize heavy industry. *Reuters*. Available at: https://www.reuters.com/business/environment/us-announces-6-bln-grants-decarbonize-heavy-industry-2023-03-08/ [accessed May 2023].

GCCA (2021). *The GCCA 2050 cement and concrete industry roadmap for net zero concrete.* Global Cement and Concrete Association (GCCA). Available at: https://gccassociation.org/concretefuture/wp-content/uploads/2021/10/GCCA-Concrete-Future-Roadmap-Document-AW.pdf.

Geist, H. J. and E. F. Lambin (2002). Proximate causes and underlying driving forces of tropical deforestation: Tropical forests are disappearing as the result of many pressures, both local and regional, acting in various combinations in different geographical locations. *Bioscience,* 52(2), 143–50.

GeSI (2015). ICT solutions for 21st century challenges. Global e-Sustainability Initiative (GeSI). Available at: https://smarter2030.gesi.org/ [accessed August 2023].

GeSI (2020). *Digital solutions for climate action.* Brussels, Belgium: Global e-Sustainability Initiative (GeSI). Available at: https://gesi.org/research/download/52.

GHG Protocol (2023). Greenhouse Gas Protocol FAQ. Available at: https://ghgprotocol.org/sites/default/files/standards_supporting/FAQ.pdf [accessed June 2023].

Ghoneim, R., G. Mete and A. Hobley (2022). Steel and cement can drive the decade of action on climate change: This is how. United Nations Industrial Development Organization (UNIDO), 'Industrial Analytics Platform'. Available at: https://iap.unido.org/articles/steel-and-cement-can-drive-decade-action-climate-change-how [accessed May 2023].

GIZ (2021). *Potential of Article 6 and other financing instruments to promote Green Hydrogen in the Steel, Cement and Mining Industries.* Bonn, Germany: Deutsche Gesellschaft für Internationale Zusammenarbeit (GIZ) GmbH. Available at: https://www.carbon-mechanisms.de/fileadmin/media/dokumente/Publikationen/Bericht/Art.-6-Green-Hydrogen-Final-ENG.pdf.

Global CCS Institute (2022). 2022 Status report: Appendices. Available at: https://status22.globalccsinstitute.com/2022-status-report/appendices/ [accessed May 2023].

Global Infrastructure Hub (2020). Pre-fabrication technology for modular construction. Global Infrastructure Hub. Available at: https://www.gihub.org/infrastructure-technology-use-cases/case-studies/pre-fabrication-technology-for-modular-construction/ [accessed July 2023].

Gomaa, M., W. Jabi, V. Soebarto and Y. M. Xie (2022). Digital manufacturing for earth construction: A critical review. *Journal of Cleaner Production,* 338, 130630.

Gomaa, M., S. Schade, D. W. Bao and Y. M. Xie (2023). Automation in rammed earth construction for industry 4.0: Precedent work, current progress and future prospect. *Journal of Cleaner Production,* 398, 136569.

Griffiths, S., B. K. Sovacool, D. D. Furszyfer Del Rio, A. M. Foley, M. D. Bazilian, J. Kim and J. M. Uratani (2023). Decarbonizing the cement and concrete industry: A systematic review of socio-technical systems, technological innovations, and policy options. *Renewable and Sustainable Energy Reviews,* 180, 113291.

Guevara Opinska, L., M. Mahmoud, C. Bene and K. Rademaekers (2021). *Moving towards zero-emission steel: Technologies available, prospects, timeline and costs.* Luxembourg: European Parliament. Available at: https://www.europarl.europa.eu/RegData/etudes/STUD/2021/695484/IPOL_STU(2021)695484_EN.pdf.

Gulda, M. P. (2021). *How digitalization will enable completely different ways of working in steelmaking.* H2 Green Steel. Available at: https://www.h2greensteel.com/stories/how-digitalization-will-enable-completely-different-ways-of-working-in-steelmaking.

Haghdadi, N., M. Laleh, M. Moyle and S. Primig (2021). Additive manufacturing of steels: A review of achievements and challenges. *Journal of Materials Science,* 56(1), 64–107.

Hanifa, M., R. Agarwal, U. Sharma, P. C. Thapliyal and L. P. Singh (2023). A review on CO_2 capture and sequestration in the construction industry: Emerging approaches and commercialised technologies. *Journal of CO_2 Utilization,* 67, 102292.

Hanley, S. (2022). Agrivoltaics – Solar panels & tomatoes may be perfect for each other. Cleantechnica. Available at: https://cleantechnica.com/2022/12/01/agrivoltaics-solar-panels-tomatoes-may-be-perfect-for-each-other/ [accessed July 2023].

Hann, S. (2022). *Is net zero enough for the material production sector?* Bristol: Eunomia Research & Consulting Ltd. Available at: https://zerowasteeurope.eu/wp-content/uploads/2022/11/Is-Net-Zero-Enough-for-the-Materials-Sector-Report-1.pdf.

Hardin, G. (1968). The tragedy of the commons. *Science,* 162(3859), 1243–48.

Havlík, P., H. Valin, M. Herrero, M. Obersteiner, E. Schmid, M. C. Rufino, A. Mosnier, P. K. Thornton, H. Böttcher, R. T. Conant, S. Frank, S. Fritz, S. Fuss, F. Kraxner and A. Notenbaert (2014). Climate change mitigation through livestock system transitions. *Proceedings of the National Academy of Sciences,* 111(10), 3709–14.

Hawkins, H.-J., R. I. M. Cargill, M. E. Van Nuland, S. C. Hagen, K. J. Field, M. Sheldrake, N. A. Soudzilovskaia and E. T. Kiers (2023). Mycorrhizal mycelium as a global carbon pool. *Current Biology,* 33(11), R560–R73.

Helldén, U. (1991). Desertification – Time for an assessment. *Ambio,* 20(8), 372–83.

Hicks Pries, C. E., C. Castanha, R. C. Porras and M. S. Torn (2017). The whole-soil carbon flux in response to warming. *Science,* 355(6332), 1420–23.

Hites, B. (2020). The growth of EAF steelmaking. Recycling Today. Available at: https://www.recyclingtoday.com/article/the-growth-of-eaf-steelmaking/ [accessed May 2023].

Hogg, D. (2006). *A changing climate for energy from waste? Final report for Friends of the Earth.* Eunomia Research & Consulting. Available at: https://www.friendsoftheearth.ie/assets/files/pdf/report_on_incineration_and_climate.pdf.

Hogg, D. (2023). *Debunking efficient recovery: The performance of EU incineration facilities.* Equanimator Ltd for Zero Waste Europe. Available at: https://zerowasteeurope.eu/library/debunking-efficient-recovery/.

ICCT (2020). *Beyond biomass? Alternative fuels from renewable electricity and carbon recycling.* The International Council on Clean Transportation (ICCT). Available at: https://theicct.org/publication/beyond-biomass-alternative-fuels-from-renewable-electricity-and-carbon-recycling/.

IEA (2018a). *The future of cooling: Opportunities for energy-efficient air conditioning.* International Energy Agency (IEA). Available at: https://iea.blob.core.windows.net/assets/0bb45525-277f-4c9c-8d0c-9c0cb5e7d525/The_Future_of_Cooling.pdf.

IEA (2018b). *Technology roadmap, Low-carbon transition in the cement industry.* Paris: International Energy Agency (IEA). Available at: https://iea.blob.core.windows.net/assets/cbaa3da1-fd61-4c2a-8719-31538f59b54f/TechnologyRoadmapLowCarbonTransitionintheCementIndustry.pdf.

IEA (2019a). *Energy Efficiency 2019.* Paris: International Energy Agency (IEA). Available at: https://www.iea.org/reports/energy-efficiency-2019.

IEA (2019b). *Global patent applications for climate change mitigation technologies – a key measure of innovation – are trending down.* Paris: International Energy Agency (IEA). Available at: https://www.iea.org/commentaries/global-patent-applications-for-climate-change-mitigation-technologies-a-key-measure-of-innovation-are-trending-down.

IEA (2019c). *Material efficiency in clean energy transitions.* Paris: International Energy Agency. Available at: https://www.iea.org/reports/material-efficiency-in-clean-energy-transitions.

IEA (2020). *Iron and steel technology roadmap.* Energy Technology Perspectives. Paris: International Energy Agency (IEA). Available at: https://iea.blob.core.windows.net/assets/eb0c8ec1-3665-4959-97d0-187ceca189a8/Iron_and_Steel_Technology_Roadmap.pdf.

IEA (2021). *Net Zero by 2050. A roadmap for the global energy sector.* Paris: International Energy Agency (EIA). Available at: https://www.iea.org/reports/net-zero-by-2050.

IEA (2022a). *Cement,* Tracking report. Paris: International Energy Agency (IEA). Available at: https://www.iea.org/reports/cement.

IEA (2022b). *Direct air capture.* Paris: International Energy Agency (IEA). Available at: https://www.iea.org/reports/direct-air-capture.

IEA (2022c). *Heating.* International Energy Agency (IEA). Available at: https://www.iea.org/reports/heating.

IEA (2022d). *Renewable heat*. International Energy Agency (IEA). Available at: https://www.iea.org/reports/renewables-2022/renewable-heat [accessed November 2023].

IEA (2023a). *Biofuels*. International Energy Agency (IEA). Available at: https://www.iea.org/energy-system/low-emission-fuels/biofuels [accessed July 2023].

IEA (2023b). *CCUS project explorer.* Available at: https://www.iea.org/data-and-statistics/data-tools/ccus-projects-explorer.

IEA (2023c). *Fossil fuel consumption subsidies 2022,* Policy report. International Energy Agency (IEA). Available at: https://www.iea.org/reports/fossil-fuels-consumption-subsidies-2022.

IEA (2023d). *Global EV outlook 2023.* International Energy Agency (IEA). Available at: https://www.iea.org/reports/global-ev-outlook-2023.

IEA (2023e). *Heat pumps*. International Energy Agency (IEA). Available at: https://www.iea.org/fuels-and-technologies/heat-pumps [accessed June 2023].

IEA (2023f). Hydrogen, *Tracking clean energy progress 2023*. International Energy Agency (IEA). Available at: https://www.iea.org/energy-system/low-emission-fuels/hydrogen#tracking [accessed August 2023].

IEA (2023g). *Transport*. International Energy Agency (IEA). Available at: https://www.iea.org/energy-system/transport.

IEA (2023h). *World energy investment 2023,* Flagship report. Paris: International Energy Agency (IEA). Available at: https://www.iea.org/reports/world-energy-investment-2023.

IEA Bioenergy (2023). *Commercial status of direct thermochemical liquefaction technologies.* International Energy Agency (IEA). Available at: https://www.ieabioenergy.com/blog/publications/commercial-status-of-direct-thermochemical-liquefaction-technologies/.

IFAD (2023). New IFAD initiative will help reduce global warming by lowering methane emissions from small-scale farming. International Fund for Agricultural Development (IFAD). Available at: https://www.ifad.org/en/web/latest/-/new-ifad-initiative-will-help-reduce-global-warming-by-lowering-methane-emissions-from-small-scale-farming.

IISD (2022). *Lighting the path: What IPCC energy pathways tell us about Paris-aligned policies and investments.* Canada: International Institute for Sustainable Development (IISD). Available at: https://www.iisd.org/system/files/2022-06/ipcc-pathways-paris-aligned-policies.pdf.

International Resource Panel (2019). *Global Resources Outlook 2019: Natural resources for the future we want.* Nairobi, Kenya: United Nations Environment Programme International Resource Panel. Available at: https://wedocs.unep.org/handle/20.500.11822/27518.

International Resource Panel (2020). *Resource efficiency and climate change: Material efficiency strategies for a low-carbon future.* Nairobi, Kenya: United Nations Environment Programme International Resource Panel. Available at: https://www.resourcepanel.org/reports/resource-efficiency-and-climate-change.

IP Australia (2018). *The blockchain innovation: A patent analytics report.* Available at: https://www.ipaustralia.gov.au/tools-and-research/professional-resources/data-research-and-reports/publications-and-reports/2022/09/30/02/59/the-blockchain-innovation-a-patent-analytics-report.

IP Australia (2019). *Machine learning innovation: A patent analytics report.* Available at: https://www.ipaustralia.gov.au/tools-and-research/professional-resources/data-research-and-reports/publications-and-reports/2022/09/30/03/31/machine-learning-innovation-a-patent-analytics-report.

IP Australia (2021). *The power of hydrogen: Patent analytics on hydrogen technologies.* Available at: https://www.ipaustralia.gov.au/tools-and-research/professional-resources/data-research-and-reports/publications-and-reports/2022/09/30/hydrogen-technology-patent-analytics.

IP Australia (2022a). Carbon capture and storage. Available at: https://app.powerbi.com/view?r=eyJrIjoiYjE1MDI2Y2ItY2Q0NC00NjUwLWE1NmYtODA4Njg0MTkzMjA4IiwidCI6IjljMGNlZDQ5LTRlMzYtNGY4MS1iOGQ3LTEwYzRhMGNiZmYyZCJ9 [accessed May 2023].

IP Australia (2022b). Low emission steel, aluminium and iron ore. Available at: https://app.powerbi.com/view?r=eyJrIjoiNGMyYjE0NjItYzcxNy00NzViLWExYjEtZGE0YjZkYzIxOGUxIiwidCI6IjljMGNlZDQ5LTRlMzYtNGY4MS1iOGQ3LTEwYzRhMGNiZmYyZCJ9 [accessed May 2023].

IP Australia (2023). Patent analytics on low emission technologies. Intellectual Property Office of Australia. Available at: https://www.ipaustralia.gov.au/tools-and-research/professional-resources/data-research-and-reports/publications-and-reports/2022/11/30/03/16/patent-analytics-on-low-emission-technologies [accessed October 2022].

IPCC (2021a). *Working Group I sixth assessment report: The physical science basis – Full report.* Geneva: Intergovernmental Panel on Climate Change (IPCC). Available at: https://www.ipcc.ch/report/sixth-assessment-report-working-group-i/.

IPCC (2021b). *Working Group I Sixth Assessment Report: The Physical Science Basis – Summary for policymakers.* Geneva: Intergovernmental Panel on Climate Change (IPCC). Available at: https://www.ipcc.ch/report/ar6/wg1/#SPM.

IPCC (2022a). *Climate change 2022: Mitigation of climate change – Full report, Working Group III contribution to IPCC sixth assessment report.* Cambridge, UK: Intergovernmental Panel on Climate Change (IPCC). Available at: https://www.ipcc.ch/report/sixth-assessment-report-working-group-3/.

IPCC (2022b). *Climate change 2022: Mitigation of climate change – Technical summary, Working Group III contribution to IPCC sixth assessment report.* Cambridge, UK: Intergovernmental Panel on Climate Change (IPCC). Available at: https://www.ipcc.ch/report/sixth-assessment-report-working-group-3/.

IPCC (2022c). *Climate change 2022: Mitigation of climate change – Summary for policymakers, Working Group III contribution to IPCC sixth assessment report.* Cambridge, UK: Intergovernmental Panel on Climate Change (IPCC). Available at: https://www.ipcc.ch/report/sixth-assessment-report-working-group-3/.

IPCC (2023). *Synthesis report (SYR) of the IPCC sixth assessment report (AR6): Summary for policymakers.* Geneva: Intergovernmental Panel on Climate Change (IPCC). Available at: https://www.ipcc.ch/report/ar6/syr/.

Ipsos (2019). *China's agriculture drone revolution.* Hong Kong: Ipsos Business Consulting. Available at: https://www.ipsos.com/sites/default/files/ct/publication/documents/2020-10/china-agriculture-drones.pdf.

IRP (2020). *Resource efficiency and climate change: Material efficiency strategies for a low-carbon future.* Nairobi: International Resource Panel (IRP) and United Nations Environment Programme (UNEP). Available at: https://www.unep.org/resources/report/resource-efficiency-and-climate-change-material-efficiency-strategies-low-carbon.

IRRI (2019a). Alternate wetting and drying. International Rice Research Institute (IRRI). Available at: https://ghgmitigation.irri.org/mitigation-technologies/alternate-wetting-and-drying [accessed July 2023].

IRRI (2019b). Dry seeded rice. International Rice Research Institute (IRRI). Available at: https://ghgmitigation.irri.org/mitigation-technologies/dry-seeded-rice [accessed July 2023].

IRRI (2019c). Laser land levelling. International Rice Research Institute (IRRI). Available at: https://ghgmitigation.irri.org/mitigation-technologies/laser-land-leveling [accessed July 2023].

IRRI (2019d). Machine transplanting. International Rice Research Institute (IRRI). Available at: https://ghgmitigation.irri.org/mitigation-technologies/machine-transplanting [accessed July 2023].

IRRI (2021). How to manage water. *Rice knowledge bank*, International Rice Research Institute (IRRI). Available at: http://www.knowledgebank.irri.org/step-by-step-production/growth/water-management [accessed July 2023].

IRRI (2023). Manual transplanting. International Rice Research Institute (IRRI). Available at: http://www.knowledgebank.irri.org/training/fact-sheets/crop-establishment/manual-transplanting#:~:text=Why%20transplant%20rice%3F,and%20has%20variable%20water%20levels. [accessed July 2023].

ITF (2023). *ITF transport outlook 2023.* International Transport Forum (ITF). Available at: https://www.oecd-ilibrary.org/transport/itf-transport-outlook-2023_b6cc9ad5-en.

ITU (2021). Indian firm's digital solution for urban waste pickers. International Transport Forum (ITF). Available at: https://www.itu.int/hub/2021/07/indian-firms-digital-solution-for-urban-waste-pickers/ [accessed July 2023].

ITU (2022a). *Measuring digital development.* International Telecommunication Union (ITU). Available at: https://www.itu.int/itu-d/reports/statistics/facts-figures-2022/.

ITU (2022b). Tech transfer and digital public goods needed for climate action. The International Telecommunication Union (ITU). Available at: https://www.itu.int/hub/2022/03/tech-transfer-digital-public-goods-climate-action-africa/ [accessed August 2023].

Ivanova, D., J. Barrett, D. Wiedenhofer, B. Macura, M. Callaghan and F. Creutzig (2020). Quantifying the potential for climate change mitigation of consumption options. *Environmental Research Letters,* 15(9).

Ivanovich, C. C., T. Sun, D. R. Gordon and I. B. Ocko (2023). Future warming from global food consumption. *Nature Climate Change,* 13(3), 297–302.

Jasonarson, I. (2020). *Digitalization for energy efficiency in energy intensive industries.* Unpublished thesis (Independent thesis advanced level), KTH.

JRC (2013). *Best Available Techniques (BAT) reference document for the production of cement, lime and magnesium oxide.* Geneva: Joint Research Centre (JRC). Available at: https://op.europa.eu/en/publication-detail/-/publication/12dbe9f3-28c6-44c9-8962-50a1359443d6.

JRC (2020). *Deep decarbonization of industry: The cement sector.* Brussels: European Commission Joint Research Centre (JRC). Available at: https://ee-ip.org/fileadmin/user_upload/IMAGES/Articles/JRC120570_decarbonisation_of_cement__fact_sheet.pdf.

Kahawalage, A. C., M. C. Melaaen and L.-A. Tokheim (2023). Opportunities and challenges of using SRF as an alternative fuel in the cement industry. *Cleaner Waste Systems,* 4, 100072.

Kang, M., S. Cho, J. Kim, S. Sohn, Y. Ryu and N. Kang (2023). On securing continuity of eddy covariance flux time-series after changing the measurement height: Correction for flux differences due to the footprint difference. *Agricultural and Forest Meteorology,* 331, 109339.

Kashyap, Y. (2022). Analysis: Costs and impacts of low-carbon technologies for steel and cement sectors in India. Climate Policy Initiative (CPI). Available at: https://www.climatepolicyinitiative.org/report-summary-costs-and-impacts-of-low-carbon-technologies-for-steel-and-cement-sectors-in-india/ [accessed May 2023].

Kaza, S., L. C. Yao, P. Bhada-Tata and F. Van Woerden (2018). *What a waste 2.0: A global snapshot of solid waste management to 2050.* Washington, DC: World Bank. Available at: https://openknowledge.worldbank.org/entities/publication/d3f9d45e-115f-559b-b14f-28552410e90a.

Kim, J., B. K. Sovacool, M. Bazilian, S. Griffiths, J. Lee, M. Yang and J. Lee (2022). Decarbonizing the iron and steel industry: A systematic review of sociotechnical systems, technological innovations, and policy options. *Energy Research & Social Science,* 89, 102565.

Kinigadner, J., B. Büttner, G. Wulfhorst and D. Vale (2020). Planning for low carbon mobility: Impacts of transport interventions and location on carbon-based accessibility. *Journal of Transport Geography,* 87, 102797.

Kreier, F. (2022). Drones bearing parcels deliver big carbon savings. *Nature.*

Kumar, P., J. Bhamu and K. S. Sangwan (2021). Analysis of barriers to Industry 4.0 adoption in manufacturing organizations: an ISM approach. *Procedia CIRP,* 98, 85–90.

Kurnik, J. and K. Devine (2022). Innovation in reducing methane emissions from the food sector: Side of rice, hold the methane. World Wildlife Fund. Available at: https://www.worldwildlife.org/blogs/sustainability-works/posts/innovation-in-reducing-methane-emissions-from-the-food-sector-side-of-rice-hold-the-methane [accessed July 2023].

Kusuma, R. T., R. B. Hiremath, P. Rajesh, B. Kumar and S. Renukappa (2022). Sustainable transition towards biomass-based cement industry: A review. *Renewable and Sustainable Energy Reviews,* 163, 112503.

Lacy, P. and J. Rutqvist (2015). *Waste to wealth: The circular economy advantage.* Accenture Strategy.

Lai, C. (2022). System of rice intensification: A solution to methane emissions and food insecurity. Earth.org. Available at: https://earth.org/system-of-rice-intensification/ [accessed July 2023].

Le Quéré, C., R. Jackson, M. Jones, A. Smith, S. Abernethy, R. Andrew, A. De-Gol, D. Willis, Y. Shan, J. Canadell, P. Friedlingstein, F. Creutzig and G. Peters (2020). Temporary reduction in daily global CO_2 emissions during the COVID-19 forced confinement. *Nature Climate Change,* 10(7), 1–7.

LeadIT (2023). Green steel tracker. Leadership Group for Industry Transition (LeadIT). Available at: https://www.industrytransition.org/green-steel-tracker/ [accessed May 2023].

Lehne, J. and F. Preston (2018). *Making concrete change: Innovation in low-carbon cement and concrete.* London: Chatham House. Available at: www.chathamhouse.org/sites/default/files/publications/research/2018-06-13-making-concrete-change-cement-lehne-preston.pdf.

Leoni, L., A. Cantini, F. De Carlo, M. Salvio, C. Martini, C. Toro and F. Martini (2021). Energy-saving technology opportunities and investments of the Italian foundry industry. *Energies,* 14(24), 8470.

Leveau, M. (2022). The FoodTech Innovation 'blind spots' of the last decade – Going beyond the hype – Part 1. Forward Fooding. Available at: https://forwardfooding.com/blog/foodtech-trends-and-insights/the-foodtech-innovation-blind-spots-go-beyond-the-hype-part-1/ [accessed 2023 June].

Li, J., M. Barwood and S. Rahimifard (2018). Robotic disassembly for increased recovery of strategically important materials from electrical vehicles. *Robotics and Computer-Integrated Manufacturing,* 50, 203–12.

Li, J., Y. Xin and L. Yuan (2009). *Hybrid rice technology development: Ensuring China's food security,* IFPRI discussion paper. Washington, D.C: International Food Policy Research Institute (IFPRI). Available at: http://www.ifpri.org/publication/hybrid-rice-technology-development.

Linquist, B., K. J. van Groenigen, M. A. Adviento-Borbe, C. Pittelkow and C. van Kessel (2012). An agronomic assessment of greenhouse gas emissions from major cereal crops. *Global Change Biology,* 18(1), 194–209.

Liu, C., Z. Chen, Y. Mao, Z. Yao, W. Zhang, W. Ye, Y. Duan and Q. Xie (2022). Analysis and optimization of grinding performance of vertical roller mill based on experimental method. *Minerals,* 12(2), 133.

Lucertini, G. and F. Musco (2020). Circular urban metabolism framework. *One Earth,* 2(2), 138–42.

Maasakkers, J. D., D. J. Varon, A. Elfarsdóttir, J. McKeever, D. Jervis, G. Mahapatra, S. Pandey, A. Lorente, T. Borsdorff, L. R. Foorthuis, B. J. Schuit, P. Tol, T. A. van Kempen, R. van Hees and I. Aben (2022). Using satellites to uncover large methane emissions from landfills. *Science Advances,* 8(32), eabn9683.

Maghazei, O. and T. Netland (2020). Drones in manufacturing: Exploring opportunities for research and practice. *Journal of Manufacturing Technology Management*, 31(6), 1237–1259.

Maltais, A., L. Linde, F. Sanchez and G. Mete (2022). *The role of international finance institutions in the transition to low-carbon steel production.* Leadership Group for Industry Transition (LeadIT). Available at: https://www.sei.org/wp-content/uploads/2022/11/report-2209a-ifis-lhv2.pdf.

MarketsandMarkets (2023a). Agricultural robots market industry analysis: Types, advantages, and forecast. MarketsandMarkets. Available at: https://www.marketsandmarkets.com/Market-Reports/agricultural-robot-market-173601759.html [accessed July 2023].

MarketsandMarkets (2023b). Agriculture drones market share, industry size and growth forecast – 2030. MarketsandMarkets. Available at: https://www.marketsandmarkets.com/Market-Reports/agriculture-drones-market-23709764.html [accessed July 2023].

MarketsandMarkets (2023c). Precision farming market size, share, industry report, revenue trends and growth drivers. MarketsandMarkets. Available at: https://www.marketsandmarkets.com/Market-Reports/precision-farming-market-1243.html [accessed October 2023].

Marmier, A. (2023). *Decarbonisation options for the cement industry.* Luxembourg: Publications Office of the European Union. Available at: https://publications.jrc.ec.europa.eu/repository/handle/JRC131246.

Martin-Roberts, E., V. Scott, S. Flude, G. Johnson, R. S. Haszeldine and S. Gilfillan (2021). Carbon capture and storage at the end of a lost decade. *One Earth,* 4(11), 1569–84.

Mastrucci, A., E. Byers, S. Pachauri and N. D. Rao (2019). Improving the SDG energy poverty targets: Residential cooling needs in the Global South. *Energy and Buildings,* 186, 405–15.

Material Economics (2018). *The circular economy – A powerful force for climate mitigation.* Available at: https://circulareconomy.europa.eu/platform/en/knowledge/circular-economy-powerful-force-climate-mitigation.

Material Economics (2019). *Industrial transformation 2050: Pathways to net-zero emissions from EU heavy industry (executive summary),* Net Zero 2050 (Executive summary). Cambridge: University of Cambridge Institute for Sustainability Leadership (CISL). Available at: https://europeanclimate.org/wp-content/uploads/2019/11/25-04-2019-industrial-transformation-2050-executive-summary.pdf.

McKinsey (2020). *Laying the foundation for zero-carbon cement.* Chemicals Practice, McKinsey & Company. Available at: https://www.naiopmd.org/wp-content/uploads/2022/08/Cement-McKinsey-laying-the-foundation-for-zero-carbon-cement-v3.pdf.

McKinsey (2022a). How a steel plant in India tapped the value of data – and won global acclaim, *Impact story.* McKinsey & Company. Available at: https://www.mckinsey.com/industries/metals-and-mining/how-we-help-clients/how-a-steel-plant-in-india-tapped-the-value-of-data-and-won-global-acclaim [accessed May 2023].

McKinsey (2022b). *Make room for alternative proteins: What it takes to build a new sector.* McKinsey & Company. Available at: https://www.mckinsey.com/capabilities/mckinsey-digital/our-insights/make-room-for-alternative-proteins-what-it-takes-to-build-a-new-sector#/.

McKinsey (2023a). Autonomous driving's future: Convenient and connected. McKinsey & Company. Available at: https://www.mckinsey.com/industries/automotive-and-assembly/our-insights/autonomous-drivings-future-convenient-and-connected [accessed September 2023].

McKinsey (2023b). *The future of mobility.* McKinsey Quarterly, McKinsey Center for Future Mobility. Available at: https://www.mckinsey.com/industries/automotive-and-assembly/our-insights/the-future-of-mobility-mobility-evolves.

Menon, J. S. and R. Sharma (2021). Nature-based solutions for co-mitigation of air pollution and urban heat in Indian cities. *Frontiers in Sustainable Cities,* 3.

Merfort, L., N. Bauer, F. Humpenöder, D. Klein, J. Strefler, A. Popp, G. Luderer and E. Kriegler (2023). State of global land regulation inadequate to control biofuel land-use-change emissions. *Nature Climate Change,* 13(7), 610–12.

MIT (2023a). Minimizing electric vehicles' impact on the grid. Massachusetts Institute of Technology (MIT). Available at: https://www.sciencedaily.com/releases/2023/03/230315132448.htm [accessed July 2023].

MIT (2023b). Soil-based carbon sequestration. Massachusetts Institute of Technology (MIT). Available at: https://climate.mit.edu/explainers/soil-based-carbon-sequestration [accessed June 2023].

Mohammadshahi, S., M. R. Tavakoli, H. Samsam-Khayani, M. Nili-Ahmadabadi and K. C. Kim (2019). Investigation of naturally ventilated shavadoons component: Architectural underground pattern on ventilation. *Tunnelling and Underground Space Technology,* 91, 102990.

Monkman, S., P. Kenward, G. Dipple, M. MacDonald and M. Raudsepp (2018). Activation of cement hydration with carbon dioxide. *Journal of Sustainable Cement-Based Materials,* 7(3), 160–81.

Mourão, J. M., I. Cameron, M. Huerta, N. Patel and R. Pereira (2020). Comparison of sinter and pellet usage in an integrated steel plant. In *ABM BRAZIL – 2013 Annual Congress.* Belo Horizonte, Brazil.

Musa, A. A., S. I. Malami, F. Alanazi, W. Ounaies, M. Alshammari and S. I. Haruna (2023). Sustainable traffic management for smart cities using internet-of-things-oriented intelligent transportation systems (ITS): Challenges and recommendations. *Sustainability,* 15(13), 9859.

Mutschler, R., M. Rüdisüli, P. Heer and S. Eggimann (2021). Benchmarking cooling and heating energy demands considering climate change, population growth and cooling device uptake. *Applied Energy,* 288, 116636.

Nawaz, A., A. U. Rehman, A. Rehman, S. Ahmad, K. H. M. Siddique and M. Farooq (2022). Increasing sustainability for rice production systems. *Journal of Cereal Science,* 103, 103400.

Net Zero Insights (2023). An overview of the green steel startups and initiatives. Available at: https://netzeroinsights.com/resources/market-insights/green-steel-startups-funding-landscape/ [accessed May 2023].

Ngige, L. (2022). Africa agrifoodtech startups raise $1bn in 5 years, but just 1% of global investment. Agfunder Network. Available at: https://agfundernews.com/africa-agrifoodtech-startups-raise-1bn-in-5-years [accessed October 2023].

Nguyen, L. D., A. Bröring, M. Pizzol and P. Popovski (2022). Analysis of distributed ledger technologies for industrial manufacturing. *Scientific Reports,* 12(1), 18055.

Nhamo, G., C. Nhemachena and S. Nhamo (2020). Using ICT indicators to measure readiness of countries to implement Industry 4.0 and the SDGs. *Environmental Economics and Policy Studies,* 22(2), 315–37.

Nicholas, S. and S. Basirat (2022). *Iron ore quality a potential headwind to green steelmaking: Technology and mining options are available to hit net-zero steel targets.* Institute for Energy Economics and Financial Analysis (IEEFA). Available at: https://ieefa.org/resources/iron-ore-quality-potential-headwind-green-steelmaking-technology-and-mining-options-are.

Nikitas, D. A. and P. M. Karlsson (2015). A worldwide state-of-the-art analysis for bus rapid transit: Looking for the success formula. *Journal of Public Transportation,* 18(1), 1–33.

Noailly, J. (2022). Directing innovation towards a low-carbon future, *Economic Research Working Paper No. 72.* Geneva: World Intellectual Property Organization (WIPO). Available at: https://www.wipo.int/publications/en/details.jsp?id=4599&plang=EN.

O'Sullivan, A., G. D. Bonnett, C. L. McIntyre, Z. Hochman and A. P. Wasson (2019). Strategies to improve the productivity, product diversity and profitability of urban agriculture. *Agricultural Systems,* 174, 133–44.

OECD (2015). *Energy efficiency in the steel sector: why it works well, but not always.* Paris: Organisation for Economic Co-operation and Development (OECD). Available at: https://www.oecd.org/sti/ind/Energy-efficiency-steel-sector-1.pdf.

OECD (2021). *Latest developments in steelmaking capacity.* Organisation for Economic Co-operation and Development (OECD). Available at: https://www.oecd.org/industry/ind/latest-developments-in-steelmaking-capacity-2021.pdf.

OECD (2022a). *Assessing steel decarbonization progress: ready for the decade of delivery?* Organisation for Economic Co-operation and Development (OECD). Available at: https://www.oecd.org/industry/ind/assessing-steel-decarbonisation-progress.pdf.

OECD (2022b). *Global plastics outlook: Policy scenarios to 2060.* Paris. Available at: https://www.oecd-ilibrary.org/environment/global-plastics-outlook_aa1edf33-en.

OECD (2022c). Plastic pollution is growing relentlessly as waste management and recycling fall short, says OECD. Available at: https://www.oecd.org/environment/plastic-pollution-is-growing-relentlessly-as-waste-management-and-recycling-fall-short.htm [accessed July 2023].

OECD (2023). *Climate change and plastic pollution,* Policy highlights. Organisation for Economic Co-operation and Development (OECD). Available at: https://www.oecd.org/environment/plastics/Policy-Highlights-Climate-change-and-plastics-pollution-Synergies-between-two-crucial-environmental-challenges.pdf.

OECD and FAO (2023). *OECD–FAO Agricultural Outlook 2023–2032.* Paris: Organisation for Economic Co-operation and Development (OECD). Available at: https://www.fao.org/documents/card/en/c/cc6361en.

Oksen, P. (2001). *Cattle, conflict and change: Animal husbandry and Fulani – Farmer interactions in Boulgou province, Burkina Faso.* Unpublished thesis (Ph.D.), Roskilde University.

Oksen, P. (2023). Climate smart technologies in adaptation – Agriculture. Sustainable Success Stories. Available at: https://sustainablesuccessstories.org/technologies/climate-smart-technolgies-adaptation-agriculture/ [accessed July 2023].

Olabi, A. G., T. Wilberforce, K. Obaideen, E. T. Sayed, N. Shehata, A. H. Alami and M. A. Abdelkareem (2023). Micromobility: Progress, benefits, challenges, policy and regulations, energy sources and storage, and its role in achieving Sustainable Development Goals. *International Journal of Thermofluids,* 17, 100292.

Paradisi, L. (2021). Understanding the future of protein. Forward Fooding. Available at: https://forwardfooding.com/blog/foodtech-trends-and-insights/understanding-the-future-of-protein/ [accessed July 2023].

Pasture.io (2023). Scientists are breeding climate-friendly cows & soon they'll be on your farm. Pasture.io. Available at: https://pasture.io/dairy-industry/breeding-climate-friendly-cows [accessed July 2023].

Patsavellas, J. and K. Salonitis (2019). The carbon footprint of manufacturing digitalization: critical literature review and future research agenda. *Procedia CIRP,* 81, 1354–59.

Peng, T., K. Kellens, R. Tang, C. Chen and G. Chen (2018). Sustainability of additive manufacturing: An overview on its energy demand and environmental impact. *Additive Manufacturing,* 21, 694–704.

PepsiCo (2023). Pepsico issues new $1.25 billion 10-year green bond as company accelerates pep+ transformation. PepsiCo. Available at: https://www.pepsico.com/our-stories/press-release/pepsico-issues-new-125-billion-10-year-green-bond-as-company-accelerates-pep-tra07202022 [accessed October 2023].

PFPI (2018). Letter from scientists to the EU Parliament regarding forest biomass. Partnership for Policy Integrity (PFPI). Available at: https://www.pfpi.net/wp-content/uploads/2018/04/UPDATE-800-signatures_Scientist-Letter-on-EU-Forest-Biomass.pdf [accessed July 2023].

Pixalytics (2023). How many earth observation satellites orbiting in 2023? Pixalytics. Available at: https://www.pixalytics.com/earth-observation-satellites-2023/ [accessed October 2023].

Pombo, O., B. Rivela and J. Neila (2019). Life cycle thinking toward sustainable development policy-making: The case of energy retrofits. *Journal of Cleaner Production,* 206, 267–81.

Poschmann, H., H. Brüggemann and D. Goldmann (2020). Disassembly 4.0: A review on using robotics in disassembly tasks as a way of automation. *Chemie Ingenieur Technik,* 92.

Potochnik, J. and A. Wijkman (2022). *From 'greening' the present system to real transformation – Transforming resource use for human wellbeing and planetary stability,* Earth4all: Deep-dive paper 12. Earth4All. Available at: https://www.clubofrome.org/wp-content/uploads/2022/10/Earth4All_Deep_Dive_Wijkman-2.pdf.

Powlson, D. S., C. M. Stirling, M. L. Jat, B. G. Gerard, C. A. Palm, P. A. Sanchez and K. G. Cassman (2014). Limited potential of no-till agriculture for climate change mitigation. *Nature Climate Change,* 4(8), 678–83.

Precedence Research (2023). Regenerative agriculture market. Precedence Research. Available at: https://www.precedenceresearch.com/regenerative-agriculture-market [accessed October 2023].

Probst, B., S. Touboul, M. Glachant and A. Dechezleprêtre (2021). Global trends in the invention and diffusion of climate change mitigation technologies. *Nature Energy,* 6, 1077–86.

Protein Directory (2023). Protein Directory – The largest alt protein database globally. Available at: https://proteindirectory.com/ [accessed June 2023].

PwC (2022). *State of climate tech 2022: Overcoming inertia in climate tech ivnesting.* Available at: https://www.pwc.com/gx/en/services/sustainability/publications/overcoming-inertia-in-climate-tech-investing.html.

Rahaee, O. (2013). Cultural identity and its effects on indigenous methods of natural ventilation passage of metal smiths in Dezful's old bazzar. *The Monthly Scientific Journal of Bagh-e Nazar,* 10(24), 39–46.

Rahman, A., M. G. Rasul, M. M. K. Khan and S. Sharma (2015). Recent development on the uses of alternative fuels in cement manufacturing process. *Fuel,* 145, 84–99.

Rainbow, R. and R. Derpsch (2011). Advances in no-till farming technologies and soil compaction management in rainfed farming systems. In Tow, P., I. Cooper, I. Partridge and C. Birch (eds), *Rainfed farming systems*. Dordrecht: Springer Netherlands, 991–1014.

Rauch, E. and D. T. Matt (2021). Status of the implementation of Industry 4.0 in SMEs and framework for smart manufacturing. In Matt, D. T., V. Modrák and H. Zsifkovits (eds), *Implementing Industry 4.0 in SMEs: Concepts, examples and applications*. Springer International Publishing, 3–26.

Reck, D. J., H. Martin and K. W. Axhausen (2022). Mode choice, substitution patterns and environmental impacts of shared and personal micro-mobility. *Transportation Research Part D: Transport and Environment,* 102, 103134.

Renaldi, R., N. D. Miranda, R. Khosla and M. D. McCulloch (2021). Patent landscape of not-in-kind active cooling technologies between 1998 and 2017. *Journal of Cleaner Production,* 296, 126507.

Richstein, J. C. and K. Neuhoff (2022). Carbon contracts-for-difference: How to de-risk innovative investments for a low-carbon industry? *iScience,* 25(8), 104700.

Ritchie, H. (2021). Cutting down forests: What are the drivers of deforestation? OurWorldinData.org. Available at: https://ourworldindata.org/what-are-drivers-deforestation [accessed August 2023].

Ritchie, H., F. Spooner and M. Roser (2021). Deforestation and forest loss. OurWorldInData.org. Available at: https://ourworldindata.org/forests-and-deforestation [accessed August 2023].

Ross, E. B. (1998). *The Malthus factor: Population, poverty, and politics in capitalist development,* London, New York: Zed Books.

Sawyer, T. (2016). *The use of limestone as an extender and its effect on concrete properties.* Unpublished thesis.

Sayem, A., P. K. Biswas, M. M. A. Khan, L. Romoli and M. Dalle Mura (2022). Critical barriers to Industry 4.0 adoption in manufacturing organizations and their mitigation strategies. *Journal of Manufacturing and Materials Processing,* 6(6), 136.

Schaart, E. (2020). Denmark's 'devilish' waste dilemma. Politico. Available at: https://www.politico.eu/article/denmark-devilish-waste-trash-energy-incineration-recycling-dilemma/ [accessed July 2023].

Schaller, B. (2021). Can sharing a ride make for less traffic? Evidence from Uber and Lyft and implications for cities. *Transport Policy,* 102, 1–10.

Schwanen, T., D. Banister and J. Anable (2011). Scientific research about climate change mitigation in transport: A critical review. *Transportation Research Part A: Policy and Practice,* 45(10), 993–1006.

SEI and CEEW (2022). *Stockholm+50: Unlocking a better future.* Stockholm: Stockholm Environment Institute (SEI). Available at: https://www.stockholm50.report/unlocking-a-better-future.pdf.

Shaohua, C., H. Murano, T. Hirano, Y. Hayashi and H. Tamura (2020). Establishment of a novel technology permitting self-sufficient, renewable energy from rice straw in paddy fields. *Journal of Cleaner Production,* 272, 122721.

Sice, C. and J. Faludi (2021). Comparing environmental impacts of metal additive manufacturing to conventional manufacturing. *Proceedings of the Design Society,* 1, 671–80.

Simoni, M., M. D. Wilkes, S. Brown, J. L. Provis, H. Kinoshita and T. Hanein (2022). Decarbonising the lime industry: State-of-the-art. *Renewable and Sustainable Energy Reviews,* 168, 112765.

Sivaram, V. (2022). Climate change. *MIT Technology Review,* 125(4).

Skinner, B. and R. Lalit (2023). With concrete, less is more. Rocky Mountain Institute (RMI). Available at: https://rmi.org/with-concrete-less-is-more/ [accessed May 2023].

Skoczinski, P., M. Carus, G. Tweddle, P. Ruiz, D. de Guzman, J. Ravenstijn, H. Käb, N. Hark, L. Dammer and A. Raschka (2023). *Bio-based building blocks and polymers: Global capacities, production and trends 2022–2027.* nova-Institute. Available at: https://renewable-carbon.eu/publications/product/bio-based-building-blocks-and-polymers-global-capacities-production-and-trends-2022-2027/.

Smith, S. (2023). 10 things you should do to get started with regenerative grazing. Noble Research Institute. Available at: https://www.noble.org/regenerative-agriculture/10-things-you-should-do-to-get-started-with-regenerative-grazing/ [accessed July 2023].

Songwe, V., N. Stern and A. Bhattacharya (2022). *Finance for climate action: scaling up investment for climate and development.* London: Grantham Research Institute on Climate Change and the Environment, London School of Economics and Political Science. Available at: https://www.lse.ac.uk/granthaminstitute/wp-content/uploads/2022/11/IHLEG-Finance-for-Climate-Action.pdf.

Sozzi, M., A. Cogato, S. Nale and S. Gatto (2018). *Patent trends in agricultural engineering.* Jelgava, Latvia: Engineering for rural development and University of Padova, Italy. Available at: https://www.tf.lbtu.lv/conference/proceedings2018/Papers/N329.pdf.

Spears, S. (2018). What is biochar? Regeneration International. Available at: https://regenerationinternational.org/2018/05/16/what-is-biochar/ [accessed June 2023].

Statistics Denmark (2018). *Precision agriculture.* Nyt fra Danmarks Statistik, Copenhagen: Statistics Denmark. Available at: https://www.dst.dk/Site/Dst/SingleFiles/GetArchiveFile.aspx?fi=formid&fo=agriculture-2018--pdf&ext.

Stevens, I., A. Garvey, J. Barrett and J. Norman (2022). *Policy options for a net-zero emissions UK steel sector,.* CREDS policy brief. Oxford, UK: Centre for Research into Energy Demand Solutions (CREDS). Available at: https://www.creds.ac.uk/publications/policy-options-for-a-net-zero-emissions-uk-steel-sector/.

Sun, F., J. Qin, Z. Wang, M. Yu, X. Wu, X. Sun and J. Qiu (2021). Energy-saving hydrogen production by chlorine-free hybrid seawater splitting coupling hydrazine degradation. *Nature Communications,* 12(1), 4182.

Svatoš-Ražnjević, H., L. Orozco and A. Menges (2022). Advanced timber construction industry: A review of 350 multi-storey timber projects from 2000 and 2021. *Buildings,* 12(4), 404.

Syngenta (2023). Syngenta Group reports record $33.4 billion sales and $5.6 billion EBITDA in 2022. Syngenta Group. Available at: https://www.syngentagroup.com/en/media/syngenta-news/year/2023/syngenta-group-reports-record-334-billion-sales-and-56-billion-ebitda [accessed July 2023].

Tabrizi, S., A. N. Rollinson, M. Hoffmann and E. Favoino (2020). *Understanding the environmental impacts of chemical recycling – Ten concerns with existing life cycle assessments.* Brussels: Zero Waste Europe. Available at: https://zerowasteeurope.eu/library/understanding-the-environmental-impacts-of-chemical-recycling-ten-concerns-with-existing-life-cycle-assessments/.

Taleb, H. M. (2014). Using passive cooling strategies to improve thermal performance and reduce energy consumption of residential buildings in U.A.E. buildings. *Frontiers of Architectural Research,* 3(2), 154–65.

Tangri, N. (2023). Waste incinerators undermine clean energy goals. *PLOS Climate,* 2(6).

The Concrete Centre (2020). *Remixed: how concrete is evolving for a net-zero built environment.* Concrete futures. Available at: https://www.concretecentre.com/TCC/media/TCCMediaLibrary/Publications/Promo%20Links/Concrete_Futures_Remixed_2020.pdf.

Tikoudis, I., L. Martinez, K. Farrow, C. García Bouyssou, O. Petrik and W. Oueslati (2021). Ridesharing services and urban transport CO_2 emissions: Simulation-based evidence from 247 cities. *Transportation Research Part D: Transport and Environment,* 97, 102923.

Touboul, S. (2021). *Technological innovation and adaptation to climate change.* Paris: Université Paris sciences et lettres. Available at: https://pastel.hal.science/tel-03610832/document.

Transport & Environment (2023). *Clean and lean: Battery metals demand from electrifying passenger transport.* Brussels: Transport & Environment. Available at: https://www.transportenvironment.org/discover/clean-and-lean-battery-metals-demand-from-electrifying-cars-vans-and-buses/.

Trappey, A. J. C., G.-B. Lin, H.-K. Chen and M.-C. Chen (2023). A comprehensive analysis of global patent landscape for recent R&D in agricultural drone technologies. *World Patent Information,* 74, 102216.

Traugott, J. (2023). California wants to make bidirectional charging mandatory for new electric vehicles. Carbuzz. Available at: https://carbuzz.com/news/california-wants-to-make-bidirectional-charging-mandatory-for-new-electric-vehicles [accessed July 2023].

Trendov, N. M., S. Varas and M. Zeng (2019). *Digital technologies in agriculture and rural areas: Status report.* Rome: Food and Agriculture Organization of the United Nations (FAO). Available at: https://www.fao.org/3/ca4985en/ca4985en.pdf.

UDP (2021). *Climate technologies in an urban context.* Copenhagen, Denmark: UNEP DTU Partnership (UDP). Available at: https://tech-action.unepccc.org/publications/climate-technologies-in-an-urban-context/.

Ueckerdt, F., C. Bauer, A. Dirnaichner, J. Everall, R. Sacchi and G. Luderer (2021). Potential and risks of hydrogen-based e-fuels in climate change mitigation. *Nature Climate Change,* 11(5), 384–93.

UK IPO (2021). *Greener buildings and heat pumps.* Newport: United Kingdom Intellectual Property Office (UK IPO). Available at: https://www.gov.uk/government/publications/a-worldwide-overview-of-greener-buildings-and-heat-pump-patents.

Umali-Deininger, D. (2022). *Greening the rice we eat.* Washington, DC: World Bank. Available at: https://blogs.worldbank.org/eastasiapacific/greening-rice-we-eat?cid=SHR_BlogSiteEmail_EN_EXT.

UN (2023). Peace, dignity and equality on a heathy planet. United Nations (UN). Available at: https://www.un.org/en/global-issues/population [accessed May 2023].

UN Habitat (2022). *World cities report 2022: Envisaging the future of cities.* Nairobi: UN Habitat. Available at: https://unhabitat.org/wcr/.

UNCTAD (2022). What is 'Industry 4.0' and what will it mean for developing countries? United Nations Conference on Trade and Development (UNCTAD). Available at: https://unctad.org/news/blog-what-industry-40-and-what-will-it-mean-developing-countries [accessed May 2023].

UNCTAD (2023a). Escalating debt challenges are inhibiting achievement of the SDGs. 221 United Nations Conference on Trade and Development (UNCTAD). Available at: https://sdgpulse.unctad.org/debt-sustainability/ [accessed August 2023].

UNCTAD (2023b). *A world of debt: A growing burden to global prosperity.* 221 United Nations Conference on Trade and Development (UNCTAD). Available at: https://unctad.org/publication/world-of-debt.

UNEP-CCC (2022). *The climate technology progress report 2022.* Copenhagen, Denmark: Copenhagen Climate Centre (CCC), UNFCCC Technology Executive Committee (TEC) and United Nations Environment Programme (UNEP). Available at: https://unepccc.org/publications/the-climate-technology-progress-report-2022/.

UNEP (2020). *Cooling emissions and policy synthesis report.* Nairobi, Paris: United Nations Environment Programme (UNEP) and International Energy Agency (IEA). Available at: https://www.unep.org/resources/report/cooling-emissions-and-policy-synthesis-report.

UNEP (2021). *From pollution to solution: A global assessment of marine litter and plastic pollution.* Nairobi: United Nations Environment Programme (UNEP). Available at: https://www.unep.org/resources/pollution-solution-global-assessment-marine-litter-and-plastic-pollution.

UNEP (2023a). *Harnessing technology in the circular economy for climate action in Africa,* CTCN knowledge brief series. Nairobi: United Nations Environment Programme (UNEP). Available at: https://www.ctc-n.org/news/climate-action-africa-harnessing-technology-circular-economy.

UNEP (2023b). *Topic sheet: Just transition.* United Nations Environment Programme (UNEP). Available at: https://wedocs.unep.org/20.500.11822/42231.

UNEP (2023c). *Turning off the tap: How the world can end plastic pollution and create a circular economy.* Nairobi: United Nations Environment Programme (UNEP). Available at: https://www.unep.org/resources/turning-off-tap-end-plastic-pollution-create-circular-economy.

UNEP FI (2023). *Climate risks in the industrials sector,* Sectoral Risk Briefings: Insights for Financial Institutions. UN Environment Programme Finance Initiative. Available at: https://www.unepfi.org/wordpress/wp-content/uploads/2023/04/Climate-Risks-in-the-Industrials-Sector.pdf.

UNFCCC (2023a). Land use, land-use change and forestry (LULUCF). United Nations Framework Convention on Climate Change (UNFCCC). Available at: https://unfccc.int/topics/land-use/workstreams/land-use--land-use-change-and-forestry-lulucf [accessed August 2023].

UNFCCC (2023b). Land use, land-use change and forestry (LULUCF). United Nations Framework Convention on Climate Change (UNFCCC). Available at: https://unfccc.int/topics/land-use/workstreams/land-use--land-use-change-and-forestry-lulucf [accessed July 2023].

UNIDO (2019). *Industrial energy efficiency improvement project in South Africa.* United Nations Industrial Development Organization (UNIDO). Available at: https://mkiee.ea.gov.mk/wp-content/uploads/2019/11/International-UNIDO-SA-IEE-Project-Arcelormittal-Saldanha-Works-Case-Study.pdf.

United Nations (2019). *The Sustainable Development Goals report 2019.* New York, NY: UN Department of Economic and Social Affairs (DESA). Available at: https://unstats.un.org/sdgs/report/2019/.

United Nations (2020). *Roadmap for digital cooperation.* Available at: https://www.un.org/en/content/digital-cooperation-roadmap/assets/pdf/Roadmap_for_Digital_Cooperation_EN.pdf.

United Nations (2022). *The Sustainable Development Goals report 2022.* UN Department of Economic and Social Affairs (DESA). Available at: https://unstats.un.org/sdgs/report/2022/.

United Nations (2023). Finance & justice. Available at: https://www.un.org/en/climatechange/raising-ambition/climate-finance [accessed October 2023].

USDA (2022). *Partnerships for climate-smart commodities.* United States Department for Agriculture (USDA). Available at: www.usda.gov/climate-solutions/climate-smart-commodities.

van den Bergh, J. and I. Savin (2021). Impact of carbon pricing on low-carbon innovation and deep decarbonisation: Controversies and path forward. *Environmental and Resource Economics,* 80(4), 705–15.

VDZ (2021). *Environmental data of the German cement industry.* Verein Deutscher Zementwerke (VDZ). Available at: https://www.vdz-online.de/fileadmin/wissensportal/publikationen/umweltschutz/Umweltdaten/VDZ-Umweltdaten_Environmental_Data_2021.pdf.

Vogl, V., M. Åhman and L. J. Nilsson (2018). Assessment of hydrogen direct reduction for fossil-free steelmaking. *Journal of Cleaner Production,* 203, 736–45.

Vogl, V., O. Olsson and B. Nykvist (2021). Phasing out the blast furnace to meet global climate targets. *Joule,* 5(10), 2646–62.

Wang, P., M. Ryberg, Y. Yang, K. Feng, S. Kara, M. Hauschild and W.-Q. Chen (2021). Efficiency stagnation in global steel production urges joint supply – and demand – side mitigation efforts. *Nature Communications,* 12(1), 2066.

WEF (2021). *Net-zero challenge: The supply chain opportunity,* Insight report. World Economic Forum (WEF). Available at: https://www3.weforum.org/docs/WEF_Net_Zero_Challenge_The_Supply_Chain_Opportunity_2021.pdf.

WEF (2022). Digital solutions can reduce global emissions by up to 20%: Here's how. World Economic Forum (WEF). Available at: https://www.weforum.org/agenda/2022/05/how-digital-solutions-can-reduce-global-emissions/ [accessed May 2023].

Werner, S. (2017). International review of district heating and cooling. *Energy,* 137.

Westerholm, N. (2023). *Unlocking the potential of local circular construction materials in urbanising Africa.* United Nations One Planet Sustainable Buildings and Construction Programme. Available at: https://www.oneplanetnetwork.org/knowledge-centre/resources/unlocking-potential-local-circular-construction-materials-urbanising.

Westervelt, A. (2023). Big oil firms touted algae as climate solution: Now all have pulled funding. *The Guardian.* Available at: https://www.theguardian.com/environment/2023/mar/17/big-oil-algae-biofuel-funding-cut-exxonmobil.

WHO (2012). *Health in the green economy: Health co-benefits of climate change mitigation – Transport sector.* World Health Organization (WHO). Available at: https://apps.who.int/iris/handle/10665/70913.

Wijewardane, S. (2022). Inventions, innovations, and new technologies: Paints and coatings for passive cooling. *Solar Compass,* 3–4, 100032.

WIPO (2022). *Global innovation index 2022: What is the future of innovation-driven growth?* Geneva: World Intellectual Property Organization (WIPO). Available at: https://www.wipo.int/global_innovation_index/en/.

WIPO (2023). *Global Innovation Index (GII).* World Intellectual Property Organization (WIPO). Available at: https://www.wipo.int/global_innovation_index/en/index.html.

Wood Mackenzie (2022). Pedal to the metal: Iron and steel's US$1.4 trillion shot at decarbonisation. *Horizons.* Available at: https://www.woodmac.com/horizons/pedal-to-the-metal-iron-and-steels-one-point-four-trillion-usd-shot-at-decarbonisation/ [accessed May 2023].

Woolley, E., Y. Luo and A. Simeone (2018). Industrial waste heat recovery: A systematic approach. *Sustainable Energy Technologies and Assessments,* 29, 50–59.

World Bank (2022). Population, total, *World population prospects: 2022 Revision.* Available at: https://data.worldbank.org/indicator/SP.POP.TOTL?end=2022&start=1973 [accessed November 2023].

World Bank (2023a). Eight Amazonian countries with the power to save the planet. The World Bank. Available at: https://www.worldbank.org/en/news/feature/2023/07/05/ocho-paises-de-la-amazonia-con-el-poder-de-salvar-el-planeta-america-latina [accessed July 2023].

World Bank (2023b). Sustainable agriculture transformation project. World Bank. Available at: https://projects.worldbank.org/en/projects-operations/project-detail/P145055 [accessed August 2023].

World Bank (2023c). Water in agriculture. World Bank. Available at: https://www.worldbank.org/en/topic/water-in-agriculture [accessed May 2023].

World Bank (2023d). World bank loan will support reducing methane, saving water in Hunan's rice paddies. World Bank Group. Available at: https://www.worldbank.org/en/news/press-release/2023/05/31/world-bank-loan-will-support-reducing-methane-saving-water-in-hunan-s-rice-paddies [accessed October 2023].

World Steel Association (2021a). Fact sheet: Scrap use in the steel industry. Available at: https://worldsteel.org/wp-content/uploads/Fact-sheet-on-scrap_2021.pdf [accessed May 2023].

World Steel Association (2021b). Raw materials: Maximising scrap use helps reduce CO_2 emissions. Available at: https://worldsteel.org/steel-topics/raw-materials/ [accessed May 2023].

World Steel Association (2021c). Steel industry key facts. Available at: https://worldsteel.org/about-steel/steel-industry-facts/ [accessed May 2023].

WRI (2023a). *The global land squeeze: Managing the growing competition for land.* World Resources Institute (WRI). Available at: https://www.wri.org/research/global-land-squeeze-managing-growing-competition-land.

WRI (2023b). Our world in data: Emissions by sector. World Reesources Institute (WRI). Available at: https://ourworldindata.org/emissions-by-sector [accessed June 2023].

WRI Brazil (2023). *Global BRT data.* World Resources Institute (WRI) Brasil Ross Center for Sustainable Cities. Available at: https://brtdata.org/.

WWF (2008). *How to turn around the trend of cement related emissions in the developing world.* Gland, Switzerland: WWF International. Available at: https://wwfint.awsassets.panda.org/downloads/english_report_lr_pdf.pdf.

Xiaodan, Y. (2022). Rice can also reduce carbon emissions! A low-carbon experiment in the field: How to build a closed loop of technology, cost, and carbon trading? *Daily Economic News* newspaper. Available at: https://www.nbd.com.cn/articles/2022-10-21/2505684.html [accessed July 2023].

Xie, H., Y. Bian, X. He, X. Guo and P. Oksen (2022). *Progress in hydrogen fuel cell technology development and deployment in China.* Geneva: WIPO, Global Challenges Division. Available at: https://dx.doi.org/10.34667/tind.44764.

Xu, H.-l., F. Qin, Q. Xu, G. Ma, F. Li and J. Li (2012). Paddy rice can be cultivated in upland conditions by film mulching to create anaerobic soil conditions. *Journal of Food Agriculture and Environment,* 10(2), 695–702.

Xu, Y., D. Zaelke, G. J. M. Velders and V. Ramanathan (2013). The role of HFCs in mitigating 21st century climate change. *Atmospheric Chemistry & Physics,* 13, 6083–89.

Zeng, Y. and R. Cecil (2021). High-grade iron ore supply to struggle to meet demand as China decarbonizes: MI. S&P Global Market Intelligence. Available at: https://www.spglobal.com/commodityinsights/en/market-insights/latest-news/metals/060821-high-grade-iron-ore-supply-to-struggle-to-meet-demand-as-china-decarbonizes-mi [accessed May 2023].

Zernicke, C., A. Hafner, A. Abecker and H. Stolpe (2023). *WEB-GIS-TOOL: Estimation of greenhouse gas savings due timber use in the urban built environment.* Oslo, Norway: World Conference on Timber Engineering 2023.

Zero Waste Europe (2020a). *Reusable VS single-use packaging: A review of environmental impact.* Brussels: Zero Waste Europe. Available at: https://zerowasteeurope.eu/library/reusable-vs-single-use-packaging-a-review-of-environmental-impact/.

Zero Waste Europe (2020b). *Why co-incineration of waste is not taxonomy-compliant and should be excluded.* Brussels: Zero Waste Europe. Available at: https://zerowasteeurope.eu/library/why-co-incineration-of-waste-is-not-taxonomy-compliant-and-should-be-excluded/.

Zero Waste Europe (2023). *Nothing left behind: Modelling material recovery and biological treatment's contribution to resource recovery and fighting climate change.* Brussels: Zero Waste Europe. Available at: https://zerowasteeurope.eu/library/nothing-left-behind-mrbt-costs-study/.

Zero Waste Scotland (2018). A scheme for Scotland. Available at: https://depositreturnscheme.zerowastescotland.org.uk/benefits#:~:text=Tackling%20climate%20change&text=The%20scheme%20will%20cut%20emissions,one%20year%20in%20the%20UK [accessed July 2023].

Zheng, J. and S. Suh (2019). Strategies to reduce the global carbon footprint of plastics. *Nature Climate Change, 9, 374–378.*

Zhijiang, X. (2023). Chinese rice farming trials cut methane emissions. China Dialogue. Available at: https://chinadialogue.net/en/food/chinas-rice-farming-trials-cut-methane-emissions-and-increase-yields/ [accessed July 2023].

www.ingramcontent.com/pod-product-compliance
Ingram Content Group UK Ltd.
Pitfield, Milton Keynes, MK11 3LW, UK
UKHW052153041026
15590UKWH00007B/2052

9 789280 535761